D0933125

ZAGATSURVEY®

MOVIE GUIDE

1,000 Top Films of All Time

Edited by Curt Gathje

Coordinated by Larry Cohn

Published and distributed by
ZAGAT SURVEY, LLC
4 Columbus Circle
New York, New York 10019
Tel: 212 977 6000
E-mail: movies@zagat.com
Web site: www.zagat.com

Acknowledgments

We appreciate the help of Carol Bidaul, founder of the DC Independent Film Festival, as well as the Arizona Film Society, MSC Film Society, Olympia Film Society, Peachtree Film Society, University Film Society and Yale Film Society.

Special thanks to Kimberly Butler, Marilyn Laurie, David Margolick, Jane Rosenthal, Arthur Schlesinger, Jr. and Bill Wolf, all of whom reviewed – and criticized – this book for us. Any improvements are theirs, any remaining faults are ours.

Thanks also to the following, each of whom edited portions of this guide: Anne Cole, Ed Dwyer, Griff Foxley, Gwen Hyman, Natalie Lebert, Laura Mitchell, Joshua Mooney, Pia Nordlinger, Maura O'Connell, Bernard Onken, Daniel Simmons and Christy Stabin. In addition, this guide would not have been possible without the hard work of our staff, especially Reni Chin, Liz Daleske, Gail Horwood, Diane Karlin, Mike Liao, Dave Makulec, Sharon Yates and Kyle Zolner.

The reviews published in this guide are based on public opinion surveys, with numerical ratings reflecting the average scores given by all survey participants who voted on each film and text based on direct quotes from, or fair paraphrasings of, participants' comments.

ISBN 1-57006-408-3

Contents

About This Survey

For 24 years, Zagat Survey has reported on the shared experiences of diners and travelers like you. In recent years, we've expanded our scope to cover entertaining, nightlife, shopping and golf. Now we are proud to bring you the ultimate moviegoers' guide, a compilation of the 1,000 best films to watch. And we've gone one step further to make this a valuable and entertaining resource – for the first time, we've partnered with **E!**, a leader in entertainment programming, who will bring this guide to life on TV. We also want to thank our sponsor, **SONY Electronics,** for its invaluable support.

With over 5,300 participants in this *Survey,* seeing an average of 2.2 movies per week (or 613,000 films annually), and with each surveyor separately rating the films they've seen for Overall Quality, Acting, Story and Production Values, we hope to have achieved a uniquely reliable guide.

Of our surveyors, 50% are women, 50% men; the breakdown by age is 24% in their 20s, 30% in their 30s, 18% in their 40s, 18% in their 50s and 10% in their 60s or above. Though living in all parts of the country and coming from highly diverse backgrounds, these surveyors share one common trait – they are all movie lovers. In producing the reviews contained in this guide, our editors have synopsized surveyors' opinions, with their exact comments shown in quotation marks. We thank each of these participants for their thoughtful comments and ratings. This guide is really "theirs."

To help our readers find the best movie for each occasion, we have prepared a number of lists – see Most Popular (page 9) and Top Ratings (pages 10–26) – and 57 handy indexes.

Though 84% of the films in this book are now available on DVD, to assist potential viewers, we have flagged those *not* available with an icon – ∅.

If you'd like to join our next *Movie Survey* or any of our upcoming *Surveys,* all you need to do is register at zagat.com and select the survey in which you'd like to participate. Each voter will receive a free copy of the resulting guide when it is published.

Since this is a first-time effort, there is sure to be room for improvement. We would appreciate your comments, suggestions and even criticisms so that we can revise our future editions. Please contact us at movies@zagat.com or by mail at Movies – Zagat Survey, 4 Columbus Circle, New York, NY 10019. We look forward to hearing from you and appreciate your help.

New York, NY
September 18, 2002

Nina and Tim
Nina and Tim Zagat

Zagat Goes to the Movies

Welcome to Zagat Survey's first *Movie Guide,* rating and reviewing 1,000 of the top films of all time. Unlike other guidebooks whose choices (and opinions) come from one or two professional critics, this book tells it from the unique perspective of avid filmgoers like you. Compiled by popular vote, it's a snapshot of the moviegoing mood at the turn of the new millennium, featuring the 1,000 pictures that garnered the most votes and highest ratings from over 5,300 surveyors. We have also included an index of Other Great Films (p. 279) that just missed the cut.

The Kane Mutiny: For years, professional critics have ranked Orson Welles' *Citizen Kane* (1941) the best movie of all time. While there's no doubt it is a seminal film in cinematic history, is it the best ever? Our surveyors didn't think so. The Top Overall vote (as well as Most Popular honors) went to Francis Ford Coppola's *The Godfather* (1972); *Citizen Kane* was ranked No. 13 in Overall Quality and No. 8 in terms of Popularity.

Oscar-worthiness: The Academy of Motion Picture Arts and Sciences has been awarding Oscars since 1927, and we wondered if its choices over the years still rang true with our surveyors. The answer is a resounding "yes," with 80% of the Best Picture winners represented in this guide. Predictably, the fallout occurred with earlier films; while every Best Picture from 1953 onward made the cut, winners from the '20s, '30s and '40s are more selectively represented. Although a few omissions were surprising (*Gentleman's Agreement, The Lost Weekend, Grand Hotel*), for the most part those that didn't get enough votes were lesser lights in the cinematic firmament (e.g. *Cavalcade, The Greatest Show on Earth, The Great Ziegfeld*).

The Best: We also polled our respondents about their all-time favorites, with the following results, in order of popularity: **Actor:** Harrison Ford, Cary Grant, Robert De Niro, Tom Hanks, Humphrey Bogart, James Stewart, Sean Connery, Al Pacino, Kevin Spacey and Paul Newman. **Actress:** Julia Roberts, Katharine Hepburn, Audrey Hepburn, Meryl Streep, Meg Ryan, Jodie Foster, Bette Davis, Ingrid Bergman, Michelle Pfeiffer and Grace Kelly. **Director:** Steven Spielberg, Alfred Hitchcock, Ron Howard, Martin Scorsese, Stanley Kubrick, Francis Ford Coppola, Woody Allen, Robert Altman, George Lucas and Frank Capra. (The absence of women and black directors reflects their limited opportunities in Hollywood in the past. Fortunately, there are signs that this is changing.)

The Worst: What irritated surveyors most? Obviously, the first answer is "bad movies." Surveyors quickly voted out such bummers as *Showgirls, Wild Wild West* and *Endless Love.* Other irritants included people talking during the picture, followed by expensive tickets, ringing cell phones, poor seats, unruly crowds and messy theaters.

What's My (Favorite) Line?: Since the movies learned to talk, they've added many unforgettable lines to our national lexicon. Here are the best of the bunch, in order of mention: "Frankly, my dear, I don't give a damn" (from *Gone with the Wind*); "I'll be back" (*The Terminator*); "Here's looking at you, kid" (*Casablanca*); "Fasten your seatbelts, it's going to be a bumpy night" (*All About Eve*); "Play it [again], Sam" (*Casablanca*); "You talkin' to me?" (*Taxi Driver*); "Badges? We don't need no stinkin' badges" (*Treasure of the Sierra Madre*); "I think this is the beginning of a beautiful friendship" (*Casablanca*); "I'll have what she's having" (*When Harry Met Sally*); and "You had me at hello" (*Jerry Maguire*). Obviously, the best single source was *Casablanca,* which one surveyor called the "runner-up to Shakespeare for classic lines." Other great one-liners are spread through this book.

Played Out: Overall, surveyors preferred films made from the 1970s onward. These pictures account for nearly two-thirds of the listings in this book. Outside of a handful of classics, films from the first half of the 20th century didn't do as well – probably because they are less available to see and appear "dated" to younger viewers. Thus, barely 100 films from the '30s and '40s received our surveyors' endorsement. As a result, even though their films were surveyed, some once-famous stars (Greta Garbo, W.C. Fields, Rudolph Valentino, Mae West) don't appear here. Still, fans of Hollywood's Golden Age won't be disappointed: the most iconic names of the silver screen (Humphrey Bogart, Bette Davis, Katharine Hepburn, John Wayne, etc.) are strongly represented.

Rating the Ratings: In 1968, the Motion Picture Association of America introduced a voluntary film ratings system designed to aid parents in deciding what movies are appropriate for children. Of the Top 1,000, 25% were not rated (that is to say, they were made pre-1968), 10% rated G, 23% rated PG, 10% rated PG-13 and 32% rated R. In short, roughly one-third of the pictures herein are acceptable for all audiences, one-third require parental guidance and one-third are meant for people over 17 years old.

In summary, we have tried to assemble a guide that's different from the rest, representing the opinions of thousands of movie fans, who are serious about film, but also understand that motion pictures are made to entertain. Everyone's a critic when it comes to the movies, and we expect (and welcome) some lively debate about the selections herein. Here's looking at you, kids.

New York, NY
September 18, 2002

Curt Gathje

Key to Ratings/Symbols

Film Name, U.S. Release, Director & Cast, Running Time, MPAA Rating

Oscar Winner, Black & White, Led to Sequel, Foreign Language, Not on DVD

Zagat Ratings

O	A	S	P
25	19	25	12

Tim & Nina's Excellent Adventure ✉◐Ⓘ🄵∅

2001. Directed by Steven Spielberg. With Harrison Ford, Julia Roberts. 90 minutes. Rated PG.

◪ This "stirring" story of a couple's "epic struggle to build a publishing empire" "against all odds" divides critics: "inspiring" ("outdoes *Citizen Kane*") vs. "strictly snoozeville" ("Bill and Ted's adventure was much better"); while most applaud Ford's "sensitive" portrayal of Tim ("amazing makeup job"), some feel Roberts' take on Nina "doesn't get all the nuances"; P.S. the black-and-white 3-D shots can be "nauseating", especially the dinner scenes.

Review, with surveyors' comments in quotes

Movies with highest overall ratings and greatest popularity are printed in CAPITAL LETTERS.

Symbols: Before each review the symbol ■ indicates responses were uniform, and ◪ means they were mixed. Other key symbols are:

✉ Oscar winner for Picture, Lead Acting, Direction, Screenplay, Foreign Film
◐ Filmed in Black & White
Ⓘ Inspired a Sequel
🄵 Foreign Language film
∅ Not yet on DVD

Ratings: Given for Overall Quality, Acting, Story and Production Values on a scale of **0** to **30**:

O Overall	A Acting	S Story	P Production Values
25	19	25	12

0–9 poor to fair
10–15 fair to good
16–19 good to very good
20–25 very good to excellent
26–30 extraordinary to perfection

Most Popular Movies

Each of our reviewers has been asked to name his or her five favorite films. The movies most frequently named, in order of their popularity, are:

1. Godfather, The
2. Casablanca
3. Star Wars
4. Gone with the Wind
5. Shawshank Redemption
6. Braveheart
7. Lord of Rings/Fellowship
8. Citizen Kane
9. Godfather Part II
10. Raiders of the Lost Ark
11. American Beauty
12. When Harry Met Sally
13. Beautiful Mind
14. It's a Wonderful Life
15. African Queen
16. Schindler's List
17. Matrix, The
18. Princess Bride
19. Wizard of Oz
20. Annie Hall
21. Usual Suspects*
22. Pretty Woman
23. Sound of Music
24. Moulin Rouge! (2001)
25. Pulp Fiction
26. 2001: A Space Odyssey
27. Gladiator
28. Affair to Remember
29. Breakfast at Tiffany's
30. Goodfellas*
31. Almost Famous
32. Saving Private Ryan
33. Singin' in the Rain*
34. Apocalypse Now
35. Lawrence of Arabia
36. Bridget Jones's Diary
37. Empire Strikes Back*
38. Shrek
39. Silence of the Lambs*
40. Animal House
41. Forrest Gump
42. All About Eve
43. Top Gun
44. Blade Runner
45. Memento*
46. E.T. The Extra-Terrestrial
47. Chocolat
48. Graduate, The
49. Dr. Strangelove
50. To Kill a Mockingbird*

Based on cumulative votes, this list reflects not just popularity on a per-viewer basis, but also the number of people who saw each film. Thus it favors more recent titles that have been seen by most surveyors over earlier ones that younger surveyors are less likely to have viewed.

* Tied with movie directly above it

Top Ratings

Overall Quality*

29 Godfather, The
Godfather Part II
Casablanca
Schindler's List
Lawrence of Arabia
To Kill a Mockingbird

28 Star Wars
Wizard of Oz
Lady Eve
Singin' in the Rain
Rear Window
It Happened One Night
Citizen Kane
Shawshank Redemption
All About Eve
African Queen
Third Man
Dr. Strangelove
Best Years of Our Lives
Man for All Seasons
Grapes of Wrath
On the Waterfront
Paths of Glory
Lion in Winter
Fantasia
Bridge on the River Kwai
Some Like It Hot
Sunset Boulevard
All Quiet on Western Front
Sound of Music
Gone with the Wind
North by Northwest
High Noon
12 Angry Men
Double Indemnity
Maltese Falcon
Psycho
Raiders of the Lost Ark

27 One Flew Over Cuckoo's Nest
My Fair Lady
Sweet Smell of Success
Snow White
Philadelphia Story
Woman of the Year
Treasure of Sierra Madre
Usual Suspects
West Side Story
Taxi Driver
Young Frankenstein
Notorious
Searchers, The**
Silence of the Lambs

By Genre

Action/Adventure

29 Lawrence of Arabia

28 Star Wars
Raiders of the Lost Ark

27 Treasure of the Sierra Madre
Apocalypse Now
Lord of Rings/Fellowship
Great Escape

26 Empire Strikes Back
Butch Cassidy
Papillon

Americana

29 To Kill a Mockingbird

28 Best Years of Our Lives
Grapes of Wrath

26 Christmas Story
Meet Me in St. Louis

25 Yankee Doodle Dandy
Music Man
All the King's Men
Stand by Me

24 American Graffiti

Animated

28 Fantasia

27 Snow White
Toy Story

26 Shrek
Beauty and the Beast (1991)
Pinocchio
Cinderella
Bambi
Lady and the Tramp
Monsters, Inc.

Biography

29 Lawrence of Arabia

28 Man for All Seasons

27 Patton
Gandhi

26 Raging Bull
Amadeus
Becket
Beautiful Mind
Last Emperor

25 Yankee Doodle Dandy

---

* See page 26 for Best Foreign Language Films and page 279 for "Other Great Films."

** Tied with movie directly above it

Children/Family
28 Wizard of Oz
Fantasia
Sound of Music
27 Snow White
It's a Wonderful Life
Christmas Carol
Princess Bride
Toy Story
Mary Poppins
26 E.T. The Extra-Terrestrial

Comedy
28 All About Eve
Dr. Strangelove
Some Like It Hot
27 Woman of the Year
Young Frankenstein
Annie Hall
Stalag 17
Graduate, The
Mister Roberts
26 MASH

Crime
29 Godfather, The
Godfather Part II
28 On the Waterfront
27 Usual Suspects
Taxi Driver
Silence of the Lambs
Sting, The
Goodfellas
26 Pulp Fiction
L.A. Confidential

Documentary
28 Shoah
27 Triumph of the Will
26 Hoop Dreams
Last Waltz
25 That's Entertainment!
Gimme Shelter
Buena Vista Social Club
Celluloid Closet
Stop Making Sense
24 Roger & Me

Drama
29 Schindler's List
To Kill a Mockingbird
28 Citizen Kane
Shawshank Redemption
African Queen
Best Years of Our Lives
Man for all Seasons
Grapes of Wrath
Lion in Winter
12 Angry Men

Epic
29 Lawrence of Arabia
28 Bridge on the River Kwai
Gone with the Wind
27 Gandhi
Doctor Zhivago
26 Ben-Hur
Last Emperor
Spartacus
Empire of the Sun
24 Longest Day

Fantasy
28 Wizard of Oz
Raiders of the Lost Ark
27 Lord of Rings/Fellowship
It's a Wonderful Life
Christmas Carol
Princess Bride
Mary Poppins
Cinderella
26 Harvey
Willy Wonka

Film Noir
28 Third Man
Sunset Boulevard
Double Indemnity
Maltese Falcon
27 Sweet Smell of Success
Chinatown
Big Sleep
Night of the Hunter
Laura
26 Touch of Evil

Horror
28 Psycho
26 Jaws
Sixth Sense
25 Exorcist, The
Wait Until Dark
Frankenstein
Alien
Shining, The
Bride of Frankenstein
24 Dracula (1992)

James Bond
26 Goldfinger
23 From Russia with Love
Dr. No
22 Thunderball
You Only Live Twice
21 Spy Who Loved Me
20 Tomorrow Never Dies
Diamonds Are Forever
19 GoldenEye
World Is Not Enough

Top Overall

Musical

28 Wizard of Oz
Singin' in the Rain
Sound of Music
27 My Fair Lady
West Side Story
Top Hat
King and I
Mary Poppins
26 Fiddler on the Roof
American in Paris

Romance

29 Casablanca
28 Lady Eve
It Happened One Night
African Queen
Some Like It Hot
Gone With The Wind
27 My Fair Lady
Philadelphia Story
Woman of the Year
Brief Encounter

Sci-Fi

28 Star Wars
27 Metropolis
26 E.T. The Extra-Terrestrial
Empire Strikes Back
Blade Runner
2001: A Space Odyssey
25 Matrix, The
Alien
Forbidden Planet
Day the Earth Stood Still

Screwball Comedy

28 Lady Eve
It Happened One Night
27 Philadelphia Story
Duck Soup
Bringing Up Baby
26 His Girl Friday
Night at the Opera
Thin Man
Born Yesterday
Animal Crackers

Silent

28 General, The
City Lights
Modern Times
27 Potemkin
Metropolis
26 Cabinet of Dr. Caligari
25 Birth of a Nation

Thriller

28 Rear Window
Third Man
North by Northwest
Psycho
27 Usual Suspects
Taxi Driver
Notorious
Silence of the Lambs
Manchurian Candidate
Vertigo

War

29 Schindler's List
28 Paths of Glory
Bridge on the River Kwai
All Quiet on Western Front
27 Apocalypse Now
Patton
Stalag 17
Great Escape
26 MASH
Saving Private Ryan

Western

28 High Noon
27 Searchers, The
Wild Bunch
Stagecoach
26 Red River
Butch Cassidy
Shane
Unforgiven
Magnificent Seven
25 Blazing Saddles

By Decade

1910s/1920s

28 General, The
27 Potemkin
Metropolis
26 Cabinet of Dr. Caligari
25 Birth of a Nation
24 Cocoanuts, The

1930s

28 Wizard of Oz
It Happened One Night
All Quiet on Western Front
Modern Times
Gone With the Wind
27 Snow White
Duck Soup
Top Hat
Wuthering Heights
39 Steps

1940s

29 Casablanca
28 Lady Eve
Citizen Kane
Best Years of Our Lives
Grapes of Wrath
Fantasia
Double Indemnity
Maltese Falcon
27 Philadelphia Story
Woman of the Year

1950s

28 Singin' in the Rain
Rear Window
All About Eve
African Queen
Third Man
On the Waterfront
Paths of Glory
Bridge on the River Kwai
Some Like It Hot
Sunset Boulevard

1960s

29 Lawrence of Arabia
To Kill a Mockingbird
28 Dr. Strangelove
Man for All Seasons
Lion in Winter
Sound of Music
Psycho
27 My Fair Lady
West Side Story
Manchurian Candidate

1970s

29 Godfather, The
Godfather Part II
28 Star Wars
27 One Flew Over Cuckoo's Nest
Taxi Driver
Young Frankenstein
Chinatown
Apocalypse Now
Patton
Annie Hall

1980s

28 Raiders of the Lost Ark
27 Gandhi
Princess Bride
Breaker Morant
26 E.T. The Extra-Terrestrial
Raging Bull
Amadeus
Empire Strikes Back
Right Stuff
Henry V

1990s

29 Schindler's List
28 Shawshank Redemption
27 Usual Suspects
Silence of the Lambs
Goodfellas
Toy Story
26 Saving Private Ryan
Beauty and the Beast
Pulp Fiction
L.A. Confidential

2000s

27 Lord of Rings/Fellowship
26 Shrek
Beautiful Mind
Monsters, Inc.
Memento
25 Requiem for a Dream
Billy Elliot
24 Harry Potter
23 Gladiator
Traffic

Top Overall

By Director

Robert Aldrich
25 Flight of the Phoenix
22 Whatever Happened to . . .
21 Dirty Dozen

Woody Allen
27 Annie Hall
26 Crimes and Misdemeanors
Manhattan

Pedro Almodóvar
25 All About My Mother
24 Women on the Verge . . .
20 Tie Me Up! Tie Me Down!

Robert Altman
26 MASH
23 McCabe & Mrs. Miller
Player, The

Hal Ashby
26 Being There
25 Harold and Maude
23 Coming Home

Ingmar Bergman
27 Seventh Seal
26 Wild Strawberries
Fanny and Alexander

Kenneth Branagh
26 Henry V
24 Hamlet
22 Dead Again

James L. Brooks
25 Terms of Endearment
23 Broadcast News
22 As Good As It Gets

Mel Brooks
27 Young Frankenstein
26 Producers, The
25 Blazing Saddles

Richard Brooks
25 Elmer Gantry
In Cold Blood
Cat on a Hot Tin Roof

Frank Capra
28 It Happened One Night
27 It's a Wonderful Life
26 Arsenic and Old Lace

Charlie Chaplin
28 City Lights
Modern Times
26 Great Dictator

Joel Coen
25 Fargo
24 Blood Simple
23 Raising Arizona

Francis Ford Coppola
29 Godfather
Godfather Part II
27 Apocalypse Now

George Cukor
27 My Fair Lady
Philadelphia Story
26 Adam's Rib

Michael Curtiz
29 Casablanca
26 Mildred Pierce
25 Yankee Doodle Dandy

Jonathan Demme
27 Silence of the Lambs
25 Stop Making Sense
24 Philadelphia

Stanley Donen
28 Singin' In the Rain
26 Charade
24 Funny Face

Clint Eastwood
26 Unforgiven
25 Outlaw Josey Wales
22 Play Misty for Me

Blake Edwards
27 Days of Wine and Roses
26 Breakfast at Tiffany's
24 Pink Panther

Federico Fellini
27 La Strada
Nights of Cabiria
26 8½

Victor Fleming
28 Wizard of Oz
Gone with the Wind
25 Captains Courageous

John Ford
28 Grapes of Wrath
27 Searchers, The
Quiet Man

Milos Forman
27 One Flew Over Cuckoo's Nest
26 Amadeus
20 Hair

Bob Fosse
26 Cabaret
24 All That Jazz
20 Sweet Charity

John Frankenheimer
27 Manchurian Candidate
26 Seven Days in May
22 Birdman of Alcatraz

Terry Gilliam
26 Monty Python/Holy Grail
24 Brazil
22 Twelve Monkeys

Lasse Hallström
25 My Life As a Dog
22 Chocolat
What's Eating Gilbert Grape

Howard Hawks
27 Big Sleep
Bringing Up Baby
26 Red River

George Roy Hill
27 Sting, The
26 Butch Cassidy
22 Slap Shot

Alfred Hitchcock
28 Rear Window
North by Northwest
Psycho

Ron Howard
26 Beautiful Mind
24 Apollo 13
22 Parenthood

John Huston
28 African Queen
Maltese Falcon
27 Treasure of Sierra Madre

James Ivory
26 Room with a View
24 Remains of the Day
22 Howards End

Norman Jewison
26 Fiddler on the Roof
24 Moonstruck
In the Heat of the Night

Philip Kaufman
26 Right Stuff
21 Unbearable Lightness of Being
19 Invasion of Body Snatchers

Elia Kazan
28 On the Waterfront
27 Streetcar Named Desire
25 Splendor in the Grass

Henry King
26 Twelve O'Clock High
24 Carousel
22 Love Is Many-Splendored

Stanley Kramer
26 Inherit the Wind
Judgment at Nuremberg
25 Guess Who's Coming to Dinner

Stanley Kubrick
28 Dr. Strangelove
Paths of Glory
26 2001: A Space Odyssey

Akira Kurosawa
29 Seven Samurai
Rashomon
27 Ran

David Lean
29 Lawrence of Arabia
28 Bridge on the River Kwai
27 Brief Encounter

Ang Lee
26 Sense and Sensibility
25 Eat Drink Man Woman
24 Crouching Tiger

Barry Levinson
25 Rain Man
Diner
23 Natural, The

George Lucas
28 Star Wars
24 American Graffiti
18 Star Wars/Phantom Menace

Sidney Lumet
28 12 Angry Men
26 Pawnbroker, The
24 Fail-Safe

Terrence Malick
25 Badlands
23 Days of Heaven
19 Thin Red Line

Louis Malle
27 Au Revoir Les Enfants
24 Atlantic City
21 My Dinner with André

Joseph L. Mankiewicz
28 All About Eve
25 Sleuth
24 Ghost and Mrs. Muir

Michael Mann
25 Insider, The
22 Last of the Mohicans
Heat

Vincente Minnelli
26 American in Paris
Band Wagon
Meet Me in St. Louis

Robert Mulligan
29 To Kill a Mockingbird
22 Same Time, Next Year
21 Summer of '42

Top Overall

Mike Nichols
27 Graduate, The
25 Who's Afraid of V. Woolf?
22 Silkwood

Alan J. Pakula
26 Sophie's Choice
25 All the President's Men
20 Klute

Arthur Penn
25 Miracle Worker
Bonnie and Clyde
24 Little Big Man

Wolfgang Petersen
28 Das Boot
20 In the Line of Fire
18 Air Force One

Sydney Pollack
25 Tootsie
Out of Africa
24 Way We Were

Otto Preminger
27 Laura
26 Anatomy of a Murder
23 Exodus

Robert Redford
25 Ordinary People
22 River Runs Through It
21 Quiz Show

Rob Reiner
27 Princess Bride
26 This Is Spinal Tap
When Harry Met Sally

Franklin J. Schaffner
27 Patton
26 Papillon
23 Planet of the Apes

Martin Scorsese
27 Taxi Driver
Goodfellas
26 Raging Bull

Ridley Scott
26 Blade Runner
25 Alien
23 Gladiator

Steven Spielberg
29 Schindler's List
28 Raiders of the Lost Ark
26 E.T. The Extra-Terrestrial

George Stevens
27 Woman of the Year
Place in the Sun
26 Shane

Robert Stevenson
27 Mary Poppins
25 Jane Eyre
24 Old Yeller

Oliver Stone
25 Platoon
22 Wall Street
20 Born on the Fourth of July

John Sturges
27 Great Escape
26 Magnificent Seven
24 Bad Day at Black Rock

François Truffaut
27 400 Blows
Day for Night
24 Jules and Jim

Peter Weir
25 Gallipoli
24 Year of Living Dangerously
Dead Poets Society

Orson Welles
28 Citizen Kane
26 Touch of Evil
25 Lady from Shanghai

James Whale
25 Frankenstein
Bride of Frankenstein
22 Invisible Man

Billy Wilder
28 Sunset Boulevard
Double Indemnity
27 Witness for the Prosecution

Robert Wise
28 Sound of Music
27 West Side Story
25 Day the Earth Stood Still

Sam Wood
26 Night at the Opera
25 For Whom the Bell Tolls
24 Day at the Races

William Wyler
28 Best Years of Our Lives
27 Roman Holiday
Wuthering Heights

Terence Young
25 Wait Until Dark
23 From Russia with Love
Dr. No

Fred Zinnemann
28 Man for All Seasons
High Noon
26 From Here to Eternity

Acting

29 Godfather Part II
Godfather, The
All About Eve
One Flew Over Cuckoo's Nest
Lion in Winter
Taxi Driver
On the Waterfront
Becket
To Kill a Mockingbird
Schindler's List
Brief Encounter
African Queen
28 Casablanca
Beautiful Mind
Streetcar Named Desire
Silence of the Lambs
Days of Wine and Roses
12 Angry Men
Gandhi
Man for All Seasons
Lady Eve
Patton
Shawshank Redemption
Lawrence of Arabia
Now, Voyager
Raging Bull
Adam's Rib
Philadelphia Story
Sweet Smell of Success
Inherit the Wind
White Heat
Cries and Whispers
Sophie's Choice
My Left Foot
Night of the Hunter
Midnight Cowboy
Born Yesterday
Kind Hearts and Coronets
Grapes of Wrath
Chinatown
Woman of the Year
Apartment, The
Caine Mutiny
Sunset Boulevard
Sleuth
Witness for the Prosecution
Bridge on the River Kwai
American History X
It Happened One Night
Third Man

By Lead Actor

Woody Allen
26 Annie Hall
Crimes and Misdemeanors
24 Manhattan

Julie Andrews
25 Sound of Music
24 Mary Poppins
Victor/Victoria

Fred Astaire
24 Funny Face
23 Top Hat
21 Band Wagon

Lauren Bacall
27 To Have and Have Not
Big Sleep
26 Key Largo

Anne Bancroft
28 Miracle Worker
27 Graduate, The
25 Agnes of God

Alan Bates
27 Zorba the Greek
25 Unmarried Woman
23 Rose, The

Warren Beatty
25 Bonnie and Clyde
Splendor in the Grass
23 McCabe & Mrs. Miller

Annette Bening
27 American Beauty
26 Grifters, The
22 American President

Ingrid Bergman
28 Casablanca
27 Notorious
Gaslight

Humphrey Bogart
29 African Queen
28 Casablanca
Caine Mutiny

Kenneth Branagh
28 Henry V
26 Hamlet
24 Dead Again

Marlon Brando
29 Godfather, The
On the Waterfront
28 Streetcar Named Desire

Top Acting

Jeff Bridges
24 Fisher King
23 Last Picture Show
Contender, The

Matthew Broderick
26 Glory
24 Election
22 Ferris Bueller's Day Off

Yul Brynner
27 Anastasia
26 King and I
21 Ten Commandments

Ellen Burstyn
27 Requiem for a Dream
26 Alice Doesn't Live Here
24 Exorcist, The

Richard Burton
29 Beckett
27 Who's Afraid of Virginia Woolf?
18 Cleopatra

Nicolas Cage
25 Moonstruck
24 Leaving Las Vegas
23 Raising Arizona

James Cagney
28 White Heat
27 Mister Roberts
25 Yankee Doodle Dandy

Michael Caine
28 Sleuth
26 Man Who Would Be King
Alfie

Charlie Chaplin
28 City Lights
27 Great Dictator
26 Modern Times

Julie Christie
26 Hamlet
Doctor Zhivago
23 McCabe and Mrs. Miller

Montgomery Clift
27 From Here to Eternity
Place in the Sun
25 Red River

George Clooney
23 O Brother, Where Art Thou?
21 Out of Sight
Thin Red Line

Glenn Close
26 Dangerous Liaisons
24 Big Chill
23 Fatal Attraction

Sean Connery
26 Man Who Would Be King
25 Wind and the Lion
24 Hunt for Red October

Gary Cooper
26 High Noon
For Whom the Bell Tolls
23 Beau Geste

Kevin Costner
24 Silverado
22 Bull Durham
Untouchables, The

Russell Crowe
28 Beautiful Mind
Insider, The
27 L.A. Confidential

Tom Cruise
27 Rain Man
26 Few Good Men
23 Magnolia

Billy Crystal
25 When Harry Met Sally
21 Analyze This
20 City Slickers

Tony Curtis
28 Sweet Smell of Success
27 Some Like It Hot
19 Operation Petticoat

John Cusack
26 Grifters, The
24 Being John Malkovich
23 Bullets Over Broadway

Willem Dafoe
25 Platoon
Shadow of the Vampire
24 Mississippi Burning

Matt Damon
26 Saving Private Ryan
25 Good Will Hunting
21 Talented Mr. Ripley

Bette Davis
29 All About Eve
28 Now, Voyager
27 Dark Victory

Geena Davis
25 Thelma & Louise
24 Accidental Tourist
20 League of Their Own

Daniel Day-Lewis
28 My Left Foot
25 In the Name of the Father
24 Age of Innocence

James Dean
27 East of Eden
24 Rebel Without a Cause
23 Giant

Catherine Deneuve
25 Belle de Jour
Indochine
23 Dancer in the Dark

Robert De Niro
29 Taxi Driver
28 Raging Bull
Deer Hunter

Johnny Depp
25 What's Eating Gilbert Grape
24 Donnie Brasco
Chocolat

Leonardo DiCaprio
25 What's Eating Gilbert Grape
17 Romeo + Juliet
16 Titanic

Kirk Douglas
27 Paths of Glory
24 Seven Days in May
Spartacus

Michael Douglas
25 China Syndrome
24 Traffic
Wonder Boys

Richard Dreyfuss
24 Apprenticeship of Duddy Kravitz
23 Goodbye Girl
American Graffiti

Faye Dunaway
28 Chinatown
25 Network
Bonnie and Clyde

Clint Eastwood
26 Unforgiven
23 Outlaw Josey Wales
Bridges of Madison County

Mia Farrow
26 Crimes and Misdemeanors
25 Hannah and Her Sisters
Rosemary's Baby

Sally Field
27 Norma Rae
25 Steel Magnolias
Absence of Malice

Ralph Fiennes
29 Schindler's List
24 End of the Affair
English Patient

Albert Finney
27 Two for the Road
24 Tom Jones
23 Erin Brockovich

Henry Fonda
28 12 Angry Men
Lady Eve
Grapes of Wrath

Jane Fonda
27 On Golden Pond
26 Coming Home
25 China Syndrome

Harrison Ford
24 Fugitive, The
Raiders of the Lost Ark
Witness

Jodie Foster
28 Silence of the Lambs
Accused, The
21 Anna and the King

Morgan Freeman
28 Shawshank Redemption
27 Driving Miss Daisy
26 Unforgiven

Clark Gable
28 It Happened One Night
27 Gone with the Wind
25 Mutiny on the Bounty (1935)

Judy Garland
26 Wizard of Oz
Star Is Born
24 Meet Me in St. Louis

Richard Gere
25 Primal Fear
22 Pretty Woman
21 Officer and a Gentleman

Mel Gibson
25 Year of Living Dangerously
Gallipoli
24 Braveheart

Cary Grant
28 Philadelphia Story
His Girl Friday
27 Bringing Up Baby

Hugh Grant
24 Bridget Jones's Diary
21 Four Weddings and a Funeral
19 Notting Hill

Alec Guinness
28 Kind Hearts and Coronets
Bridge on the River Kwai
26 Lavender Hill Mob

Top Acting

Gene Hackman
26 Unforgiven
French Connection
24 Mississippi Burning

Tom Hanks
27 Philadelphia
26 Forrest Gump
Saving Private Ryan

Ed Harris
28 Beautiful Mind
27 Glengarry Glen Ross
26 Pollock

Rex Harrison
27 My Fair Lady
25 Ghost and Mrs. Muir
18 Cleopatra

Audrey Hepburn
27 My Fair Lady
Two for the Road
26 Roman Holiday

Katharine Hepburn
29 Lion in Winter
African Queen
28 Adam's Rib

Charlton Heston
24 Touch of Evil
23 Ben-Hur
21 Ten Commandments

Dustin Hoffman
28 Midnight Cowboy
27 Graduate, The
Rain Man

William Holden
28 Born Yesterday
Sunset Boulevard
Bridge on the River Kwai

Anthony Hopkins
28 Silence of the Lambs
27 Elephant Man
Remains of the Day

Holly Hunter
25 Broadcast News
24 Piano, The
23 Raising Arizona

William Hurt
25 Children of a Lesser God
Body Heat
Kiss of the Spider Woman

Anjelica Huston
26 Crimes and Misdemeanors
Grifters, The
24 Prizzi's Honor

Jeremy Irons
25 French Lieutenant's Woman
24 Mission, The
23 Dead Ringers

Shirley Jones
27 Elmer Gantry
24 Music Man
22 Oklahoma!

Diane Keaton
26 Annie Hall
24 Manhattan
20 Father of the Bride

Gene Kelly
28 Inherit the Wind
26 Singin' in the Rain
23 American in Paris

Grace Kelly
27 Rear Window
26 High Noon
25 To Catch a Thief

Deborah Kerr
27 From Here to Eternity
26 King and I
25 Affair to Remember

Nicole Kidman
25 Others, The
23 Moulin Rouge!
21 To Die For

Kevin Kline
28 Sophie's Choice
24 Fish Called Wanda
Big Chill

Burt Lancaster
28 Sweet Smell of Success
27 Elmer Gantry
Atlantic City

Jack Lemmon
28 Days of Wine and Roses
Apartment, The
27 Odd Couple

Peter Lorre
28 Casablanca
27 Maltese Falcon
26 M

Myrna Loy
27 Best Years of Our Lives
25 Thin Man
24 Mr. Blandings . . .

Shirley MacLaine
28 Apartment, The
27 Being There
26 Terms of Endearment

Tobey Maguire
24 Wonder Boys
Cider House Rules
21 Pleasantville

John Malkovich
26 Dangerous Liaisons
Killing Fields
25 Shadow of the Vampire

Marx Brothers
25 Duck Soup
Night at the Opera
24 Animal Crackers

Matthew McConaughey
24 Amistad
21 Contact
18 Time to Kill

Frances McDormand
27 Fargo
25 Man Who Wasn't There
Blood Simple

Kelly McGillis
28 Accused, The
24 Witness
18 Top Gun

Ewan McGregor
23 Moulin Rouge! (2001)
22 Trainspotting
16 Star Wars Episode 1

Steve McQueen
27 Papillon
26 Sand Pebbles
Great Escape

Marilyn Monroe
27 Some Like It Hot
23 Seven Year Itch
21 Gentlemen Prefer Blondes

Yves Montand
27 Jean de Florette
26 Wages of Fear
25 Z

Bill Murray
25 Rushmore
24 Royal Tenenbaums
21 Ghostbusters

Paul Newman
27 Cat on a Hot Tin Roof
Cool Hand Luke
26 Hustler, The

Jack Nicholson
29 One Flew Over Cuckoo's Nest
28 Chinatown
27 Five Easy Pieces

Nick Nolte
25 Affliction
24 Cape Fear
21 Prince of Tides

Edward Norton
28 American History X
25 Fight Club
Primal Fear

Kim Novak
26 Vertigo
24 Picnic
22 Bell, Book and Candle

Laurence Olivier
28 Sleuth
27 Wuthering Heights
Rebecca

Peter O'Toole
29 Lion in Winter
Becket
28 Lawrence of Arabia

Al Pacino
29 Godfather Part II
Godfather, The
28 Insider, The

Gwyneth Paltrow
25 Shakespeare In Love
24 Royal Tenenbaums
23 Emma

Guy Pearce
27 L.A. Confidential
25 Memento
24 Adventures of Priscilla . . .

Gregory Peck
29 To Kill a Mockingbird
26 Cape Fear (1962)
Roman Holiday

Sean Penn
26 Dead Man Walking
21 Thin Red Line
19 Fast Times at Ridgemont High

Joe Pesci
28 Raging Bull
27 Goodfellas
24 My Cousin Vinny

Michelle Pfeiffer
26 Dangerous Liaisons
24 Age of Innocence
23 Scarface

Brad Pitt
25 Fight Club
23 Seven
Twelve Monkeys

Top Acting

Sidney Poitier
27 In the Heat of the Night
Guess Who's Coming to Dinner
26 Lilies of the Field

William Powell
27 Mister Roberts
25 Thin Man
My Man Godfrey

Claude Rains
28 Casablanca
Now, Voyager
27 Notorious

Robert Redford
26 Sting, The
Butch Cassidy
All the President's Men

Tim Robbins
28 Shawshank Redemption
23 Player, The
22 Bull Durham

Julia Roberts
23 Erin Brockovich
22 Pretty Woman
19 My Best Friend's Wedding

Edward G. Robinson
27 Double Indemnity
26 Key Largo
21 Ten Commandments

Rosalind Russell
28 His Girl Friday
25 Auntie Mame
24 Picnic

Winona Ryder
24 Age of Innocence
23 Little Women
22 Girl, Interrupted

Susan Sarandon
27 Atlantic City
26 Dead Man Walking
25 Thelma & Louise

Peter Sellers
28 Dr. Strangelove
27 Being There
24 Lolita

Omar Sharif
28 Lawrence of Arabia
26 Doctor Zhivago
25 Funny Girl

Jean Simmons
27 Elmer Gantry
24 Spartacus
21 Guys and Dolls

Frank Sinatra
27 From Here to Eternity
26 Manchurian Candidate
23 On the Town

Will Smith
24 Six Degrees of Separation
20 Men In Black
19 Enemy of the State

Sissy Spacek
27 Badlands
Coal Miner's Daughter
26 In the Bedroom

Kevin Spacey
28 Usual Suspects
27 L.A. Confidential
American Beauty

Rod Steiger
29 On the Waterfront
28 Pawnbroker, The
27 In the Heat of the Night

James Stewart
28 Philadelphia Story
27 Rear Window
Anatomy of a Murder

Ben Stiller
24 Royal Tenenbaums
21 Meet the Parents
19 There's Something About Mary

Meryl Streep
28 Sophie's Choice
Deer Hunter
26 Silkwood

Barbra Streisand
25 Funny Girl
Way We Were
21 Prince of Tides

Elizabeth Taylor
27 Who's Afraid of Virginia Woolf?
Cat on a Hot Tin Roof
Place in the Sun

Emma Thompson
27 Sense and Sensibility
Remains of the Day
26 Howards End

Billy Bob Thornton
27 Sling Blade
25 Man Who Wasn't There
22 Simple Plan

Spencer Tracy
28 Adam's Rib
Inherit the Wind
Woman of the Year

John Travolta
26 Pulp Fiction
19 Saturday Night Fever
Face/Off

Jean-Louis Trintignant
26 Conformist, The
25 Z
24 Man and a Woman

Kathleen Turner
25 Body Heat
24 Prizzi's Honor
Accidental Tourist

Jon Voight
28 Midnight Cowboy
26 Coming Home
Deliverance

Denzel Washington
27 Philadelphia
Training Day
26 Hurricane

John Wayne
25 Red River
Searchers, The
Quiet Man

Sigourney Weaver
25 Year of Living Dangerously
22 Alien
Dave

Orson Welles
28 Third Man
27 Citizen Kane
Jane Eyre

Gene Wilder
26 Producers, The
Young Frankenstein
22 Blazing Saddles

Robin Williams
26 Awakenings
25 Dead Poets Society
Good Will Hunting

Bruce Willis
26 Pulp Fiction
25 Sixth Sense
23 Twelve Monkeys

Kate Winslet
27 Sense and Sensibility
25 Heavenly Creatures
16 Titanic

Reese Witherspoon
24 Election
21 Pleasantville
20 Legally Blonde

Natalie Wood
25 Splendor in the Grass
24 West Side Story
Rebel Without a Cause

Best Story

29 Godfather, The
To Kill a Mockingbird
28 Schindler's List
Godfather Part II
Casablanca
Shawshank Redemption
Usual Suspects
All Quiet on Western Front
Star Wars
Paths of Glory
Witness for the Prosecution
Grapes of Wrath
Wizard of Oz
Manchurian Candidate
Best Years of Our Lives
Double Indemnity
Rear Window
Christmas Carol
Seven Days in May
27 Man for All Seasons
All About Eve
Henry V
Wuthering Heights
Citizen Kane
Great Escape
Dr. Strangelove
Wages of Fear
Raiders of the Lost Ark
12 Angry Men
Breaker Morant
Bridge on the River Kwai
Romeo and Juliet (1968)
39 Steps
Place in the Sun
Strangers on a Train
Psycho
Dial M for Murder
Gone with the Wind
Christmas Story
House of Games
It's a Wonderful Life
Rebecca
Searchers, The
Sting, The
One Flew Over Cuckoo's Nest
Killing Fields
Sunset Boulevard
Third Man
Lord of Rings/Fellowship
Princess Bride

By Subject/Style

Camp Classic
25 La Cage aux Folles
Mildred Pierce
24 Auntie Mame
23 Imitation of Life
Whatever Happened to . . .

Chick Flick
26 Sense and Sensibility
25 When Harry Met Sally . . .
Roman Holiday
Affair to Remember
Way We Were

Food-Themed
26 Babette's Feast
25 Like Water for Chocolate
Wedding Banquet
24 Tom Jones
Eat Drink Man Woman

Guy Movie
27 Great Escape
26 Goodfellas
Papillon
25 French Connection
Hunt for Red October

Independent
27 Henry V
25 This is Spinal Tap
Blood Simple
24 Being John Malkovich
Room with a View

Literary Adaptation
29 Godfather
To Kill a Mockingbird
28 Shawshank Redemption
All Quiet on Western Front
Grapes of Wrath

Sports
26 Hoop Dreams
25 Chariots of Fire
Rocky
24 Raging Bull
Hoosiers

Stage Adaptation
28 Witness for the Prosecution
27 Man for All Seasons
Henry V
Romeo and Juliet
Dial M for Murder

Top Production Values

29 Fantasia
Lawrence of Arabia
Lord of Rings/Fellowship
Godfather, The
Star Wars
Godfather Part II
Wizard of Oz
Schindler's List
Gone with the Wind

28 Empire Strikes Back
Matrix, The
Last Emperor
Saving Private Ryan
Singin' in the Rain
Toy Story
Raiders of the Lost Ark
Doctor Zhivago
Citizen Kane
Sound of Music
Shrek
Monsters, Inc.
Ben-Hur
Apocalypse Now
Return of the Jedi
Bridge on the River Kwai
Third Man
Nightmare Before Christmas

27 2001: A Space Odyssey
North by Northwest
Searchers, The
Beauty and the Beast (1991)
West Side Story
Jurassic Park
My Fair Lady
Patton
Braveheart
King and I
Brazil
Gandhi
American in Paris
Blade Runner
Harry Potter
Wild Bunch
Casablanca
E.T. The Extra-Terrestrial
Quiet Man
Who Framed Roger Rabbit
Fantasia 2000
Sunset Boulevard
Psycho

By Category

Animation

29 Fantasia

28 Toy Story
Shrek
Monsters, Inc.
Nightmare Before Christmas

Cinematography – B&W

29 Schindler's List

28 Third Man

27 Children of Paradise
Paths of Glory
Raging Bull

Cinematography – Color

29 Lawrence of Arabia
Lord of Rings/Fellowship
Gone with the Wind

28 Last Emperor
Saving Private Ryan

Costumes

28 Last Emperor

27 My Fair Lady
King and I
American in Paris
Barry Lyndon

Editing

26 Raging Bull
Jaws

25 High Noon
Traffic

24 Bullitt

Scenery

29 Lawrence of Arabia

28 Last Emperor
Raiders of the Lost Ark
Doctor Zhivago
Sound of Music

Sets

29 Godfather Part II

28 Ben-Hur

27 West Side Story
My Fair Lady
American in Paris

Special Effects

29 Lord of Rings/Fellowship
Star Wars

28 Empire Strikes Back
Matrix, The
Return of the Jedi

Best Foreign Language Films

29 Seven Samurai
Rashomon
28 Shoah
Children of Paradise
Beauty and the Beast (1947)
Grand Illusion
Das Boot
27 Ran
Bicycle Thief
Seventh Seal
Life Is Beautiful
La Strada
Au Revoir Les Enfants
Jean de Florette
Nights of Cabiria
Triumph of the Will*
400 Blows
Wages of Fear
Day for Night
26 Cinema Paradiso
Conformist, The
Babette's Feast
8½
Wild Strawberries
Amarcord
Black Orpheus
Fanny and Alexander*
Z
Cries and Whispers
Alexander Nevsky
Amélie
M
Diabolique
25 Blue Angel
Antonia's Line
Garden of Finzi-Continis
Farewell My Concubine
La Dolce Vita
All About My Mother
My Life As a Dog
Like Water for Chocolate
Breathless
Eat Drink Man Woman
24 Jules and Jim
Crouching Tiger
La Cage aux Folles
Swept Away
Il Postino
Man and a Woman
Belle de Jour

By Country

France
28 Shoah
Children of Paradise
Beauty and the Beast (1947)
Grand Illusion
27 Au Revoir Les Enfants
Jean de Florette

Germany
28 Das Boot
27 Triumph of the Will
26 M
25 Blue Angel
24 Wings of Desire
23 Run Lola Run

Italy
27 Bicycle Thief
Life is Beautiful
La Strada
Nights of Cabiria
26 Cinema Paradiso
Conformist, The

Japan
29 Seven Samurai
Rashomon
27 Ran
23 Akira

Spain
25 All About my Mother
24 Women on the Verge
20 Tie Me Up! Tie Me Down!

Sweden
27 Seventh Seal
26 Wild Strawberries
Fanny and Alexander
Cries and Whispers
25 My Life as a Dog
20 Elvira Madigan

* Tied with movie directly above it

Movie Directory

Absence of Malice 21 | 25 | 21 | 20

1981. Directed by Sydney Pollack. With Paul Newman, Sally Field, Bob Balaban. 116 minutes. Rated PG.

◪ "Newman and Field ignite the screen" in this "textured" "hard-hitting" courtroom drama demonstrating how "guilt by association" causes a "newspaper to ruin a man's career"; most say that the "irresponsible press" is a topic made for the movies, but some feel this "slight" effort "should have been better" – starting with the "not-believable ending."

Absent-Minded Professor, The ◑ⓘ∅ 19 | 17 | 19 | 17

1961. Directed by Robert Stevenson. With Fred MacMurray, Nancy Olson, Keenan Wynn. 97 minutes. Rated PG.

◪ Despite its "charming", "classic Disney" formula, this "bouncy tale" involving an invention dubbed "flubber" divides voters: flubbergasted fans claim it "stands up well over time", but deflators find it "kinda corny", adding it "may not appeal" to small fry, since its black-and-white cinematography "looks old"; although popular enough to inspire a couple of remakes, the "original is the best."

Abyss, The 20 | 19 | 19 | 25

1989. Directed by James Cameron. With Ed Harris, Mary Elizabeth Mastrantonio. 146 minutes. Rated PG-13.

■ "Eye-popping" special effects – notably the "break-out use of morphing" – are the raison d'être of this "underwater opus", a "fun" cocktail comprised of a "little sci-fi, a little action and a little romance"; it's also a little "long" and "sputters" at the finale, so diehards recommend the (even longer) "director's cut", which "fleshes out the far-too-abrupt ending in the original version."

Accidental Tourist, The ∅ 20 | 24 | 21 | 19

1988. Directed by Lawrence Kasdan. With William Hurt, Kathleen Turner, Geena Davis. 121 minutes. Rated PG.

◪ This very "zany" romantic drama about love, loss and "alphabetizing the groceries in your cupboard" is "as good as " Anne Tyler's best-seller and might "break and mend your heart in one sitting"; its "perfect cast" includes a "terrific" Hurt and an "offbeat", "pitch-perfect" Davis (who "copped an Oscar"), though some argue the picture is "too quirky", "overrated and inert" for "mainstream" audiences.

Accused, The ✉ 23 | 28 | 23 | 21

1988. Directed by Jonathan Kaplan. With Kelly McGillis, Jodie Foster, Bernie Coulson. 108 minutes. Rated R.

■ Not for the "faint of heart", this "white-knuckle" thriller about a "gang rape" and its courtroom consequences is "based on true events" and dominated by a "phenomenal" Foster, who won a "thoroughly deserved" Oscar for her "captivating performance"; the "excruciating", "very graphic" reenactment of the crime is "definitely for mature audiences" – but far from gratuitous given the picture's "socially responsible" message.

Adam's Rib ◑ 26 | 28 | 25 | 23

1949. Directed by George Cukor. With Spencer Tracy, Katharine Hepburn, Judy Holliday. 101 minutes. Not Rated.

■ "Chemistry abounds" in this "sparkling" Tracy-Hepburn matchup, "probably the best pairing" of these "two pros", who are so "delightful" that many "wish they'd made even more movies together"; plotwise, this "battle-of-the-sexes" comedy concerns "married attorneys on opposing sides of a case", but fans say it's worth watching for the "scintillating" "repartee" and "effortless comedic timing" alone.

Adventures of Priscilla, Queen of the Desert, The 23 | 24 | 22 | 22

1994. Directed by Stephan Elliott. With Terence Stamp, Guy Pearce, Hugo Weaving. 104 minutes. Rated R.

■ "Outlandish drag queens" and the "Australian outback" collide in this "razor-sharp" road comedy, a "flaming" "romp" about "boas, false eyelashes" and a bus "ride through the desert" that's a "nice combination of pathos and fluff"; highlights include Stamp's "campy" performance as a "post-op transsexual looking for love" and a "fabulous" soundtrack that will thrill "ABBA fans"; P.S. yup, "that's really Guy Pearce!"

Adventures of Robin Hood, The ∅ 25 | 22 | 24 | 24

1938. Directed by Michael Curtiz, William Keighley. With Errol Flynn, Olivia de Havilland. 102 minutes. Not Rated.

■ This "swashbuckliest swashbuckler of them all" is the "definitive telling" of the tale, filmed in "gorgeous Technicolor" and "acted with verve" by a "charismatic" Flynn and a "perfect" de Havilland; ok, it might be "a bit dated", but its "lightning-quick dialogue", "exciting" swordplay and those famous "green tights" are "still engaging" enough to inspire a "whole genre of films" – plus a "whole lot of parodies."

Affair to Remember, An 26 | 25 | 25 | 23

1957. Directed by Leo McCarey. With Cary Grant, Deborah Kerr, Richard Denning. 119 minutes. Not Rated.

■ The "ultimate chick flick", this "three-hankie" "tearjerker" begins with a "glamorous" "shipboard romance" that turns "tragic" after an "unexpected twist" at the "Empire State Building"; though the "inspiration for many other" weepies (notably *Sleepless in Seattle*), this one's the "standard", thanks to the "captivating banter", ultra-"suave Grant" and some "classic NY" scenery; just don't bother to see it with your boyfriend – men "don't get it."

Affliction 20 | 25 | 19 | 19

1998. Directed by Paul Schrader. With Nick Nolte, Sissy Spacek, James Coburn. 113 minutes. Rated R.

◪ Granted, it's "grim, grim, grim", but this "disquieting" adaptation of Russell Banks' novel of "family dysfunction" in New Hampshire is still "eminently watchable" due to its "strong performances": Nolte's "wrenching" work and Coburn's "scary", Oscar-winning turn in particular; though admittedly a "great exposé on abuse", some of the afflicted find it so "mind-numbingly downbeat" that they want to "slash their wrists" afterward.

AFRICAN QUEEN, THE ✉ 28 | 29 | 26 | 26

1951. Directed by John Huston. With Humphrey Bogart, Katharine Hepburn. 105 minutes. Not Rated.

■ "Curmudgeonly riverboat captain" Bogart and "feisty missionary" Hepburn "sizzle" as they take a "trip up a hellish river" and "discover love, courage" and the "best use of leeches since the Middle Ages" in this "beautifully crafted" drama; its "legendary reputation" owes a lot to Huston's "no-nonsense direction", James Agee's "witty" screenplay, the fine "location shots" of "deepest Africa" and, of course, that "undeniable chemistry" between the two leads; in sum, "they don't make them like this anymore."

After Hours ∅ 21 | 20 | 22 | 19

1985. Directed by Martin Scorsese. With Griffin Dunne, Rosanna Arquette, Teri Garr. 96 minutes. Rated R.

■ From the ever-"creative" Scorsese comes this "offbeat" "cult" curio, a "pitch-black comedy" set in '80s SoHo recounting the after-hours adventures of a "straight-laced guy" out on the town and out of cash in a "pre-ATM" world; the "numerous subplots" (involving an "ice cream truck", a "headbanger nightclub" and a potty-mouthed sculptress) strike the straightlaced as "confusing" verging on "weird", but most tout its "razor-sharp performances" and "deft" wit.

Age of Innocence, The 22 | 24 | 22 | 26

1993. Directed by Martin Scorsese. With Daniel Day-Lewis, Michelle Pfeiffer, Winona Ryder. 139 minutes. Rated PG.

■ "Scorsese does Edith Wharton justice" in this "exquisite period drama" concerning "forbidden love" among "upper-class NYers" in the "opulent" "Gilded Age"; Day-Lewis gives a "subtle, understated" performance as the "tortured" lover, while the "gorgeous production" supplies a "sumptuous feast for the eyes" that "captures the smallest details in a languorous way" – maybe that's why the pace is a little on the "slow" side.

Agnes of God 21 | 25 | 22 | 19

1985. Directed by Norman Jewison. With Jane Fonda, Anne Bancroft, Meg Tilly. 98 minutes. Rated PG-13.

◪ Make sure to "be in a serious mood" for this "disturbing" yet "powerful" drama about a "hysterical nun who may or may not be pregnant"; while there's some mighty "serious acting by some great women", voters split on the story ("compelling" vs. "convoluted") and the overall quality ("thought-provoking" vs. "underbaked"); either way, it's "worth sitting through just for the ending."

Air Force One 18 | 19 | 18 | 21

1997. Directed by Wolfgang Petersen. With Harrison Ford, Gary Oldman, Glenn Close. 124 minutes. Rated R.

◪ The "furrowed-browed" Ford plays a "butt-kicking" American president whose plane is hijacked by a "Russian madman" in this "escapist" thriller, a roiling stew of "edge-of-your-recliner" "suspense" and "million-dollar stunts"; sure, cynics nix its "far-fetched", "action-by-the-numbers" plot but admit that this piece of "harmless, jingoistic fun" "works best with a big bowl of popcorn" nearby.

Airplane! Ⓘ 24 | 19 | 20 | 19

1980. Directed by Jim Abrahams, David Zucker, Jerry Zucker. With Robert Hays, Julie Hagerty, Lloyd Bridges, Leslie Nielsen, Peter Graves. 88 minutes. Rated PG.

■ "Funny as heck", this "laugh-a-second spoof" mocks "'70s-era disaster films" with a "scatter-gag" barrage of "relentless slapstick", "constant plays on words" and the "best appearance by Ethel Merman in decades"; granted, it's "infantile" and some of the humor might be "politically incorrect" today, but there are so many "one-liners you'll remember years later" – 'don't call me Shirley!' – that it's no surprise this flick "launched a thousand imitators."

Akira 23 | – | 21 | 26

1988. Directed by Katsuhiro Otomo. Animated. 124 minutes. Rated R.

◪ "Defining the anime genre", this "groundbreaking" "classic" "based on the Japanese comic" book is "blazingly kinetic", although "more violent than it needs to be" and thus "not for younger viewers"; the "confusing" sci-fi plot (something to do with "how power corrupts") might "make you wonder if something was lost in translation", but it's so "visually stunning" you won't care.

Aladdin 24 | – | 22 | 25

1992. Directed by Ron Clements, John Musker. Animated. 90 minutes. Rated G.

■ Disney's "fast-moving" animated version of the Aladdin story is "stolen" by Robin Williams' "infectiously manic", "whirlwind" vocal performance as a "genius" genie; overall, its "likable characters" and "humorous storyline" appeal to both "adults and kids alike", while the "enchanting" Oscar-winning soundtrack will leave you "singing for days."

Alamo, The 18 | 18 | 20 | 21

1960. Directed by John Wayne. With John Wayne, Richard Widmark, Laurence Harvey. 167 minutes. Not Rated.

◪ A "big-as-Texas" slice of "classic Americana", this "entertaining" rendition of the Battle of the Alamo still "appeals as a period film", although it strikes some as "overblown", "hokum history" with a "surprisingly boring" Wayne as Davy Crockett; even so, that "slam-bang, operatic finale" "mostly justifies" the "dreary opening hour."

Alexander Nevsky ◑ 🅵 26 | 22 | 25 | 26

1938. Directed by Sergei Eisenstein. With Nikolai Cherkassov. 107 minutes. Not Rated.

◪ "Propaganda" was never better than this "exceptional" war epic, made to rally Soviet support for Stalin; shot in "haunting" black-and-white and set to a "superb Prokofiev score", it recounts the trials and tribulations of a 13th-century Russian prince, and even if the "clanky" script "ultimately collapses under the weight of all the ideological baggage", it's still a "triumph of expressionism" from "genius" director Eisenstein.

Alfie Ⓘ 22 | 26 | 22 | 20

1966. Directed by Lewis Gilbert. With Michael Caine, Shelley Winters, Vivien Merchant. 114 minutes. Not Rated.

◪ This "little charmer" of a drama stars the "phenomenal" Caine in the career-making role of a "philandering playboy who gets his comeuppance" after dalliances with a flock of '60s birds; although it seems "a bit dated" and might be "politically incorrect" today, its "brutally honest" script still "asks the important questions" – and there's an "excellent" Sonny Rollins score as a bonus.

Alice Doesn't Live Here Anymore ✉ ∅ 24 | 26 | 23 | 21

1974. Directed by Martin Scorsese. With Ellen Burstyn, Kris Kristofferson, Jodie Foster. 112 minutes. Rated PG.

■ In this "early Scorsese" drama, Burstyn "won an Oscar" for her role as a "blue-collar" gal "trying to find herself" after a marriage breakup, and the "poignant", very "real" outcome marked a "watershed" for "feminists" in a "time when men and women were changing their roles"; forget that it "begat an insipid television series" – it's "worth seeing for the tomboyish Foster alone."

Alice in Wonderland 24 | – | 25 | 25

1951. Directed by Clyde Geronimi, Wilfred Jackson, Hamilton Luske. Animated. 75 minutes. Rated G.

■ Disney's wonderfully "wacky" animation transforms Lewis Carroll's children's book into an "intelligent cartoon" rife with "hidden messages" and a slightly "schizophrenic" edge to boot; indeed, "family entertainment" mavens say this "imaginative" production is such a "terrific adaptation" that it "almost makes you forget the classic Tenniel illustrations."

Alien Ⓘ 25 | 22 | 25 | 26

1979. Directed by Ridley Scott. With Sigourney Weaver, Tom Skerritt, Veronica Cartwright. 117 minutes. Rated R.

■ "Often imitated but never equaled", this "fierce" sci-fi "horror classic" could pass as a "Hitchcock-in-space" thriller thanks to its "jaw-dropping visuals" and "heart-pounding" plot about an outer space "survey team" that inadvertently brings a "new guest" home to dinner; "Weaver rocks" in "macho-man" mode and is only upstaged by the "slimy", "really gross" title character, the "best movie monster this side of Frankenstein."

Aliens Ⓘ 23 | 21 | 22 | 26

1986. Directed by James Cameron. With Sigourney Weaver, Michael Biehn, Bill Paxton. 137 minutes. Rated R.

◪ This "second installment" in the *Alien* franchise is just as "scream-out-loud scary" as its predecessor, with a "*Rambo*-esque" emphasis (i.e. more "big guns and bloody fight scenes"); expect the "same high-quality production values" and "edge-of-your-seat tension", and if there's debate as to whether it "trumps" or "just lives up to" the original, one thing's certain: Weaver is still one "bad-ass" chick.

ALL ABOUT EVE ✉◑ 28 | 29 | 27 | 26

1950. Directed by Joseph L. Mankiewicz. With Bette Davis, Anne Baxter, Gary Merrill. 138 minutes. Not Rated.

■ "Fasten your seatbelts" – the "ladies lunch on each other" in this "scalding", "wickedly funny" look at the "vicious world of showbiz"; a "boffo" Davis is "electrifying" as the "fading star" (opposite a "strong" Baxter as the rising one), but both are indebted to Mankiewicz's "perfect script", a "catty" catalog of "sharp-tongued dialogue" that "puts today's scenarios to shame"; in sum, this is one of the "best backstage, backstabbing bitchfests of all time."

All About My Mother ✉F 25 | 26 | 25 | 23

1999. Directed by Pedro Almodóvar. With Cecilia Roth, Penélope Cruz, Marisa Paredes. 101 minutes. Rated R.

◪ Though "all the major characters are women", this "captivating story" via Spanish director Almodóvar is definitely "not a chick flick": rather, this "unusual", Oscar-winning drama about a mother searching for her dead son's transsexual dad provides a very "modern definition of what makes a family"; fans single out Roth's "stunning" work and Cruz's "breakout performance" – that is, when they're not "crying their hearts out" or "laughing their heads off."

ALL QUIET ON THE WESTERN FRONT ✉◑ 28 | 26 | 28 | 25

1930. Directed by Lewis Milestone. With Lew Ayres, Louis Wolheim, Raymond Griffith. 131 minutes. Not Rated.

■ "One of the first anti-war films" (and the "last word" on the subject for many), this "devastating" WWI saga is a "harrowing", "heartbreaking" glimpse at the "unglorious nature" of battle; more than 70 years later, it "still packs a wallop", and though a little "slow" by modern standards, this "faithful adaptation of the novel" will "stay with you."

All That Jazz ∅ 24 | 23 | 22 | 26

1979. Directed by Bob Fosse. With Roy Scheider, Jessica Lange, Ann Reinking, John Lithgow. 123 minutes. Rated R.

■ A "brilliantly original" "autobiopic" from Bob Fosse about Bob Fosse, this "prescient" drama might be "self-indulgent" and plainly "inspired by *8½*", but it's also a "fantastic" "warts-and-all" "character sketch" with, no surprise, "imaginative choreography"; look for a "great star turn" by Scheider, an "early" appearance by Lange and lots of "sardonic" dialogue; funniest/saddest line: 'it's showtime!'

All the King's Men ✉◑ 25 | 26 | 25 | 22

1949. Directed by Robert Rossen. With Broderick Crawford, John Ireland, Mercedes McCambridge. 109 minutes. Not Rated.

■ The "American dream goes sour" in this "classic political drama" adapted from the Pulitzer prize–winning novel about the rise and fall of a Huey Long–esque politician "corrupted by power"; this Best Picture winner is memorable for its "strong story" – and "even stronger acting by Crawford" (who also won a statuette).

All the President's Men 25 | 26 | 26 | 23

1976. Directed by Alan J. Pakula. With Robert Redford, Dustin Hoffman, Jason Robards. 138 minutes. Rated PG.

■ "History comes alive" in this "truth-is-stranger-than-fiction" account of the "Watergate" scandal, a "riveting", torn-"from-the-headlines thriller" that "captures you every time" "even though you know the outcome"; as reporters Woodward and Bernstein, Redford and Hoffman are truly "memorable" (ditto those "ties and sideburns"), and though this "gripping" effort brings "clarity to the events of that confusing time", many still ask "who is Deep Throat?"

Almost Famous ✉ 23 | 24 | 24 | 22

2000. Directed by Cameron Crowe. With Billy Crudup, Frances McDormand, Kate Hudson. 122 minutes. Rated R.

■ "Almost perfect" filmmaking, director Crowe's "feel-good" "semi-autobiographical story" about his experiences as a "teenage" "*Rolling Stone* reporter" "on the road with a rock band" is half "coming-of-age" romance, half "love song" to the '70s; while Crudup's "underrated" rocker and McDormand's "outstanding" mom earn kudos, "Hudson steals the show" as the "vulnerable groupie."

Altered States 19 | 20 | 20 | 20

1980. Directed by Ken Russell. With William Hurt, Blair Brown, Bob Balaban. 102 minutes. Rated R.

◪ "Sometimes you don't know which end is up" in this "mind-bending" sci-fi "journey" starring Hurt as a scientist experimenting with sensory deprivation via an isolation chamber and select "hallucinogens"; although the "trippy" visuals and "convoluted" plot were considered "shocking" at the time, it may now look "like a relic from another era."

Amadeus ✉ 26 | 27 | 25 | 27

1984. Directed by Milos Forman. With F. Murray Abraham, Tom Hulce, Elizabeth Berridge. 158 minutes. Rated PG.

◪ "Genius thwarted by mediocrity" is the theme of this "lively" Mozart biopic that's admittedly "not historically accurate", given its depiction of the "tortured" composer as a cross between a "twerp" and a "rock god"; awash in "lush period details", "timeless music" and "surprisingly nuanced performances" by Abraham and Hulce, it even manages to "make classical music seem racy" – and was quite the Oscar magnet, taking home eight of them.

Amarcord ✉ F — 26 | 25 | 25 | 26

1975. Directed by Federico Fellini. With Magali Noël, Bruno Zanin, Pupella Maggio. 127 minutes. Rated R.

■ "Fellini's warmhearted look back to his childhood", this Foreign Language Oscar winner is a "wonderful depiction" of "small-town life" in 1930s "fascist Italy", an "evocative" film that's simultaneously "lyric, tragic, vulgar and comic"; fans say this "beautiful reminiscence" reveals the famed director "at his most accessible" – and most "surreal."

Amélie F — 26 | 26 | 24 | 25

2001. Directed by Jean-Pierre Jeunet. With Audrey Tautou, Mathieu Kassovitz. 122 minutes. Rated R.

■ "Sweet as *sucre*", this "candy-coated" "French picture postcard" of a romance concerns a "modern-day Pollyanna from Montmartre" "who wants to fix everyone's life" to make up for "what's missing in hers"; in the title role, a "new star has arrived" in "gamine" Tautou, a "21st-century Audrey Hepburn" whose "doe-eyed", "cute-as-a-button" looks alone will "put a huge grin on your face"; indeed, this "brimming-with-goodwill" picture is so "magical", you'll "hardly notice the subtitles."

American Beauty ✉ — 24 | 27 | 23 | 24

1999. Directed by Sam Mendes. With Kevin Spacey, Annette Bening, Wes Bentley. 121 minutes. Rated R.

◪ The "desperation of modern suburban life" is the theme of this "engrossing" Best Picture winner that polarizes viewers: fans hail this tale of a man's "midlife awakening" and "resurrection" as a "truthful commentary on American society", but thornier types fuss it's a "pretentious", "angry" tract "disguised as existentialist philosophy"; nonetheless, there are plenty of bouquets for Spacey's "dead-on" performance and Alan Ball's "seriously meaty", "rapier-like screenplay."

American Graffiti ⓘ — 24 | 23 | 23 | 23

1973. Directed by George Lucas. With Richard Dreyfuss, Ron Howard, Cindy Williams. 110 minutes. Rated PG.

■ "Spot future stars" (including an early Harrison Ford) in this "end-of-an-era" dramedy that "launched a dozen careers" and proves that "Lucas once directed actors, not just pixels"; "covering one night" in 1962 – "but what a night" – it "captures a time and place" in teenage, West Coast America by mixing "cool cars", "period jukebox hits" and "Wolfman Jack" into a "classic growing-up story" that really "makes nostalgia compelling."

American History X 25 | 28 | 24 | 23

1998. Directed by Tony Kaye. With Edward Norton, Edward Furlong, Beverly D'Angelo. 119 minutes. Rated R.

■ "Neo-Nazi violence" and "racism" lie at the heart of this "scalding" drama about "white supremacists" that's "like a punch in the gut" thanks to the "gifted" Norton's "all-too-convincing" portrait of a "scary" "skinhead"; though surely "horrifying", this "powerful" film will also "make you think."

American in Paris, An ✉ 26 | 23 | 22 | 27

1951. Directed by Vincente Minnelli. With Gene Kelly, Leslie Caron, Oscar Levant. 113 minutes. Not Rated.

■ A "debonair" Kelly and "beautiful Caron" "dance up a storm" in this "unforgettable" Gershwin musical that might tempt you "to visit Paris" *tout suite*; sure, the "silly story" is a bit "hackneyed", but "who cares?" when the production's so "visually compelling" (especially that climactic ballet "integrating Impressionist art" in its settings); no surprise, it took home six Oscars, including Best Picture.

American Pie ⓘⓘ 19 | 16 | 18 | 18

1999. Directed by Paul Weitz. With Jason Biggs, Shannon Elizabeth, Tara Reid. 95 minutes. Rated R.

◪ "You'll never look at an apple pie the same way" after a gander at this "drop-dead funny" slice of "raunch" about some teenage dudes, "hormones a-raging", who "vow to lose their virginity on prom night"; while bluenoses berate its "sophomoric" "toilet humor" as "moronic", "baked-goods" buyers say its "laugh-a-minute" plot is an "*intelligent* gross-out", the "Gen-X" version of "*Porky's*."

American President, The 21 | 22 | 21 | 21

1995. Directed by Rob Reiner. With Michael Douglas, Annette Bening, Martin Sheen. 114 minutes. Rated PG-13.

◪ "Only in Hollywood" could the "President openly date a lobbyist", but no one "believes it for a second – or cares" – since this "feel-good" romance is so darned "entertaining"; voters like Douglas' "humanized" Chief Exec and Bening's "luminous" gal pal but reject the "rose-colored" script and its "telegraphed happy ending", sighing "pass the popcorn."

American Tail, An ⓘⓘ ∅ 21 | – | 21 | 22

1986. Directed by Don Bluth. Animated. 77 minutes. Rated G.

■ "One of the first good non-Disney" pieces of animation, this "wonderful" "story of the immigrant experience" follows the adventures of a Russian mouse separated from his kin after arriving in America; a "real family favorite", its "clever" concept with a "touch of pathos" makes many "hearts melt."

American Werewolf in London, An ⓘⓘ 20 | 17 | 21 | 21

1981. Directed by John Landis. With David Naughton, Jenny Agutter, Griffin Dunne. 97 minutes. Rated R.

■ "Filmed with style and wit", this "tragicomic gorefest" "shows some bite" as it follows the misadventures of two

American "zombies" abroad; best remembered for its "transformation scene" combining "superior makeup" and "amazing special effects" – and second-best known for Agutter's "hot shower scene" – this one's so "suspenseful and creepy" that it "helped revitalize the horror genre" in the early '80s.

Amistad 21 | 24 | 22 | 24

1997. Directed by Steven Spielberg. With Morgan Freeman, Djimon Hounsou, Anthony Hopkins. 152 minutes. Rated R.

◪ Examining the "dark underside of American history", this "little-known" true story of 19th-century "Africans forced into slavery" "starts on a slave ship and culminates in court"; while some say this "gripping" albeit "difficult" story is an "underappreciated" Spielberg opus, others find it so "heavy-handed" and "manipulative" that they're left "out to sea."

Analyze This Ⓘ 18 | 21 | 18 | 18

1999. Directed by Harold Ramis. With Robert De Niro, Billy Crystal, Lisa Kudrow. 103 minutes. Rated R.

◪ "*Sopranos*" nuts see some familiar plot threads in this "funny Mafia movie" featuring the "hilarious pairing" of "De Niro as a mobster with anxiety attacks" and Crystal as his reluctant "shrink"; though some analysts shrug it off as a "flat" "trifle", supporters call it an "amusing send-up" that may be "ridiculous, but it works."

Anastasia ✉∅ 23 | 27 | 24 | 23

1956. Directed by Anatole Litvak. With Ingrid Bergman, Yul Brynner, Helen Hayes. 105 minutes. Not Rated.

■ The Oscar-winning, ever "appealing" Bergman and a "great" Brynner make quite a "combo" in this dramatic biography of Anastasia, the legendary daughter of the last Russian czar and pretender to the throne – or is she?; told with "sympathy and empathy", it's a "cuddle-up-with-your-honey" picture with acting "so good you find yourself rooting for those inept royals"; "is it true?" – c'mon, "does it matter?"

Anastasia 20 | – | 19 | 22

1997. Directed by Don Bluth, Gary Goldman. Animated. 94 minutes. Rated G.

◪ "Disney isn't the only one" making "amazing animation" these days: this cartoon version of a lost (and found) Russian princess is an "astonishingly good feature", although it might "sanitize history" and "doesn't seem to be kid material"; still, it's a "visually appealing" CinemaScope extravaganza oozing "style", even if the "bat steals the show."

Anatomy of a Murder ◑ 26 | 27 | 27 | 24

1959. Directed by Otto Preminger. With James Stewart, Lee Remick, Ben Gazzara. 160 minutes. Not Rated.

■ Stewart "pulls out all the stops" as a "down-to-earth" lawyer in this courtroom drama that's a "spellbinding" look at a "sensational" "backwoods" revenge killing; "considered risqué" in the '50s given Remick's "sultry" turn and its use of the then-verboten word "'panties'", it remains as "riveting" as ever; P.S. "Duke Ellington and his band" lay down the cool progressive-jazz soundtrack.

Andromeda Strain, The 20 | 18 | 25 | 20

1971. Directed by Robert Wise. With Arthur Hill, David Wayne, James Olson, Kate Reid. 131 minutes. Rated G.

◪ "Science provides the thrills" in this piece of "thinking man's sci-fi" based on the early "Michael Crichton thriller" concerning a "dangerous" virus from outer space; though it may be "low-tech" (with "out-of-date special effects" and "sprayed-on perspiration"), it supplies enough "palpable" "tension" to keep things "taut and interesting to the end."

Angels with Dirty Faces ◑∅ 24 | 24 | 22 | 20

1938. Directed by Michael Curtiz. With James Cagney, Pat O'Brien, Humphrey Bogart. 97 minutes. Not Rated.

■ Two toughs from the slums take different career paths – one becoming a "low-life criminal", the other a priest – in this "cautionary melodrama" made in the days when "good was good and bad was bad"; "cliché-ridden" though it may be, this "hard-as-nails drama" was designed to "scare the bejesus out of would-be delinquents" – or at least have them "doing Cagney impersonations for weeks" afterward.

Animal Crackers ◑ 26 | 24 | 18 | 20

1930. Directed by Victor Heerman. With the Marx Brothers, Lillian Roth, Margaret Dumont. 97 minutes. Rated G.

■ "Hooray for Captain Spaulding!"; this "timeless" "Marx Brothers romp" is best remembered for Groucho's "priceless entrance" and "fabulously stupid" quips ("I shot an elephant in my pajamas, but how he got in my pajamas, I'll never know"); needless to say, the "storyline isn't the point" here, but the "zany" pace doesn't leave time for logic anyway.

Animal House 24 | 20 | 21 | 20

1978. Directed by John Landis. With John Belushi, Tim Matheson, Tom Hulce. 109 minutes. Rated R.

■ "Lowbrow", "raunchy and vulgar", this much-admired "granddaddy of the frat boy gross-out comedies" features the much-"missed" Belushi "at his side-splitting best" as Bluto Blutarsky, a "seven-year college" vet; "no, it ain't Shakespeare", but rather a "textbook" study of "toga parties", "road trips", "food fights" and "anarchic libidos on parade" that's so much of a "guy's movie" that some fellas say they "thought it was a documentary."

Anna and the King 19 | 21 | 21 | 24

1999. Directed by Andy Tennant. With Jodie Foster, Chow Yun-Fat, Tom Felton. 148 minutes. Rated PG-13.

◪ Take a "trip to Thailand" via this "touching" romance that's a "nonmusical rendition" of *The King and I,* based on the true story of Brit school teacher Anna Leonowens; though "slow" pacing and the "absence of chemistry" between Foster and Yun-Fat leave things "rather flat", at least this "lush-as-hell" production ("magnificent scenery", "elaborate costumes") is "gorgeous to look at."

Annie 19 | 19 | 20 | 20

1982. Directed by John Huston. With Albert Finney, Carol Burnett, Aileen Quinn. 126 minutes. Rated PG.

◪ Little Orphan "Annie's rags-to-riches" saga morphs into a "colorful" "children's musical" with a "splendid cast" in this "stylized" "adaptation of the comic strip" that first bowed on Broadway; parents say it's "perfect for kids", and even those who find it "bloated" and "boring" find themselves leaving the theater humming 'Tomorrow.'

ANNIE HALL ✉ 27 | 26 | 25 | 24

1977. Directed by Woody Allen. With Woody Allen, Diane Keaton, Tony Roberts. 93 minutes. Rated PG.

■ "Every neurotic's favorite comedy", this Oscar-winning, "quintessential" Allen film about an "insecure" "Jewish nebbish" smitten with a nutty, "la-di-da"–spouting "shiksa" is "among his deftest creations"; its "pitch-perfect NY" setting, "pure-genius script" and "very funny" set pieces (the "lobster-cooking episode", the "split-screen family dinner scene") make for "essential Woody": "witty, insightful and in love."

Antonia's Line ✉ F 25 | 26 | 25 | 24

1995. Directed by Marleen Gorris. With Willeke van Ammelrooy, Els Dottermans. 102 minutes. Rated R.

■ "About women and for women", this "liberating" drama recounts 50 years in one lady's life, told in "flashback" from her "death bed"; "shockingly feminist" to chauvinists, its "charming performances", "empowering message" and "touching script" are so "unforgettable" that it more than "deserves the Best Foreign Film Oscar" it received.

Antz 20 | – | 19 | 23

1998. Directed by Eric Darnell, Tim Johnson. Animated. 87 minutes. Rated PG.

◪ Opinion splitz on this fully computer-animated feature about an insect's "rebellion" against conformity; fans buzz that this "highly creative" film "for all ages" tells a "well-executed" story, yet drones swat it for "ugly animation" and a "subversive socialist subtext" that's "not recommended" for "younger children"; P.S. Woody Allen's voice-over as a "neurotic ant is a must-hear."

Apartment, The ✉◑ 25 | 28 | 25 | 23

1960. Directed by Billy Wilder. With Jack Lemmon, Shirley MacLaine, Fred MacMurray. 125 minutes. Not Rated.

■ "Sex in the big, bad city" has never been as "realistic" or "touching" as in this "biting", "sad-edged romance" from

Billy Wilder, recounting the exploits of a "hapless" "junior exec in love with his boss' mistress"; it pits a "baby-faced" Lemmon opposite a "tender" MacLaine and "understated" MacMurray, and besides being "very amusing", it's also a "powerful social comment masquerading as comedy."

APOCALYPSE NOW 27 | 27 | 25 | 28

1979. Directed by Francis Ford Coppola. With Martin Sheen, Marlon Brando, Robert Duvall. 153 minutes. Rated R.

■ The "Vietnam nightmare" meets Joseph "Conrad's *Heart of Darkness*" in this "landmark" Coppola opus that's one part "gut churner", one part "acid trip" as it examines the "insanity of war"; true, it's "long", the "last half hour is disappointing" and many wonder "what the heck Brando's saying", but ultimately this "sprawling" "meditation on the human mind" just plain "grabs you"; P.S. the expanded version (*Apocalypse Now Redux*) divides voters.

Apollo 13 24 | 24 | 25 | 26

1995. Directed by Ron Howard. With Tom Hanks, Bill Paxton, Kevin Bacon, Gary Sinise. 140 minutes. Rated PG.

■ "Even though you [presumably] know the outcome", this "space race" drama based on the "remarkable true story" of the "perilous voyage of Apollo 13" stays "incredibly suspenseful" until the very end; with a roster of "big-name actors" exuding the "right stuff", it delivers "get-up-and-cheer escapism" that might be "a tad corny" but will "make you proud to be an American" – "isn't history wonderful?"

Apprenticeship of Duddy Kravitz, The ∅ 22 | 24 | 24 | 20

1974. Directed by Ted Kotcheff. With Richard Dreyfuss, Micheline Lanctôt, Jack Warden. 120 minutes. Rated PG.

■ A "nice Jewish boy in Montreal comes of age" and tries to ascend the "slippery slope of success" in this "little-known comic gem" "tinged with sadness"; a "moving" adaptation of Mordecai Richler's novel, it's a "genius" "showcase for Dreyfuss" as the titular "hustling" "mensch."

Around the World in 80 Days ✉∅ 22 | 20 | 22 | 25

1956. Directed by Michael Anderson. With David Niven, Cantinflas, Shirley MacLaine. 175 minutes. Rated G.

◪ "It's the scenery, stupid" that makes this globe-trotting "epic" "travelogue" based on "Jules Verne's classic book" "worth watching", though lots of "stars popping up in cute cameo roles" also add to the "visual cornucopia"; however, some find it a "boring", "three-hour ride around the world" and "can't believe" it snagged a Best Picture Oscar.

Arsenic and Old Lace ◑ 26 | 26 | 25 | 22

1944. Directed by Frank Capra. With Cary Grant, Priscilla Lane, Raymond Massey. 118 minutes. Not Rated.

■ "Elderberry wine" makes for "murderous fun" in this "macabre" black comedy about two "vengeful old ladies" "killing off" bachelors while "chewing the scenery"; as their nephew, a "frantic" Grant "hams it up unashamedly" and delivers the "world's best double takes" in this "far-fetched" but "oh-so-funny" adaptation of the Broadway hit.

Arthur Ⓘ 20 | 21 | 19 | 19

1981. Directed by Steve Gordon. With Dudley Moore, Liza Minnelli, John Gielgud. 117 minutes. Rated PG.

◪ There's "not a dull moment" in this "silly" yet "tender" romantic comedy about a "falling-down-drunk" "millionaire" looking for love; although top billing goes to "sexy short guy" Dudley Moore opposite "Liza Minnelli as Liza Minnelli", this "priceless" picture arguably belongs to the "terrific", Oscar-winning Gielgud, who delivers its most "classic line" – "I'll alert the media" – "as if he were playing Hamlet."

As Good As It Gets ✉ 22 | 25 | 21 | 21

1997. Directed by James L. Brooks. With Jack Nicholson, Helen Hunt, Greg Kinnear. 139 minutes. Rated PG-13.

◪ Fans feel the "title says it all": this "smart comedy" about the "unlikely pairing" of a "cantankerous" "obsessive-compulsive jerk" and a "kooky" "single-mom" "waitress" crackles with "sharp", "NY neurotic" dialogue; but even though both Hunt and Nicholson grabbed Oscars for their "tour-de-force" turns, some shrug they "play themselves" in this "overhyped", "overrated" and "predictable" flick.

Asphalt Jungle, The ◑∅ 24 | 24 | 24 | 23

1950. Directed by John Huston. With Sterling Hayden, Louis Calhern, Sam Jaffe. 112 minutes. Not Rated.

■ Sure, this "prime example of juicy film noir" is one of the "original caper" pictures, about a "carefully planned" "jewel heist gone terribly wrong", but it's also appealing for an "early" turn by Marilyn Monroe in a "blow-you-away" bit part; otherwise, this "dark tale" of "greed" and "emotion" supplies enough "twists and compelling characters" to make it "one of Huston's most underated films."

Atlantic City 24 | 27 | 22 | 22

1980. Directed by Louis Malle. With Burt Lancaster, Susan Sarandon, Kate Reid. 104 minutes. Rated R.

■ This "valentine to a lost city" pairs a "stunning" Lancaster and Sarandon as unlikely lovers "trying to redeem their lives" in the "bleak atmosphere" of a "dying" town; "sad, bittersweet" and "overlooked", it boasts a "superb" John Guare script full of "characters worth caring about" but is most remembered for the scene of "our heroine bathing herself with sliced lemons."

Auntie Mame ∅ 25 | 25 | 24 | 25

1958. Directed by Morton DaCosta. With Rosalind Russell, Forrest Tucker, Coral Browne. 143 minutes. Not Rated.

◪ "Defining diva-dom for generations", this "stylish" comedy about a wide-eyed kid's "wacky rich" auntie stars a "larger-than-life Russell" as a "great old broad"–cum–"force of nature"; it might be "overlong and underplotted", but "great one-liners" barbed with "sharp wit" ("life is a banquet and most poor suckers are starving to death") assure its reputation as the "campiest of camp classics."

AU REVOIR LES ENFANTS F ∅ 27 | 26 | 27 | 24

1987. Directed by Louis Malle. With Gaspard Manesse, Francine Racette. 104 minutes. Rated PG.

■ "Powerful and haunting", this "must-see" drama explores "anti-Semitism" in WWII "occupied France" via its depiction of a "Jewish boy hidden" in a French school; though there's certainly "no happy ending" to this "well-orchestrated" film, it "brings the events of the Holocaust to a personal level" so devastatingly that you'll "never forget" it.

Austin Powers: International Man of Mystery Ⓘ 19 | 18 | 17 | 19

1997. Directed by Jay Roach. With Mike Myers, Elizabeth Hurley, Michael York. 90 minutes. Rated PG-13.

◪ "No-brainer" alert: this "shagadelic" "spoof of James Bond movies" delivers "tons of laughs" with "dumb" jokes and overall "retro '60s silliness" – "oh, behave!" – courtesy of "comic genius" Myers in a dual role as a spy with "mossy teeth" and a villain with a pet pussycat; there's debate over its "crude" "toilet humor" but wide agreement that you needn't "bother with the sequel."

Awakenings 22 | 26 | 23 | 20

1990. Directed by Penny Marshall. With Robert De Niro, Robin Williams, John Heard. 121 minutes. Rated PG-13.

■ A "true story" about the search for a "cure for comatose patients" gets some "thought-provoking" treatment in this "touching" drama, featuring Williams "playing it straight" for a change opposite a "memorable" De Niro; while the hard-hearted berate its "sentimental", "hanky-wringing" edge, most find it both "amusing and moving", despite the "potentially mawkish" subject matter.

Babe Ⓘ 25 | 22 | 25 | 26

1995. Directed by Chris Noonan. With James Cromwell, Magda Szubanski, Danny Mann. 89 minutes. Rated G.

■ "Believe the hype": fans are in "hog heaven" over this "porcine" comedy "marvel" about a "talking pig" who "wants to be a sheepherder so he won't get eaten"; "cute without being cutesy", it features Oscar-winning "computer effects" that allow "animals to interact" with humans so realistically that it may "turn you into a vegetarian."

Babes in Toyland ◑ ∅ 22 | 19 | 20 | 23

1934. Directed by Gus Meins, Charles H. Rogers. With Laurel & Hardy. 77 minutes. Rated G.

■ It may be "lightweight stuff for serious Laurel and Hardy fans", but this "charming" musical comedy based on the

"Victor Herbert operetta" about "toys come to life" is a "timeless" "holiday treat" for the rest of us; expect some "darker moments to balance the sunny ones", and though its a "handsome production", "don't expect special effects."

Babette's Feast ✉ F 26 | 26 | 26 | 25

1987. Directed by Gabriel Axel. With Stéphane Audran, Bibi Andersson, Jarl Kulle. 102 minutes. Rated G.

■ "Sumptuous enough to make vegetarians drool" (though "slow as molasses"), this "classic foodie" dramedy is an "unusual" tale based on the Isak Dinesen story about the "power of redemption" cooked up in one "magnificent meal"; "still mouthwatering after all these years", this "intriguing" Danish treat is so "delectable" and "savory" that it could be the "Zagat signature movie."

Baby Boom 19 | 20 | 20 | 18

1987. Directed by Charles Shyer. With Diane Keaton, Sam Shepard, Harold Ramis. 103 minutes. Rated PG.

◪ "Career vs. home and family" is the theme of this "very '80s" "light comedy" starring a "sharp, understated" Keaton as a "woman who wants it all" – and gets it when she inherits a baby and hooks up with Shepard; though tough guys dismiss it as a "feel-good chick flick", "warm-and-fuzzy" folk find it a "likable" tale of "triumphant romance."

Backdraft 18 | 18 | 18 | 23

1991. Directed by Ron Howard. With Kurt Russell, William Baldwin, Scott Glenn, Robert De Niro. 132 minutes. Rated R.

◪ "Big fires and cute firemen" sum up the appeal of this disaster thriller aflame with a "stellar cast" and "eye-opening", "amazingly realistic" special effects; ok, the "melodramatic" "storyline's a bit soft" and the actors struggle with the "moronic dialogue", but at least the "action sequences" will "keep you hanging on until the end."

Back to the Future Ⅱ 23 | 20 | 25 | 24

1985. Directed by Robert Zemeckis. With Michael J. Fox, Christopher Lloyd, Lea Thompson. 111 minutes. Rated PG.

■ A "time-traveling DeLorean" propels the "delectably dimpled Fox" into a "fun ride to the past" (and an opportunity to observe his parents as "goofy teenagers") in this "perfect blend of sci-fi, fantasy and pop culture"; "irrepressibly entertaining" and immensely popular, it spawned an "incredible ride" at the Universal theme park as well as two "terrible sequels."

Bad Day at Black Rock ∅ 24 | 28 | 24 | 22

1955. Directed by John Sturges. With Spencer Tracy, Robert Ryan, Anne Francis. 81 minutes. Not Rated.

■ This "taut little thriller" is "mean, lean" moviemaking about "bigotry and intolerance" in a "small town with a secret", starring an "excellent" Tracy in "one of his more unusual roles"; somewhat "forgotten" today, it's "just as relevant as it was in the post-McCarthy '50s", "giving you plenty to think about" as it "profiles American prejudices."

Badlands 25 | 27 | 24 | 24

1973. Directed by Terrence Malick. With Martin Sheen, Sissy Spacek, Warren Oates. 95 minutes. Rated PG.

■ The "banality of evil" is dissected in this "dark, disturbing" depiction of a true-life teen crime spree; playing "shallow", "disaffected" lovers on the run, a "very young" Spacek and Sheen are "first rate" (with an "especially haunting voice-over" by Sissy), while Malick's "trademark sweeping cinematography" acts as "visually stunning" counterpoint to the "bitingly tragic" story; in short, it's "gutsy", "twisted" and "not nearly as well known as it should be."

Bad News Bears, The Ⓘ 18 | 16 | 19 | 15

1976. Directed by Michael Ritchie. With Walter Matthau, Tatum O'Neal, Vic Morrow. 102 minutes. Rated PG.

◪ A "must-see for any Little Leaguer", this "cute" sports comedy pitches a story about a curmudgeonly drunk who somehow transforms a "truly awful" "kids' baseball" team into local champions; though perhaps "better then than now" (with "foul but funny language" that might raise parental eyebrows), its two sequels are definitely "bad news for moviegoers."

Bad Seed, The ◑∅ 22 | 23 | 25 | 20

1956. Directed by Mervyn LeRoy. With Nancy Kelly, Patty McCormack, Eileen Heckart. 129 minutes. Not Rated.

■ "Not for the faint of heart", this "very creepy" thriller is the story of a "perky little deranged girl" who's the "world's most evil child" (think "Ted Bundy in a pinafore"); "unsettling and unforgettable" in its time, it's still "way, way over the top", and even if the Broadway play "had a better ending", this one will positively "send chills down your spine."

Bambi ∅ 26 | – | 25 | 26

1942. Directed by David Hand. Animated. 70 minutes. Rated G.

■ "Don't forget those tissues" before settling into this dear coming-of-age story that's best remembered for the "absolutely heart-wrenching" "death of Bambi's mother", a "cruel lesson in life" that will "make you think twice about showing it" to "very young children"; otherwise, it's arguably the "most beautiful" example of vintage Disney animation "when Walt was at the helm", "warm and fuzzy" but "not mawkish."

Bananas 23 | 20 | 22 | 19

1971. Directed by Woody Allen. With Woody Allen, Louise Lasser, Carlos Montalban. 82 minutes. Rated PG-13.

◪ "For Allen purists mostly", this "early" comic romance "relies heavily on sight gags and slapstick humor" in its "anarchic" story of a nebbish turned "Latin American dictator" that's a "zany" satire to some, but "dated", "intermittently funny" "shtick" to others; P.S. hang on for cameos from Howard Cosell and a "young" Sylvester Stallone as a "thug on the subway."

Band Wagon, The ∅ 26 | 21 | 20 | 26

1953. Directed by Vincente Minnelli. With Fred Astaire, Cyd Charisse, Nanette Fabray. 111 minutes. Not Rated.

■ A "worthy companion to *Singin' in the Rain*", this "solid musical" comedy boasts the "most romantic moment in movie history" – the "hauntingly lovely 'Dancing in the Dark' number in Central Park" – performed by Astaire and Charisse in "top form"; thanks to its "fantastic music" and "delightful cast", nostalgists sigh "they don't make 'em like this anymore."

Bang the Drum Slowly ∅ 23 | 25 | 24 | 18

1973. Directed by John Hancock. With Michael Moriarty, Robert De Niro, Vincent Gardenia. 96 minutes. Rated PG.

■ Moriarty and De Niro deliver "two moving performances" in this memorably "sad" drama about a hayseed baseball catcher with a terminal illness and the star pitcher who befriends him; both a "real tearjerker" and a "powerful story of friendship", it's a "well done", "humbling" experience that's "maintained its staying power" over the years.

Barry Lyndon 20 | 18 | 21 | 27

1975. Directed by Stanley Kubrick. With Ryan O'Neal, Marisa Berenson, Leon Vitali. 184 minutes. Rated PG.

◪ "Kubrick's classic adaptation" of the "Thackeray novel" depicts the "rise and fall of an Irish lad whose luck finally runs dry" with "amazing period detail" and "gorgeous photography"; but although this "thing of beauty" is a "feast for the eyes", the "acting's from hunger" and the "dull, plodding" pace leaves some sighing "what you see isn't what you get."

Barton Fink ∅ 20 | 24 | 19 | 22

1991. Directed by Joel Coen. With John Turturro, John Goodman, Judy Davis. 116 minutes. Rated R.

◪ "Delightfully weird" and "offbeat", this Coen brothers drama about a gone-Hollywood playwright with a colossal case of writer's block "alternates between fascinating and frustrating" given a "surreal", "terribly odd" storyline that's "brain candy" for intellectuals; despite "fantastic acting" from an "exceptional" Turturro and "absolutely sinister" Goodman, this "out-there" picture is "not for everyone."

Basic Instinct 19 | 19 | 20 | 19

1992. Directed by Paul Verhoeven. With Michael Douglas, Sharon Stone, Jeanne Tripplehorn. 123 minutes. Rated R.

◪ Aside from Sharon Stone's notorious "uncrossed legs" "money shot", this "leering erotic thriller" offers enough "noir-esque dialogue" and "gratuitous sex" to make for one "highly provocative" "hormone movie"; though detractors deem it "unintentionally funny" "trash", "mired in leftover '80s hedonism", fans find it "surprisingly entertaining" – just "don't make the mistake of watching it with your parents."

Batman Ⓘ 20 | 19 | 19 | 24

1989. Directed by Tim Burton. With Michael Keaton, Jack Nicholson, Kim Basinger. 126 minutes. Rated PG-13.

■ The "first and best of the bat franchise", this "brilliantly shot" fantasy-adventure flick reflects the "dark side of the comic book" thanks to the "dynamic duo" of "visionary" director Burton and "top-notch" "caped crusader" Keaton; Nicholson's an "awesome" Joker and the "*Blade Runner*"-esque Gotham City is "realized to stunning effect", so even if the "sequels stink", this "stylish" "superhero" saga still "rocks."

Beau Geste ◑∅ 25 | 23 | 25 | 22

1939. Directed by William A. Wellman. With Gary Cooper, Ray Milland, Robert Preston. 120 minutes. Not Rated.

■ "Heroic heroes and villainous villains" populate this "ultimate" war picture about "friendship and honor" that's "perhaps the best Foreign Legion movie" ever made; ok, there are "no special effects" and it might seem "corny" today, but this "black-and-white classic" still supplies plenty of "first-class adventure" right up to that "majestic ending."

Beautiful Mind, A ✉ 26 | 28 | 25 | 25

2001. Directed by Ron Howard. With Russell Crowe, Ed Harris, Jennifer Connelly. 134 minutes. Rated PG-13.

■ "What *Rain Man* did for autism", this "absorbing" Oscar winner about a "brilliant mathematician's" "battle with mental illness" "does for schizophrenia", revealing the "thin line between genius and insanity"; "enlightening, but not preachy" and "phenomenally acted" by Crowe and Connelly, it "celebrates the triumph of the human spirit" – though sticklers say its "cleaned-up", "Hollywoodized" script "strays too far from historical accuracy."

BEAUTY AND THE BEAST ◑Ⓕ 28 | 25 | 27 | 28

1947. Directed by Jean Cocteau. With Jean Marais, Josette Day, Marcel André. 93 minutes. Not Rated.

■ Enter an "eccentric", "highly stylized universe" in this "hallucinatory" take on the classic "fairy tale" that's both "dreamlike" and "complex" owing to director "Cocteau's wit and imagination"; "still unsurpassed by more lavish productions", this "amazing visual feast" demonstrates the artistry possible with "ancient technology" – and enough "sexuality beneath the surface" to keep things throbbing.

Beauty and the Beast 26 | – | 25 | 27

1991. Directed by Gary Trousdale, Kirk Wise. Animated. 84 minutes. Rated G.

■ A "sensational score" complements a cast of "lovable characters" in this "magical" "milepost" that "set the bar for a new wave of animated classics"; told with a "fresh approach", it has an "intelligent" "heroine with chutzpah" trilling "catchy", "singable songs" that will "keep tots of all ages entranced"; in short, this "modern masterpiece" – the first animated film ever nominated for Best Picture – is nothing less than "Disney at its high-flying best."

Becket ✉∅ 26 | 29 | 26 | 26

1964. Directed by Peter Glenville. With Richard Burton, Peter O'Toole, John Gielgud. 148 minutes. Not Rated.

■ "Big drama writ large", this biopic about England's King Henry II and his "deep bond with Thomas Becket" features the "brilliant teaming" of "two high-powered actors" – the "winning" O'Toole and "wonderful" Burton – in "histrionic, bellowing performances"; sure, it's "a bit talky", but otherwise this "beautifully filmed period piece" is living proof of the way "history should be experienced."

Bedazzled ∅ 20 | 19 | 21 | 16

1967. Directed by Stanley Donen. With Dudley Moore, Peter Cook, Raquel Welch. 104 minutes. Not Rated.

■ This "immensely clever" "takeoff on the Faust legend" relocated to "swinging '60s London" is a "wickedly funny" comedy full of "vintage Brit humor" and "witty" "double entendres" in its story of "poor dweeb Moore selling his soul" to the devil in exchange for "true love"; ok, it may be "slow in spots", but it's still "far superior to the 2000 remake."

Beetlejuice 20 | 19 | 21 | 22

1988. Directed by Tim Burton. With Michael Keaton, Geena Davis, Alec Baldwin. 92 minutes. Rated PG.

■ "Netherworld antics" animate this "demented haunted-house comedy", a "bizarre" yet "enchanting" flick from "twisted" director Burton that's "endlessly inventive and endearingly funny"; built around a "genius" performance by Keaton as the "wonderfully disgusting" title character, it's also notable for a "macabre" turn from the then-"emerging Winona Ryder" as a very "unusual teenager."

Before Night Falls 22 | 26 | 22 | 20

2000. Directed by Julian Schnabel. With Javier Bardem, Johnny Depp. 133 minutes. Rated R.

■ Based on the true life story of "gay Cuban poet" Reinaldo Arenas, this "historically significant" biodrama is a "serious" reminder not to "take freedom for granted" as it details the hero's struggles against an "oppressive regime" bent on "silencing" him; look for an "excellent" Bardem in a "beautiful", "fully realized" performance.

Being John Malkovich 22 | 24 | 24 | 22

1999. Directed by Spike Jonze. With John Cusack, Cameron Diaz, John Malkovich. 112 minutes. Rated R.

◪ "'Original' does not even begin to describe" this "surreal romp" that mixes "dark fantasy" with "smart comedy" in its "off-the-wall" story of a regular guy who finds a portal that takes him "inside the head" of actor John Malkovich; though it "rewards rather than insults the audience's intelligence", it's definitely "not for everybody", being either "engrossing", "audacious fun" or "confusing as hell"; your call.

Being There 26 | 27 | 25 | 23

1979. Directed by Hal Ashby. With Peter Sellers, Shirley MacLaine, Melvyn Douglas. 130 minutes. Rated PG.

■ "Politics and hypocrisy" get a skewering in this "classic allegory" about a "slow-thinking" gardener who proves that "80 percent of life is just showing up"; "Sellers glows" in this "faithful" adaptation of "Jerzy Kosinski's masterpiece story", which might "require patience with its slow pace" but does "allow viewers to form their own conclusions."

Bell, Book and Candle 22 | 22 | 22 | 21

1958. Directed by Richard Quine. With Kim Novak, James Stewart, Jack Lemmon. 106 minutes. Not Rated.

■ Stewart and Novak "have fun with witchcraft" in this romantic comedy based on the Broadway hit about a "man falling for a woman who's a witch"; fans claim that this "old chestnut" was responsible for many cats being "named Pyewacket" and note that the "enchanting" title is a reference to the Roman Catholic rite of exorcism.

Belle de Jour F 24 | 25 | 23 | 23

1968. Directed by Luis Buñuel. With Catherine Deneuve, Jean Sorel. 101 minutes. Rated R.

■ Deneuve was "never sexier" than in this "marvelously perverse" French drama, a peek at the "dark side" of a "chichi housewife" pent up in "bourgeois" wedlock whose "S&M fantasies" compel her to take a "side job" at the local bordello; more "Dali painting" than *Playboy* centerfold, it's a "stylish", "complex" window into director Buñuel's "surreal world", and the leading lady's "intense", "alluring" performance spices up the "slow" spots.

Bells Are Ringing ∅ 24 | 24 | 22 | 22

1960. Directed by Vincente Minnelli. With Judy Holliday, Dean Martin. 127 minutes. Not Rated.

◪ An already "funny" Broadway musical becomes a "fine vehicle" for the "wonderful", "show-stealing" Holliday in this story of a singing switchboard girl hung up on a playwright (the slightly "out-of-his-league" Martin); yet despite a "classic" score and a "famous song" – 'The Party's Over' – some find this "stage-bound" production a bit "outdated."

Ben-Hur ✉ 26 | 23 | 25 | 28

1959. Directed by William Wyler. With Charlton Heston, Jack Hawkins, Stephen Boyd. 212 minutes. Rated G.

■ Unleashed four decades "before Gladiator", this "bigger than big" sword-and-sandals "masterpiece" features Heston exuding "hammy", bare-chested "bravura" as a

Judean prince betrayed into Roman slavery only to seek payback via "breathtaking" bouts of action (including that "stunner" of a "chariot race"); a colossal hit and major Oscar magnet, it "epitomizes" the "grand" "Hollywood historical epic", built on "biblical" bedrock.

Benji Ⓘ 19 | 16 | 18 | 17

1974. Directed by Joe Camp. With Patsy Garrett, Peter Breck. 86 minutes. Rated G.

■ *The* "must-see" flick for the "mid-'70s" single-digit demo, this fetching "doggy adventure" features a star turn from a "cute", shaggy-browed mutt who trots to the rescue after his young owners are kidnapped; nostalgists recall a "sappy" but "wonderful" "childhood favorite", albeit with "low-rent" production values.

BEST YEARS OF OUR LIVES, THE ⊠◑ 28 | 27 | 28 | 25

1946. Directed by William Wyler. With Myrna Loy, Fredric March, Dana Andrews, Teresa Wright. 172 minutes. Not Rated.

■ "Have the Kleenex handy" – there's no denying the "pure heart" of this "compelling" drama exploring the "uneasy readjustment" of three WWII "vets coming home" to Main Street USA; its all-around "riveting" acting and "no-miss script" "perfectly capture" the "next-door" post-war mood, bringing home Best Picture (plus six more Oscars) and resonating as a "quintessentially American" "period piece."

Beverly Hills Cop Ⓘ 20 | 19 | 19 | 19

1984. Directed by Martin Brest. With Eddie Murphy, Judge Reinhold, John Ashton. 105 minutes. Rated R.

◪ This action/comedy "breakthrough" is a "star vehicle" for Murphy, cast as an "inner-city" flatfoot with a "trademark laugh" who upstages his "goofy" El Lay counterparts in pursuit of a friend's killer; though the typically "'80s" foolery and "cheesy storyline" have cooled over time, this "hoot" still works as "feel-good" fare to fill a "Saturday afternoon."

BICYCLE THIEF, THE ⊠◑F 27 | 26 | 27 | 24

1948. Directed by Vittorio De Sica. With Lamberto Maggiorani, Enzo Staiola. 93 minutes. Not Rated.

■ "Poetry put on film", this early slice of "Italian neorealism" is "so sad" but so "beautifully executed" that it's ultimately "not a downer"; using "nonprofessional actors" in a drama of a father and "adorable" son searching impoverished post-war Rome for the stolen bike that's key to their livelihood, director De Sica tugs hearts with a "timeless" "pathos" that's most "affecting" for its "charm and simplicity."

Big 23 | 24 | 24 | 22

1988. Directed by Penny Marshall. With Tom Hanks, Elizabeth Perkins, Robert Loggia. 104 minutes. Rated PG.

■ Getting literal with its "inner child", this "cute" "kid-in-a-man's-body" comedy stars a "winning", "never-so-lovable"

Hanks, who "makes the movie" (and moves into the big time) as a 13-year-old who "becomes an adult overnight" and gains entrée to NYC's corporate playground; though some of the "fantasy" is "on the sappy side", a large contingent calls it "sweet", "amusing" and "most rewatchable."

Big Chill, The 23 | 24 | 22 | 21

1983. Directed by Lawrence Kasdan. With Glenn Close, William Hurt, Kevin Kline, Jeff Goldblum, Mary Kay Place, JoBeth Williams, Tom Berenger. 105 minutes. Rated R.

◪ Trace the tracks of their tears as this '60s-era "nostalgia" trip tries to "define a generation" via a "superb ensemble cast", an "iconic soundtrack" and the "soul-searching" premise of "boomers regathering" at a friend's funeral (fun fact: Kevin Costner "plays the stiff"); anyone bummed by the "contrived" setup and "insufferably" "smug" "yuppie angst" can still groove to the "perfect" selection of tunes.

Big Lebowski, The 20 | 22 | 19 | 20

1998. Directed by Joel Coen. With Jeff Bridges, John Goodman, Julianne Moore. 117 minutes. Rated R.

◪ The brothers Coen "strike again" with this "shaggy-dog" comedy, an "homage to slobs" that gets rolling when Bridges' "aging" "slacker/stoner character" (aka the Dude) and his "bizarre" "bowling buddies" become embroiled in the "kidnapping of a trophy wife"; though an "acquired taste" and "strange for its own sake" ("dude, where's my plot?"), it has "cult" followers citing "quotable" lines and swearing "you'll laugh."

Big Night 24 | 26 | 23 | 23

1996. Directed by Campbell Scott, Stanley Tucci. With Stanley Tucci, Tony Shalhoub, Minnie Driver. 107 minutes. Rated R.

■ "Yum": this "quirky", "thoroughly enjoyable" dramatic "feast" tracks two "Italian immigrant brothers" in their "endearing" effort to keep their restaurant and culinary "vision" alive on the '50s-era Jersey coast; hailed as an "overlooked" "gem", its slow-simmering pace allows admirers to "savor" "brilliant performances" that are rivaled only by "stunning food shots" – "don't catch it on an empty stomach."

BIG SLEEP, THE ◑ 27 | 27 | 24 | 24

1946. Directed by Howard Hawks. With Humphrey Bogart, Lauren Bacall. 114 minutes. Not Rated.

■ "Whodunit? who cares?" as long as the legendary "Bogey and Bacall" keep up the "snappy" patter and "heavy-lidded" "chemistry" in this "dizzying" film noir "classic" featuring Bogart as a "fast-talking" gumshoe Philip Marlowe prowling Raymond Chandler territory (1940s Los Angeles at its most "atmospheric"); if the notoriously "incomprehensible plot" is seriously in need of a clue, at least the "crackling" pace and "salty" repartee always "entertain and enthrall."

Billy Elliot 25 | 26 | 25 | 23

2000. Directed by Stephen Daldry. With Julie Walters, Jamie Bell. 110 minutes. Rated PG-13.

■ It takes *Swan Lake* to break the "working-class shackles" of a Northern England mining town in this "charming", "well-acted" "coming-of-age" drama about a "boy who loves ballet" and his hardscrabble dad; behind the "thick British accents", devotees discover a "captivating" if "unlikely tale" propelled by "talent, desire" and lots of "fancy footwork", with an "uplifting" finale that's apt to inspire "a good cry."

Birdcage, The 22 | 25 | 22 | 22

1996. Directed by Mike Nichols. With Robin Williams, Nathan Lane, Gene Hackman. 117 minutes. Rated R.

■ Reset in South Beach, director Nichols' "slick" take on the "classic" French farce *La Cage aux Folles* soars "over the top" on the wings of the "perfect comedic combination" of Williams and Lane, cast as a pair of "flamboyant" gay cabaret owners obliged to "play it straight" for their son's "uptight" in-laws-to-be; busy with burlesque and "insight", it's widely welcomed as a "laugh-out-loud" "blast", though a handful of holdouts chirp "stick with the original."

Birdman of Alcatraz ◑ 22 | 25 | 22 | 20

1962. Directed by John Frankenheimer. With Burt Lancaster, Karl Malden. 147 minutes. Not Rated.

■ Lancaster is "at the top of his game" in this saga of "a man, a prison and some birds", the "fascinating" bio of Rock lifer Robert Stroud, who struggles under the screws' authority but "finds love and friendship" when he becomes a famed ornithologist from his solitary cell; it's generally judged a "keeper" as a "gritty" but "entertaining" penal drama that's also a "touching" "examination of survival."

Birds, The 24 | 20 | 24 | 25

1963. Directed by Alfred Hitchcock. With Tippi Hedren, Rod Taylor, Jessica Tandy. 119 minutes. Rated PG-13.

◪ "Nature strikes back, Hitchcock style", in this "improbably terrifying" "nail-biter" about "birds gone mad" that "still packs enough of a punch" to leave the timid "traumatized"; though critics aren't chirping about the "hokey", "no-rhyme-or-reason" plot that takes "too long to get going", ultimately you'll "never think of pigeons in the same way" after a gander at this one; best scene: "Tippi in the attic."

Birth of a Nation, The ◑ 25 | 20 | 19 | 27

1915. Directed by D.W. Griffith. With Lillian Gish, Mae Marsh, Henry B. Walthall. 190 minutes. Not Rated.

◪ A "masterful" technical feat that could be the "most influential movie ever made", Griffith's "landmark" silent epic "wrote the book" on "camera movement" and "cinema as storytelling" while offering a "morally irresponsible" version of Reconstruction replete with "blatantly racist" "stereotyping" and the "Ku Klux Klan presented as heroes";

so even though this work marks the "birth of the feature" film, be prepared for a storyline that's a "mess" – "even by 1915" standards.

Bishop's Wife, The ◑ 24 | 24 | 24 | 23

1947. Directed by Henry Koster. With Cary Grant, Loretta Young, David Niven. 105 minutes. Not Rated.

■ Although "less well known" than some of its "holiday movie" peers, this "Christmasy" romance stars Grant as a "guardian angel" blessed with "elegance and style" ("duh!") who's sent to "restore faith" to a clergyman and his spouse but "falls in love" along the way; overall, it's an "amusing, touching" display of "old-fashioned" "star power" that sentimental souls will "never forget."

Blackboard Jungle ◑∅ 23 | 24 | 22 | 19

1955. Directed by Richard Brooks. With Glenn Ford, Anne Francis, Vic Morrow, Sidney Poitier. 101 minutes. Not Rated.

◪ See "the '50s in a new way" via this "gripping, gritty" drama, a standout of the "juvenile delinquent genre" set in an "inner-city school" where "danger is only a heartbeat away" as idealistic teacher Ford is forced to "tame" a horde of malevolent punks; notable for Hollywood's "first use of a rock 'n' roll" soundtrack, it may "feel a bit dated", though cynics shrug "schools haven't changed" that much.

Black Orpheus ✉ F 26 | 23 | 25 | 25

1959. Directed by Marcel Camus. With Marpessa Dawn, Breno Mello. 100 minutes. Rated PG.

■ "Brazilian backdrops" and "bossa nova" rhythms cast their "spell" over Greek legend in this "enchanting", "lyrical" foreign flick, an "exotic retelling" of the Orpheus and Eurydice myth transposed to "modern-day Rio" during Carnival; "sexy", "lush" and full of "beautiful shots" of "cinema verité" revelry, it takes its Dionysian devotees to Hades and back in "unmatched" style – and oh, that "moving-in-your-seat" soundtrack!

Black Stallion, The ⓫ 24 | 20 | 23 | 25

1979. Directed by Carroll Ballard. With Mickey Rooney, Kelly Reno, Teri Garr. 118 minutes. Rated G.

■ Equestrians of "all ages" ponder the "bond between boy and horse" in this "captivating" family film, about a Arabian steed who's shipwrecked with a youngster on a desert island only to be entered in a turf race after they're rescued and resettled to a Western ranch; though saddled with a "somber" side, it "wins the roses" with a "skillful blend" of "breathtaking" scenery and "luminous cinematography."

Blade Runner 26 | 22 | 25 | 27

1982. Directed by Ridley Scott. With Harrison Ford, Rutger Hauer, Sean Young. 117 minutes. Rated R.

■ This "awesome" "blueprint" for "modern sci-fi" is a "visually stunning" picture best watched with "your brain switched on"; an ultra-"stylish" "noir take" on LA as a 21st-century "dystopia" where "commercialism and biotech run amok", it's also a "hard-boiled" "morality play" with one of "Ford's best acting jobs" as a PI "hunting cyborg replicants while falling in love with one"; connoisseurs run right for the "superior director's cut."

Blazing Saddles 25 | 22 | 23 | 23

1974. Directed by Mel Brooks. With Cleavon Little, Gene Wilder, Harvey Korman. 93 minutes. Rated R.

■ "You'll never look at a horse the same way" after a peek at this "hilarious", "decidedly un-PC" comedy via Mel Brooks, an "off-the-wall" Wild West "spoof" that "insults everyone" with a mix of "slapstick", "eminently quotable" "one-liners" and infamously "tasteless" routines (like the sound effects–ridden "campfire scene"); consensus calls it "enjoyable" if "overdone" – in comparison, *The Producers* will seem like a model of sensitivity.

Blood Simple 24 | 25 | 25 | 22

1984. Directed by Joel Coen. With Frances McDormand, John Getz, Dan Hedaya. 97 minutes. Rated R.

■ "Complex" is more like it as the Coen brothers' first feature "pumps new blood" into the "low-budget crime thriller" in this "brilliant" "film noir homage" filled with "wicked" "thrills delivered with a drawl"; it's a "twisty", "nerve-jangling" tale of betrayal and revenge in a dusty Texas town, told with a "quirky" slant that "foreshadows" the filmmakers' "masterpiece, *Fargo*."

Blowup ∅ 26 | 23 | 25 | 25

1966. Directed by Michelangelo Antonioni. With David Hemmings, Vanessa Redgrave, Sarah Miles. 111 minutes. Not Rated.

■ "Forget *Austin Powers*", baby, "this is the *real* Swinging London": a "riveting" "existential thriller" via director Antonioni that tracks a "mod" "fashion photographer" obsessed by both Redgrave and a "mysterious death in a park"; hipsters hail it as an "enigmatic" (or "infuriating") milestone of the "alienation genre" possessed by the "spirit of the '60s" – and that tasty "period flavor" is still "too cool for words."

Blue Angel, The ◐ F 25 | 27 | 24 | 22

1931. Directed by Josef von Sternberg. With Marlene Dietrich, Emil Jannings. 99 minutes. Not Rated.

■ Behold the "magnificent Dietrich" "at her best" in this "Weimar-era" German drama, the story of "naughty Lola", a garter-flashing chanteuse who "seduces an old fool" of a schoolmaster and expedites his "descent into the gutter"; though it's a "dated" dose of "ennui and moral rot" in a "world now lost", fräulein Marlene's "tour-de-force", career-launching performance is "music to the eyes" and "still powerful."

Blues Brothers, The ⓫ 22 | 19 | 19 | 21

1980. Directed by John Landis. With John Belushi, Dan Aykroyd, John Candy. 133 minutes. Rated R.

■ "Ignore the plot" and "get out the popcorn" for this "good-time" comedy, powered by Belushi and Aykroyd on a "full tank of gas" as sibs Jake and Elwood, who accept a "mission from God" to provoke "hilarity" and find out "how many cars they can wreck"; if it's (ahem) "not a critics' choice", those with a hankering for "hot" "soul 'n' blues" numbers liberally chased with "dumb fun" insist "you gotta love it."

Blue Velvet 22 | 23 | 20 | 23

1986. Directed by David Lynch. With Kyle MacLachlan, Isabella Rossellini, Dennis Hopper. 120 minutes. Rated R.

◩ "One sick puppy of a movie", this "kinky" yet totally "enthralling" look at the "seedy underbelly" "beneath the surface of suburbia" is "love-it-or-hate-it" filmmaking from the "warped" mind of "surrealist auteur Lynch"; despite applause for Hopper's "memorably creepy" portrayal of the "gas-inhaling pervert" ("worth seeing for the Pabst Blue Ribbon scene alone"), sensitive souls find the flick "ugly, pointless" and "not as good as its reputation."

Body Heat 24 | 25 | 25 | 23

1981. Directed by Lawrence Kasdan. With William Hurt, Kathleen Turner. 113 minutes. Rated R.

■ "Whew!" this "palpably steamy" "noir thriller" stars "what-a-babe" Turner as a trophy wife who "burns up the screen" as she seduces "small-town lawyer" Hurt into a "spiraling" web of "deceit" that "keeps you guessing" to the last frame; in short, it's a sexed-up "version of the old help-me-kill-my-husband story", a kind of "*Double Indemnity* for a new generation."

Bonnie and Clyde 25 | 25 | 24 | 25

1967. Directed by Arthur Penn. With Warren Beatty, Faye Dunaway, Gene Hackman, Estelle Parsons. 111 minutes. Not Rated.

■ More a piece of "film history than real history", this "stunning" 1930s "crime-spree" biopic "broke a lot of old rules" in its "revisionist" take on the title characters, real-life "losers" reconceived by Beatty and Dunaway as the "screen's best-ever antiheroes"; the "letter-perfect" cast, "impeccable" direction and "gorgeously gory" photography all add up to way-"ahead-of-its-time" moviemaking, even if the "indelible images" of the "bloody ballet at the end" unsettle the squeamish.

Boogie Nights 19 | 21 | 19 | 19

1997. Directed by Paul Thomas Anderson. With Mark Wahlberg, Burt Reynolds, Julianne Moore. 152 minutes. Rated R.

■ Set in the '70s "disco era", this "dead-on look" at the "ins and outs (so to speak) of the porn industry" features "inspired performances" – "Burt returns!", "Marky Mark grows up!" – even if the "XXX film stars" portrayed "don't have much going on upstairs"; though the "sex-drugs-and-roller-skates" plot is "shamelessly entertaining" for the "first 2/3" of the picture, the "violent", "depressing" final act can be "emotionally draining."

Born Free Ⓘ∅ 24 | 19 | 24 | 23

1966. Directed by James Hill. With Virginia McKenna, Bill Travers, Geoffrey Keen. 95 minutes. Rated PG.

■ The "theme song alone" is enough to set off "shameless weeping" as this "well-told" family flick unfolds, focusing on a husband and wife in "wild Africa" and their effort to "protect the lioness Elsa"; a "major tearjerker" in its day, it remains "vivid" for boomers who tell of "loving it as a child" even though it's "so sad."

Born on the Fourth of July ✉ 20 | 21 | 20 | 20

1989. Directed by Oliver Stone. With Tom Cruise, Kyra Sedgwick, Willem Dafoe. 145 minutes. Rated R.

◪ "Cruise excels" in one of Stone's "most accomplished works", a "potent", "well-done" bio of "Vietnam vet Ron Kovic" that's an "intense", "heart-wrenching" study of "flag-waving patriotism"; though it draws fire for being "contrived" and "overwrought" ("my, aren't we important?"), it does offer convincing "proof that Tom can act."

Born Yesterday ✉◑ 26 | 28 | 25 | 23

1950. Directed by George Cukor. With Judy Holliday, Broderick Crawford, William Holden. 103 minutes. Not Rated.

■ "Still magical today", this "zany" "screwball comedy" has to do with a "not-so-dumb blonde" who undergoes a *My Fair Lady*–like transformation and "breaks out of her bimbo chains"; thanks to a unique voice and "great timing", the "perfectly cast" Holliday took home an Oscar for her "pure gold" performance, a "pièce de résistance" that the 1993 remake "can't match."

Boys Don't Cry ✉ 23 | 27 | 23 | 21

1999. Directed by Kimberly Peirce. With Hilary Swank, Chloë Sevigny, Peter Sarsgaard. 118 minutes. Rated R.

■ Turning a "dark situation" into a "tough", "eye-opening" study of "intolerance", this "disturbing" drama is a "faithful telling of the story of Teena Brandon", a small-town girl who "dresses and acts the part" of a boy, leading to "powerful" complications; though the "strong", Oscar-winning Swank is "beyond convincing", the "brutal" ending is "not easy to watch", but "will stay with you" – "unfortunately, it's true."

Boyz N the Hood 23 | 22 | 24 | 21

1991. Directed by John Singleton. With Ice Cube, Cuba Gooding Jr., Laurence Fishburne. 107 minutes. Rated R.

■ The "gangsta flick" that "sets the bar" for the competition is also a "sincere drama" that "keeps it real" as it takes a "hard-core" "look at ghetto" "gang wars in South Central" LA; an "important" breakthrough with some "surprising acting turns", it's a "fantastic first film" from Singleton, whose later work doesn't "get anywhere near this one."

Braveheart ✉ 26 | 24 | 25 | 27

1995. Directed by Mel Gibson. With Mel Gibson, Sophie Marceau, Catherine McCormack. 177 minutes. Rated R.

◪ "It's got everything" say fans of this "awe-inspiring" medieval "history lesson" about an "underdog" Scottish hero ("Mel in a kilt" and "war paint") "knocking heads" in an anti-Brit "rebellion", while "wooing" lassies on the side; the "gory", "hackin'-and-hewin'" battles, "heartfelt" acting and "huge scope" help justify Gibson's Best Director win, even if some warn of three "long", "melodramatic" hours.

Brazil 24 | 23 | 23 | 27

1985. Directed by Terry Gilliam. With Jonathan Pryce, Robert De Niro, Bob Hoskins. 131 minutes. Rated R.

◪ Even as "fantasy", Monty Python alum Gilliam's "twisted", "utterly original" vision of a "part-Orwell, part-Python" future is "a little out there"; it demands "perseverance" – what with its "baffling" "whirlwind" of "bizarre" effects and chin-scratching "black comedy" plot about one man's struggle with a "Kafka-esque" "bureaucracy" – but rewards those who hang on with a "totally crazy ride."

Breaker Morant 27 | 27 | 27 | 24

1980. Directed by Bruce Beresford. With Jack Thompson, Edward Woodward, Bryan Brown. 107 minutes. Rated PG.

■ "Guy's-flick" fans salute this "solid" "Aussie" drama of "kangaroo" justice, a "small masterpiece" in its "gripping" depiction of "betrayal" at a military trial during the Boer War; told with "moving" "realism", it tackles the "question of morals in warfare" using a "top-notch" cast to "demonstrate bravery" and "bravura", turning the fate of "appointed scapegoats" into an "inspiration" – "fine film", mate.

Breakfast at Tiffany's 26 | 26 | 24 | 24

1961. Directed by Blake Edwards. With Audrey Hepburn, George Peppard, Patricia Neal. 115 minutes. Rated PG.

■ In the "role she was born to play", a "mesmerizing" Hepburn brings Truman Capote's "messed-up" "free spirit" Holly Golightly to life in "peerless style"; fans find everything about it "irresistible" – "Henry Mancini's divine score", the "love-letter-to-NY" cinematography, Audrey's "timeless clothes" – and call this "dream-making, heartbreaking" tribute to the "power of romance" their "all-time" "favorite."

Breakfast Club, The 22 | 21 | 22 | 19

1985. Directed by John Hughes. With Emilio Estevez, Anthony Michael Hall, Judd Nelson, Molly Ringwald. 92 minutes. Rated R.

■ Any card-carrying "child of the '80s" is apt to "know all the lines" of this "engaging" high school yukfest, a "Gen-X" "time capsule" about a group of "brat pack" "all-stars" "stuck in detention" and left to compare and contrast "confused personalities"; a "hoot" with a "sensitive" side, it's rerun "ad infinitum", since it "speaks to teenagers in a way that *American Pie* will never be able to."

Breaking Away ✉ 24 | 21 | 24 | 20

1979. Directed by Peter Yates. With Dennis Christopher, Dennis Quaid, Daniel Stern. 100 minutes. Rated PG.

■ A "rousing ride", this "*Rocky*-esque" "Hoosier tale" is a "coming-of-age" drama on two wheels, with Christopher leading a cast of "cutie-pie" "underdogs" as a cyclist who pedals straight into a "town-and-gown" "class conflict"; it's cheered on as a "big-hearted" "buddy film" that delivers a "socko" "bike race" finale.

Breaking the Waves 23 | 27 | 20 | 20

1996. Directed by Lars von Trier. With Emily Watson, Stellan Skarsgård. 153 minutes. Rated R.

◪ "Be prepared" for "emotionally devastating" doings in this "raw" drama of "delusion" and "doomed romance" about a "dim-witted girl" who "sacrifices everything for her paralyzed husband"; most pronounce it "strange" yet "so well done it's painful" (the "musical interludes give one time to weep"), though foes wave it off as a "silly" parable that's a "depressing" depiction of "female martyrdom."

Breathless ◑ F 25 | 24 | 21 | 23

1961. Directed by Jean-Luc Godard. With Jean-Paul Belmondo, Jean Seberg. 87 minutes. Not Rated.

■ "*So* hip" and as "refreshing" now as at its debut, this French "New Wave masterpiece" breathes "pure pleasure" into a "silly gangster story" with "luscious" leads Belmondo and Seberg as lovers on the lam (even the late-'50s Paris setting is a "terrific character"); while scholars speak of genre-"defining" technical feats – the "jump cut is born!" – most simply find it "charming" and way "ahead of its time."

Bride of Frankenstein ◑ 25 | 21 | 23 | 23

1935. Directed by James Whale. With Boris Karloff, Colin Clive, Elsa Lanchester. 75 minutes. Not Rated.

■ Bolt-necked "Frankie" gets "his one shot at love" in this "excellent sequel" to the hoary "'30s horror" "classic", wherein Karloff reprises his signature role with "panache" and Lanchester's shocked fiancée simply has "great hair"; fright fiends cherish the "creepy" results as "campy", "funny" and not a little "whacked."

BRIDGE ON THE RIVER KWAI, THE ✉ 28 | 28 | 27 | 28

1957. Directed by David Lean. With William Holden, Alec Guinness, Jack Hawkins. 161 minutes. Rated PG.

■ Those "stiff upper lips" do some "memorable" whistling in director Lean's "grand", "engrossing" "Japanese POW camp" epic, an "old-fashioned" yarn about the "timeless themes" of "honor", "conviction" and the "madness" of war; a lock for the top Oscars of 1957, it "succeeds" mightily with "great performances" – led "heart and soul" by a "hubris"-afflicted Guinness – enhanced by "splashy" scenery and an "explosive ending."

Bridges of Madison County, The 19 | 23 | 20 | 20

1995. Directed by Clint Eastwood. With Clint Eastwood, Meryl Streep, Annie Corley. 135 minutes. Rated PG-13.

◪ Director/leading man Eastwood unveils his "gentle side" in this "bittersweet" romance recounting the "middle-aged" "passion" between a "roving" photographer and a "lonely housewife" (the "spot- on" Streep); some cite the "banal", "snail's-pace" plot as a big "yawn", but to sentimentalists it's "lovably sappy" – and "way better" than the "treacly" book.

Bridget Jones's Diary 21 | 23 | 22 | 21

2001. Directed by Sharon Maguire. With Renée Zellweger, Hugh Grant, Colin Firth. 97 minutes. Rated R.

■ This "everygirl" "chick flick" is a "charming" romance that logs the progress of the "fab" Zellweger, doing a "knockout job" in the title role as a "twentysomething singleton" "Londoner" "desperately seeking a spouse" but beleaguered by "faux pas", "weight gain" and a "perfect cad" of a boss; followers find it "hilarious yet so true" but won't commit as to whether it "nails the book" or not.

BRIEF ENCOUNTER ◑ 27 | 29 | 27 | 25

1946. Directed by David Lean. With Celia Johnson, Trevor Howard, Stanley Holloway. 86 minutes. Not Rated.

■ For a "truly romantic" fix, this "quiet" "masterpiece of yearning" from David Lean (via Noël Coward) is "right up there" in the running as the "definitive" "tearjerker"; the "never better" Johnson and Howard play "ordinary people" whose meeting on a commuter line develops into a "short but intense" "connection", with swells of Rachmaninoff to seal the deal; in brief, an "unforgettable" excursion.

Bringing Up Baby ◑∅ 27 | 27 | 24 | 24

1938. Directed by Howard Hawks. With Katharine Hepburn, Cary Grant. 102 minutes. Not Rated.

■ "One continuous roar", director Hawks' "screwiest of screwball comedies" is propelled at a "frenetic pace" by the Hepburn-Grant "chemistry" and a "tons-of-fun" scenario touching on "dinosaur bones, crazy rich folk" and a lost leopard; it's an old-school "madcap" "champ", and fans of "farce" still bring it up as the "funniest movie ever."

Broadcast News 23 | 25 | 22 | 20

1987. Directed by James L. Brooks. With William Hurt, Albert Brooks, Holly Hunter. 127 minutes. Rated R.

■ "Appearance over substance" is the subject of this "smart" "send-up of the media" about a "love triangle" in a "career-driven", *Network*-esque TV newsroom that hums with "behind-the scenes" one-upmanship and "absurdity"; nominated for a slew of Oscars (but winner of none), this "underrated", "ahead-of-its-time" comedy remains "totally engaging", due to the efforts of its "sharp-as-a-tack" cast.

Broadway Danny Rose ◑ 22 | 22 | 22 | 20

1984. Directed by Woody Allen. With Woody Allen, Mia Farrow, Nick Apollo Forte. 84 minutes. Rated PG.

◪ Woody and Mia (in rosier days) light up this comedy about a "Mafia tootsie who melts" for the "ultimate mensch", a small-time talent agent clinging to the "underbelly" of "borscht-belt" showbiz; although infused with a "NY sensibility", the "shaggy-dog" plot "doesn't quite deliver", so surveyors split: "average" vs. "best-kept secret."

Buck Privates ◑Ⓘ 22 | 19 | 16 | 18

1941. Directed by Arthur Lubin. With Abbott & Costello, the Andrews Sisters. 84 minutes. Not Rated.

■ A coupla clowns go to boot camp and "frivolity" ensues in this "classic Abbott and Costello" comedy, which "evokes an era" thanks to the "duo's rapid-fire patter" and USO-worthy tunes by the "Andrews Sisters at their peak"; despite "patchwork" plotting, it "ranks up there" in Bud and Lou's oeuvre and works as a swell "Sunday morning" indulgence.

Buena Vista Social Club 25 | – | 24 | 24

1999. Directed by Wim Wenders. Documentary. 101 minutes. Rated G.

■ "Revelatory – and danceable" – this documentary is a "love letter to a vanishing breed" of musicians, "aging" vets of the "Afro-Cuban jazz" scene who volunteer "personal histories" of "trials and tribulations" in the "shadow of Castro", interspersed with "irresistible" live jams; it "builds slowly" in a haze of "washed-out tropical colors" to a narrative of "great charm" and "insight", backed by a soundtrack that's as "captivating" as they come.

Bug's Life, A 24 | – | 22 | 26

1998. Directed by John Lasseter, Andrew Stanton. Animated. 96 minutes. Rated G.

■ "Even parents" bug out on the "mind-blowing creativity" of the Disney/Pixar team's "step-ahead animation" in this "cute" parable of "insect politics" rendered in "sharp, colorful" computer graphics that "look incredible", even if the "social satire" is "geared for kids"; most maintain it's "superior to *Antz*" as family fare and advise sticking around for the fake outtakes as the credits roll (the "best part").

Bull Durham 22 | 22 | 22 | 20

1988. Directed by Ron Shelton. With Kevin Costner, Susan Sarandon, Tim Robbins. 108 minutes. Rated R.

■ "Life and love in minor-league baseball" equal "diverting" comedy in this "funny and realistic" sports pic, juiced by "sexy", "laid-back acting" from Sarandon and Costner, a "great pair" out to take the "American spirit" into extra innings; fans cheer it on as a "sweet", "smart" "home run" that's "one of the best" of the hardball yarns.

Bullets Over Broadway 21 | 23 | 21 | 21

1994. Directed by Woody Allen. With John Cusack, Dianne Wiest, Jennifer Tilly. 98 minutes. Rated R.

■ A "quirky, colorful" shot of "period" atmosphere, this "backstage comedy" concerns a Jazz Age dramatist and a "gangster who rewrites his Broadway play"; it's "likable" enough for its "witty dialogue", "well-executed story" and "over-the-top" cast, though as usual for a "post-*Hannah*" Allen opus, some wish it were "just a little funnier."

Bullitt 22 | 20 | 20 | 24

1968. Directed by Peter Yates. With Steve McQueen, Robert Vaughn, Jacqueline Bisset. 113 minutes. Rated PG.

◪ Arguably "the mother of all cop films", this "solid" action thriller stars an "icy-cool" McQueen, "acting by not acting" as a no-bull SFPD detective who takes on killers and a corrupt system; set in Frisco "before too many high-rises" arrived, it's famed for a "definitive car chase" ("wheee!") that's "still the best" after "countless" knockoffs, though some find the ride "pretty straightforward" plotwise.

Bus Stop 21 | 21 | 20 | 20

1956. Directed by Joshua Logan. With Marilyn Monroe, Don Murray, Eileen Heckart. 96 minutes. Not Rated.

◪ Proving herself "at home on the range", Monroe brings "depth" to romantic comedy in "one of her best roles", as a "sweet, vulnerable" "Western chantoosie" with "impossible dreams" adrift in an otherwise "slightly sappy" tale of a cowpoke's "crazy love" (via a William Inge play); though Marilyn proves she's more than "just a pretty face", skeptics of her "serious actress" mode say they "want to get off."

Butch Cassidy & the Sundance Kid ✉ ⓫ 26 | 26 | 25 | 25

1969. Directed by George Roy Hill. With Paul Newman, Robert Redford, Katharine Ross. 110 minutes. Rated PG.

■ "Compulsive charmers" Newman and Redford play a pair of wisecracking, "magnetic" "antiheroes" trying to stay ahead of the law in this "outstanding" Western "buddy movie", loaded with "adventure and humor"; it fuses a "snappy" script, Burt Bacharach soundtrack and "too many classic scenes to count" into a "sentimental favorite" that's "never boring" from start to "unforgettable" finish.

Bye Bye Birdie 19 | 18 | 18 | 20

1963. Directed by George Sidney. With Janet Leigh, Dick Van Dyke, Ann-Margret. 112 minutes. Rated G.

◪ The high "fun quotient" bolsters this "upbeat" musical from the "long-ago world" of 1963, a look at the hoopla surrounding an Elvis-like singer's farewell gig before he goes off to the army; though Ann-Margret is "one heck of a talented" "sex kitten" doing some athletic song-and-dance numbers that – whew! – "stay with you", foes wave it off as "cheesy" fare that's "woefully dated now."

Cabaret ✉ 26 | 25 | 25 | 27

1972. Directed by Bob Fosse. With Liza Minnelli, Michael York, Joel Grey. 124 minutes. Rated PG.

■ Comprised of equal parts "love, angst", "singing, dancing and Nazis", this "seminal modern musical" set in "pre-WWII Berlin" is a "touchstone" of the genre that "hasn't lost its luster"; old chums cheer Fosse's "superb direction" and the "starmaking performances" from Minnelli and Grey (who all took home Oscars), and even though the mood of the piece can careen from "dark" to "raunchy", it's always "fun to watch."

Cabinet of Dr. Caligari, The ◑ 26 | 21 | 24 | 26

1921. Directed by Robert Wiene. With Conrad Veidt, Werner Kraus. 67 minutes. Not Rated.

■ "They don't get any freakier" than this "fascinating antique", a "menacingly atmospheric" silent horror flick that uses "German expressionism" and "twisted sets" to kindle a "nightmare" tale of murder told by a "tortured mind"; "stark, powerful" and "spooky" right down to the pioneering "surprise ending", it's "still being imitated" and still makes many modern chillers "look lame."

Caddyshack Ⓘ 24 | 20 | 19 | 19

1980. Directed by Harold Ramis. With Chevy Chase, Rodney Dangerfield, Bill Murray. 99 minutes. Rated R.

■ "Dumb as it is", this "goofy" comedy of "golfers gone amok" is a "classic" of "unironic" (some say "sophomoric") humor featuring the "priceless" ensemble of Chase, Murray, Dangerfield and a fake gopher; "ok, it's a guy thing", but it "stands the test of time" as "oft-quoted" "mindless fun."

Caine Mutiny, The 27 | 28 | 26 | 23

1954. Directed by Edward Dmytryk. With Humphrey Bogart, Jose Ferrer. 124 minutes. Not Rated.

■ This "briny" blend of "powerful wartime story" and "engrossing" courtroom drama gets its ballast from Bogart's "brilliant", "pull-out-all-the-stops" turn as Queeg, the "demented sea captain" compulsively "click, click, clicking" a set of "steel balls"; the "classic script" follows a "totally believable" high-seas rebellion to a Navy court-martial and is "must-see" material for maritime mavens.

Camelot 21 | 21 | 23 | 23

1967. Directed by Joshua Logan. With Richard Harris, Vanessa Redgrave, Franco Nero. 179 minutes. Rated G.

◪ Lerner and Loewe's Broadway musical of the "well-worn" King Arthur legend receives "faithful" treatment as royal duo

Harris and Redgrave rule over a round table of pomp and "passion in medieval England"; admirers of the "gorgeous" sets and "beautiful music" sing its praises as a "magical" "diversion", though dissenters take a tilt at the "ponderous" "excess" and note "no one in the cast can carry a tune."

Candidate, The ✉ 20 | 22 | 22 | 20

1972. Directed by Michael Ritchie. With Robert Redford, Peter Boyle, Melvyn Douglas. 109 minutes. Rated PG.

■ A "prescient" civics lesson, this political drama tracks a "social activist seduced into selling his soul" when he runs for the Senate from California; a "most convincing" Redford leads the pack of "top-notch performances" as the novice campaigner who's "in far over his head", presenting an "accurate" if "cynical view" of the process that registers as "timely" 30 years later.

Cape Fear ◑ 25 | 26 | 26 | 23

1962. Directed by J. Lee Thompson. With Gregory Peck, Robert Mitchum, Polly Bergen. 105 minutes. Not Rated.

■ It's high tide for "rage and revenge" in this "doozy" of a noir thriller, a "gritty" "nail-biter" starring Peck as an upright dad who "gets down in the gutter" to protect his family from the "deeply frightening" ex-con Mitchum, at large in the marsh and "as evil as they come"; most rate it "scarier than the remake", "without the histrionics."

Cape Fear 20 | 24 | 21 | 20

1991. Directed by Martin Scorsese. With Robert De Niro, Nick Nolte, Jessica Lange. 128 minutes. Rated R.

◪ Count on "fear for sure" as Scorsese's "well-done" redo of the killer '62 thriller heads for "over-the-top territory", working up "sustained suspense" as a "terrifying" De Niro "has a ball" portraying a vengeance-bent "wacko"; it's an "edge-of-your-seat" ride, but admirers of the original can't hack the "unnecessary violence"; P.S. the "cameos" from the "previous cast" are a "nice touch."

Captain Blood ◑∅ 23 | 21 | 20 | 21

1935. Directed by Michael Curtiz. With Errol Flynn, Olivia de Havilland, Basil Rathbone. 119 minutes. Not Rated.

■ Avast, there's "salty" "popcorn fun" aplenty in this "smashing" "swashbuckler", featuring "Flynn's first starring role" as an enslaved wretch who becomes a "devil-may-care" pirate of the Caribbean; armchair buccaneers jump on board for the "roguish" baddies, "high-seas action" and "devil-may-care" "men in tights", not minding that the old vessel is "on the creaky side."

Captains Courageous ✉◑∅ 25 | 26 | 24 | 21

1937. Directed by Victor Fleming. With Spencer Tracy, Freddie Bartholomew, Lionel Barrymore. 115 minutes. Not Rated.

■ Fashioned from a Kipling tale that's "every boy's dream of excitement", this "tearjerker"–cum–adventure story stars

Bartholomew as a bratty rich kid who's rescued at sea and matures under the helm of a salty sailor, the Oscar-winning Tracy; the lad's "highly touching" transformation is conveyed through "phenomenal" acting that's "too often forgotten."

Carnal Knowledge 22 | 26 | 21 | 21

1971. Directed by Mike Nichols. With Jack Nicholson, Candice Bergen, Art Garfunkel, Ann-Margret. 98 minutes. Rated R.

■ "Literate people talk dirty" in this "bitter but engrossing" look at "two self-absorbed buddies who measure life in terms of their sexual conquests", and though these "pretty sad characters" can be "hard to watch", the "perfect cast" expertly evokes its theme of "innocence lost"; still, the jaded jeer what was "bold for its time" is now rather "tame."

Carousel 24 | 22 | 22 | 25

1956. Directed by Henry King. With Gordon MacRae, Shirley Jones. 128 minutes. Not Rated.

◪ "Girl meets wrong boy" at the traveling show in this silver screen go-round of Rodgers and Hammerstein's "sentimental" musical, which draws on a "lovely" score and "fine cast" of "first-rate" singers to spin a tale that's "romantic, sad" and "not always pretty"; a "neglected great" to some, it's also seen as a squandering of "talent" on a "corny", "tarnished-with-age" storyline.

Carrie Ⓘ 22 | 22 | 23 | 21

1976. Directed by Brian De Palma. With Sissy Spacek, Piper Laurie, Amy Irving. 98 minutes. Rated R.

■ "Stephen King done right", this "bloody good" horror pic headlines Spacek as a "bug-eyed" "telekinetic outcast" (with a "nut bar" of a mom) who repays the "casual cruelty of high-schoolers" with a prom-night "flip-out" that's gorier than a bucket of "pig's blood"; with "character-oriented" carnage that's a cut above "shock schlock", it's "white knuckles all the way" to that "grabber" of an ending.

CASABLANCA ✉◑ 29 | 28 | 28 | 27

1942. Directed by Michael Curtiz. With Humphrey Bogart, Ingrid Bergman, Paul Henreid, Claude Rains. 102 minutes. Rated PG.

■ We'll always have the "magic" of this "most compelling" of romances, a showcase for "legendary" turns from an "enigmatic" Bogart, "radiant" Bergman and "top-shelf" supporting cast set against the "unforgettable" backdrop of occupied North Africa; the "fast-paced" plot of passion and "intrigue" is an "unsurpassed" model of "old-fashioned storytelling" and a "runner-up to Shakespeare" for "classic lines" – there's no choice but to "play it again and again."

Casino 21 | 24 | 21 | 22

1995. Directed by Martin Scorsese. With Robert De Niro, Sharon Stone, Joe Pesci. 178 minutes. Rated R.

◪ A crash course in "pre-corporate casino management", Scorsese's "flashy" crime saga of "mob life" in "seedy

Vegas" relates a "dark" tale that deals out "violence, drugs and self-loathing" in spades; proponents lay their money down for De Niro as a dapper hood, Pesci's "insane mob guy" bit and a "sizzling" Stone proving she "can actually act"; still, those who yawn it's "way too long" say bets are off, since they could be "watching *Goodfellas* instead."

Cast Away 20 | 25 | 18 | 23

2000. Directed by Robert Zemeckis. With Tom Hanks, Helen Hunt. 143 minutes. Rated PG-13.

◪ "Hanks does Crusoe" in this "well-made" adventure based on Tom's "almost-one-man show" as a "pudgy FedEx" pilot "marooned" after a crash landing and forced to "slim down", don a "loincloth" and start "talking to a volleyball"; though "feeling his pain and loneliness" may be "inspiring", foes say the action's beached by "slow-moving" stretches and a "trite" windup that's a "predictable" "snoozer."

Cat Ballou ✉ 21 | 22 | 19 | 20

1965. Directed by Elliot Silverstein. With Lee Marvin, Jane Fonda, Michael Callan. 97 minutes. Not Rated.

■ "Not your typical Western", this comic oater "with a heart" stars Fonda as a righteous lady outlaw but is stolen by Oscar-winner Marvin, who horses around in two roles, including that of a whiskey-addled gunslinger; a "hoot in its day", it's nearing its ninth life but is still "fun to watch."

Cat on a Hot Tin Roof 25 | 27 | 24 | 23

1958. Directed by Richard Brooks. With Elizabeth Taylor, Paul Newman, Burl Ives. 108 minutes. Not Rated.

■ "Man, these people have problems": "steamy Liz" "in that white slip" and a "dynamite" Newman "couldn't possibly look better" as they "burn up the screen" in this "sex-soaked" Tennessee Williams drama of "love, rejection" and "Southern family politics"; the "towering" Ives presides as the ragin' Big Daddy, adding an "incredibly interesting" *Lear*-like thread to all that "eye candy."

Celluloid Closet, The 25 | – | – | 24

1995. Directed by Robert Epstein, Jeff Friedman. Documentary. 102 minutes. Rated R.

■ Learn to "appreciate" certain classics in a "whole new" way via this documentary "revelation" that traces "gay themes and undercurrents" in Hollywood history using film clips and "insightful" interviews; it takes an "unsparing look at prejudice" that's also a "very entertaining" glimpse into a "crowded closet" – even if some wish there were more than "mild surprises behind the door."

Charade 26 | 25 | 26 | 25

1963. Directed by Stanley Donen. With Cary Grant, Audrey Hepburn, Walter Matthau. 113 minutes. Not Rated.

■ Expect "plenty of plot twists" in this "quintessential romantic comedy/thriller" (the "best Hitchcock flick that

Hitchcock didn't make") about the scramble for a missing fortune; its very "easy-on-the-eyes" stars, "luscious Paris" scenery, magical "Mancini melodies" and "Audrey's fab wardrobe" make for "perfect" moviemaking – "murder was never so much fun."

Chariots of Fire ✉ 26 | 25 | 25 | 25

1981. Directed by Hugh Hudson. With Ben Cross, Ian Charleson, Ian Holm. 123 minutes. Rated PG.

■ Remembered for "running off with" a Best Picture Oscar, this "inspiring" drama paces itself in "superb" style as it follows the "trials and triumph" of a British track team bound for the 1924 Olympics; thanks to "uplifting" legwork and a very "hummable" soundtrack, it breaks the tape as a "never boring" movie that's "suitable for all ages."

Charly ✉∅ 21 | 25 | 22 | 17

1968. Directed by Ralph Nelson. With Cliff Robertson, Claire Bloom, Leon Janney. 103 minutes. Rated PG.

■ A bright idea grafting drama onto a "believable" sci-fi scenario, this "original" flick gives Best Actor honoree Robertson a chance to "shine" in his "best performance", as a "man who goes from retardation to genius and back again" after a round of brain surgery; tutor Bloom adds romantic interest to make the doings "supremely touching" – "if a bit sappy" for cynics.

Chasing Amy 20 | 19 | 20 | 17

1997. Directed by Kevin Smith. With Ben Affleck, Joey Lauren Adams, Jason Lee. 111 minutes. Rated R.

◪ Director Smith's trademarks – "Jersey-speak", "coarse humor", "semi-realistic situations" – are all apparent in this "offbeat" romantic comedy, featuring Affleck in the role of a comic-book scribe bewitched by a lesbian with a "nails-on-chalkboard" voice; it "rocks" fans with an "entertainingly different" mix of "smart" talk and "slacker cool", but those who take flight claim it's a "sentimental", "pretentious" ode to "geek life" that's "not really funny."

Cheaper By the Dozen Ⓡ∅ 22 | 22 | 23 | 19

1950. Directed by Walter Lang. With Clifton Webb, Jeanne Crain, Myrna Loy. 85 minutes. Not Rated.

■ Set at the turn of the last century, this "warm family comedy" relates the "wonderful", fact-based story of a pair of efficiency experts bringing up 12 "cute" children, with a "droll" Webb stealing the show as the "pompous" head of the brood; sure, it strays into "precious" territory but oldsters attest it "wears well over time."

Chicken Run 23 | – | 23 | 27

2000. Directed by Peter Lord, Nick Park. Animated. 84 minutes. Rated G.

■ Pure "poultry in motion", this "ingenious", "touching" barnyard saga uses "fantastic" claymation to portray a "darn appealing" bunch of British fowl and their "valiant struggle" to get off the farm; "subtle references" make it a "hilarious take" on all the *Stalag 17*–style POW pics, so while kids can enjoy the "innocent" animated escapade, it "doesn't chicken out" on "tongue-in-cheek", grown-up undertones; in an eggshell, a "good run for the money."

Children of a Lesser God ✉ 23 | 25 | 22 | 21

1986. Directed by Randa Haines. With Marlee Matlin, William Hurt, Piper Laurie. 119 minutes. Rated R.

◪ This "touching" drama "does justice to the original play" on the strength of "sexy, compelling" turns from Hurt as a speech teacher at a school for the deaf and Best Actress winner Matlin, "signing throughout" as a hearing-impaired woman with a complex past; expect "moving scenes" as their intimacy develops, and though an "enjoyable" intro to the "deaf community", it might be a "little overdramatized."

CHILDREN OF PARADISE ◑ F 28 | 27 | 27 | 26

1946. Directed by Marcel Carné. With Arletty, Jean-Louis Barrault, Pierre Renoir. 190 minutes. Not Rated.

■ Filmed in France "under the noses of the Nazis", this "legendary" romance "lovingly recreates" "1840s Paris" in a "multilayered" story of a "lovesick" mime's passion for a vampish stage siren; built on "profound" themes and "stylized" performances (that come off as "melodramatic" but are rich with "beauty and feeling"), it "continues to fascinate" as a "masterpiece of world cinema" and the big screen's "greatest tribute to live theater."

China Syndrome, The 22 | 25 | 24 | 20

1979. Directed by James Bridges. With Jack Lemmon, Jane Fonda, Michael Douglas. 122 minutes. Rated PG.

◪ The going gets "scary" as a nuclear power facility heads for meltdown in this "intelligent thriller" with a "solid" cast, including a "terrific" Lemmon as the plant supervisor and "Fonda at her peak" as a frustrated TV reporter; the "could-happen" story is "well-crafted", but conservatives contend that the "melodramatic" matchup of "bad-guy corporate players" against "good-guy idealists" makes it into the "definitive liberal" "message film."

CHINATOWN ✉ Ⓘ 27 | 28 | 26 | 26

1974. Directed by Roman Polanski. With Jack Nicholson, Faye Dunaway, John Huston. 131 minutes. Rated R.

■ This "taut drama" about "stolen water" and "bottled-up emotion" in 1930s LA is a "nearly perfect" exercise in "Technicolor film noir" that manages to be simultaneously "funny, bleak and knowing"; credit the "dynamite" cast, "deft" direction, "ravishingly beautiful" cinematography and "superb script" (that's capped by a "shocking", "untypical-Hollywood ending") for its success; most memorable scene: Dunaway's "slap"-happy "she's-my-sister-she's-my-daughter" tour de force.

Chocolat 🅵 | 22 | 24 | 22 | 23

2000. Directed by Lasse Hallström. With Juliette Binoche, Alfred Molina, Johnny Depp. 121 minutes. Rated PG-13.

◪ A "yummy" "escape" "bordering on a fairy tale", this "funny, warm" romance finds "lovely" "rebel spirit" Binoche pitted against "petty-minded villagers" when she opens a chocolate emporium in a French hamlet and takes up with "dreamboat" Depp; the blend of a "beautiful setting" mixed with some "uplifting" "whimsy" makes it a "tasty bonbon" – though a few complain of "saccharine" overdose.

CHRISTMAS CAROL, A ◑ | 27 | 26 | 28 | 23

(aka Scrooge)

1951. Directed by Brian Desmond Hurst. With Alastair Sim, Kathleen Harrison, Mervyn Johns. 86 minutes. Not Rated.

■ "Sim is the best Scrooge ever" in this Dickens of a "holiday delight", a "magical adaptation" of the "timeless" fable concerning a rich old paragon of "grouchiness" transformed by a Yuletide visit from a posse of ghosts; cherished as "superb" family fare that "inspires" without drowning in the "happily-ever-after tone" of other versions, it has fans replaying it "religiously" because there's "no way" to do "Christmas without it."

Christmas Story, A | 26 | 23 | 27 | 22

1983. Directed by Bob Clark. With Peter Billingsley, Melinda Dillon, Darren McGavin. 94 minutes. Rated PG.

■ A "sweet but not sugary" look at the "debacle that's Christmas in America", this "irresistible" family fave takes a "fond glimpse back" with a "funny-till-it-hurts" "exposition of a '50s childhood" centered on a kid bent on a "BB gun" under the tree; "most rewatchable" and "quotable" thanks to its "excellent cast and script", it's "good clean fun" for all ages and now widely deemed a seasonal "must."

Cider House Rules, The ✉ | 22 | 24 | 23 | 22

1999. Directed by Lasse Hallström. With Tobey Maguire, Charlize Theron, Michael Caine. 126 minutes. Rated PG-13.

◪ Presenting "life choices" in an "idyllic" '30s-era Maine orphanage, this "thought-provoking tearjerker" is a story of "compassion" with some "tough subject matter sneaked in" that gives Maguire his "breakout role" and proves "Caine really can act"; despite a few objections to the "cloying" tone and "watered-down" treatment of John Irving's novel, "satisfied" customers rule it an "absorbing" "feel-good" flick that "doesn't pander to the Hallmark crowd."

Cinderella ∅ | 26 | – | 25 | 26

1950. Directed by Clyde Geronimi, Wilfred Jackson, Hamilton Luske. Animated. 74 minutes. Rated G.

■ "You know the drill": "breathtaking" animation from "Disney's golden age" merges with the stuff "countless girlish dreams" are made of in this "beautiful fantasy" about an "overworked, abused orphan" who bags Prince

Charming, with a little help from her fairy godmother and some "industrious" finely feathered friends; if "short on characterization", it remains an "old-fashioned" "favorite" that's a shoe-in to be a "classic for generations to come."

Cinderella Liberty ∅ 19 | 23 | 20 | 17

1973. Directed by Mark Rydell. With James Caan, Marsha Mason, Kirk Calloway. 117 minutes. Rated R.

■ "Great chemistry" between the leads buoys this "honest" but "often-overlooked" romance about a lonesome shore-patrol swabbie who falls for a "tender-hearted prostitute" and becomes a father figure to her "mixed-race son"; an "excellent" Caan plays well against Mason's "sympathetic, funny" portrayal of the "hooker who doesn't know any other way to live"; all in all, a shipshape effort.

Cinema Paradiso ✉ F 26 | 26 | 26 | 25

1988. Directed by Giuseppe Tornatore. With Philippe Noiret, Jacques Perrin. 123 minutes. Rated R.

■ This Italian "heart-warmer" is an "endearing" look at "love and loss" as well as a "nostalgic valentine" to the "magic of cinema"; based on the "utterly charming" story of a "projectionist in the local movie house" who "mentors a fatherless child", it rolls a "colorful" cast, "*bellissimo*" camerawork and a "lovely" score into an "engrossing", frankly "sentimental" film – "bring a hankie" for that last reel.

CITIZEN KANE ✉◑ 28 | 27 | 27 | 28

1941. Directed by Orson Welles. With Orson Welles, Joseph Cotten, Agnes Moorehead. 119 minutes. Rated PG.

■ "Loosely based on the life of William Randolph Hearst", this "magnum opus" about a "ruthless" "megalomaniac" who "mourns the loss of his innocent childhood" is an "undisputed masterpiece" that's "often imitated, never duplicated" and "as fresh as ever"; directed by and starring wunderkind Welles, it "revolutionized the cinema" and forever changed the meaning of the word "rosebud" – "by comparison, all other films are home movies."

CITY LIGHTS ◑ 28 | 28 | 26 | 25

1931. Directed by Charles Chaplin. With Charles Chaplin, Virginia Cherrill. 87 minutes. Not Rated.

■ "Humor, pathos and poignancy" make this silent "Chaplin masterpiece" glow with "old-fashioned sentimentality" as the Little Tramp's "devotion for a blind flower girl" leads to a series of "classic" sequences; from famed bits like the "balletic boxing match" to the "heartbreaking" closing, this early flicker is a testament to a master "on top of his game."

City Slickers Ⓘ 20 | 20 | 20 | 19

1991. Directed by Ron Underwood. With Billy Crystal, Daniel Stern, Jack Palance. 112 minutes. Rated PG-13.

■ "Yee-haw!"; a "super" Crystal rides high in this "tons-of-fun" "buddy comedy" about three NYers who go west for a dude-ranch vacation and wind up having a "midlife crisis during a cattle drive"; the "right-on" cast (particularly the "just-too-funny Palance") has a way with "wisdom and great one-liners", rounding up applause for "good fun" that doesn't shy from its "moving" side.

Clear and Present Danger 20 | 21 | 22 | 20

1994. Directed by Phillip Noyce. With Harrison Ford, Willem Dafoe, Anne Archer. 141 minutes. Rated PG-13. D-1

■ Clearly "great popcorn fodder", this "provocative action" flick is "one of the better Clancy adaptations", with Ford in "fine form" reprising his role as "what-a-man" CIA agent Jack Ryan going mano a mano with a Colombian dope cartel; though in danger of dismissal as "escapist stuff", it's so "exciting" and "patriotic", you can't help but root for this "smart movie hero" who "really kicks butt."

Cleopatra 19 | 18 | 19 | 25

1963. Directed by Joseph L. Mankiewicz. With Elizabeth Taylor, Richard Burton, Rex Harrison. 192 minutes. Not Rated.

◪ "Grand, gaudy and tons of fun", this epic bio of the queen of the Nile (renowned for "breaking all production-cost records") is either a "guilty pleasure" or an "incredible waste of time"; devotees dig its "huge scale", over-the-top "entertainment" value and Liz's "exquisite" beauty, but cynics nix the flick's "bloated" look and "draggy" pace, advising that you "hit the clicker" immediately after Cleo's "showstopping entrance into Rome."

Clerks ◑ 23 | 17 | 22 | 16

1994. Directed by Kevin Smith. With Brian O'Halloran, Jeff Anderson, Marilyn Ghigliotti. 92 minutes. Rated R.

■ "Crude" acting and "bottom-of-the-barrel production" values are redeemed by "wicked" "black humor" and "inspired", "raunchy" dialogue in this "microbudget indie" effort, a "fast-paced" comedy that pumps life into the "dead-end job" scene with a "realistic" look at "minimart" wage slavery; the "first foray" in Smith's "New Jersey series", it's a "slacker" "cult classic" that's "painfully funny" but unsafe for the "squeamish."

Clockwork Orange, A 25 | 24 | 24 | 25

1971. Directed by Stanley Kubrick. With Malcolm McDowell, Patrick Magee. 137 minutes. Rated R.

■ "Not for the weak of heart", this "ingenious Kubrick" sci-fi parable is a "bold", "nightmarish" "mix of sex, ultraviolence" and "mind control" set in a "freaky", "futuristic" Britain; following the travails of "unhinged" "bad boy" McDowell (the "sinister yet strangely likable" head of a "vicious gang of droogies") through his "chilling" crimes to his "brainwashing" rehab, it threads "brilliant visuals" and "twisted" "social satire" into "riveting", "artful stuff" – helped by a bit of the old "Ludwig van."

Close Encounters of the Third Kind 24 | 22 | 25 | 27

1977. Directed by Steven Spielberg. With Richard Dreyfuss, François Truffaut, Teri Garr. 135 minutes. Rated PG.

■ "It's ok to believe in UFOs" thanks to this "landmark" sci-fi "spectacle", a "mesmerizing", "believable contact film" wherein Spielberg's "sense of wonder" first embraces the "aliens-come-to-earth" formula; the "hopeful" plotline involves a race to "figure it all out" when strange signals arrive from the sky, and the result is a "mind-blowing" "visual treat" with plenty of "heart" (and "mountains of mashed potatoes") that delivers a "jaw-dropping" climax with a "sentimental streak" a light-year wide.

Clueless 21 | 19 | 20 | 20

1995. Directed by Amy Heckerling. With Alicia Silverstone, Paul Rudd, Brittany Murphy. 97 minutes. Rated PG-13.

■ Totally "sneaky-smart", this "lively" "update of *Emma*" with a "90210" twist is a "winning" comedy about LA's "spoiled rich" kids and stars a "delightful", "not-quite-acting" Silverstone, who juggles romantic uncertainty, a variety of "Valley" "catch phrases" and a "'90s" wardrobe "to die for"; despite a few hints of "fluff" – "whatever" – it offers "pure enjoyment" as a "pivotal teen movie" and some of the "sharpest" "bubblegum" out there.

Coal Miner's Daughter ⊠∅ 24 | 27 | 23 | 22

1980. Directed by Michael Apted. With Sissy Spacek, Tommy Lee Jones, Levon Helm. 125 minutes. Rated PG.

■ Kentucky moonshine and "bravura performances" brighten this "charming biopic" of country crooner Loretta Lynn, led by the "remarkable", Oscar-winning Spacek, "in character in every sense" as the daughter of Appalachia who "makes it huge" in Nashville; a down-home, "down-to-earth fairy tale", its "realistic portrayal" of a star's "rise to fame" and bout with burnout plays like an "interesting" C&W take on *Behind the Music.*

Cocoanuts, The ◑ 24 | 22 | 19 | 19

1929. Directed by Robert Florey, Joseph Santley. With the Marx Brothers, Kay Francis. 96 minutes. Not Rated.

◪ Never mind "technical primitiveness", this "first Marx Brothers" comedy is as "zany" as their later work and still has "enough snap to make you long for more"; though this "crude" rendering of the sibs' Broadway show is burdened with "trite musical numbers" and a "weak" story involving real estate in the Sunshine State, die-hard Marxists say ya "gotta love" it as an "intriguing mess" that's at worst a guarantee of "better things to come."

Cocoon Ⓘ∅ 20 | 21 | 21 | 20

1985. Directed by Ron Howard. With Don Ameche, Wilford Brimley, Hume Cronyn. 117 minutes. Rated PG-13.

■ "Old duffers" meet "pod people" in this "warm" sci-fi tale, which spins a "clever story" of an intergalactic meet-up between extraterrestrials and Florida rest-home residents, whose backyard pool becomes a fountain of youth; the "delightful" setup and "complete characters" give some of Hollywood's elder statesmen room to "romp", while director Howard makes it all "credible" – if a bit too "warm and cuddly" for some.

Color Purple, The 26 | 27 | 26 | 25

1985. Directed by Steven Spielberg. With Whoopi Goldberg, Danny Glover, Oprah Winfrey. 154 minutes. Rated PG-13.

■ A "heartfelt" reading of Alice Walker's "breakthrough" best-seller via Steven Spielberg, this "moving" drama of "empowerment" "really hits home" with its depiction of a "post-slavery black family" in the deep South and a wronged woman's "redemption and liberation"; the "breathtaking" lenswork, "Goldberg's best-ever showing" and a "brilliant" supporting cast ("Oprah can act!") make for a "teary" "triumph" that some cite as "Oscar's biggest snub."

Coming Home ✉ 23 | 26 | 23 | 21

1978. Directed by Hal Ashby. With Jane Fonda, Jon Voight, Bruce Dern, Penelope Milford. 126 minutes. Rated R.

■ "Jon and Jane are magic together" in this "ultimate anti-war message" drama–cum–love triangle involving a paraplegic Vietnam vet, an "inconveniently married" hospital volunteer and a gung-ho marine; expect "moving performances" (Voight and Fonda took home Oscars) and "loads of emotion" that manage to convey a "coming of age for both the characters – and the times."

Coming to America 18 | 18 | 17 | 17

1988. Directed by John Landis. With Eddie Murphy, Arsenio Hall, James Earl Jones. 116 minutes. Rated R.

■ "Sidesplitting", "multiple-character tour de force" showcasing the talents of "total riot" Murphy and "hilarious" Hall in a "goofy", "fish-out-of-water" comedy about an African prince who logically "heads to Queens" to find a royal mate; hard-core groupies who can "repeat the whole movie by heart" reveal their favorite scene: "pre-*ER* Eriq Le Salle's Soul Glow" routine.

Conformist, The F ∅ 26 | 26 | 27 | 26

1971. Directed by Bernardo Bertolucci. With Jean-Louis Trintignant, Stefania Sandrelli, Dominique Sanda. 115 minutes. Rated R.

■ Director "Bertolucci is at his absolute best" in this "supercool, superstylized" Italian psychological drama set in the '30s about an "emotionally troubled civil servant" turned "fascist agent"; nonconformists warn "beware the dubbed version" but concur that Vittorio Storaro's "haunting", "*magnifico*" cinematography transcends dialogue; hottest moment: that "erotic tango" between Sanda and Sandrelli.

Contact 20 | 21 | 20 | 22

1997. Directed by Robert Zemeckis. With Jodie Foster, Matthew McConaughey, Tom Skerritt. 153 minutes. Rated PG.

◪ This "thinking person's" sci-fi flick addresses the "Big Question" – "are we alone" in the universe?; true believers cite the "excellent special effects", "fascinating" story and a fine Foster "near the top of her form", but the alienated dismiss it as "long-winded", "preachy" and "emotionally void", opting to "read Carl Sagan's excellent book" instead.

Contender, The 19 | 23 | 20 | 19

2000. Directed by Rod Lurie. With Joan Allen, Gary Oldman, Jeff Bridges. 126 minutes. Rated R.

◪ In this Clinton White House–ish "Washington soap opera" (with enough "twists and turns" to keep you "guessing till the end"), a "scrappy" female pol "stays true to her principles" at great cost to her reputation and career; though Allen is "superb" and Bridges would make a "fine" real-life prez, some pundits protest the drama's "tackling of big issues" as "overblown" "melodrama."

Conversation, The 25 | 26 | 25 | 23

1974. Directed by Francis Ford Coppola. With Gene Hackman, John Cazale, Frederic Forrest. 113 minutes. Rated PG.

■ A "brilliant", "gripping" thriller about a "paranoid" surveillance specialist who comes undone, this "little-known" Coppola feature features a "virtuoso performance by Hackman", whose gradual "deterioration is amazing" (there's also an appearance by a very young, virtually unknown Harrison Ford); though a bit "slow-moving", the script is so "superbly constructed" that "if this flick doesn't put you on edge, nothing will."

Cool Hand Luke 26 | 27 | 24 | 22

1967. Directed by Stuart Rosenberg. With Paul Newman, George Kennedy, Strother Martin. 126 minutes. Not Rated.

■ "One of the best movie lines ever" ('what we have here is a failure to communicate') and that "famous hard-boiled egg eating scene" make this "damn great" Deep South prison drama memorable – not to mention the efforts of "consummate pro" Newman playing one cool con on a "chain gang", abetted by a "strong" Kennedy, who grabbed an Oscar for his supporting work.

Cool Runnings 18 | 16 | 21 | 17

1993. Directed by Jon Turteltaub. With John Candy, Doug E. Doug, Leon, Malik Yoba. 98 minutes. Rated PG.

■ Granted, it might be "silly", but this "cute", "underrated" comedy "based on the true" tale of the '88 Olympics' "Jamaican bobsled team" is "fun for the whole family" (despite "a bit too much profanity"); cheerleaders say its "come-from-behind" story will "touch anyone's heart", particularly those who "miss John Candy", whose "sweet" performance is a standout here.

Cousin, Cousine F ∅ 21 | 20 | 21 | 19

1975. Directed by Jean-Charles Tacchella. With Marie-Christine Barrault, Victor Lanoux. 95 minutes. Rated R.

■ This "sweet but naughty" French farce about romantically involved cousins-by-marriage offers a "refreshing", "truly charming" take on family dynamics; while comparison shoppers say it's "much better than the American" remake (*Cousins*), those suffering from memory lapses "can't recall anything" except – *zut alors!* – Barrault's "naked breasts."

Cries and Whispers F 26 | 28 | 24 | 26

1972. Directed by Ingmar Bergman. With Harriet Andersson, Liv Ullmann, Ingrid Thulin. 106 minutes. Rated R.

■ "Compelling is an understatement" when it comes to this "tortured masterpiece", a "raw", "close-in study of three sisters and their prickly relationship" that's "quintessential Bergman"; although it's "well acted" and "handsomely mounted" (with Oscar-winning cinematography and especially "gorgeous use of color"), its depiction of "pain" is so "hard to watch" that some ask "are you sure 'angst' isn't a Swedish word?"

Crimes and Misdemeanors 26 | 26 | 25 | 24

1989. Directed by Woody Allen. With Woody Allen, Mia Farrow, Anjelica Huston, Martin Landau. 107 minutes. Rated PG-13.

■ "Crime *does* pay" in this "deeply serious" Allen dramedy with dual plotlines, one about a murderous philanderer, the other a "socially inept" filmmaker; "ruthlessly truthful", it manages to be alternately "scathing", "thought-provoking" and "hilarious", with "dead-on casting" and an "expert" scenario to boot.

Crimson Tide 21 | 24 | 22 | 22

1995. Directed by Tony Scott. With Denzel Washington, Gene Hackman, George Dzundza. 116 minutes. Rated R.

◪ "Gripping", "tightly plotted" action flick relating the "macho machinations aboard a submarine" as two officers square off over a nuclear launch that could trigger an "unprovoked war"; given the "smart", "thought-provoking" acting of "big-screen titans" Washington and Hackman, you can expect a "first-rate" ride, even if some shrug it off as a "*Hunt for Red October* wanna-be."

Crouching Tiger, Hidden Dragon ✉ F 24 | 23 | 21 | 28

2000. Directed by Ang Lee. With Chow Yun-Fat, Michelle Yeoh, Zhang Ziyi. 120 minutes. Rated PG-13.

■ Whether it's a "kung fu chick flick", a "thinking person's" martial arts film or "'chop-socky' translated into art", this "surreal" fantasy is full of "eye-popping, choreographed fight sequences" that are half "ballet", half "Bruce Lee"; most memorable for its "strong female characters" and that "encounter in the bamboo forest", it's nothing less than a "breath of fresh air on the stale movie landscape."

Crying Game, The ✉ 22 | 24 | 24 | 20

1992. Directed by Neil Jordan. With Stephen Rea, Miranda Richardson, Forest Whitaker, Jaye Davidson. 112 minutes. Rated R.

■ "Violence and pathos" are served in the "right amounts" in this "disturbing" British drama about an "IRA recruit who's not really committed to his cause"; most famed for its whopper of a "surprise twist" (that leaves some "still flabbergasted"), this "intense vision of terrorism" offers enough nuanced "questions about race, sex and country" to justify a Best Screenplay Oscar.

Damn Yankees! ∅ 24 | 23 | 23 | 24

1958. Directed by George Abbott, Stanley Donen. With Gwen Verdon, Tab Hunter, Ray Walston. 111 minutes. Not Rated.

■ This "successful screen adaptation" of the *Faust*-influenced Broadway musical recounts how a "man makes a pact with the devil" to guarantee that the "Washington Senators win the pennant"; reprising their stage roles, Walston is at his "evil best" as Lucifer, while the "too-rarely-seen" Verdon gets what she wants as his sidekick, Lola; it's a "perfect evocation of the national optimism of the '50s" with a "great score" and a bonus: "Bob Fosse's mambo."

Dancer in the Dark 22 | 23 | 20 | 22

2000. Directed by Lars von Trier. With Björk, Catherine Deneuve, David Morse. 140 minutes. Rated R.

◪ A "musical like no other", this "dynamic" if "depressing" film "pushes the genre to the limit" in its account of an immigrant Czech "factory worker going blind who finds redemption only in music"; while foes find it "difficult to watch" – "even painful" – artistes laud its "wondrously strange" feel and praise pop star Björk's "amazing" "acting chops" and "compelling" vocal work.

Dances with Wolves ✉ 23 | 20 | 22 | 25

1990. Directed by Kevin Costner. With Kevin Costner, Mary McDonnell, Graham Greene. 183 minutes. Rated PG-13.

◪ For once, "American Indians" are portrayed in a "human light" in this "picturesque, sweeping epic" about a Civil War soldier (Costner) who goes West, joins the Sioux and finds love (McDonnell) along the way; although "beautifully shot" and quite the Oscar magnet (seven statuettes, including Best Picture), this "guy flick that women love" has critics citing a "monotonous", way-"too-long" running time.

Dangerous Liaisons ✉ 24 | 26 | 24 | 26

1988. Directed by Stephen Frears. With Glenn Close, John Malkovich, Michelle Pfeiffer. 119 minutes. Rated R.

■ "Malkovich quietly chews up the scenery" opposite "perfectly evil" "ice queen" Close in this "flawless" drama set in "decadent", 17th-century France rife with "treachery, betrayal and sexual games" among the "effete upper classes" ("no wonder the peasants revolted"); still, its "sumptuous production" and Oscar-winning screenplay make the "manipulating" characters more palatable.

Dark Crystal, The 24 | – | 24 | 26

1982. Directed by Jim Henson, Frank Oz. With puppet characters. 93 minutes. Rated PG.

■ "Sinister muppets" take the stage in this "classic" "all-puppet feature", a "magical fairy tale" with an "otherworldly good and evil" storyline that represents the "culmination of Jim Henson's imagination"; while the "stunning visuals" please crowds, some warn that the "dark", un-"cutesy" plot "may be too scary" for smaller fry.

Dark Victory ◑ 25 | 27 | 23 | 23

1939. Directed by Edmund Goulding. With Bette Davis, George Brent, Humphrey Bogart. 104 minutes. Not Rated.

■ "Sensational" Bette at her "Warner Brothers peak" "turns camp into classic" in this melodramatic "tearjerker" about an heiress who's got everything – including a brain tumor; sob sisters say it's "worth every hanky" for Davis' "valiant" turn (one of the "best performances of 1939") and keep their eye out for a "young Ronald Reagan" in a supporting role.

DAS BOOT F 28 | 26 | 26 | 27

1982. Directed by Wolfgang Petersen. With Jürgen Prochnow, Herbert Grönemeyer. 149 minutes. Rated R.

■ When it comes to "underwater über alles" action, it's hard to top this "sweaty, claustrophobic" saga of "doomed German sailors" engaged in a "battle of egos" in a U-boat at the "bottom of the ocean"; though it's almost an "anti-recruiting film" given its "horrifying", "harrowing" realism, it exhibits enough "depth" to prove that "fear has no nationality" – you'll almost "root for" the Nazis.

Dave 21 | 22 | 22 | 20

1993. Directed by Ivan Reitman. With Kevin Kline, Sigourney Weaver, Frank Langella. 110 minutes. Rated PG-13.

■ "Kline's adorable, as usual" in this "funny" political satire about an average "doofus" who looks so much like the President that he's asked to pinch-hit and winds up putting "faith back in government"; a latter-day "*Mr. Smith Goes to Washington*", this "feel-good" comedy has a "serious message", though conspiracy theorists say the message is "proof that liberals really do run Hollywood."

Day at the Races, A ◑ 24 | 21 | 20 | 19

1937. Directed by Sam Wood. With the Marx Brothers, Maureen O'Sullivan, Margaret Dumont. 111 minutes. Not Rated.

◪ The "Marx Brothers at their zenith of zaniness" horse around in this "very funny" comedy about a veterinarian turned human doctor trying to save a cash-strapped sanitarium; though some say it's a "slightly second-tier" also-ran (only "sporadically funny" and even a tad "racist"), it was nevertheless one of the boys' "biggest box office hits."

Day for Night ✉ F ∅ 27 | 25 | 25 | 25

1973. Directed by François Truffaut. With Jaqueline Bisset, Valentina Cortese, Jean-Pierre Léaud. 115 minutes. Rated PG.

■ "Truffaut's homage to American filmmaking", this "quintessential movie about making movies" "perfectly captures" all the "behind-the-scenes" "neuroses" and "joy" from an insider's point of view; though it shows the director "at his lightest", the "magical" result was both "charming" and "wacky" enough for it to take home a Best Foreign Language picture Oscar.

Days of Heaven 23 | 21 | 20 | 25

1978. Directed by Terrence Malick. With Richard Gere, Brooke Adams, Sam Shepard. 95 minutes. Rated PG.

◪ "Underseen but not underappreciated", this "gorgeous" if "bleak" drama detailing a love triangle between two dirt-poor migrant workers and a loaded landowner "broke new ground" in its use of "beautiful cinematography" to take the place of conventional exposition; though it "speaks volumes without much dialogue", low-attention-span types yawn "not terribly compelling."

Days of Wine and Roses ◑ ∅ 27 | 28 | 25 | 24

1962. Directed by Blake Edwards. With Jack Lemmon, Lee Remick, Charles Bickford. 117 minutes. Not Rated.

■ For a "tough look" at a "serious issue", this "harrowing" drama about the "ravages of alcoholism" was a "huge breakthrough in its day" and remains "relevant" thanks to "tear-your-heart-out" performances from Lemmon and Remick as "desperate" young marrieds "lost in the bottom of the bottle"; "Henry Mancini's haunting title song" won the Oscar and "says it all."

Day the Earth Stood Still, The ◑ ∅ 25 | 20 | 26 | 21

1951. Directed by Robert Wise. With Michael Rennie, Patricia Neal, Sam Jaffe. 92 minutes. Rated G.

◪ "'50s-era real-life fears about the fate of humanity" are the backbone of this "earnest" "Cold War sci-fi" flick about a "benevolent alien" invasion of Washington DC; sure, the "less-is-more special effects" seem "dated" and "primitive by today's standards", but the "underlying message" – "world peace or else!" – makes this one "very enlightened for its time."

Dead Again 22 | 24 | 24 | 22

1991. Directed by Kenneth Branagh. With Kenneth Branagh, Andy Garcia, Emma Thompson. 107 minutes. Rated R.

■ There are "good twists and mind tricks" aplenty in this "stylish, pseudo-noir thriller" about a detective ("Branagh with a great American accent") drawn into a decades-old murder mystery; deadheads dig its "riveting performances", "Dali-esque imagery" and that "wonderful twist at the end", swearing you'll never look at a "pair of scissors" the same way after seeing this "over-the-top" "nail-biter."

Dead Man Walking ✉ 23 | 26 | 23 | 21

1995. Directed by Tim Robbins. With Susan Sarandon, Sean Penn, Robert Prosky. 122 minutes. Rated R.

■ "Based on a true story", this "enlightening" study of "capital punishment" is also a "profound lesson in human compassion" thanks to "poignant" turns from a "riveting" Penn as a "condemned killer" and the Oscar-winning Sarandon as a nun bent on leading him to "redemption"; although "unsettling and disturbing" overall, the picture "provides both sides of the death-penalty argument" in an "objective", "unflinching" manner.

Dead Poets Society ✉ 24 | 25 | 24 | 23

1989. Directed by Peter Weir. With Robin Williams, Robert Sean Leonard, Ethan Hawke. 128 minutes. Rated PG.

■ "Living with rules" vs. "living with passion" gets the big-screen treatment in this "uplifting" drama about a "inspirational teacher" who admonishes his students with a ringing "'carpe diem!'"; thanks to the Oscar-winning screenplay and Williams' ultra-"convincing" turn as the "influential mentor", many say this "wake-up call" of a movie should be "mandatory classroom viewing."

Dead Ringers 18 | 23 | 19 | 19

1988. Directed by David Cronenberg. With Jeremy Irons, Geneviève Bujold. 115 minutes. Rated R.

◪ Ok, it's "beyond weird", but this "cold, clinical" tale of "twin gynecologists" "descending into madness" strikes followers of things "depraved" as "deliciously creepy", given its fascination with "prescription drugs", "kinky sex" and "bizarre" surgical instruments; despite Irons' "astounding dual performance", very vocal opponents call it "really offensive" with "no redeeming value", maybe the "ickiest movie ever"; proceed at your own risk.

Death on the Nile 19 | 20 | 23 | 21

1978. Directed by John Guillermin. With Peter Ustinov, Bette Davis, Angela Lansbury. 140 minutes. Rated PG.

◪ "Everyone looks properly shifty-eyed and guilty" in this "decent" adaptation of the Agatha Christie whodunit that takes place on a cruise down the River Nile; though foes grouse it's a "lightweight" "follow-up to *Murder on the Orient Express*" cast with "out-of-work actors", fans find it "suspenseful" enough and single out the "outrageous" Lansbury and Oscar-winning costumes for praise.

Deer Hunter, The ✉ 26 | 28 | 24 | 24

1978. Directed by Michael Cimino. With Robert De Niro, Christopher Walken, Meryl Streep, John Cazale, John Savage. 183 minutes. Rated R.

■ "Ordinary guys from an ordinary American town" undergo the "ravages" of Vietnam in this "unforgettable war film", a "deeply moving", "epic-in-every-way" work that netted five Oscars (including Best Picture); brace yourself for "tough-as-nails" performances from De Niro and Walken, some "profound" if "heavy-handed symbolism" plotwise and a wrenching "Russian roulette scene" that will "leave you drained"; P.S. it also features "someone new named Streep."

Deliverance 25 | 26 | 25 | 23

1972. Directed by John Boorman. With Jon Voight, Burt Reynolds, Ned Beatty. 109 minutes. Rated R.

■ This "allegorical nightmare" about four "city slickers" on a "weekend canoe trip" "did for camping in the woods what *Jaws* did for swimming in the ocean", mainly because of that infamous "squeal-like-a-pig" "rape scene" (to the tune of "those damn 'Dueling Banjos'"); more important, it also "proves that thought and testosterone can coexist" and "debunks the long-held myth that Reynolds can't act."

Diabolique ◑ F 26 | 25 | 28 | 23

1955. Directed by Henri-Georges Clouzot. With Simone Signoret, Vera Clouzot. 116 minutes. Not Rated.

■ "Leave it to the French" to serve up this "nasty little thriller" about a murderous love triangle set in a boarding school that "scares the socks" off surveyors; granted, it "looks pretty primitive today", but ultimately "Signoret still smolders", the "clever plot twists" keep coming and "whoa, what an ending!"; P.S. "skip the tepid Sharon Stone remake."

Dial M for Murder 25 | 24 | 27 | 24

1954. Directed by Alfred Hitchcock. With Ray Milland, Grace Kelly, Robert Cummings. 105 minutes. Rated PG.

■ A "jilted husband seeks revenge on his philandering wife" in this "taut thriller" via Alfred Hitchcock, whose "distinctive touch" transforms a "stagey story" into a "suspenseful" movie (fun fact: it was "originally shot in 3-D"); actingwise, "Kelly shines", Milland is "subtly sinister" and Cummings "drags down every scene he appears in"; try the remake, *A Perfect Murder*, for an up-to-date take on the same topic.

Diamonds Are Forever 20 | 18 | 18 | 21

1971. Directed by Guy Hamilton. With Sean Connery, Jill St. John, Charles Gray. 125 minutes. Rated PG.

◪ "007 goes Vegas, baby" in this sixth installment of the series, chock-full of the usual "gadgets" and gals, including the "hot", high-"cheekboned" St. John; in his next-to-last appearance as the stirred-but-never-shaken spy, Connery's at his "dashing, womanizing best" while Gray, as a "hilarious Howard Hughes type", makes a "great villain"; still, Fleming fanatics fret it's "one of the sillier" in the canon.

Diary of Anne Frank, The ◑ ∅ 23 | 23 | 26 | 21

1959. Directed by George Stevens. With Millie Perkins, Shelley Winters, Richard Beymer. 180 minutes. Not Rated.

■ "Every young person should see" this "true story" of a Jewish family hiding from the Nazis in an Amsterdam attic that "brings to life a dark time in history"; "man's inhumanity to man" is depicted "from a child's point of view" in this "well-done transfer from the stage", and "though we know the outcome", the "suspense" is truly "heartbreaking."

Die Hard Ⓘ 23 | 19 | 22 | 24

1988. Directed by John McTiernan. With Bruce Willis, Bonnie Bedelia, Alan Rickman. 131 minutes. Rated R.

■ This "flawless" "granddaddy of the '80s action" flick spawned "countless imitations but no equals" thanks to its "thrill-a-minute" mix of suspense, explosions and "comic one-liners"; die-hard diehards tout Willis' "ass-kicking" turn as a "loser whom fate requires to be a hero" as well as "chic bad guy" Rickman, who supplies the "cool quips and fashion tips."

Diner 25 | 25 | 23 | 22

1982. Directed by Barry Levinson. With Steve Guttenberg, Mickey Rourke, Kevin Bacon. 110 minutes. Rated R.

■ Levinson's first Baltimore drama "centers on the lives of a group of '50s high school grads" "who spent their youth in diners"; a "finely observed" "guy flick" that's both "smart and funny", it features a "wonderful ensemble cast" that delivers the snappy patter so "brilliantly" it served as a "springboard" for the careers of "many future stars."

Dinosaur 19 | – | 17 | 24

2000. Directed by Eric Leighton, Ralph Zondag. Animated. 82 minutes. Rated PG.

◪ "Kids interested in dinosaurs" dig this Disney flick for its "extraordinary computer animation", "wonderful music" and "fabulous" (albeit "violent") "meteor shower" scene; but despite some "exciting moments", soreheads lament that it's "lacking in the plot department" and not much more than a "dull remake of *The Land Before Time.*"

Dirty Dancing 21 | 17 | 20 | 20

1987. Directed by Emile Ardolino. With Patrick Swayze, Jennifer Grey, Jerry Orbach. 96 minutes. Rated PG-13.

■ Whether it's a "girls'-night-in" "entertainment" or a "Sunday afternoon" "vacation", this "cult classic" is the cinematic equivalent of "comfort food" and even works as an "excellent date movie"; its "heart-melting story" centers on the romance between "hot, sexy teen dream" Swayze and "cute gamine" Grey, who "shake their booties" "like the Solid Gold dancers" to pop hits in a "'60s Catskills resort"; P.S. keep an eye open for the "most intense PG-13 love scene ever."

Dirty Dozen, The 21 | 19 | 22 | 20

1967. Directed by Robert Aldrich. With Lee Marvin, Ernest Borgnine, Charles Bronson. 145 minutes. Not Rated.

■ This "delightful" war adventure exudes a "healthy dose of cynicism" in telling the tale of a "merry band of cutthroats" "brought together to do good in WWII"; the "early-in-their-careers" actors are "awesome", "super-macho" types (particularly "ultimate tough guy" Marvin as their leader), while the "rough-and-tumble", action-packed plot still seems "fun after all these years."

Dirty Harry Ⓘ 21 | 18 | 20 | 19

1971. Directed by Don Siegel. With Clint Eastwood, Harry Guardino, Reni Santoni. 102 minutes. Rated R.

■ Clint's at his "steely-eyed, gravelly voiced best" in this "modern cop" flick that "struck a chord in the '70s" and "created a fast-and-furious" subgenre "solid" enough to "spawn a host of imitators"; throw in some "great views of San Francisco" and a moodily "muted jazz score" and you just might "feel lucky, punk."

Discreet Charm of the Bourgeoisie, The ✉ F 24 | 23 | 23 | 22

1972. Directed by Luis Buñuel. With Fernando Rey, Delphine Seyrig, Stéphane Audran. 102 minutes. Rated PG.

■ "Controversial" in its day, this Oscar-winning "satirical portrait of the French bourgeoisie" tells the "elliptical" tale of "six people in search of a hot meal" who are "confounded at every turn" by bizarre goings-on; Buñuel serves up enough "dream-within-a-dream sequences" to turn this dark comedy into a "thoughtful, surreal delight" that furthers his rep as the "Dali of cinema."

Diva F 24 | 20 | 24 | 24

1982. Directed by Jean-Jacques Beineix. With Wilhelmenia Fernandez, Frederic Andrei. 123 minutes. Rated R.

■ Perhaps the "greatest opera/action flick ever", this "oh-so-stylish" French thriller creates a "complicated world" about a "scooter-riding kid" "obsessed" by a "reclusive soprano"; "glorious to look at", with "wonderful images of Paris" energized by "beautiful music", it's most memorable for that "fast-paced motorcycle chase" in the Métro.

D.O.A. ◑ 22 | 22 | 26 | 21

1950. Directed by Rudolph Maté. With Edmond O'Brien, Pamela Britton, Luther Adler. 83 minutes. Not Rated.

◪ "One of the best opening lines" – "I want to report a murder . . . mine" – sets in motion the "intriguing plot" of this "elaborate time-runs-backward" drama in which an "innocent man" "must find his own killer before he dies"; set against a backdrop of "great location shots of LA and San Francisco", it's "gritty, bleak" noir that's "compelling as hell", even if a few deadbeats declare it "promises more than it delivers."

Doctor Zhivago ✉ 27 | 26 | 26 | 28

1965. Directed by David Lean. With Omar Sharif, Julie Christie, Geraldine Chaplin. 197 minutes. Rated PG-13.

◪ Lean's "timeless" – others say "long" – Oscar-winning evocation of Boris Pasternak's "sweeping" novel of "love and war" is the "epic to end all epics", merging "brilliant historical storytelling" with "romantic extravaganza"; set during the "Russian Revolution", it "humanized the USSR during the Cold War" due to the "tear-jerking" relationship between Christie and Sharif – though its "balalaika"-heavy "theme song" and the scenes in that "shimmering", "winter wonderland" of an "ice palace" resonate most.

Dog Day Afternoon ✉ 24 | 27 | 22 | 20

1975. Directed by Sidney Lumet. With Al Pacino, John Cazale, Chris Sarandon. 124 minutes. Rated R.

■ This "funny/sad" tale of a real-life botched "bank heist" committed by "hapless" "amateurs" is transformed into a "deep, character-driven" example of director Lumet "at his best"; expect "great performances from the entire cast" ("right down to the pizza delivery guy"), with particular kudos to an "ass-kicking" Pacino and a "brilliant" Sarandon as his "gay lover."

Donnie Brasco 20 | 24 | 22 | 20

1997. Directed by Mike Newell. With Al Pacino, Johnny Depp, Anne Heche. 127 minutes. Rated R.

■ In this true story, an undercover FBI agent "befriends the man he's supposed to entrap" and takes you "inside the inner workings of the mob" to reveal a "more realistic side to the underworld"; a "sympathetic", "nuanced" Pacino does the "gangster-as-loser" thing right, while Depp's titular turn is similarly "excellent"; like the 'family' it portrays, this one "never lets go of you."

Do the Right Thing 23 | 23 | 22 | 21

1989. Directed by Spike Lee. With Spike Lee, Danny Aiello, Ossie Davis, Ruby Dee. 120 minutes. Rated R.

■ "Italian-American pizza parlor owners in Brooklyn" and the "African-American community who patronize the shop" clash "on the hottest day of the year" in this "anatomy of a race riot" from Spike Lee, who "deftly balances tragedy with comedy" to telegraph a "message as clear as black and white" that still "resonates years later"; P.S. look for then-up-and-comers Martin Lawrence and Rosie Perez in minor roles.

DOUBLE INDEMNITY ◑ 28 | 27 | 28 | 25

1944. Directed by Billy Wilder. With Fred MacMurray, Barbara Stanwyck, Edward G. Robinson. 107 minutes. Not Rated.

■ "From the chiaroscuro settings to the world-weary voiceover", Wilder's "refreshingly sour" slice of "hard-boiled" noir "sets the standard for the genre"; the story of "another dumb cluck done in by a woman", it features a "fast-talking" MacMurray, a "knockout" Stanwyck ("love the anklet") and a "fantastic" Robinson, with enough plot "twists" and sly "killer banter" to make it the cinematic equivalent of "bonded bourbon"; best scene: shopping at the "supermarket."

Dracula ◑ Ⓘ | 24 | 21 | 23 | 20

1931. Directed by Tod Browning. With Bela Lugosi, Helen Chandler, Dwight Frye. 75 minutes. Not Rated.

■ Granted, the "special effects are nonexistent", but this "definitive Dracula" is still "scarier than anything made today", leaving "plenty of room for imagination" thanks to Lugosi's "riveting" take on the "immortal vampire"; though it uses music sparingly to evoke an "eerie atmosphere", a new, souped-up DVD with a "Philip Glass score" is highly touted; best line: "I never drink . . . *wine.*"

Dracula | 20 | 19 | 22 | 25

1992. Directed by Francis Ford Coppola. With Gary Oldman, Winona Ryder, Anthony Hopkins, Keanu Reeves. 130 minutes. Rated R.

◪ "You can sink your teeth" into director Coppola's "highly underrated" "retelling of Bram Stoker's tale" of a "lovelorn", bloodthirsty Romanian count; "stylish" costumes, Oscar-winning sets, a "stunning" Oldman and the spectacle of "Tom Waits eating bugs" make for "visionary" moviemaking, even if some nix the "laughable miscasting" of Reeves.

Dressed to Kill | 20 | 22 | 19 | 20

1980. Directed by Brian De Palma. With Michael Caine, Angie Dickinson, Nancy Allen. 105 minutes. Rated R.

◪ "Swirling camera work, split screens, tracking shots that go on for miles" – yup, it's another "stylishly bloody" De Palma thriller, replete with "violent slashings, sensuous showers and sexual confusion" as it tells the adventures of a "happy hooker, an unhappy housewife and a shrink"; though an "inspiring" Angie provides the "sexy" "goose bumps", the unmoved say it's "too derivative of Hitchcock."

Driving Miss Daisy ✉ | 24 | 27 | 23 | 22

1989. Directed by Bruce Beresford. With Morgan Freeman, Jessica Tandy, Dan Aykroyd. 99 minutes. Rated PG.

■ "Race relations" in the South and the "loss of dignity" that can come with aging are "wonderfully depicted" in this "heartwarming" story of an "unconventional friendship" between a matriarch and her chauffeur; the "sterling" Tandy and Freeman exhibit "incredible onscreen chemistry" (she drove home with an Oscar) in this "uplifting yet down-to-earth" drama.

Dr. No | 23 | 20 | 22 | 23

1963. Directed by Terence Young. With Sean Connery, Ursula Andress. 110 minutes. Rated PG.

■ The "first Bond outing" is a "lean and mean" thriller "unhindered by political correctness", with "fewer gadgets" and gals than usual (though the image of Andress in that "white bikini" is "seared forever onto many a man's brain"); while the "dashing" Connery "makes it all look effortless", "purists" note this "unadulterated" "template" is the "closest they ever came to Ian Fleming's vision."

DR. STRANGELOVE ◑ 28 | 28 | 27 | 26

1964. Directed by Stanley Kubrick. With Peter Sellers, George C. Scott, Sterling Hayden. 93 minutes. Rated PG.

■ "Nuclear annihilation was never funnier" than in Kubrick's "stinging" "Cold War satire", a "chillingly comic" look at "distressingly familiar government officials" and their "precious bodily fluids"; as members of "our military at work", Scott is "magnificent" and Sellers "phenomenal" (in "three, count 'em, roles"), while "Slim Pickens riding the bomb" remains one of the cinema's most indelible images; doomsday devotees dub it "apocalypse now and forever."

Drugstore Cowboy 19 | 21 | 19 | 18

1989. Directed by Gus Van Sant. With Matt Dillon, Kelly Lynch, James Le Gros. 100 minutes. Rated R.

◪ Van Sant's grittily "accurate depiction" of narcotics addicts robbing drugstores for drugs is loaded with "precise, unexpected performances" and a surprise bonus: William Burroughs as a junkie ex-priest; though habit-ues hail it as a "highly original dark comedy", nonsupporters say it "doesn't hold up well."

DUCK SOUP ◑ 27 | 25 | 23 | 22

1933. Directed by Leo McCarey. With the Marx Brothers, Margaret Dumont. 70 minutes. Not Rated.

■ "Hail, hail Freedonia" cry fans of the "anarchic" Marx foursome, whose trademark "lunacy" is at its "peak" in this "brilliant political satire" about a "mythical dictatorship"; rife with "absurdly funny" bits – including the "legendary mirror scene with Groucho and Harpo" – it's the brothers' "finest hour" and voted top of the Marxes in this *Survey.*

Dumbo 24 | – | 23 | 24

1941. Directed by Ben Sharpsteen. Animated. 64 minutes. Rated G.

◪ "Elephants fly" in this "short but sweet" animated Disney classic message movie "about the importance of being yourself"; though the politically correct disparage its "racist undertones" and find it "too sad" for smaller fry, fans laud its "fabulous", Oscar-winning score and "unforgettable sequences" – particularly the "tripped-out" "hallucination" of those pink pachyderms on parade.

Easter Parade ∅ 22 | 21 | 17 | 24

1948. Directed by Charles Walters. With Judy Garland, Fred Astaire, Ann Miller. 107 minutes. Not Rated.

■ "It isn't really Easter" till you've watched this "grand Irving Berlin musical" boasting 17 songs and "lots of frills upon it" – including those swells "Fred and Judy" at their "singing, acting and dancing best" in their "only screen appearance together"; the slender storyline has a "suave" Astaire trying to make a star out of chorus girl Garland, but this "wonderful" MGM "showcase" transcends its plot with sheer star power.

East of Edén ∅ 24 | 27 | 24 | 23

1955. Directed by Elia Kazan. With James Dean, Julie Harris, Raymond Massey. 115 minutes. Not Rated.

■ An "unforgettable" Dean eats "every actor on the set for breakfast" in his "searing" big-screen debut as the "proverbial bad seed" in this adaptation of John Steinbeck's "riveting" story of "sibling rivalry"; sure, there are also "beautiful" CinemaScope panoramas and an Oscar-winning turn from Jo Van Fleet, but Jimmy makes it "memorable" – "to think he only made three films is amazing."

Easy Rider 23 | 23 | 20 | 20

1969. Directed by Dennis Hopper. With Peter Fonda, Dennis Hopper, Jack Nicholson. 94 minutes. Rated R.

◪ "Sex, drugs and rock 'n' roll" hit the silver screen in this "seminal" "road movie" that "defined a generation" by capturing the "anarchistic" essence of the "tumultuous" '60s; famed for "Nicholson's starmaking performance" and Hopper's "manic", "revolutionary" direction, this "trippy" "time capsule" might have also "invented the music video" thanks to that "amazing soundtrack"; still, Gen-Y types protest it "doesn't hold up" today, unless you "get high" first.

Eat Drink Man Woman F 25 | 24 | 24 | 24

1994. Directed by Ang Lee. With Sihung Lung, Wu Chien-Lien, Yang Kuei-Mei, Wang Yu-Wen. 123 minutes. Not Rated.

■ Gourmands eat up this "tasty" Taiwanese "window into a different culture" that tells the story of a traditional "Asian father who shows his love by cooking for his headstrong daughters"; director Lee's "visual feast" contrasts "ticklish relationships" with "stupendous food scenes" so adroitly that many "get hungry just thinking about it."

Eating Raoul ∅ 18 | 18 | 21 | 15

1982. Directed by Paul Bartel. With Paul Bartel, Mary Woronov, Robert Beltran. 90 minutes. Rated R.

■ "Not everyone can stomach" this "blacker-than-black" "bizarro" "cult" comedy, but there's agreement that its "absurd" plot (about a Moral Majority–esque couple luring swingers to their deaths) is the "trailer-park" version of "*Sweeney Todd*"; "kind of sick", this "deadpan" "low-budget" "B movie" is also kind of "fun" – and "probably for grown-ups only."

Educating Rita 18 | 21 | 19 | 18

1983. Directed by Lewis Gilbert. With Michael Caine, Julie Walters. 110 minutes. Rated PG-13.

■ Caine and Walters exhibit "great chemistry" together in this "interesting" tale of an "alcoholic professor" who tutors a "working-class hairdresser" in English Lit; though the "pseudo-*Pygmalion*" plotline "isn't quite convincing" for some, others relate perfectly to the "believable" title character, a "woman who won't allow herself to be held back by family or social class."

Edward Scissorhands 21 | 22 | 22 | 24

1990. Directed by Tim Burton. With Johnny Depp, Winona Ryder, Dianne Wiest. 100 minutes. Rated PG-13.

■ Burton's "oddball" opus spins a "sweet", "delightfully bent" "love story" around an ultimate "outsider" – a "misfit boy with garden tools for hands" – living in "conformist suburbia"; "Depp shows he has the big-screen stuff" (and "makes a hell of a topiary"), while the "primary-colored" art direction creates an "alternative universe that's disturbingly close to home"; best line: Wiest's perky "Avon calling!"

Ed Wood ◑ 20 | 23 | 19 | 21

1994. Directed by Tim Burton. With Johnny Depp, Martin Landau, Sarah Jessica Parker. 127 minutes. Rated R.

■ "Schlockmeister" director Ed Wood gets the Tim Burton treatment in this "loving tribute" to the famed "Hollywood hack" that's also an "entertaining glimpse into grade Z filmmaking"; look for an "enthusiastic", "totally sympathetic" Depp in the title role opposite an Oscar-winning Landau as a "drugged-out" Bela Lugosi – "never before have the talentless been so brilliantly rendered by the talented."

8½ ✉◑🅵 26 | 26 | 24 | 26

1963. Directed by Federico Fellini. With Marcello Mastroianni, Claudia Cardinale, Anouk Aimée. 145 minutes. Not Rated.

■ "Navel-gazing has never been more profound" than in this "semi-autobiographical" "Italian masterpiece" from the "extraordinary" Fellini about a blocked "director trying to make a film" by using his "inner life as material for his work"; told in "stream of consciousness", it also features "luscious" art direction and a "career-defining turn by Mastroianni" – no wonder many call this "heartfelt" flick the "definitive movie about movies."

El Cid ∅ 19 | 16 | 20 | 23

1961. Directed by Anthony Mann. With Charlton Heston, Sophia Loren, Raf Vallone. 182 minutes. Not Rated.

◪ This early '60s epic is a "guy's delight" that finds Heston once again inhabiting the skin of a "larger-than-life" figure, this time the legendary 11th-century Spanish nobleman who defended his country against the Moors; "lots of action" and a "great score by Miklos Rozsa" elate thrill-seekers, though foes lambaste it as "bombastic and overblown."

Election 22 | 24 | 22 | 20

1999. Directed by Alexander Payne. With Reese Witherspoon, Matthew Broderick. 103 minutes. Rated R.

■ "Student council elections" as an "allegory for real political life" underscore this "whip-smart" "black comedy" about a "goody two-shoes" "high-school overachiever" and a teacher bent on putting a stop to her rise; voters find "no fraud" in this "spot-on" "social satire", adding that "unless you were home-schooled, you'll relate."

Elephant Man, The ◑ 24 | 27 | 25 | 23

1980. Directed by David Lynch. With Anthony Hopkins, John Hurt, Anne Bancroft. 125 minutes. Rated PG.

■ The "dignity in deformity" is defined in this "unflinching" "true story" from David Lynch about a "Victorian-era" freak who "tests the compassion of a horrified society"; "brilliant acting and makeup" make it a "gloriously Gothic" "voyage into the human heart" – a "perfect match of director and material", it will "touch you deep inside."

Elizabeth 24 | 27 | 23 | 26

1998. Directed by Shekhar Kapur. With Cate Blanchett, Geoffrey Rush, Joseph Fiennes. 124 minutes. Rated R.

■ "Captivating" Cate "displays unbelievable range" in this bio of England's "Virgin Queen" that follows her progress from "lusty young woman" to "ice-cold, calculating icon"; though it "feels like a fantasy version of Elizabeth I's life" to skeptics, scholars swear it's "historically on the mark", with "beautiful sets", "excellent costume design" and a "gripping" storyline.

Elmer Gantry ✉ 25 | 27 | 24 | 23

1960. Directed by Richard Brooks. With Burt Lancaster, Jean Simmons, Shirley Jones. 146 minutes. Not Rated.

■ Disciples of this "rip-roaring" adaptation of the Sinclair Lewis novel testify that Lancaster's Oscar-winning, "fire-and-brimstone" performance as a "street preacher"–cum–"con man" in a "hypocritical" traveling ministry is the "best of his career" (while some "get religion" watching Jones' take on a jilted prostitute); its "excellent script" detailing a "flesh vs. the spirit" conflict also took home a statuette.

Elvira Madigan F 20 | 19 | 20 | 24

1967. Directed by Bo Widerberg. With Pia Degermark, Thommy Berggren. 91 minutes. Rated PG.

◪ Both "visually stunning" and "wonderfully dated", this "seductive" Swedish sobfest recounts the "heartbreaking" affair between "two AWOL lovers" – a tightrope walker and a married army officer – who are "beautiful" and, of course, "doomed"; although memorable for its "lovely scenery" and the Mozart string concerto it popularized, it's forgettable to those who see it as "tiresome" "romantic fluff."

Emma 22 | 23 | 23 | 24

1996. Directed by Douglas McGrath. With Gwyneth Paltrow, Jeremy Northam, Greta Scacchi. 121 minutes. Rated PG.

■ Jane Austen's "charming" story of "matchmaking at its best and worst" gets an "engaging" spin in this "delightful period piece" starring a "perfect" Paltrow opposite a "laconically charming" Northam; its "cheery" tone and dryly "humorous approach" make it a natural to "watch back-to-back with *Clueless*, since they're both based on the same novel."

Emperor's New Groove, The 20 | – | 18 | 20

2000. Directed by Mark Dindal. Animated. 78 minutes. Rated G.

◪ A "selfish, smart-mouthed emperor becomes a llama" with humbling results in this "quirky", "overlooked cartoon" that effortlessly merges both "standard and CGI animation" with "superb voice acting"; sure, aesthetes complain of a "low-budget", "slapped-together" look, but most find it "highly entertaining" with "lots of great gags" and a script that's "actually funny."

Empire of the Sun 25 | 23 | 24 | 26

1987. Directed by Steven Spielberg. With Christian Bale, John Malkovich. 154 minutes. Rated PG.

■ Perhaps Spielberg's most "underappreciated" film, this "touching story of a British child's internment in a WWII Japanese prison camp" is an "ambitious" epic replete with "dazzling performances", "David Lean–worthy" imagery and an "especially moving John Williams score"; maybe the "storyline drags" a bit midway, but overall its "sheer power and intensity" supply plenty of "magic moments."

Empire Strikes Back, The ⓫ ∅ 26 | 21 | 26 | 28

1980. Directed by Irvin Kershner. With Mark Hamill, Harrison Ford, Carrie Fisher, Billy Dee Williams. 124 minutes. Rated PG.

■ The "darkest of the *Star Wars* series", this "worthy" first sequel features more "depth" in its characterizations and the "best storyline so far", "revealing many important secrets" as the "cosmic struggle continues"; "blissfully free of wooden dialogue", it might be the "most adult" of the "original trilogy", while that open-ended "cliff-hanger" of a finale supplies a suitably "spectacular" windup.

Enchanted April ∅ 24 | 26 | 22 | 25

1992. Directed by Mike Newell. With Joan Plowright, Miranda Richardson. 95 minutes. Rated PG.

■ For a "wonderfully rich pick-me-up", try this "genteel" "getaway" of a movie about four "risk-taking" women who "leave their dreary English lives behind" and are "transformed" during an April vacation in "lush, sunny" Tuscany; the perfect "antidote to winter", it's "more complex than it first appears", and Plowright's "terrific performance" will brighten any "rainy day."

End of the Affair, The 20 | 24 | 20 | 22

1999. Directed by Neil Jordan. With Ralph Fiennes, Julianne Moore, Stephen Rea. 102 minutes. Rated R.

■ "Faith, love and loss" underlie this "terrific" adaptation of Graham Greene's "tragic romance" set in "rainy" WWII London about a "conflicted, adulterous Englishwoman" and her "jealous, angry lover"; this "difficult story" succeeds thanks to a "flashback"-heavy, "multi-layered" scenario and "wonderful screen chemistry" between a "powerful" Fiennes and a "smoldering" Moore modeling "glamorous slips and retro suits."

Enemy of the State 19 | 19 | 20 | 21

1998. Directed by Tony Scott. With Will Smith, Gene Hackman, Jon Voight. 131 minutes. Rated R.

■ "Privacy and civil liberties" issues take center stage in this "engaging", "paranoid" thriller about "Big Brother"–ish "government agents" chasing after a "DC lawyer" who's unwittingly holding an incriminating videotape; so "fast moving" that there's barely time to "catch your breath", it mixes "high-tech" effects with a "low-concept" idea to come up with something "very exciting" indeed.

English Patient, The ✉ 22 | 24 | 21 | 25

1996. Directed by Anthony Minghella. With Ralph Fiennes, Juliette Binoche, Kristin Scott Thomas. 160 minutes. Rated R.

◪ "Love it or hate it", there's no question that this "lush" WWII "romance" (winner of nine Oscars) boasts an "old-Hollywood scope", "poetic" cinematography, "brilliant writing" and "magnetic" performances from Fiennes and Scott Thomas as star-crossed lovers "in the desert sands of North Africa"; but those who "agree with Elaine on *Seinfeld*" claim this patient requires "patience", given a pace so "laborious" that it's "recommended for treating insomnia."

Enter the Dragon 23 | 16 | 17 | 20

1973. Directed by Robert Clouse. With Bruce Lee, John Saxon, Jim Kelly. 98 minutes. Rated R.

■ "Martial arts" mavens maintain that this "all-time best kung fu" flicker is "butt-kicker" "Lee's magnum opus", the "standard by which all karate films are judged"; sure, the "production's cheesy" and its "James Bond" "rip-off" plot is "unoriginal", but the "balletic, ballistic" fight scenes are so "spectacular" that this one "spawned many forgettable imitators" – not to mention many "video games."

Eraserhead ◑∅ 21 | 17 | 17 | 19

1977. Directed by David Lynch. With Jack Nance, Charlotte Stewart. 90 minutes. Not Rated.

■ Director Lynch's "trippy", "dread-inducing" debut is an "eerie glimpse of a marriage gone horribly awry" that "replicates the logic of a nightmare" (i.e. "you don't know what's going on half the time"); gird yourself for some "disturbing pictures, disturbing music" and "no discernable plot", but at least this "cult classic" is "willing to take risks."

Erin Brockovich ✉ 21 | 23 | 23 | 21

2000. Directed by Steven Soderbergh. With Julia Roberts, Albert Finney, Aaron Eckhart. 130 minutes. Rated R.

■ "Roberts proves her worth" with a "boffo", Oscar-winning turn in this "uplifting", "push-up bra"–laden "true story" about "standing up to a big corporation and winning"; ok, its "socially conscious", "don't-mess-with-the-little-people" screenplay might owe a lot to "*Norma Rae*", but ultimately this "polished production" works as both a "star vehicle and a compelling story."

E.T. The Extra-Terrestrial 26 | 22 | 26 | 27

1982. Directed by Steven Spielberg. With Dee Wallace, Henry Thomas, Drew Barrymore. 115 minutes. Rated PG.

■ Arguably the "*Wizard of Oz* for a new generation", this "irresistible" sci-fi "fairy tale" is the "endearing story of a boy", the "cutest alien of all time" and their attempts to "phone home"; there's agreement that Spielberg's "incredibly imaginative" "genius strikes again", managing to express "every human emotion in less than two hours", so gather the "entire family" along with a "big bowl of Reese's Pieces" and get ready for some "true magic."

Evil Dead, The Ⓘ 22 | 14 | 18 | 17

1982. Directed by Sam Raimi. With Bruce Campbell, Ellen Sandweiss, Betsy Baker. 85 minutes. Rated NC-17.

■ "Not for the weak-stomached", this "scary, scary, scary" "gorefest" with "abundant blood" and lots of "energy" is "dumb", "campy horror at its best"; alright, the acting's "questionable", the dialogue "lame", the story "hackneyed" and the effects very "low-budget", but it "blows Hollywood blockbusters away" simply because it's "so much fun"; P.S. its sequel, *Evil Dead II*, is even "better."

Evita 19 | 17 | 21 | 24

1996. Directed by Alan Parker. With Madonna, Antonio Banderas, Jonathan Pryce. 134 minutes. Rated PG.

◪ "Sleazy politics come alive" in this "visually rich" "celluloid version" of the stage musical based on the life of Argentina's Eva Peron, an all-singing, dialogue-free production that phrase-makers dub an "extended MTV video"; though surveyors split on Madonna's title turn ("surprisingly good" vs. "doesn't have the chops"), the "smoldering", "powerful" Banderas is a hit and overall this "entertaining" epic is at the very least "watchable."

Exodus ∅ 23 | 23 | 26 | 25

1960. Directed by Otto Preminger. With Paul Newman, Eva Marie Saint, Sal Mineo. 210 minutes. Not Rated.

■ An "all-star cast" drives this story of the "founding of modern Israel", a "stunning", "satisfying" Preminger epic "faithfully" adapted from Leon Uris' best-seller; fans single out the star turn from a "too-gorgeous-for-words" Newman "in his prime", and if the plot has some "bathos" mixed into its "high drama", it's ultimately a "moving" moving picture.

Exorcist, The ✉Ⓘ 25 | 24 | 26 | 25

1973. Directed by William Friedkin. With Ellen Burstyn, Max von Sydow, Linda Blair. 122 minutes. Rated R.

■ "Horror and religion" collide in this "head-spinning", "nightmare-inducing" "shocker" about a child possessed by the devil that "grossed out America" with its "revolting" language and that infamous "pea-soup vomit scene"; though some say it's "slid into camp" over the years, most maintain it's still "one of the scariest movies ever" – but stick to the "original" cut that's much more "terrifying" than the recent 'restored' reissue.

Fabulous Baker Boys, The 20 | 22 | 18 | 19

1989. Directed by Steven Kloves. With Jeff Bridges, Michelle Pfeiffer, Beau Bridges. 114 minutes. Rated R.

■ "Sibling rivalry" gets "compelling" treatment in this "great date movie" about two "journeyman musicians" competing for the attentions of their "slinky, sexy" girl singer; the Bridges brothers exude the "art of cool" and Pfeiffer "slithers around so deliciously" that no one minds that this "slice-of-life" story "doesn't go anywhere", given the "enjoyable" ride; most memorable scene, no question: Michelle "draped over a piano" crooning 'Makin' Whoopee' ("who knew she could sing?").

Face/Off 18 | 19 | 18 | 21

1997. Directed by John Woo. With John Travolta, Nicolas Cage, Joan Allen. 138 minutes. Rated R.

◪ "Hong Kong auteur Woo" "goes Hollywood" in this "hyperkinetic" action flick that "fires on all pistons", despite an "unashamedly preposterous scenario" in which "over-the-top" archenemies Travolta and Cage "switch places" (and faces); be prepared for "twists and turns galore", "lots of violence" and enough "mindless fun" to put this one at the top of your "guilty pleasures list."

Fahrenheit 451 21 | 19 | 25 | 19

1966. Directed by François Truffaut. With Oskar Werner, Julie Christie, Cyril Cusack. 110 minutes. Not Rated.

◪ "Truffaut's first English-language picture" is an "excellent adaptation" of Ray Bradbury's "Big Brother"–ish sci-fi novel, a "social commentary" about "censorship" by "book burning" in the not-too-distant future (the title is the temperature at which paper ignites); though zealots praise the "thoughtful" presentation of an "important topic", nonbelievers flame it as "plodding" and suggest you "read the book" instead.

Fail-Safe ◑ 24 | 25 | 26 | 21

1964. Directed by Sidney Lumet. With Henry Fonda, Walter Matthau, Larry Hagman. 112 minutes. Not Rated.

■ The "Cold War gets hot" in this "chilling", "hypnotic" "nuclear-war melodrama" about a U.S. President forced to make "horrifying choices" as an atom bomb hurtles toward Moscow; fans note the storyline's strikingly similar to *Dr. Strangelove* (though decidedly laugh-free) but insist its "what if?" plot is "gripping – and hopefully not prophetic."

Fame ∅ 21 | 18 | 21 | 20

1980. Directed by Alan Parker. With Irene Cara, Lee Curreri, Eddie Barth, Laura Dean. 134 minutes. Rated R.

■ "Little girls who sing in front of the mirror" relate to this "feel-good" musical set in "NY's High School of Performing

Arts", where "talented", "leg warmer–wearing teenagers" spend their days "dancing in the streets" and "struggling for fame"; ok, it's a bit "overdone" and "very dated now", but "crank up the volume" and you'll "enjoy the energy" all the same.

Fanny and Alexander ✉ F ∅ 26 | 25 | 25 | 26

1982. Directed by Ingmar Bergman. With Pernilla Allwin, Bertil Guve, Gunn Wallgren. 188 minutes. Rated R.

■ "Proof that Bergman wasn't miserable all the time", this "semi-autobiographical look back at his childhood" in Sweden "told from two siblings' point of view" features the "master" "at his most accessible"; sure, the "pacing's slow" and the film "long" (in fact, it's a pared-down version of a six-hour TV miniseries), yet the overall "visual magnificence" makes for something "rich and interesting."

FANTASIA ⓘ 28 | – | – | 29

1940. Directed by Ben Sharpsteen et al. Animated. 120 minutes. Rated G.

■ Walt Disney's "magnificent merger" of "mind-blowing" animation with a "symphonic orchestra" conducted by "highbrow maestro Leopold Stokowski" is a piece of "unbeatably creative" "eye candy" that's "never been equaled"; though a "flop when it first came out", it was later revived as a "'60s head movie" (thanks to trippy sequences like those "dancing hippos in tutus" and "Mickey Mouse as the sorcerer's apprentice"); modernists maintain this "original music video" remains a "perfect way to introduce a child to classical" sounds.

Fantasia 2000 24 | – | – | 27

1999. Directed by James Algar et al. Animated. 75 minutes. Rated G.

◪ The "perfect companion" to the 1940 "classic", this "worthy" sequel marrying animation to music of great composers is "terrific Disney" that might be "more for adults than kids" for a change; it "keeps the spirit of the original beautifully" (right down to the "cloying celebrity" intros to each vignette), and though the "flamingo-with-the-yo-yo" scene enthralls many, the "best segment" is "'Rhapsody in Blue' via Al Hirschfeld"; P.S. purists insist it's "best on an IMAX screen."

Fantastic Voyage 19 | 12 | 23 | 21

1966. Directed by Richard Fleischer. With Stephen Boyd, Raquel Welch, Edmond O'Brien. 100 minutes. Rated PG.

◪ "Outrageous in its day", this sci-fi fantasy for "thinking" folks "still wows" the wide-eyed with its story about scientists miniaturized and then "injected into a human body" to repair a blood clot; despite "wooden acting" and a "dumb ending", the "special effects are impressive for its time" – and Raquel sure looks swell in and out of that skintight diving outfit.

Farewell My Concubine F 25 | 26 | 24 | 26
1993. Directed by Chen Kaige. With Leslie Cheung, Gong Li, Zhang Feng-Yi. 171 minutes. Rated R.
■ "Worthy of David Lean on every level", this "sumptuous", "epic achievement" traces a complex friendship between two Peking Opera singers over a "fascinating sweep of history" spanning Chinese culture from the '30s to the '70s; "stunning both visually and emotionally", it boasts "superb acting" and "outstanding scenery", but make sure to sit up straight: its "overlong" running time can be "draining."

Fargo ✉ 25 | 27 | 25 | 25
1996. Directed by Joel Coen. With Frances McDormand, William H. Macy, Steve Buscemi. 98 minutes. Rated R.
■ This "comic noir" treatment of "crime in the heartland" shows "how funny Minnesota can be" in the hands of the Coen brothers, who "spin a folksy", violent yarn that makes the "outrageous seem everyday" and the "mundane interesting"; but the pièce de résistance is McDormand's "deadpan", Oscar-winning performance as a "pregnant" "crime-stopper" whose "goofy dialogue" alone is – "you betcha" – worth the price of admission.

Fast Times at Ridgemont High 22 | 19 | 21 | 18
1982. Directed by Amy Heckerling. With Sean Penn, Judge Reinhold, Jennifer Jason Leigh, Phoebe Cates. 92 minutes. Rated R.
■ One of the "crown jewels of the teen-comedy" genre, this "totally killer" "coming-of-age" "favorite" is an indelible "snapshot of the '80s" that made a star of Penn in the immortal role of "surfer stoner dude" Jeff Spicoli; adapted from Cameron Crowe's book, it showcases a "sprawling cast in interweaving stories" (like a "teenage *Nashville*") and, among other things, "inspired a generation of in-school pizza orderers"; best "gratuitous scene": "Phoebe Cates on the diving board."

Fatal Attraction 22 | 23 | 23 | 21
1987. Directed by Adrian Lyne. With Michael Douglas, Glenn Close, Anne Archer. 119 minutes. Rated R.
■ "Anyone contemplating an extramarital affair" should take a hard look at this "genuinely creepy" "cautionary tale", dominated by a "demented" Close as a "licentious hubby's worst nightmare"; though the plot "goes overboard" occasionally and Douglas "plays the same character as in 47 other movies", the picture had tremendous "cultural impact" in its day and is "still hair-raising" – particularly the "yikes"-inducing "boiled-bunny" scene.

Father of the Bride ◑ⅡØ 23 | 25 | 21 | 20
1950. Directed by Vincente Minnelli. With Spencer Tracy, Joan Bennett, Elizabeth Taylor. 92 minutes. Not Rated.
◪ Hollywood legends Tracy (in the "harried" title role) and Taylor ("never lovelier" as the bride) walk down the

aisle together in this "heartwarming" chestnut about the "havoc surrounding the planning of a wedding"; while most vow it's something that "all fathers and daughters should watch" together, a few pronounce it "dated and slow."

Father of the Bride ⓫ 20 | 20 | 19 | 20

1991. Directed by Charles Shyer. With Steve Martin, Diane Keaton, Martin Short. 105 minutes. Rated PG.

◪ "Faster-moving than the original", this "thoroughly engaging" comedy captures the "chaos and hilarity of wedding planning" thanks to a "hilarious" Martin (as the "clueless dad") and an equally "hysterical" Short; sure, it can be "tame" and rather "silly", but ultimately it goes down "like soothing chocolate pudding"; better yet, it "won't inflict pain on guys", even though it's a bona fide "chick flick."

Ferris Bueller's Day Off 23 | 22 | 23 | 21

1986. Directed by John Hughes. With Matthew Broderick, Alan Ruck, Mia Sara. 98 minutes. Rated PG-13.

■ "Every teenager's fantasy" of "ditching high school" for the day is realized in this "brilliant comedy" about a "sly slacker" on the loose in Chicago who "gets away with everything" and "does it with style"; the "smug-mugged" Broderick exudes "bravado" in the role that "launched his career", while "under-appreciated" director Hughes offhandedly produces a picture so "influential" that it "belongs in a time capsule of the '80s."

Few Good Men, A 23 | 26 | 23 | 22

1992. Directed by Rob Reiner. With Tom Cruise, Jack Nicholson, Demi Moore. 138 minutes. Rated R.

■ "Star-driven", "crackerjack courtroom drama" about a military murder investigation that's both "intelligent and entertaining"; no question, there are more than a few good performances, especially the "adorable-as-ever" Cruise in a "gritty", change-of-pace role playing against Nicholson's "riveting" if "pompous" marine colonel, who delivers the picture's most "infamous line: 'you can't handle the truth.'"

Fiddler on the Roof 26 | 25 | 27 | 26

1971. Directed by Norman Jewison. With Topol, Leonard Frey, Norma Crane. 181 minutes. Rated G.

■ One of the "last of the epic musicals", this "uplifting" adaptation of the "Broadway classic" finds "wide-screen resonance" in its "memorable" score and "elaborate production" values; despite the unmusical subject matter (19th-century "Jews fleeing the pogroms"), it's still a "joyous" film that's as "moving as a moving picture can be."

Field of Dreams 22 | 21 | 23 | 22

1989. Directed by Phil Alden Robinson. With Kevin Costner, Amy Madigan, Ray Liotta. 107 minutes. Rated PG.

■ "Even non–sports fans can love" this "feel-good" fantasy/drama about "baseball, ghosts" and "one man's search to find himself" in an Iowa cornfield; its "realistic sporting sequences, great storyline" and "touching" Costner turn ("before he lost it") make for a flick that "gets better every time you see it"; even those who find it too "sentimental" agree it's a "must-see for any father and son."

Fifth Element, The 19 | 15 | 19 | 23

1997. Directed by Luc Besson. With Bruce Willis, Gary Oldman, Milla Jovovich. 126 minutes. Rated PG-13.

◪ "Hyperkinetic", "loud" and "fast-paced", this "slick" sci-fi "actionfest" is about as substantial as a "big ball of cotton candy, but a hoot nonetheless"; sure, "Willis saves the planet – again" – but in this "loopy" "send-up of the genre", the "tongue-in-cheek" plot plays second fiddle to the "visually spectacular" effects; still, shirkers shrug it off as a "messy example of why more isn't always better."

Fight Club 23 | 25 | 24 | 24

1999. Directed by David Fincher. With Brad Pitt, Edward Norton, Helena Bonham Carter. 139 minutes. Rated R.

■ "Love-it-or-hate-it" filmmaking is alive and well in this "testosterone-ridden" "cult classic" that uses "top-notch effects", "twisted humor" and a "killer" soundtrack in its depiction of "ultraviolent, disenfranchised males"; an "amazing Norton" and "underrated Pitt" provide the fireworks in this "gore"-drenched drama, with a "surprise finish" that's either "mind-blowing" or "nonsensical."

First Blood: Rambo Ⓘ 18 | 13 | 19 | 18

1982. Directed by Ted Kotcheff. With Sylvester Stallone, Richard Crenna, Brian Dennehy. 97 minutes. Rated R.

◪ A "great kick-butt movie" "bolstered by a muscular score", this "simplistic but satisfying revenge tale" about a Vietnam vet harassed by small-town cops "delivers some punch"; the "studly", "steroidal" Stallone makes a bloody decent "action god", if not a silver-tongued thespian ("he should never talk"), though connoisseurs caution it's his "last good movie before getting lost in sequel land."

Fish Called Wanda, A 23 | 24 | 22 | 21

1988. Directed by Charles Crichton. With John Cleese, Jamie Lee Curtis, Kevin Kline. 108 minutes. Rated R.

■ It's easy getting hooked on this "nonstop", "kitchen-sink comedy" about a "heist" perpetrated by a "bumbling gang" portrayed by a "few chaps of Python fame" as well as the "show-stealing", Oscar-winning Kline; be prepared for "lots of giggles", but "forget political correctness", as "stutterers" and some unfortunate "goldfish" are gleefully abused.

Fisher King, The 21 | 24 | 21 | 21

1991. Directed by Terry Gilliam. With Jeff Bridges, Robin Williams, Mercedes Ruehl. 137 minutes. Rated R.

◪ Grail-seekers gravitate to this "strange" mix of "comedy, fantasy and drama", a "powerful" story of a high-flying radio shock jock who falls to earth only to be rescued by a homeless man; some find the plot "confusing" and "a little too out there", but loyal subjects say the "incredible visual effects in the Grand Central Station" scene alone "make it worth watching."

Fistful of Dollars, A Ⓘ 19 | 17 | 18 | 17

1967. Directed by Sergio Leone. With Clint Eastwood, Marianne Koch, Mario Brega. 99 minutes. Rated R.

◪ The "pasta flows" in this "early spaghetti Western" as Clint "defines coolness" with his "prototypical" "Man With No Name" caught between two rival families; though a "couple notches down from *The Good, The Bad and the Ugly*" ("maybe something was lost in the translation"), this "classic" is "still fun on a Saturday afternoon."

Five Easy Pieces 24 | 27 | 22 | 21

1970. Directed by Bob Rafelson. With Jack Nicholson, Karen Black, Lois Smith. 96 minutes. Rated R.

■ "Nicholson's at the height of his powers" in this very "deliberately paced character study" about "disaffection", "wasted ambition and dreams" that's a "must-see for Jack fans"; it "captures the restlessness of its era" with an expert "mix of comedy and serious drama" – and offers explicit instructions on "how *not* to be a waitress" in that "unforgettable" "chicken-salad sandwich" scene.

Fletch Ⓘ 19 | 18 | 18 | 16

1985. Directed by Michael Ritchie. With Chevy Chase, Joe Don Baker, Tim Matheson. 98 minutes. Rated PG.

■ This "goofball" "cult" comedy represents "Chase's peak" in his "ultimate" role as an "undercover reporter who changes his ID more often than his underwear"; fools for "tomfoolery" swear it's "possibly the most quotable movie" ever, thanks to a flurry of "great one-liners" that only get "funnier every time you see it."

Flight of the Phoenix, The ∅ 25 | 26 | 24 | 21

1965. Directed by Robert Aldrich. With James Stewart, Richard Attenborough, Peter Finch. 147 minutes. Not Rated.

■ "Jimmy Stewart can fly anything" and does in this post–*Spirit of St. Louis* "adventure" flicker about a desert plane crash that leaves its survivors facing a "seemingly hopeless future"; "realistically shot" and "brilliantly acted", it's a "feel-good", "can-do" kind of picture "without violence" that "really stays with you."

Fly, The Ⓘ 20 | 18 | 22 | 18

1958. Directed by Kurt Neumann. With Vincent Price, David Hedison, Patricia Owens. 94 minutes. Not Rated.

■ The "golden age of B movies" lives on in this wonderfully "camp" "classic" about a scientist "who pushes the envelope too far and becomes a fly"; fans buzz it remains "truly horrifying", especially that "unforgettable" shot of our hero "stuck in the spider's web" ("help me!") that "makes up for any quaintness in the execution."

Fly Away Home 22 | 20 | 24 | 24

1996. Directed by Carroll Ballard. With Anna Paquin, Jeff Daniels, Dana Delany. 107 minutes. Rated PG.

■ Get out your "biggest bowl of popcorn" for this "deeply felt family film" about a young girl, her estranged dad and the flock of baby geese she takes under her wing; fans "honk" about its "captivating story" and "beautiful" Canadian scenery, saying it's "not just for kids", but rather a "quite uplifting", "lovely movie for all."

Forbidden Planet 25 | 18 | 25 | 24

1956. Directed by Fred M. Wilcox. With Walter Pidgeon, Anne Francis, Leslie Nielsen. 98 minutes. Rated G.

■ Its long-before-digital FX "may seem quaint" today, but otherwise this "top-notch" "psychological thriller" is "still lots of fun" and represents the "true start of the sci-fi genre" to many; despite a compelling storyline about an outer-space rescue attempt "based on Shakespeare's *Tempest*" and some halfway decent acting from the humans, "Robby the Robot is the real star" here.

Forrest Gump ✉ 24 | 26 | 24 | 25

1994. Directed by Robert Zemeckis. With Tom Hanks, Robin Wright, Gary Sinise. 142 minutes. Rated PG-13.

◪ "Even macho guys" get misty over this "sentimental" story of "hope and perseverance" that explores recent American history through the "unlikely eyes" of a "simple-minded", Zelig-like hero (the "triumphant", Oscar-winning Hanks); though picky viewers find "not much assortment in this box of chocolates", they're overruled by "enchanted" believers who say its "basic good-heartedness" makes it "remarkably touching."

Fort Apache ◑ 23 | 22 | 23 | 22

1948. Directed by John Ford. With John Wayne, Henry Fonda, Shirley Temple. 125 minutes. Not Rated.

■ This "great" Golden-Age-of-Hollywood Western is the first of the Ford trilogy that both mythologized and humanized the cavalry; Fonda's effectively "cast against type" as a by-the-numbers commander who takes over a frontier fort and can't connect with his men or the local Indians, while Wayne is "perfect" as the more understanding captain with whom he clashes; tame for the TV generation, its fight scenes are "remarkable for its era."

48 HRS. Ⓘ 19 | 18 | 18 | 17

1982. Directed by Walter Hill. With Nick Nolte, Eddie Murphy, Annette O'Toole. 92 minutes. Rated R.

■ The "blueprint" for "buddy action flicks", this "profanely entertaining" crime thriller about a "surly white cop teaming up with a loud-mouthed black convict" features "stroke-of-genius" casting in its "quintessential pairing" of Nolte and Murphy; ok, it's "brainless fun" and a "little too violent", but worth catching for Eddie's "starmaking" screen debut alone – especially his "great rendition of 'Roxanne.'"

42nd Street ◑ 24 | 18 | 20 | 26

1933. Directed by Lloyd Bacon. With Ruby Keeler, Ginger Rogers, Bebe Daniels. 89 minutes. Not Rated.

■ Alright, it's a "bit corny by modern standards", but this "brassy" "mother of all backstage musicals" showcases choreographer "Busby Berkeley at his glossy best" applying his "inventive" genius to all those "dancing feet"; "every actress' dream" come true, it's a real "classic", so just ignore the "hackneyed" plot and "Keeler's clunky" footwork.

For Whom the Bell Tolls 25 | 26 | 26 | 22

1943. Directed by Sam Wood. With Gary Cooper, Ingrid Bergman, Katina Paxinou. 170 minutes. Not Rated.

◪ Papa-ficionados swear this adaptation of Hemingway's Pulitzer Prize–winning novel about an American fighting fascism in '30s Spain "gets every single nuance right", from its "poignant", "old-fashioned love story" right down to the convincing battle sequences; though a minority dubs it "schmaltz in macho drag", it strikes a chord as a "true classic by any measure" for most.

For Your Eyes Only 18 | 16 | 18 | 21

1981. Directed by John Glen. With Roger Moore, Carole Bouquet, Topol, Julian Glover. 127 minutes. Rated PG.

■ A "solid" entry in the Bond blitz, this spy flicker focuses less on "supergadgets" and more on Moore, leading many to label it his "best" outing as the ever-suave 007; the "realistic villains", "exotic locations" and "jaw-dropping" ski chases entice "even die-hard nonfans" – although the "fight scenes are never believable."

Foul Play ∅ 21 | 19 | 20 | 19

1978. Directed by Colin Higgins. With Goldie Hawn, Chevy Chase, Dudley Moore. 116 minutes. Rated PG.

■ Goldie "at her cute, giggly best" and a "terrific" Chevy make a "charming couple" in this "lightweight murder mystery" that's a loose "takeoff on Hitchcock's *The Man Who Knew Too Much*"; its "international-assassination plot" seesaws between "hilarity and suspense", while Moore deftly walks away with the picture as a lecherous swinger with a memorably equipped bachelor pad.

400 BLOWS, THE ◑ⅡF 27 | 26 | 25 | 24

1959. Directed by François Truffaut. With Jean-Pierre Léaud, Robert Beauvais. 94 minutes. Not Rated.

■ "Anyone who survived adolescence" can relate to this "benchmark" French "coming-of-age" film, a "semi-autobiographical" effort that marked Truffaut's directorial debut; as his "great alter ego", Léaud "depicts the pain and joy of growing up" in a winsomely "giddy" performance, though the picture earned its "place in film history" by "breaking a lot of rules" while demonstrating a "true love of movies."

Four Weddings and a Funeral 21 | 21 | 21 | 20

1994. Directed by Mike Newell. With Hugh Grant, Andie MacDowell, Kristin Scott Thomas. 117 minutes. Rated R.

◪ This "fabulously entertaining" marriage of "sweet and savvy" wrings "unexpected" laughs out of the "ups and downs of modern love" and "every bad wedding" you've ever endured; notable for "putting Hugh Grant on the map", it also boasts a "sparkling script" and a "quirky" ensemble cast, though the less said about the "wooden", "whiny" MacDowell the better.

Fox and the Hound, The 18 | – | 19 | 18

1981. Directed by Ted Berman, Richard Rich, Art Stevens. Animated. 83 minutes. Rated G.

◪ As the title canines become unlikely pals, kids can learn about the "meaning of friendship" from this "cute" Disney film, but it's not all tail-wagging "family" fun: the "bittersweet" tone "tugs at those heartstrings with no mercy", and bashers bark at the "copy-machine" quality of the early '80s animation.

Frankenstein ◑Ⓘ 25 | 21 | 25 | 23

1931. Directed by James Whale. With Boris Karloff, Colin Clive, Mae Clarke. 71 minutes. Not Rated.

■ The "granddaddy of all horror films" adds a touch of "pathos" and "camp" to its story of a mad scientist who "goes against nature" and builds a creature "prone to violence"; beyond monster-mashing, it also explores the "themes of loneliness and mass hysteria" via Karloff's "heartbreaking" ghoul, and though "a bit overacted", it's still "goose-bumps time when Colin Clive shouts 'it's alive!'"

Freaky Friday ∅ 18 | 17 | 21 | 16

1977. Directed by Gary Nelson. With Barbara Harris, Jodie Foster, John Astin. 95 minutes. Rated G.

■ A "kooky" idea – a teenage girl and her mom trade bodies for a day – powers this "fun" '70s "family film" that's a step up from the "usual body-swapping" comedies; thanks to a "smart script" and "brilliant" performances from Harris and Foster, some mothers and daughters watch it together for a "great bonding experience."

French Connection, The ✉Ⓘ 25 | 26 | 25 | 24

1971. Directed by William Friedkin. With Gene Hackman, Roy Scheider, Fernando Rey. 104 minutes. Rated R.

■ Famed for the "most harrowing car chase ever", this "seminal hard-boiled cop drama" is a "fast-paced" "exposé of the drug underworld" that's also "superbly cast and acted", starting with Hackman's "explosive", Oscar-winning turn as the tough-talking 'Popeye' Doyle; sure, it might seem "dated" to modernists, but that's "only because it's aped so frequently."

French Lieutenant's Woman, The 22 | 25 | 21 | 23

1981. Directed by Karel Reisz. With Meryl Streep, Jeremy Irons, Hilton McRae. 127 minutes. Rated R.

■ "Streep is fantastic" in this "original" romance detailing parallel relationships: one involving an upper-class gent and a lower-class lass in Victorian England, the other between the contemporary actors playing them; granted, Harold Pinter's scenario might be "a bit confusing at the get-go", but ultimately this "excellent" adaptation of John Fowles' novel is both "worthwhile and really cool."

Frequency 19 | 20 | 22 | 19

2000. Directed by Gregory Hoblit. With Dennis Quaid, James Caviezel. 118 minutes. Rated PG-13.

◪ Sure, it might be "unbelievable", but this "initially overlooked" "time-travel" tale generates lots of "surprise" with its "truly original story" about a young man who talks to his late father via ham radio; despite "metropolis-size plot holes", it's still "touching", with a baseball subplot that's "especially fun" for fans of NY's 1969 "Miracle Mets."

Fried Green Tomatoes 23 | 25 | 23 | 22

1991. Directed by Jon Avnet. With Kathy Bates, Jessica Tandy, Mary Stuart Masterson, Mary-Louise Parker. 130 minutes. Rated PG-13.

■ "Southern-fried memories" are on the menu of this "heartwarming" dramedy detailing how a "pathetic excuse for a woman" transforms herself into a "take-charge wonder"; its "sweet story" might feature a dash of "male bashing", but it's "genuinely touching and involving" – no wonder many fried-food fans find this "feel-good" "tear-jerking" "chick flick" so gosh darn "yummy."

From Here to Eternity ✉◑ 26 | 27 | 24 | 24

1953. Directed by Fred Zinnemann. With Burt Lancaster, Montgomery Clift, Deborah Kerr, Frank Sinatra, Donna Reed. 118 minutes. Not Rated.

■ Based on James Jones' "powerful" novel, this "gold standard" of war dramas depicts military life in Honolulu's Pearl Harbor just before the Japanese attack; the "all-star cast" (including an Oscar-winning "Ol' Blue Eyes") and a "technically brilliant" production make this a "telling", "compelling" "classic" – though it's best remembered for Burt and Deborah's iconic "kissing-on-the-beach" scene.

From Russia With Love 23 | 21 | 23 | 23

1964. Directed by Terence Young. With Sean Connery, Robert Shaw, Lotte Lenya. 115 minutes. Rated PG.

■ Ride the "Orient Express from Istanbul to Venice" – with plenty of stops for "exotic locales", "scantily clad" gals and "great fight scenes" – in this early James Bonder; the "formula never works better" thanks to an "incomparable" Connery pitted against "non-cartoon" villains, especially the "wonderful" Lenya at her most "sadomasochistic."

Fugitive, The 23 | 24 | 24 | 23

1993. Directed by Andrew Davis. With Harrison Ford, Tommy Lee Jones. 127 minutes. Rated PG-13.

■ From the "ultimate adrenaline rush" of the opening "train wreck" to the "smashing grand finale", you're likely to be "on the edge of your seat" throughout this "thinking person's action flick", based on the "long-ago" TV series about a doctor unjustly accused of murder; the "cat-and-mouse" plot lends a "Hitchcockian" feel to the proceedings, while Ford and Jones deliver "pitch-perfect performances."

Full Metal Jacket 24 | 25 | 22 | 25

1987. Directed by Stanley Kubrick. With Matthew Modine, Adam Baldwin, Vincent D'Onofrio. 116 minutes. Rated R.

◪ "Kubrick does Vietnam" in this "intense" war picture that's really "two amazing films in one": first up is the "disturbingly funny" depiction of "boot-camp" basic training, followed by an abrupt about-face to the "total hell" of the front-line war; "first-rate production and acting" keep things "compelling" throughout, even if peaceniks feel the "uneven" second half is a tad too "violent."

Full Monty, The 22 | 22 | 24 | 19

1997. Directed by Peter Cattaneo. With Robert Carlyle, Mark Addy, Tom Wilkinson. 91 minutes. Rated R.

■ Out-of-work, out-of-shape "blokes" put together a "Chippendale's-type" strip act as a "creative response to unemployment" in this "riotous" English comedy that mixes "bumps and grinds" with "serious social themes"; its "enthusiastic" if "unknown" ensemble cast shake their booties to a "terrific" pop soundtrack, though most prefer it "with subtitles" to decipher those "British accents."

Funny Face 24 | 24 | 21 | 25

1957. Directed by Stanley Donen. With Audrey Hepburn, Fred Astaire, Kay Thompson. 103 minutes. Not Rated.

■ "Cinderella" goes to Paris in this "fashion industry musical" wherein a "gracefully aging", "debonair" Astaire turns a "bookish" Hepburn into an "ethereal", "luminous" supermodel; despite "no story to speak of", it's "thoroughly enchanting" thanks to "magic" dancing and Gershwin's "s'wonderfully" "dreamy" score; best number: Thompson's "steal-the-movie" rendition of 'Think Pink.'

Funny Girl ✉ Ⓘ 26 | 25 | 24 | 26

1968. Directed by William Wyler. With Barbra Streisand, Omar Sharif, Walter Pidgeon. 151 minutes. Rated G.

■ "Hello, gorgeous!"; Babs' "big movie debut" in one of the "last great traditional Hollywood musicals" made her the "greatest star" thanks to some "chutzpah", some "charm" and a voice "like buttah"; indeed, her Oscar-winning turn as comedienne Fanny Brice is so "socko" that it's easy to ignore the "schmaltzy" plot about the "man who got away."

Funny Thing Happened on the Way to the Forum, A 22 | 22 | 21 | 20

1966. Directed by Richard Lester. With Zero Mostel, Phil Silvers, Buster Keaton. 99 minutes. Not Rated.

◪ For "comedy tonight", try this "total farce" of a musical that depicts Ancient Rome as a freewheeling toga party; sure, "Zero's the greatest" at provoking "laugh after laugh", but fans of the "quite different" stage version find it "stupid" "schlock" with "a lot lost in the translation to the screen."

Gallipoli 25 | 25 | 25 | 24

1981. Directed by Peter Weir. With Mel Gibson, Mark Lee, Bill Kerr, David Argue. 110 minutes. Rated PG.

■ A young, "fresh-faced" Gibson "comes of age" as an actor in this "oh-so-sad war movie" about a "disastrous WWI" battle in Turkey that points up the "pointlessness" of combat; "one of the best of the Australian New Wave" films, it winds up with a "ten-hanky tragic ending" that "tugs at the heartstrings without being corny."

GANDHI ✉ 27 | 28 | 27 | 27

1982. Directed by Richard Attenborough. With Ben Kingsley, Candice Bergen. 188 minutes. Rated PG.

■ "Big Hollywood at its best", this "meticulously detailed" bio of the Indian leader is "*The Ten Commandments* of the '80s", "long but riveting" and "emotionally wrenching"; Kingsley's "searing", Oscar-winning portrayal of the figure "who brought the British Empire to its knees" is the movie's "glorious centerpiece", and if a few find it "ponderous" and "overblown", there's no debate that it "captures the spiritual essence of the man perfectly."

Garden of the Finzi-Continis, The ✉ F 25 | 24 | 27 | 25

1971. Directed by Vittorio De Sica. With Dominique Sanda, Lino Capolicchio, Helmut Berger. 94 minutes. Rated R.

■ "Complacency leads to disaster" in this "haunting" WWII drama about "upper-class Italian Jews" who "close their eyes to the looming evil" of fascism by believing that "money and position will insulate them"; "gripping and emotional", it's notable for being one of De Sica's last films and for making the "beautiful" young Sanda a star.

Gaslight ✉◑∅ 26 | 27 | 26 | 24

1944. Directed by George Cukor. With Ingrid Bergman, Charles Boyer, Joseph Cotten. 114 minutes. Not Rated.

■ Anything but light, this "high-tension" thriller stars a "glowing", Oscar-winning Bergman as a newlywed who thinks she's "going insane – or is she?"; "mesmerized" fans say the "original" storyline "maintains the suspense to the end", helped along by an atmospheric "Victorian" setting and a particularly "villainous villain" in Boyer; P.S. look for a "very young Angela Lansbury" in her "screen debut."

GENERAL, THE ◑ 28 | 27 | 26 | 27

1927. Directed by Clyde Bruckman, Buster Keaton. With Buster Keaton, Marion Mack. 75 minutes. Not Rated.

■ One of the "most remarkable" silent films, this pioneering effort "establishes gags still used today" in its story of a Civil War–era Southern engineer in relentless, hapless pursuit of a stolen locomotive; the "Great Stoneface's" most "ambitious" work, it also incorporates some "amazing physical comedy" (Keaton "does all his own stunts") that must be "seen to be believed."

Gentlemen Prefer Blondes 23 | 21 | 20 | 24

1953. Directed by Howard Hawks. With Jane Russell, Marilyn Monroe, Charles Coburn. 91 minutes. Rated PG.

◪ You'll probably prefer Monroe's "ingenious, ingenuous" "dumb blonde" to the "nonexistent storyline" in this "guilty-pleasure" musical comedy, a "deliciously over-the-top" story of "gold diggers" on the make made all the more vivid in "spectacular Technicolor"; it's "one for the time capsule", if only for Marilyn's "dazzling", iconic rendition of 'Diamonds Are a Girl's Best Friend.'

Ghost ✉ 21 | 21 | 22 | 21

1990. Directed by Jerry Zucker. With Patrick Swayze, Demi Moore, Whoopi Goldberg. 128 minutes. Rated PG-13.

◪ There's "action for the boys and romance for the girls" in this comic "tearjerker" that's got "hot" "date movie" written all over it; sure, its story of a dead man watching over his surviving lover is "improbable" (and "sappy and manipulative", according to cynics), yet Moore and Swayze make it seem so "sexy", while the "priceless", Oscar-winning Goldberg "delivers the laughs."

Ghost and Mrs. Muir, The ◑∅ 24 | 25 | 25 | 22

1947. Directed by Joseph L. Mankiewicz. With Rex Harrison, Gene Tierney. 104 minutes. Not Rated.

■ This "timeless" "romantic fantasy" details the unlikely "love story" between a "beautiful" widow and a "crusty old" sea captain who's "full of life" – even though he's a "ghost"; the "otherworldly", "very funny" romance that ensues avoids being "sentimental goop" thanks to "superb performances" from Tierney, Harrison and little "8-year-old Natalie Wood."

Ghostbusters Ⓘ 21 | 18 | 21 | 23

1984. Directed by Ivan Reitman. With Bill Murray, Dan Aykroyd, Sigourney Weaver, Harold Ramis. 107 minutes. Rated PG.

■ "Kooky, spooky" and flat-out "funny", this "classic '80s" "sci-fi comedy" about 'paranormal investigators' banishing ghosts from NYC is "one of the best stupid movies ever", so "not much thinking is required"; "wonderful special effects" and a wonderfully "sarcastic Murray" are its highlights, though its most lasting achievement is that it "made the word 'slime' into a verb."

Ghost World 23 | 26 | 22 | 21

2001. Directed by Terry Zwigoff. With Thora Birch, Steve Buscemi, Scarlett Johansson. 111 minutes. Rated R.

■ A "witty" look at two "nonconformist" girls trapped in a "homogenized" suburb, this "random" comedy is a "nice departure from the typical teen angst film"; the "quirky" but "believable" characters sport "great thrift-store clothes", while the "phenomenal Buscemi" is "pitch-perfect."

Giant ⊠∅ 24 | 23 | 24 | 24

1956. Directed by George Stevens. With Elizabeth Taylor, Rock Hudson, James Dean. 201 minutes. Rated G.

◪ As "sprawling" as the Lone Star state itself, this "all-out wonderful" Texas "epic" about money, love and oil "burns with star power", featuring some mighty "big names" – Liz, Rock and Jimmy (in his last role) – "in their prime"; cynics say this "way too long" example of "Hollywood bloat" is just "cornball hooey", but fans insist this "colossal '50s production" "holds your interest."

Gigi ⊠ 24 | 23 | 23 | 26

1958. Directed by Vincente Minnelli. With Leslie Caron, Maurice Chevalier, Louis Jourdan. 119 minutes. Rated G.

■ "Thank heaven" for this "fine rendering" of Lerner and Loewe's hit Broadway musical, an "unorthodox love story" about a "turn-of-the-century" Parisian courtesan and the client who wants to marry her; winner of nine Oscars, this "stunner" boasts a "radiant" Caron, a suave Jourdan, an "*amusant*" Chevalier and "top-notch production values", so even if the end result might look like a "lavish" wad of "cotton candy", "just give in" and enjoy it.

Gilda ◑ 24 | 23 | 21 | 23

1946. Directed by Charles Vidor. With Rita Hayworth, Glenn Ford, George Macready. 110 minutes. Not Rated.

■ Noir was never more "delectable" than in this "solid" love triangle starring a "delicious" "Hayworth in her signature role" as the "glamorous", hair-tossing Gilda; though her "modified striptease" in the 'Put the Blame on Mame' number is the "only reason to see it" for some, others find enough "mystery and suspense" to make it "memorable."

Gimme Shelter 25 | – | 21 | 22

1970. Directed by Albert Maysles, David Maysles, Charlotte Zwerin. Documentary. With the Rolling Stones. 91 minutes. Rated R.

■ Originally commissioned by the Rolling Stones as a "simple concert" flick, this "rockumentary" took on a "darker side" after filmmakers inadvertently recorded a "real murder" at the group's infamous Altamont gig; the result is a "grim, gritty look" at the "turbulent '60s" "spiraling out of control", with a "complicated storyline" and "classic" soundtrack that put modern "music videos to shame"; hottest moment: the "amazing" Tina Turner at the mike.

Girl, Interrupted 18 | 22 | 18 | 18

1999. Directed by James Mangold. With Winona Ryder, Angelina Jolie, Brittany Murphy. 127 minutes. Rated R.
◪ "Haunting if overwrought" drama providing a "hair-raising glimpse" inside a "mental institution" headlining a "convincing" Ryder as a "troubled" patient, though Jolie "steals the show" (and an Oscar) portraying the "sexiest crazy person" ever captured on film; fans insist it's a "compelling" "emotional trip", but others say it's so insanely "soapy" that it "should have been a 'Cosmo' article."

Gladiator ✉ 23 | 23 | 22 | 27

2000. Directed by Ridley Scott. With Russell Crowe, Joaquin Phoenix, Oliver Reed. 155 minutes. Rated R.
◪ "Everything a big Hollywood blockbuster should be", this "old-fashioned" "sword-and-sandal" extravaganza features lots of "action, adventure and backstabbing" in its story of a Roman general turned wretched slave; the "intense", Oscar-winning Crowe oozes "testosterone" and the "lavish" "recreation of Ancient Rome" brings the "Coliseum to life", but thumbs-downers dismiss it as "bombastic" "beefcake."

Glengarry Glen Ross 23 | 27 | 22 | 20

1992. Directed by James Foley. With Al Pacino, Jack Lemmon, Ed Harris, Alec Baldwin. 100 minutes. Rated R.
■ "High-pressure" real-estate salesmen "with an axe about to fall on their jobs" get the David Mamet treatment in this "dark", "lacerating drama" about the "predatory world of business"; its "talky", expletive-laden scenario can be "intensely disturbing", but ultimately it "shows what can be done with a small cast, limited sets and Godzilla talent."

Glory 25 | 26 | 26 | 26

1989. Directed by Edward Zwick. With Matthew Broderick, Denzel Washington, Morgan Freeman. 122 minutes. Rated R.
■ Based on the "true story" about the "first black Civil War regiment and the white Union officer who led them", this "powerful" "period piece" is a fine "evocation of a story few people know"; expect "stunning" acting and "great battle scenes", even if it "doesn't end the way you want it to."

GODFATHER, THE ✉ Ⓘ 29 | 29 | 29 | 29

1972. Directed by Francis Ford Coppola. With Marlon Brando, Al Pacino, Diane Keaton, Robert Duvall, James Caan, John Cazale. 175 minutes. Rated R.
■ Perhaps the "best three hours you can spend sitting still", this "ultimate gangster film" and "cultural phenomenon" is

ranked both Top Overall and Most Popular film in this *Survey*; an "absolutely flawless" "American epic", it recounts the "operatic" lives of the Corleone family via an "intricate" plot, "bravura photography" and "iconic performances" from Brando and Pacino; in fact, the end result is so "killer" that "nothing else comes close – except maybe the sequel"; favorite line: "leave the gun, take the cannoli."

GODFATHER PART II, THE ✉ ⓘ 29 | 29 | 28 | 29

1974. Directed by Francis Ford Coppola. With Al Pacino, Robert Duvall, Diane Keaton, Robert De Niro, John Cazale. 200 minutes. Rated R.

■ A "real rarity – a sequel as good as the original" – this "true masterpiece" "stands on its own laurels" as it "delves deeper into the Corleone family" saga; a "moody meditation on the emptiness of power", its "complex" plot "masterfully intercuts" two stories separated by a half-century into a "taut", "heartbreaking tale of innocence lost", and though "never overshadowing its big brother", it just might be "even more subtle and sublime"; most chilling moment: the "kiss between Michael and Fredo."

Gods and Monsters ✉ 23 | 27 | 23 | 22

1998. Directed by Bill Condon. With Ian McKellen, Brendan Fraser, Lynn Redgrave. 105 minutes. Rated R.

■ McKellen's "brilliant" performance is the backbone of this "innovative biopic" detailing an "encounter between a hedge clipper and a has-been" moviemaker that's based on the life of 1930s "gay director" James Whale; partisans point to the "smart", Oscar-winning script as proof of why "independent films are such a delight."

Gods Must Be Crazy, The ⓘ ∅ 22 | 17 | 23 | 18

1981. Directed by Jamie Uys. With Marius Weyers, Sandra Prinsloo, N!xau. 109 minutes. Rated PG.

◪ "Consumerism meets primitive African bushmen" when a Coke bottle "falls out of the sky" in this "cult" "culture-clash" comedy that "proves you don't need a big Hollywood budget" to be "original and witty"; despite bare-bones production and middling acting, this "diamond in the rough" still has plenty of "universal appeal" thanks to "creative" ideas and "more sight gags than the Marx Brothers."

GoldenEye 19 | 19 | 19 | 23

1995. Directed by Martin Campbell. With Pierce Brosnan, Sean Bean, Famke Janssen. 130 minutes. Rated PG-13.

■ "Born to play the part" of the "never-fazed secret agent", Brosnan brings the 007 "franchise" "back from the dead" with a "suave" turn opposite Janssen's "great villainess" in this "entertaining" "modern Bond" flick; though the "convoluted storyline" about globe-busting weaponry in post-Soviet Russia is a "little clunky", overall it "gets the job done" with "outstanding action", "amazing special effects" and a "refreshing lack of hokeyness."

Goldfinger 26 | 23 | 25 | 25

1964. Directed by Guy Hamilton. With Sean Connery, Honor Blackman, Gert Frobe. 112 minutes. Rated PG.

■ Rated the Top 007 picture in this *Survey,* this "classic" has it all: "formidable villains", the "coolest gadgets", an "out-of-this-world", "robbing-Fort-Knox" plot, a "fabulous theme song" "belted out by Shirley Bassey" and perhaps the "best-named" babe of them all, the one-and-only "Pussy Galore"; most memorable exchange: "do you expect me to talk? – no, Mr. Bond, I expect you to *die!*"

GONE WITH THE WIND ✉ 28 | 27 | 27 | 29

1939. Directed by Victor Fleming. With Clark Gable, Vivien Leigh, Leslie Howard, Olivia de Havilland, Hattie McDaniel, Butterfly McQueen. 238 minutes. Rated G.

■ A bona fide piece of "American pop culture", this Civil War "melodrama" based on Margaret Mitchell's "beloved" book is a "timeless", "sweeping" saga of love and loss in dwindling Dixieland; frankly, legions of admirers "*do* give a damn", rating it an "epic with a capital E" for its incredibly "beautiful production", "amazing" costumes and "perfect cast", especially Gable's "dashing" Rhett and Leigh's "performance of a lifetime" as the "feisty", "fiddle-dee-deeing" Scarlett; sure, it's a "long sit", yet in the end this "gorgeous" "triumph" "still thrills."

Goodbye, Columbus ∅ 19 | 19 | 20 | 19

1969. Directed by Larry Peerce. With Richard Benjamin, Ali MacGraw, Jack Klugman. 102 minutes. Rated PG.

◪ Based on Philip Roth's then-provocative novella, this frank romantic comedy "might seem dated" now, but nostalgists remember its "good performances", especially MacGraw's tour-de-force turn as a "crush"-worthy "Jewish princess"; foes say that it "should have been better", considering the source material.

Goodbye Girl, The ✉ 21 | 23 | 20 | 20

1977. Directed by Herbert Ross. With Richard Dreyfuss, Marsha Mason, Paul Benedict. 110 minutes. Rated PG.

■ "Exactly what a romantic comedy should be", this "sweet, feel-good movie" whips up some "well-done froth" about a "likable", lovelorn single mom forced to share an apartment with an unlikable, "lovable actor"; one of "Neil Simon's best" screenplays, this surprise hit garnered a clutch of Oscar nominations and won one for Dreyfuss' "charismatic" turn.

GOODFELLAS 27 | 27 | 26 | 25

1990. Directed by Martin Scorsese. With Robert De Niro, Ray Liotta, Joe Pesci. 146 minutes. Rated R.

■ "Not for the faint of heart", "mob-master" Scorsese's "harrowing modern gangster" classic careens from "hysterically funny to terrifyingly violent" owing to an "electrifying" screenplay based on the "true story" of "'made' guys and greed" that reveals "mobsters as human beings" – albeit "vicious and heartless" ones; "beautiful lensing" and "stellar performances" make this one boil with "brutal power."

Good Morning, Vietnam 22 | 24 | 22 | 22

1987. Directed by Barry Levinson. With Robin Williams, Forest Whitaker, Bruno Kirby. 119 minutes. Rated R.

■ Get a "different perspective on the Vietnam war" from this "bittersweet" tale of an army radio DJ in Saigon that "strikes just the right balance between comedy and drama", capturing the "reality" while still provoking beaucoup "laughs"; Williams "at his manic best" not only supplies the expected "hilarious ad-libbing" but shows off some "impressive acting skills" too.

Good, the Bad and the Ugly, The 24 | 21 | 23 | 23

1967. Directed by Sergio Leone. With Clint Eastwood, Lee Van Cleef, Eli Wallach. 161 minutes. Rated R.

■ A "delicious spaghetti Western" drenched in "tasty dramatic marinara sauce", this Clint-essential "Man-With-No-Name" oater about three Civil War–era gunmen battling over Confederate treasure is a "true classic of the genre"; sure, Eastwood's "penetrating glare" is "hypnotic", but some say Wallach "steals the show" by injecting "subtle comedy" into the mix, while Ennio Morricone's "memorable score" will "stick in your head for days."

Good Will Hunting ✉ 24 | 25 | 24 | 22

1997. Directed by Gus Van Sant. With Robin Williams, Matt Damon, Ben Affleck. 126 minutes. Rated R.

◪ Written by the "then-unknown" Damon and Affleck, this "intelligent" drama is built on an "uplifting", "powerful" screenplay about a "troubled" "petty criminal" who's coincidentally a "brilliant" "math genius"; its "searing yet subtle" performances include an Oscar-winning turn from Williams at his "most moving", and though the ill-willed badmouth it as "predictable" and "improbable", overall most folks "like them apples."

Goonies, The 23 | 19 | 23 | 21

1985. Directed by Richard Donner. With Sean Astin, Josh Brolin, Corey Feldman. 114 minutes. Rated PG.

◪ One of the "best kids' adventures ever", this "smart, finely crafted" "family movie" is a fun "roller-coaster ride" "for all ages" (and a bona fide "nostalgia" trip for "Gen-Xers") about a gang of "pre-teen treasure hunters" who wield "go-go gadgets" and thwart bad guys; ok, it may have "some flaws", but at least it "doesn't take itself too seriously."

Gorillas in the Mist 19 | 21 | 20 | 21

1988. Directed by Michael Apted. With Sigourney Weaver, Bryan Brown, Julie Harris. 129 minutes. Rated PG-13.

■ "African jungles" supply the "beautiful setting" in this "fascinating bio" of primatologist Dian Fossey, the story of a complex woman who abandons humanity in favor of a group of endangered mountain gorillas; Weaver delivers a "great performance", the special effects blend real and artificial apes seamlessly and the "ending will stay with you."

Gosford Park ✉ 23 | 27 | 21 | 25

2001. Directed by Robert Altman. With Alan Bates, Maggie Smith, Helen Mirren. 137 minutes. Rated R.

◪ "Agatha Christie meets *Upstairs, Downstairs*" in this "jolly good show" of a "whodunit" that's an "insightful", "behind-the-scenes" "skewering of the British class system" set in a "'30s country estate"; "one of Altman's best", it features "rich atmosphere", "scintillating dialogue" and a "bloody great" ensemble cast "acting up a storm", and if cynics nix its "convoluted", "hard-to-follow" plot, fans claim it "gets better every time you see it."

GRADUATE, THE ✉ 27 | 27 | 26 | 24

1967. Directed by Mike Nichols. With Dustin Hoffman, Anne Bancroft, Katharine Ross. 105 minutes. Rated PG.

■ *The* "benchmark coming-of-age comedy", this "funny", "knowing" look at a "confused" "young man" and his "older seductress" is the "definitive '60s alienation" flick and "somehow never ages"; credit its "witty script", Mike Nichols' "ahead-of-its-time direction", a "groovy" Simon-and-Garfunkel soundtrack and "superb" turns from the "fab" Hoffman and the "unforgettable" Bancroft as – "koo-koo-ka-choo" – Mrs. Robinson; best word: "plastics."

Grand Canyon 18 | 21 | 18 | 18

1991. Directed by Lawrence Kasdan. With Danny Glover, Kevin Kline, Steve Martin. 134 minutes. Rated R.

◪ In this ambitious "meaning-of-life" drama, director Kasdan brings together a group of "average people leading average lives" to tell some "extraordinary stories" about "destiny and hope"; though some find the "fragmented", "confusing" result too "out there", most allow that this "surprisingly moving" picture "just misses being great."

GRAND ILLUSION ◑ 🄵 28 | 28 | 27 | 26

1938. Directed by Jean Renoir. With Jean Gabin, Erich von Stroheim, Pierre Fresnay. 114 minutes. Not Rated.

■ "It's no illusion": this "compelling" WWI "masterpiece" has "inspired generations" with its "crushing" "portrayal of the futility of war" and is "still as powerful as ever"; director Renoir "shows how it should be done" in this "ahead-of-its-time" picture that's on "everyone's greatest list" simply because it "touches on every human emotion."

GRAPES OF WRATH, THE ✉◑∅ 28 | 28 | 28 | 25

1940. Directed by John Ford. With Henry Fonda, Jane Darwell, John Carradine. 128 minutes. Not Rated.

■ "Every frame is a work of art" in this "faithful rendition" of Steinbeck's "eloquent" novel about dispossessed

"Depression"-era farmers living through "desperate" times; quite possibly "Ford's best", it's a "classic for a reason" and "ranks high on the list of great American films" as an "important statement about life", the "depth of man's sorrow and the zenith of man's spirit."

Grease Ⓘ 23 | 19 | 21 | 23

1978. Directed by Randal Kleiser. With John Travolta, Olivia Newton-John, Stockard Channing. 110 minutes. Rated PG.

■ "Fun" is the word for this "campy" comedy "classic", a "high-energy" "adaptation of the Broadway musical" that's a "'70s" take on a "hokey '50s" story enacted by some of the "oldest high-school students ever"; still, the "hunky Travolta" and "stunning Newton-John" "light up the screen", and the "slick production" numbers are so "irresistible" that "cult followers" watch this "guilty pleasure" "over and over."

Great Dictator, The ◑ 26 | 27 | 25 | 23

1940. Directed by Charles Chaplin. With Charles Chaplin, Jack Oakie, Paulette Goddard. 124 minutes. Not Rated.

■ The normally "silent Chaplin" "fearlessly" takes "aim at Hitler" in this rare "talkie", a "scathing satire of fascist tyranny" in which he "plays two roles": a Jewish barber and "rabid" dictator "Adenoid Hynkel", a "brilliant parody" of Der Führer; although "overly sentimental" and "preachy" to some, most find this "masterpiece of physical comedy" "thought-provoking and perpetually relevant."

GREAT ESCAPE, THE 27 | 26 | 27 | 26

1963. Directed by John Sturges. With Steve McQueen, James Garner, Richard Attenborough. 169 minutes. Not Rated.

■ "Guy movies don't get any better" than this "absorbing" "prison break" flick "based on a true escape" from a WWII "German war camp"; featuring McQueen backed up by a "phenomenal", "all-star" ensemble, it also boasts "excellent writing", a "hummable score" and "flawless action" scenes, including the "best motorcycle scene ever filmed"; though on the "long" side, it's "worth every minute."

Great Race, The 20 | 18 | 20 | 20

1965. Directed by Blake Edwards. With Jack Lemmon, Tony Curtis, Natalie Wood. 150 minutes. Not Rated.

■ Director Edwards revs up the engines in this "kitschy" "family" comedy about a turn-of-the-century auto race from NY to Paris, with plenty of "must-see" settings along the way; a tip-top "ensemble cast" supplies "over-the-top" performances, but the pièce de résistance is the "best pie fight in movie history"; in a word, it's a "hoot."

Great Santini, The 22 | 27 | 21 | 21

1979. Directed by Lewis John Carlino. With Robert Duvall, Blythe Danner, Michael O'Keefe. 115 minutes. Rated PG.

■ "Adapted from the painful Pat Conroy novel", this intense "dissection" of a "dysfunctional family" offers a "look inside the mind" of a "domineering" marine – "outstandingly" played by the "frighteningly good Duvall" – who treats his wife and kids like soldiers under his command; you'll "love him or hate him (or maybe both)", but in any event his "imperfect life" will "stay with you."

Green Mile, The 23 | 25 | 23 | 24

1999. Directed by Frank Darabont. With Tom Hanks, David Morse, Michael Clarke Duncan. 188 minutes. Rated R.
■ Stephen King's "harrowing" serial novel is "wonderfully translated to the screen" in this "disturbing drama" that "tugs at your emotions" with its "touching depiction" of "humanity at its best and worst"; despite "fine acting" (Hanks' "powerful" death-row prison guard and Duncan's "excellent" condemned man are standouts), this "very long" Mile makes some "wish it was an hour shorter."

Gremlins (II) 19 | 14 | 20 | 20

1984. Directed by Joe Dante. With Zach Galligan, Phoebe Cates, Hoyt Axton. 106 minutes. Rated PG.
◪ This "black comedy" features a "cuddly", "too-cute-for-words" pet who breeds "scary" offspring when exposed to bright light, water or being "fed after midnight"; although "lots of fun", some parents warn "proceed with caution": it has a "dark side", i.e. those "mean-spirited", "nightmare"-inducing gremlins who are too violent for smaller fry.

Grifters, The 22 | 26 | 23 | 21

1990. Directed by Stephen Frears. With Anjelica Huston, John Cusack, Annette Bening. 119 minutes. Rated R.
■ Despite "soulless characters" and a "cynical" theme, this very "adult" piece of "hard-core film noir" is a "first-class" study of "low-life culture" (the "twisted" plot concerns a "mommy and her long-lost son who are reunited" only to "go down in flames"); while the "whole film gels" around the "powerhouse" "work of all three leads", some say the "real star" is "Donald Westlake's superb" script.

Groundhog Day 22 | 20 | 24 | 20

1993. Directed by Harold Ramis. With Bill Murray, Andie MacDowell, Chris Elliott. 101 minutes. Rated PG.
■ An "intelligent" "existential romp", this "literate comedy" has an "original concept": a "jerk" is forced to "live the same day over and over until he gets it right" and "becomes a lovable man"; ok, it's a "one-joke premise" that can get "tedious", but for most it "works like a charm" thanks to the "hilarious" Murray, who transcends his "usual smart-ass" persona to come up with something "surprisingly deep."

Grumpy Old Men (II) 21 | 24 | 20 | 20

1993. Directed by Donald Petrie. With Jack Lemmon, Walter Matthau, Ann-Margret. 103 minutes. Rated PG-13.
■ Though "made for the *Murder, She Wrote*" crowd, this "lighthearted comedy" works for both "young and old",

reuniting the "classic Matthau-and-Lemmon" team playing retired Minnesotans "vying for the affections" of a "comely" new neighbor (the "not-hard-to-watch Ann-Margret"); sure, "we've seen it all before", but these "well-loved icons" still provoke a "ton of laughs."

Guess Who's Coming to Dinner ✉ 25 | 27 | 25 | 22

1967. Directed by Stanley Kramer. With Spencer Tracy, Sidney Poitier, Katharine Hepburn. 108 minutes. Not Rated.
◪ "Daring for its day", this '60s "commentary on race relations" is the "final film of one of Hollywood's finest couples", "class acts Hepburn and Tracy", at their most "powerful"; sure, its "controversial subject" of "interracial marriage" might seem a bit "stagy" and "dated" now, but its "poignant and charming" treatment assures that the "issues remain" relevant.

Gunfight at the O.K. Corral ∅ 20 | 21 | 20 | 21

1957. Directed by John Sturges. With Burt Lancaster, Kirk Douglas, Rhonda Fleming. 122 minutes. Not Rated.
◪ Always "entertaining", this Western recounts the famed 19th-century shoot-out between rival gangs in Tombstone, AZ; despite two Hollywood icons "playing off each other wonderfully" – the rugged Lancaster (as Wyatt Earp) and the cleft-chinned Douglas (Doc Holliday) – foes fume this "too-long" production doesn't "move the way it should."

Gunga Din ◑∅ 25 | 24 | 25 | 24

1939. Directed by George Stevens. With Cary Grant, Victor McLaglen, Douglas Fairbanks Jr. 117 minutes. Not Rated.
■ This "rousing adventure flick" from the "golden age of Hollywood" recounts the "golden age of the British Empire" via the "story of three soldiers in imperial India" and the titular native lad who befriends them; some snappy "byplay between Grant, McLaglen and Fairbanks" makes it a "buddy film" prototype, though a few are troubled by the "superior", "racist attitude" of the colonialists.

Guns of Navarone, The ⓫ 23 | 22 | 24 | 23

1961. Directed by J. Lee Thompson. With Gregory Peck, David Niven, Anthony Quinn. 158 minutes. Rated PG.
■ "Even people who hate war movies love" this "big", "star-studded" production about WWII Allied commandos plotting to destroy Nazi artillery on an Aegean island; "pounding" suspense and a "splendid cast" place this "classic" action-adventurer "head-and-shoulders above" the rest – and that "climactic sequence" will have you "holding your breath."

Guys and Dolls 24 | 21 | 24 | 24

1955. Directed by Joseph L. Mankiewicz. With Marlon Brando, Jean Simmons, Frank Sinatra. 150 minutes. Not Rated.
◪ "Brando sings!" in this "colorful" musical rendition of the "Damon Runyon stories" about "gamblers, evangelists" and racehorses, all dolled up into one "heavyweight"

extravaganza set around Times Square, rife with "catchy tunes" and "showstopping" numbers; foes think Marlon's "miscast", pointing to his "bored", "sexually smug" rendition of 'Luck Be a Lady.'

Gypsy 20 | 21 | 22 | 22

1962. Directed by Mervyn LeRoy. With Rosalind Russell, Natalie Wood, Karl Malden. 143 minutes. Not Rated.

◪ "Stripper Gypsy Rose Lee's life" is the basis of this "terrific" musical about the "original backstage mother" and her "passionate" efforts to make her kids into stars; ok, it's "kind of windy" and Wood (in the title role) "doesn't really strip", while the "brilliant miscasting" of a "shrill" Russell leads many to say the part "should have gone to Ethel Merman", who delivered the "real goods" on Broadway.

Hair 20 | 18 | 21 | 21

1979. Directed by Milos Forman. With John Savage, Treat Williams, Beverly D'Angelo. 121 minutes. Rated PG.

◪ The groovy "Broadway musical" that "defined the psychedelic '60s" gets a "terrific" big-screen transfer in this story of a Midwestern kid bound for Vietnam dallying with Central Park hippies; even though "Treat's a treat" in a role that "epitomizes the loving craziness" of the time, some say the "flower-child imagery" is "sadly faded."

Hairspray 19 | 17 | 18 | 18

1988. Directed by John Waters. With Divine, Ricki Lake, Sonny Bono, Ruth Brown. 91 minutes. Rated PG.

◪ "Grab a can of Aquanet" and get ready to "shake a tailfeather": this "hilariously campy" story of a "fat girl who lives to dance" is underground director Waters' "mainstream" ode to his "beloved Baltimore" in the '60s and his "most family-friendly" flick (it even "unflinchingly looks at racism"); though "Divine's divine" and the "absolutely perfect" Lake wears her "big hair" well, "deviant" devotees hedge it's "kind of tame, but still fun."

Halloween ⓫ 22 | 16 | 20 | 19

1978. Directed by John Carpenter. With Donald Pleasence, Jamie Lee Curtis. 91 minutes. Rated R.

■ "Changing the face of horror movies forever", this "almost bloodless chiller shows that gore doesn't equal terror" as it depicts a "masked psycho stalker" who preys on "rowdy teens"; despite "zero-budget" production values and so-so acting (but mighty "great screaming by Jamie Lee"), this "influential" "slasher" flick spawned a slew of sequels and "still holds up" simply because it's so "genuinely scary."

Hamlet 24 | 26 | 26 | 25

1996. Directed by Kenneth Branagh. With Kenneth Branagh, Julie Christie, Derek Jacobi. 242 minutes. Rated PG-13.

◪ This oft-done (maybe even "overdone") Shakespearean tragedy gets "expansive" treatment from "modern master"

Branagh, who uses the Bard's full text, resulting in a "four-hour adaptation"; though "engrossing, suspenseful" and "beautifully" "reimagined" to fans, those who sigh "enough already" claim it's "*too much* of a good thing."

Hannah and Her Sisters ✉ 24 | 25 | 23 | 23

1986. Directed by Woody Allen. With Mia Farrow, Barbara Hershey, Dianne Wiest. 103 minutes. Rated PG-13.

■ A "nice balance of jokes and philosophy", this "pertinent" romantic comedy about three sisters and their "struggle with the meaning of life" "brims with so much intelligence and heart" that many call it "Allen's most life-affirming" picture; featuring "all-around wonderful" acting, it's a "valentine" to "NYers in all their neurotic glory" that manages to "convey a message without tempering the laugh-out-loud humor."

Happiness 23 | 25 | 22 | 20

1998. Directed by Todd Solondz. With Jane Adams, Jon Lovitz, Philip Seymour Hoffman. 134 minutes. Not Rated.

◪ Forget the "truly ironic title": this extremely "dark" "feel-bad" comedy is "*American Beauty* with a lot more acid", so "unrelentingly bleak" that it's "not for the faint of heart"; given some "taboo subject matter" (e.g. "pedophilia", "masturbation"), the unhappy call it a "sicko" "train wreck" that's "probably the worst first-date movie ever", but fans tout its "brave" if "perverted" take on the "middle classes."

Hard Day's Night, A ◑ 24 | 19 | 19 | 24

1964. Directed by Richard Lester. With the Beatles, Wilfrid Brambell. 87 minutes. Rated G.

■ "Before there was MTV", there was this "best rock movie ever", an "ahead-of-its-time" "groundbreaker" shot with documentary-style "quick edits" that brilliantly convey the "lunacy" and the "pure joy of Beatlemania" in the "days of innocence"; it's "still a film of wonder", and, of course, there's that "incredible soundtrack" of "Fab Four" classics.

Harold and Maude 25 | 25 | 25 | 21

1972. Directed by Hal Ashby. With Ruth Gordon, Bud Cort, Vivian Pickles. 91 minutes. Rated PG.

■ Ok, it "starts with a hanging", but this "counterculture" "cult classic" "gets funnier", managing to be both "morbid" and "absurdly wonderful" in its "May-December story" of a "death-obsessed" kid who finds love with a "free-spirited old lady"; while "not for everyone", this "original" features a "phenomenal" Gordon (the "sexiest" septuagenarian ever) and a "gem" of a "Cat Stevens soundtrack."

Harry Potter and the Sorcerer's Stone Ⓘ 24 | 23 | 25 | 27

2001. Directed by Chris Columbus. With Daniel Radcliffe, Rupert Grint, Emma Watson. 152 minutes. Rated PG.

■ It's "Hogwarts brought to magic life": this "reverent" screen adaptation of the ultra-"popular children's book" about a school for young witches and wizards is simply "spellbinding" – nothing less than a "21st-century *Wizard of Oz*"; fans zero in on the "eye-popping special effects", "outstanding" ensemble cast and "perfect" scenario that "gets every character right", "just like you imagined them"; still, the "length and scariness factors" might mean it's "wasted on little kids."

Harvey ◑ 26 | 27 | 25 | 22

1950. Directed by Henry Koster. With James Stewart, Josephine Hull, Peggy Dow. 104 minutes. Not Rated.

■ "So sweet and genuine that it's never become dated", this "classic comedy" concerning an "adorable sot" and his "imaginary" "six-foot rabbit" is such an "enchanting, grown-up fairy tale" that the "word 'heartwarming' was coined for it"; the "delightful performances" from Stewart and Hull (who scored a Best Supporting Oscar) elevate this "feel-good" flick into the "can't-miss" category.

Hatari! 21 | 17 | 18 | 23

1962. Directed by Howard Hawks. With John Wayne, Hardy Kruger, Elsa Martinelli. 157 minutes. Not Rated.

◪ "Great African location shots" and a "fab" Henry Mancini score make this "somewhat forgotten" action/adventurer "better than its reputation" (even if its rather "dull" plot about "wild animal" trappers lacks "political correctness" for some); though it's a "lesser" vehicle for the "bigger-than-life" Wayne, at least "Red Buttons is less annoying than usual", and the "beautiful photography" supplies the "entertainment value."

Heat 22 | 25 | 19 | 22

1995. Directed by Michael Mann. With Al Pacino, Robert De Niro, Val Kilmer, Jon Voight. 171 minutes. Rated R.

◪ "Both the cop and robber are heroes" in this "operatic" "crime epic", a "star-studded killfest that's an action lover's dream" and cinematically historic, since "legends" "Pacino and De Niro are finally on-screen together" (their "face-to-face" "coffeehouse scene" is a "knockout"); yet "despite a captivating cast and storyline", "they could have done a better job in the editing room" – "there's a perfect two-hour movie" lurking in this sprawling, 171-minute marathon.

Heathers 21 | 19 | 22 | 18

1989. Directed by Micheal Lehmann. With Winona Ryder, Christian Slater, Shannen Doherty. 102 minutes. Rated R.

■ The "pinnacle of '80s dark humor" – maybe even "before its time" – this "out-there" "black comedy" is "twisted" and "proud of it" as it provides an important lesson in "teen peer pressure": "popularity can kill"; though admittedly "not for everyone" (especially the "lighthearted or light-stomached"), it did "launch Slater's and Ryder's careers", and the "deliciously biting dialogue is full of comebacks you wish you'd thought of."

Heaven Can Wait 21 | 19 | 22 | 19

1978. Directed by Warren Beatty, Buck Henry. With Warren Beatty, Julie Christie, Dyan Cannon. 101 minutes. Rated PG.

■ An "enjoyable remake of *Here Comes Mr. Jordan*", this "amusing" comedy/fantasy mix of true love and the afterlife is kind of "far-fetched, but it works"; sure, "Buck Henry's script is as good as the original", the art direction won an Oscar and a "likable" Beatty at least "tries to be sincere", but the "hysterical" Charles Grodin "steals the show."

Heavenly Creatures 24 | 25 | 26 | 24

1994. Directed by Peter Jackson. With Kate Winslet, Melanie Lynskey, Clive Merrison. 99 minutes. Rated R.

■ One part "fantasy", one part "true crime", this "absolutely riveting" drama about "two teens" plotting "matricide" is a "surreal", "haunting descent into the imagination" as it details an "attachment that turns deadly"; Winslet's "career-launching" performance is so "astounding" that some say "*this* is the movie" that the *Titanic* star "should have gotten an Oscar nomination for."

Heavy Metal Ⓘ 20 | – | – | 21

1981. Directed by Gerald Potterton. Animated. 86 minutes. Rated R.

◪ "Based on the sci-fi comic book of the same name", this "cult" cartoon "classic" is a novel "departure for animation", given its "adult-oriented" content and "heavy metal" score; some shrug it "wavers between entertaining and dull", since this "strung-together" "anthology" of hard-rock-flavored "vignettes" is more than "a little choppy" (it "makes no sense without alcohol").

Hello, Dolly! ∅ 20 | 19 | 20 | 23

1969. Directed by Gene Kelly. With Barbra Streisand, Walter Matthau, Michael Crawford. 146 minutes. Rated G.

◪ This "big, over-the-top" musical concerning a turn-of-the-century matchmaker is a "colorful" romp with "fabulous" dance numbers and all the "beautiful music from the Broadway show"; but goodbye Charlies call it a "leaden", "overblown spectacle", citing "one of the most unappealing romantic couplings imaginable": a "miscast" Streisand ("who knew Dolly Levi was 25 years old?") playing opposite an "embarrassing" Matthau.

Help! 19 | 16 | 15 | 20

1965. Directed by Richard Lester. With the Beatles, Leo McKern, Eleanor Bron. 90 minutes. Rated G.

■ "Sing along with the hits from 1965" that enliven this "zany musical comedy", a "perfectly enjoyable" if "silly John-Paul-George-and-Ringo romp" that's really not much more than a "platform to take advantage of the Beatles' popularity"; still, the "story's ok" ("at least there's a plot this time"), the international "locations are great" and, "of course, the soundtrack is terrific."

Henry V 26 | 28 | 27 | 26

1989. Directed by Kenneth Branagh. With Kenneth Branagh, Derek Jacobi. 137 minutes. Rated PG-13.

■ "Brush up on your Shakespeare" via this "revisionist" adaptation of the Bard's "difficult" history play about an English monarch at war with France over Normandy; "both spectacular and approachable", it makes the 17th-century dialogue "completely understandable to modern ears", and first-time director Branagh's "lavish, lusty" brio is so "brilliant" that many acolytes ask "Sir Laurence who?"

High Anxiety ∅ 21 | 19 | 19 | 19

1977. Directed by Mel Brooks. With Mel Brooks, Madeline Kahn, Cloris Leachman. 94 minutes. Rated PG.

■ "Hitch would have laughed" at this "totally goofy" comic homage from the "totally insane" Mel Brooks that's a "send-up" of the Hitchcockian oeuvre, particularly *Psycho* and *Vertigo*; only problem is, "you must know the material he's spoofing in order to get the jokes" or else this pretty "silly" picture "doesn't really hang together."

HIGH NOON ✉◑ 28 | 26 | 26 | 25

1952. Directed by Fred Zinnemann. With Gary Cooper, Grace Kelly, Lloyd Bridges. 85 minutes. Not Rated.

■ Voted the "best Western" in this *Survey*, this "tense drama" filmed in "real time" "breaks the mold" by combining all the "grit of the West" with a "strong comment on the McCarthyist '50s" and a touch of "Greek drama" to boot; as a "single-minded sheriff" with "principles", Cooper took home an Oscar, though many admit they're drawn to this "classic" "allegory" for its "theme song" alone; in short, it's "absolutely tops" – nothing else "comes close."

High Plains Drifter 18 | 19 | 20 | 19

1972. Directed by Clint Eastwood. With Clint Eastwood, Verna Bloom, Marianna Hill. 105 minutes. Rated R.

◪ "Perennial badass" Eastwood plays a "violent" "avenging angel" in this "powerful" if by-the-numbers Western in which "everyone gets what they deserve"; connoisseurs say it's Clint's "defining moment", though the less enamored rate it an "acquired taste", "not up to the standard of some of his others."

High Society ∅ 23 | 22 | 22 | 23

1956. Directed by Charles Walters. With Bing Crosby, Grace Kelly, Frank Sinatra. 107 minutes. Not Rated.

■ "What a swell party" is this "Cole Porter" "musical rendition" of "*The Philadelphia Story*", a "sophisticated comedy of manners" set in a "Newport mansion" inhabited by some "fantastic talent": a "gorgeous Grace", "swingin' Bing" and "delightful Sinatra", who "make it all look so easy"; sure, the original might be "far superior" plotwise, but fans dub this "softer" take the "Tiffany" of the singing-and-dancing genre.

Hilary and Jackie 21 | 26 | 22 | 21

1998. Directed by Anand Tucker. With Emily Watson, Rachel Griffiths, David Morrissey. 121 minutes. Rated R.

■ "Poignant and touching", this "overlooked" bio-drama tells the true story of the prickly "relationship between two sisters", one a cellist who's "battling MS" as well as other "personal" demons; "outstanding lead performances from Watson and Griffiths" lend appeal to more than just "classical music fans", though some say it can be "difficult to watch", given the "tragic" storyline.

His Girl Friday ◑ 26 | 28 | 24 | 22

1940. Directed by Howard Hawks. With Cary Grant, Rosalind Russell, Ralph Bellamy. 92 minutes. Not Rated.

■ "Pay attention" now: the "superfast-moving plot" "comes at you at 100 mph" in this "biting" "screwball" comedy that's a "wonderful adaptation" of "*The Front Page*"; Grant and Russell "snap and crackle" as a "newspaper editor and star reporter chasing the story of a lifetime – and each other" – and if the "breakneck speed" of this "roller-coaster ride" can be "exhausting", the payoff is "absolute hilarity."

Holiday Inn ◑ 23 | 20 | 20 | 23

1942. Directed by Mark Sandrich. With Bing Crosby, Fred Astaire, Marjorie Reynolds. 100 minutes. Not Rated.

■ "Crooner Bing" and "hoofer Astaire" are "rivals" in this "lively" "musical romance" that's chock-full of "Irving Berlin favorites" but most remembered for introducing the "show-stealing 'White Christmas'" to the world; sure, the plot's pretty "lightweight", but at least the songs of this "holiday bonbon" will "stick in your brain well into the new year."

Home Alone Ⓘ 19 | 17 | 20 | 19

1990. Directed by Chris Columbus. With Macaulay Culkin, Joe Pesci, Daniel Stern. 103 minutes. Rated PG.

■ "Every parent's nightmare" – and "every child's fantasy" – this "ultimate sleepover movie" made Culkin a "star" as a "self-sufficient" "kid who defends himself against robbers" after his vacation-bound family accidentally "leaves him at home"; though its "loony premise" is "full of funny sight gags" (and wraps up with a de rigueur "heartwarming ending"), some warn it can be too "violent" for smaller fry: "this is Bugs Bunny vs. Yosemite Sam for real."

Hoop Dreams ∅ 26 | – | 26 | 23

1994. Directed by Steve James. Documentary. 170 minutes. Rated PG-13.

■ "Two young athletes who dream of NBA fame" as a way "to escape the inner city" are the subjects of this "gritty, gripping" documentary, a "slam-dunk" "exposé" of "naive boys" that's "quite moving" if a "tad long"; "superb editing" makes it feel more like a "drama" than a real-life story, but don't look for a "Hollywood ending": this one's so "devastatingly real", it just might "break your heart."

Hoosiers 23 | 22 | 24 | 19

1986. Directed by David Anspaugh. With Gene Hackman, Barbara Hershey, Dennis Hopper. 114 minutes. Rated PG.

■ A modern-day "David and Goliath on the basketball court", this "inspirational" "classic of the small-town-team-rises-up genre" is a "corporate team builder" kind of flick; as the "motivational" but "down-and-out coach trying to make a comeback in the boonies", Hackman captures the spirit of "rural" hoops culture and supplies this "underdog story" with some "real heart."

Horse Feathers ◑ 24 | 22 | 20 | 18

1932. Directed by Norman Z. McLeod. With the Marx Brothers, Thelma Todd. 68 minutes. Not Rated.

■ "One of the Marxes' zaniest comedies" showcases the boys in "peak form" in an ivy-covered college setting, in which Groucho is the incoming university president; expect the usual "breezy" "lunacy" "based on years of vaudeville antics" – especially the "hilarious" "French-farcical wooing of Todd" – and ignore that "abrupt ending."

House of Games 24 | 23 | 27 | 21

1987. Directed by David Mamet. With Lindsay Crouse, Joe Mantegna, Lilia Skala. 102 minutes. Rated R.

■ "Cold characters and clipped conversations" make this "mind-bending thriller" pure "vintage Mamet" "at his most manipulative"; its "twisty" con-game plot (something like "*The Sting,* all grown-up") "keeps you guessing", and though the dialogue reminds some of "cartoons talking", it remains "chilling on many levels", with a "head-spinning" ending that will stick with you "long after the movie's over."

House of Wax ∅ 21 | 18 | 21 | 20

1953. Directed by Andre de Toth. With Vincent Price, Frank Lovejoy, Phyllis Kirk. 90 minutes. Rated PG.

■ "Look out for the giant vat of wax!": this "entertaining" "horror melodrama" was one of the first flicks made in "3-D", but fans say it's "still fun" "even without the glasses"; featuring a "priceless Price", a "chiller" story and "atmospheric", "gaslight-era" sets, it's the "stuff of nightmares", forever "spooky."

Howards End ✉ 22 | 26 | 21 | 25

1992. Directed by James Ivory. With Anthony Hopkins, Emma Thompson, Vanessa Redgrave, Helena Bonham Carter. 140 minutes. Rated PG.

◪ "Another Merchant-Ivory masterpiece", this "period piece" adaptation of the E.M. Forster novel concerns a "snobby upper-class" British family scheming to cut an interloper out of their "mother's will"; though Anglophiles laud the lovely cinematography and appearances by "some of the best actors of our time" (including a "superb" Hopkins and Oscar-winning Thompson), phobes fret it's "way too slow."

How to Marry a Millionaire 22 | 20 | 19 | 22

1953. Directed by Jean Negulesco. With Betty Grable, Marilyn Monroe, Lauren Bacall. 95 minutes. Not Rated.

■ "Fabulous gowns and mink coats are the stars" of this "rather entertaining" romantic comedy, a "guilty pleasure" about three gold diggers on the loose in Manhattan; "Lauren and Marilyn are charming in their own ways", while its "fascinating look" at women's roles in "'50s society" makes many feminists sigh "thank goodness for progress."

Hunchback of Notre Dame, The 19 | – | 19 | 21

1996. Directed by Gary Trousdale, Kirk Wise. Animated. 91 minutes. Rated G.

◪ "Disney does Victor Hugo" in this "underrated" bell-ringer that's "edgier than most animated fluff" and thus "more rewarding" for adults, given its "opera"-esque feel and "dark subtleties"; but cynics nix it as a bit "too sinister for children" and fear that the "forgettable songs" and "stupid talking gargoyles" must have the author "turning in his grave."

Hunger, The ∅ 20 | 21 | 20 | 20

1983. Directed by Tony Scott. With Catherine Deneuve, David Bowie, Susan Sarandon. 100 minutes. Rated R.

■ Deliciously "scary and erotic", this "stylish" "modern-day vampire film" "gets the blood moving" with a "to-die-for cast", including a "surprisingly effective Bowie" opposite Deneuve and Sarandon as two very "hot" vamps ("Buffy wouldn't stand a chance against them"); a pop Goth score by Bauhaus helps the atmospherics, but ultimately this one's best remembered for that notorious "lesbian" interlude.

Hunt for Red October, The 24 | 24 | 25 | 24

1990. Directed by John McTiernan. With Sean Connery, Alec Baldwin, Scott Glenn. 134 minutes. Rated PG. D-I

■ The "first and best Jack Ryan thriller", this "thoroughly entertaining" "Cold War" "guy flick" about a "renegade" "Russian submarine captain" combines "heart-pounding" suspense with "characters you can root for" (i.e. the "powerhouse" Connery and "holding-his-own" Baldwin); the "involving", "twisting plot" supplies enough "tense", "white-knuckle" moments to make it every bit "as good as the book."

Hurricane, The 21 | 26 | 21 | 21

1999. Directed by Norman Jewison. With Denzel Washington, Liev Schreiber. 145 minutes. Rated R.

■ Denzel's "excellent", "Oscar-worthy" performance is the glue in this true story about a hardscrabble middleweight boxer wrongly convicted of a triple murder; alternately "exciting and poignant", the script "really emphasizes human emotion", but it's Washington's "tremendous" performance that makes this miscarriage-of-justice movie so moving.

Hustler, The ◑ Ⓘ 25 | 26 | 24 | 22

1961. Directed by Robert Rossen. With Paul Newman, Jackie Gleason, Piper Laurie. 134 minutes. Not Rated.

■ "Dark, tense and beautifully delivered", this "ultimate movie about winning" is also a "love poem to the game of pool", featuring "Newman on a roll" opposite Gleason in a rare dramatic turn that nearly "steals the picture"; it's "convincing", "gripping" stuff, and though Paul reprised the character in "*The Color of Money*", connoisseurs claim this first take is so "much better."

Il Postino F 24 | 25 | 24 | 24

1995. Directed by Michael Radford. With Massimo Troisi, Philippe Noiret. 108 minutes. Rated PG.

■ A "charming" mix of "poetry and postal services", this "small treasure" "could only have been made in Italy", given its "lyrical", "humble" airs; the "sweet tale" of a "simple peasant" postman "with the heart of a poet", it manages to be both a "great love story" and a "haunting" tale of "inspiration", with "bravura performances" and "beautiful scenery" that come together for "winning" moviemaking.

Imitation of Life ∅ 21 | 22 | 23 | 22

1959. Directed by Douglas Sirk. With Lana Turner, John Gavin, Sandra Dee. 125 minutes. Not Rated.

◪ Bring "two boxes of Kleenex" before settling into this melodramatic Turner vehicle, a "classy" if "campy" "B movie" about a black woman who passes for white; a remake of the 1934 Claudette Colbert "tearjerker", this time around it's "all gussied up in pretty color" with the "racial theme toned down", leading realists to rate it a "ridiculous", "sudsy" soap opera.

In Cold Blood ◑ ∅ 25 | 26 | 26 | 22

1967. Directed by Richard Brooks. With Robert Blake, Scott Wilson, John Forsythe. 134 minutes. Rated R.

■ Brooks' "brilliant" adaptation of Truman Capote's "true-crime" "spellbinder" is "one of the most chilling films" about random murders "ever made" ("remember when not showing blood was more scary than showing it?"); recorded "in an almost documentary style" and all the more frightening thanks to Quincy Jones' evocative score, it "still works today" as an example of "powerful" albeit "disturbing" moviemaking.

Independence Day 19 | 16 | 18 | 24

1996. Directed by Roland Emmerich. With Will Smith, Bill Pullman, Jeff Goldblum. 145 minutes. Rated PG-13.

◪ "*E.T.* with an attitude", this "ultimate flying-saucer movie" might be a "remake of *War of the Worlds*" and "splashy trash" with a "plot as thin as a dime" that's "all noise and no substance", but at least it "doesn't take itself too seriously"; so grab some "popcorn" and hold on for a "helluva lot of fun."

Indiana Jones and the Last Crusade ∅ 24 | 23 | 23 | 26

1989. Directed by Steven Spielberg. With Harrison Ford, Sean Connery, Denholm Elliott. 127 minutes. Rated PG-13.

■ "Almost as good as the first" installment, this third foray in the "Indy adventure" series is a "search-for-the-Holy-Grail" tale that alternates "lighthearted humor" with plenty of "gee-whiz", "close-call action sequences"; Ford is "sexy, smart and tough" as the "perfect hero", but Connery (as his dad) "takes the cake" in this fond salute to "old-fashioned Saturday afternoon movie serials" "brought up to date."

Indiana Jones and the Temple of Doom Ⓘ∅ 22 | 21 | 21 | 25

1984. Directed by Steven Spielberg. With Harrison Ford, Kate Capshaw, Quan Ke Huy. 118 minutes. Rated PG.

◪ "Ford rules the day and saves the world" – again – in this "take-me-away" action/adventure story, the "follow-up to *Raiders*" that "goes more for shock value than the original" (though as exhilaratingly "over the top" as ever); still, doomsayers say its "hooey"-heavy plot and "dark feel" can be "far too grisly for younger viewers", dismissing it as a "blip in the trilogy"; most indelible image: those "chilled monkey brains."

Indochine ✉ F 23 | 25 | 23 | 25

1992. Directed by Régis Wargnier. With Catherine Deneuve, Vincent Perez. 152 minutes. Rated PG-13.

■ A "haunting", "epic" "tale of French Indochina", this Foreign Language Oscar winner details an "absolutely enthralling romance" played out against the background of a country in turmoil; as a "beautiful" rubber plantation owner, Deneuve "looks smashing in great clothes", and if the end result is a "little too picture perfect" for some, "hey! it's the movies."

Inherit the Wind ◑ 26 | 28 | 27 | 22

1960. Directed by Stanley Kramer. With Spencer Tracy, Fredric March, Gene Kelly. 128 minutes. Rated PG.

■ "You'll go ape" for this "superb" "fictionalized account of the Scopes monkey trial", based on the true story of a teacher trying to bring Darwin into his Tennessee classroom; a "magnificent Tracy and March" are "at the top of their game" trying to "reconcile creationism with evolution" in this "still relevant" "thought-provoker" – no wonder many call it the "ultimate in intelligent courtroom drama."

In-Laws, The ∅ 24 | 24 | 24 | 20

1979. Directed by Arthur Hiller. With Peter Falk, Alan Arkin, Richard Libertini. 103 minutes. Rated PG-13.

■ If you have any "weird" relatives-by-marriage, you'll "laugh out loud" at this "sidesplitting" comedy pitting a "chameleonic Falk" against a "befuddled Arkin" ("one of the great pairings of the cinema") as about-to-be in-laws;

"totally crazy and unpredictable", it's "worth watching" if only to "find out where *Meet the Parents* came from."

Insider, The 25 | 28 | 25 | 23

1999. Directed by Michael Mann. With Al Pacino, Russell Crowe, Christopher Plummer. 157 minutes. Rated R.

■ Crowe turns in a "quietly intense" performance (while Pacino is intense but definitely not quiet), in this dramatic thriller about a tobacco company "whistle-blower" trying to "do the right thing no matter what the consequences"; although a "disillusioning behind-the-scenes look" at "big business, the media and public opinion", it's "absolutely riveting" and an "inspirational" profile in "courage."

Interview with the Vampire 19 | 19 | 20 | 22

1994. Directed by Neil Jordan. With Tom Cruise, Brad Pitt, Antonio Banderas, Christian Slater. 123 minutes. Rated R.

■ "Cover up your neck"; this "entertaining Gothic horror flick about a maladjusted trio of immortal vampires" is "almost as good" as Anne Rice's "overwrought" best-selling book; sure, it might be "too beautiful" for words and they "could have cut out some of the gore", but with "pretty boys" Brad, Tom and Antonio playing "yummy bloodsuckers", "what's not to like?"

In the Bedroom 22 | 26 | 20 | 21

2001. Directed by Todd Field. With Sissy Spacek, Tom Wilkinson, Marisa Tomei. 130 minutes. Rated R.

◪ "Less is more" in this "intense" drama about murder, revenge and family "dysfunction" that's the kind of picture in which the "silences say more than any of the dialogue"; though "Spacek and Wilkinson are superb" and "first-time director" Field "does an amazing job", critics sigh it's a "made-for-Lifetime movie" that's "dark, depressing and 20 minutes too long."

In the Heat of the Night ⊠Ⓘ 24 | 27 | 24 | 22

1967. Directed by Norman Jewison. With Sidney Poitier, Rod Steiger, Warren Oates. 109 minutes. Rated PG.

◪ The "faint smell of dead honeysuckle hangs over" this "excellent" crime drama, a "brave statement on race relations" about a "black Yankee cop" suspected of murder in a small Southern town; it "generated a fair amount of controversy in its day" and was quite the Oscar magnet, taking home five statuettes including Best Picture and Best Actor for the "perfect Steiger."

In the Line of Fire 20 | 20 | 21 | 19

1993. Directed by Wolfgang Petersen. With Clint Eastwood, John Malkovich. 128 minutes. Rated R.

■ "Eastwood is perfect" as an "aging but resourceful" Secret Service agent – "vulnerable, tough and world-weary" – battling a "would-be Presidential assassin" in this "solid action" thriller; throw in a "truly creepy" Malkovich as the "coldly reptilian" villain and you have a "completely engrossing" flick that's more than "effective", right up to the "suspenseful climax."

In the Name of the Father 23 | 25 | 24 | 21

1993. Directed by Jim Sheridan. With Daniel Day-Lewis, Emma Thompson, Pete Postlethwaite. 133 minutes. Rated R.

■ This "shattering" look at "desperate times" in Northern Ireland is a "riveting" "true story" about a "father and son jailed for a crime they did not commit"; "Day-Lewis is mesmerizing" and "totally believable" in this "troubling" account of "love and respect" amid a "terrible civil war."

Invasion of the Body Snatchers ◑ 24 | 19 | 25 | 19

1956. Directed by Don Siegel. With Kevin McCarthy, Dana Wynter, Larry Gates. 80 minutes. Not Rated.

■ "Don't fall asleep!"; this '50s slice of "paranoid science fiction" posits that there are "alien" "pod people among us" "plotting to take over our hearts and minds"; alright, it's a "classic Red Scare parable", but "still perfectly effective today" despite "wooden acting" and that studio-enforced optimistic ending; P.S. "forget the remake – this is the one that gives you the chills."

Invasion of the Body Snatchers 19 | 18 | 21 | 18

1978. Directed by Philip Kaufman. With Donald Sutherland, Brooke Adams, Jeff Goldblum. 115 minutes. Rated PG.

◪ You'll be "looking for pods in the basement" after seeing this "thought-provoking", "very different" remake of the "classic" sci-fi thriller about an insidious alien invasion; this time around, the McCarthyist subtext has been replaced by 'Me Decade' pop psychobabble, and if "less fun" than the original, it's still pretty darn "scary."

Invisible Man, The ◑⓫ 22 | 20 | 21 | 20

1933. Directed by James Whale. With Claude Rains, Gloria Stuart, William Harrigan. 71 minutes. Not Rated.

■ "Fabulous effects" ("especially for its time") and some slyly "campy" moments make this "classic" creature feature worthy of "every movie lover's repertoire"; the tale of an inventor whose invisibility serum transforms him into a crazed killer, it stars an engrossing Rains in the "scary" title role, whose amazing performance has more to do with vocalizing than visibility.

Irma La Douce 21 | 23 | 20 | 21

1963. Directed by Billy Wilder. With Shirley MacLaine, Jack Lemmon, Lou Jacobi. 147 minutes. Not Rated.

■ A surprisingly "sweet" comedy from the usually acerbic Billy Wilder, this story of an honest Parisian cop who falls for a prostitute, becomes her unwilling pimp, then schemes to keep her off the streets is "funny and well done"; MacLaine plays the "hooker with a heart of gold" perfectly, while Lemmon mugs winningly in a dual role.

Iron Giant, The 24 | – | 25 | 25

1999. Directed by Brad Bird. Animated. 86 minutes. Rated PG.

■ "Markedly different from other animated films", this story of a "quirky" "boy and an enormous robot from outer space" is both a "sly satire of the '50s" and a "tender" "message" flick about "tolerance and non-violence"; "criminally underrated" (it "slipped through the cracks due to poor marketing"), it's "entertaining" and "deserves to be seen."

IT HAPPENED ONE NIGHT ✉◑ 28 | 28 | 26 | 25

1934. Directed by Frank Capra. With Clark Gable, Claudette Colbert. 105 minutes. Not Rated.

■ "Gable and Colbert are swell together" in this "great Depression spirit-lifter", the "mother of all screwball comedies" about a "wisecracking tabloid reporter" and a "snooty heiress" "on the run"; the first picture to "sweep all the major Oscars", it was also considered rather "racy for its time": indeed, Gable's baring of his chest in the famed "walls of Jericho" sequence sent the "undershirt industry" into a tizzy.

It's a Mad Mad Mad Mad World 24 | 21 | 22 | 23

1963. Directed by Stanley Kramer. With Spencer Tracy, Milton Berle, Sid Caesar, Buddy Hackett, Mickey Rooney, Ethel Merman. 192 minutes. Rated G.

■ The ultimate "car comedy", this "sprawling" "gut-buster" features a "huge cast" of "crème de la crème" comedians in an "every-man-for-himself" "race to find a hidden fortune"; sure, it's a "long long long long movie", but it's "still terrifically entertaining" with plenty of "silly slapstick" and "great cameos" to keep things lively; best moment: "Jonathan Winters single-handedly tearing up a gas station."

IT'S A WONDERFUL LIFE ◑ 27 | 27 | 27 | 25

1946. Directed by Frank Capra. With James Stewart, Donna Reed, Henry Travers. 130 minutes. Not Rated.

■ "Nobody tells a story like Capra", and this "inspirational" film "strikes a fundamental chord with lots of people" via its "small-town" story about a "good guy" coping with "hard times" and proving "how one life can make a difference"; sure, it's a "little schmaltzy" and "surprisingly dark", but most say "it's a wonderful picture" and "Christmas wouldn't be Christmas without it" – even if you've seen it a "million times" on TV.

Jagged Edge 22 | 22 | 22 | 20

1985. Directed by Richard Marquand. With Glenn Close, Jeff Bridges, Peter Coyote. 108 minutes. Rated R.

■ This "entertaining murder" thriller tells the tale of a "grisly homicide and a sensational trial intertwined with a forbidden love affair"; "great performances" from "'80s diva" Close (as a lawyer with principles) and Bridges (as the client endowed with troubling "charm") keep it so "exciting and suspenseful" that you'll be "guessing to the very end."

James and the Giant Peach 20 | – | 20 | 24

1996. Directed by Henry Selick. Animated. 79 minutes. Rated PG.

"Fantastic effects", a kinetic visual style and bushels of "charm" give this "quirky" cartoon a "different look and feel from the typical animated movie"; the story of a boy and a house-size fruit, it blends "live-action" shots with "stop-motion" and digital animation, though the result is "too edgy" and "bizarre" for those who claim Roald Dahl's "book is much better."

Jane Eyre ◑∅ 25 | 27 | 26 | 22

1944. Directed by Robert Stevenson. With Orson Welles, Joan Fontaine, Margaret O'Brien. 97 minutes. Not Rated.

■ A "moody rendition of the Brontë novel", this "damn good" "Gothic romance" concerns a "frail" governess, a rich landowner and a houseful of dark secrets; expect plenty of "gloom and doom from the get-go" followed by atmospheric "shadows" and "Orson scowling" throughout – but as for that "disappointingly contrived ending", blame the author, not Hollywood.

Jaws Ⓘ 26 | 22 | 25 | 26

1975. Directed by Steven Spielberg. With Roy Scheider, Robert Shaw, Richard Dreyfuss. 124 minutes. Rated PG-13.

■ "Sink your teeth" into this "classic summer" scarefest that "still gets the adrenaline pumping", since it's got "everything": "horrifying shark attacks", "missing limbs", "crackling" John Williams music and even "fully developed characters"; it "launched the Spielberg juggernaut" by cleverly "making you fear what you don't see", and if the title character looks a bit dated today, the "seasick" wonder "will it ever be safe to go back in the water?"

JEAN DE FLORETTE Ⓘ F 27 | 27 | 26 | 26

1987. Directed by Claude Berri. With Yves Montand, Gérard Depardieu. 120 minutes. Rated PG.

■ "As Balzacian as French cinema can get", this "epic" drama about farmers feuding over a natural spring in the "pastoral paradise of Provence" is "stunningly beautiful" and "totally compelling"; since it's only the "first half of a genuinely tragic tale", "make sure to see *Manon of the Spring*" (its sequel) afterward to get the full scope of this truly "unforgettable story."

Jeremiah Johnson 23 | 21 | 23 | 22

1972. Directed by Sydney Pollack. With Robert Redford, Will Geer, Stefan Gierasch. 108 minutes. Rated PG.

■ "One of the earliest Westerns to change the old movie stereotypes of Indian ways", this saga relates the story of an American soldier turned "mountain man" and his pitched, emotional battle with Crow Nation warriors; a precursor of *Dances with Wolves,* it showcases Redford "at his best" and is a "classic" to true believers.

Jerk, The 22 | 21 | 19 | 18

1979. Directed by Carl Reiner. With Steve Martin, Bernadette Peters, Catlin Adams. 94 minutes. Rated R.

■ Opening with "one of the best lines ever" – "I was born a poor black child" – this "absolutely hysterical" "rags-to-riches-to-rags" comedy captures the "wacky early Steve Martin" in all his "zany" glory (with ample support from Peters as his "sweetly naive love interest"); some snort it's "totally silly", but "that's exactly the point."

Jerry Maguire 21 | 22 | 21 | 20

1996. Directed by Cameron Crowe. With Tom Cruise, Cuba Gooding Jr., Renée Zellweger. 138 minutes. Rated R.

■ A "gutsy sports agent" "sees the light" and "rediscovers his soul" in this "crowd-pleasing" dramedy that blends "football and love" into an "honest", "better-than-average" brew; in the "tailor-made" title role, "Tom terrific" plays "Mr. Show Me the Money" with excellent backup from the Oscar-winning Gooding and "little kid" Jonathan Lipnicki (who "steals the movie"); best line: "you had me at hello."

Jesus Christ Superstar 21 | 18 | 22 | 21

1973. Directed by Norman Jewison. With Ted Neeley, Carl Anderson, Yvonne Elliman. 108 minutes. Rated G.

◪ "Old flower children" find religion in this "visually arresting" "rock opera", a "fantastic" depiction of "Christ's humanity" featuring "hottie" Neeley in the title role and possibly the "best Lloyd Webber score" ever; heretics say it's "overindulgent" and "not as good as the stage show", speculating that the "cast was stoned the entire time" and thus it all "made sense to them."

JFK 19 | 20 | 20 | 21

1991. Directed by Oliver Stone. With Kevin Costner, Kevin Bacon, Tommy Lee Jones. 189 minutes. Rated R.

◪ This "riveting", "revisionist" "conspiracy theory" drama about "what really happened on November 22, 1963" is, at the very least, a look at "what *might* have happened"; zealots swear it "makes a pretty good case" and delivers some "pull-out-all-the-stops" punches, but debunkers dub it "powerful paranoia" with "too many ifs, buts and maybes to be credible"; in the end, "whether truth or fiction", it remains as "controversial" as ever.

Journey to the Center of the Earth ∅ 19 | 16 | 21 | 18

1959. Directed by Henry Levin. With James Mason, Pat Boone, Arlene Dahl. 132 minutes. Rated G.

■ "Bernard Herrmann's score lends enchantment" to this "enjoyable" production based on "Jules Verne's fantastical tale" of underground exploration that's a "fun" sci-fi "romp" worth seeking out in a "widescreen" format; sure, it's a tad "overwrought" and "hokey", but "kiddies" like its "Disney-esque" flavor and "superior special effects."

Judgment at Nuremberg ✉◑∅ 26 | 27 | 25 | 22

1961. Directed by Stanley Kramer. With Spencer Tracy, Burt Lancaster, Richard Widmark. 178 minutes. Not Rated.

■ Based on the "historic" 1948 Nazi war criminal trials, this "excellent courtroom drama" "asks some tough questions" and boasts "uniformly fine" players "often cast against type", as well as a "brilliant", Oscar-winning script; though the issues it raises are "unsettling", it remains a "relevant" "movie that everyone should see."

Jules and Jim ◑🅵 24 | 26 | 24 | 23

1962. Directed by François Truffaut. With Jeanne Moreau, Oskar Werner, Henri Serre. 100 minutes. Not Rated.

■ One of the "milestones of the French New Wave", this "charming" "Truffaut masterpiece" is the "ultimate" "love triangle", wherein Moreau's "enigmatic beauty" makes her the "elusive muse" of two best friends; the "chemistry" between the players is "haunting and lyrical", and though that "bad-dream" ending is mighty "sad", the "fascinating story" proves "how complicated life can be."

Jumanji 18 | 18 | 19 | 22

1995. Directed by Joe Johnston. With Robin Williams, Bonnie Hunt, Kirsten Dunst. 104 minutes. Rated PG.

◪ "You'll see rolling dice in a whole different light" after a look at this "smartly done" adventure fantasy about a "mysterious board game" that swallows a young boy and coughs him up a quarter-century later – "along with a number of rampaging animals"; despite a "very cool concept" with "lots of action" and "loud CGI effects", it's "too scary for younger children" and ultimately might be a better "theme-park ride than movie."

Jungle Book, The 23 | – | 23 | 24

1967. Directed by Wolfgang Reitherman. Animated. 78 minutes. Rated G.

■ Kipling's "Tarzan-like character and all his friends" pop up in this "charming" Disney cartoon (the last overseen by Walt) that "makes an impression" with a "crowd-pleasing" story full of "family fun"; it might not be the studio's "best animation", but its "enchanting" soundtrack has enough "delightful songs" to make for a thing of "pure joy."

Jurassic Park Ⓘ 22 | 16 | 22 | 27

1993. Directed by Steven Spielberg. With Sam Neill, Laura Dern, Jeff Goldblum. 127 minutes. Rated PG-13.

◪ "Humans are upstaged by dinosaurs" in this sci-fi "thrill ride" from the "astounding" Spielberg set in an extinct-creatures-come-to-life theme park that's "every child's dream come true"; don't expect much from the "lame story" and "weak" actors (nothing more than "dinochow"), but hold on for "white-knuckle", "roller-coaster" pacing and "astounding special effects" so "truly frightening" that they "might scare younger viewers."

Karate Kid, The Ⓣ 19 | 16 | 20 | 17

1984. Directed by John G. Avildsen. With Ralph Macchio, Pat Morita, Elisabeth Shue. 126 minutes. Rated PG.

◪ "*Rocky* for teenagers", this "classic" "underdog-wins-the-day story" matches a "kid finding it hard to fit in" with a martial-arts "mentor" who teaches him control through "discipline and loyalty"; balancing "solid values" with "doses of action", this "not-typical teen movie" has the "coming-of-age" thing down pat while being "inspiring" and "entertaining throughout."

Key Largo ◑ 26 | 26 | 23 | 23

1948. Directed by John Huston. With Humphrey Bogart, Edward G. Robinson, Lauren Bacall. 101 minutes. Not Rated.

■ "Tough guys and dolls bring back the golden Warner Brothers days" in this "hard-hitting" noir showcase about a group held hostage by a "super-rat" of a gangster – until "anti-hero" Bogart shows up; near the "top of Huston's body of work", it features a "highly suspenseful" plot, "stellar performances" and some "vintage" "Bogey and Bacall" moments – "'nuff said."

Killers, The ◑∅ 25 | 25 | 25 | 23

1946. Directed by Robert Siodmak. With Burt Lancaster, Ava Gardner, Edmond O'Brien. 105 minutes. Not Rated.

■ "Lancaster makes a powerful film debut" backed up by an "outstanding" Gardner in this "riveting" flick "expanded from the Hemingway short story" about a mysterious small-town murder and its aftermath; it gets to the "core of film noir" through a burbling mix of "moral ambiguity, sexual tension and crime", and the "opening ten minutes" are something to see.

Killing Fields, The 26 | 26 | 27 | 25

1984. Directed by Roland Joffé. With Sam Waterston, Haing S. Ngor, John Malkovich. 141 minutes. Rated R.

■ "Friendship is tested by war" in this "harrowing" "true story" "told through the eyes of a journalist" relating the "atrocities in Cambodia" and the "horrors of the Khmer Rouge" following the U.S. pullout from Vietnam; "worthy Oscar-winner Ngor" (a real-life survivor of this "holocaust") turns in a "bravely honest" performance that "will move you to tears" and "make you think" a lot.

Kind Hearts and Coronets ◑ 26 | 28 | 26 | 24

1949. Directed by Robert Hamer. With Alec Guinness, Dennis Price, Valerie Hobson. 106 minutes. Not Rated.

■ For "quintessential" "English humor" that "gets better with each viewing", try this "matchless black comedy" about the disinherited scion of a noble clan who tries to achieve dukedom through serial murder; in an inspired twist, his victims – all eight of them – are played by the one-and-only Alec Guinness, whose performance squarely places this one on the "forever best list."

King and I, The ✉ 27 | 26 | 25 | 27

1956. Directed by Walter Lang. With Yul Brynner, Deborah Kerr, Rita Moreno. 133 minutes. Rated G.

■ The "'Shall We Dance' scene" alone is "worth the price of admission" to this regally "sumptuous" version of Rodgers and Hammerstein's "terrific, old-fashioned" Broadway musical; although it may be "historically inaccurate", "who cares?" given the "stunning production", "gorgeous score" and "totally engaging" team of the "lovely Kerr" "getting to know" Oscar-winner Brynner; in sum, "bravos all around."

King Kong ◑Ⓘ∅ 25 | 15 | 24 | 24

1933. Directed by Merian C. Cooper, Ernest B. Schoedsack. With Fay Wray, Robert Armstrong, Bruce Cabot. 100 minutes. Rated PG.

■ This "granddaddy of all monster flicks" "still rules the roost" as an "essential piece of cinema history" and the inspiration for "countless" imitators; ok, the "stop-motion" special effects are "Stone Age–stuff by today's production standards", but this "warped beauty-and-the-beast saga" remains memorable for its "indelible" imagery, that iconic "climax atop the Empire State Building" and most of all for the "irreplaceable" Fay Wray, "filmdom's finest screamer."

King of Comedy, The ∅ 23 | 26 | 23 | 21

1983. Directed by Martin Scorsese. With Robert De Niro, Jerry Lewis, Sandra Bernhard. 101 minutes. Rated PG.

■ "Sharp, insightful and totally original", this pitch-black comedy about a wanna-be comedian and the talk-show host he stalks is a different kind of "De Niro psycho flick" that's "complex and unsettling, but kind of fun"; as the stalkee, Lewis is both "funny and sad" ("maybe the French do know something"), and the picture itself is the "most underrated of Scorsese's career."

King Solomon's Mines 20 | 18 | 20 | 22

1950. Directed by Compton Bennett, Andrew Marton. With Stewart Granger, Deborah Kerr. 103 minutes. Not Rated.

◪ "Location filming on the breathtakingly beautiful African continent" is the raison d'être of this H. Rider Haggard "chestnut" that's "hardly the most realistic" action flick, but a "good enough rendition" for most; it delivers some "romance" (via its "matinee idol" stars) and some "camp" (that "noble savages" subtext), but whether it's truly "Indiana Jones *before* Indiana Jones" is your call.

Kiss Me Kate ∅ 24 | 21 | 24 | 25

1953. Directed by George Sidney. With Howard Keel, Kathryn Grayson, Ann Miller. 109 minutes. Not Rated.

■ "Cole Porter's Broadway smash" "gets the Hollywood treatment" in this "sparkling film version" that's a reworking of "*The Taming of the Shrew*" "fortified with song and dance"; even though the "principals lack star power", you can still "brush up on your Shakespeare" nicely with "great musical numbers" and "exciting dancing", which come together famously in Miller's "knock-'em-dead" turn in 'Too Darn Hot.'

Kiss of the Spider Woman ⊠∅ 22 | 25 | 22 | 21

1985. Directed by Hector Babenco. With William Hurt, Raul Julia, Sonia Braga. 120 minutes. Rated R.

■ An "odd couple" – a political activist and a gay pederast – inhabit the same "prison cell" in this "intense drama" "based on the Manuel Puig novel" that deals with "love, discrimination, corruption and redemption"; though "worth seeing" for its "moving" script and Hurt's Oscar-winning turn, it may be a bit too much for "mainstream audiences."

Klute ⊠ 20 | 23 | 21 | 19

1971. Directed by Alan J. Pakula. With Jane Fonda, Donald Sutherland, Roy Scheider. 114 minutes. Rated R.

■ Oscar-winner Fonda stars as an "unhappy hooker" "stalked by a killer" but protected by an "excellent" Sutherland as the cop who humanizes her in this "heart-pounding" thriller; it "avoids all the clichés" of the genre via a chillingly matter-of-fact script, and if a bit "forgotten", at least Jane's shag "hairdo" is memorable.

Kramer vs. Kramer ⊠ 23 | 26 | 23 | 21

1979. Directed by Robert Benton. With Dustin Hoffman, Meryl Streep, Justin Henry. 105 minutes. Rated PG.

■ "All about the acting", this "riveting drama" won Oscars for Hoffman and Streep as a "married couple" undergoing the "trauma of divorce and child custody"; overturning the "gender-biased view of parenting", its depiction of a growing "father-son relationship" is the core of the story, though ultimately its "heart-wrenching" theme "hits you hard" – "there are no winners" in this split-up.

La Cage aux Folles Ⓘ🅵 24 | 26 | 25 | 22

1979. Directed by Edouard Molinaro. With Michel Serrault, Ugo Tognazzi, Remy Laurent. 100 minutes. Rated R.

■ "Funnier than the American remake", the "Broadway musical" and the "two sequels", this "absurd" French "farce" is "light-years ahead of its time" recounting the story of a gay couple forced to "play it straight" in order to impress prospective in-laws; "overacted to perfection" by an "unbeatable" cast, it defines flaming, "fun-filled frivolity", even if a few cluck it's become "a bit faded" with time.

L.A. Confidential ⊠ 26 | 27 | 25 | 26

1997. Directed by Curtis Hanson. With Kevin Spacey, Russell Crowe, Guy Pearce, Kim Basinger. 138 minutes. Rated R.

■ "Every nuance is perfect" in this "steamy" "period" crime drama, an "explosive exposé" about "crooks, hookers" and "police corruption" in '50s LA that's "sharp", "detailed" and "violent as hell"; though it "made a star of Crowe", the overall "dead-on casting" advances the "case for an ensemble acting award", while the "smart", Oscar-winning script has "all the grit" of a "film noir" classic, boosted by "21st-century production values."

La Dolce Vita ◑ F ∅ 25 | 25 | 23 | 25

1961. Directed by Federico Fellini. With Marcello Mastroianni, Anita Ekberg, Anouk Aimée. 167 minutes. Not Rated.

■ "Celebrity-obsessed culture" goes under the microscope in this "scandalous" study of "decadence", "damnation and redemption" as seen in '60s Rome through the eyes of a jaded gossip columnist (Mastroianni "at his best") fed up with the "sweet life"; arguably "Fellini's most famous" film, it's a "decidedly unglamorous look at glamour" that "introduced the word 'paparazzi'" into the world lexicon; most iconic scene: "Anita Ekberg in the Trevi Fountain."

Lady and the Tramp 26 | – | 24 | 25

1955. Directed by Wilfred Jackson, Hamilton Luske, Clyde Geronimi. Animated. 75 minutes. Rated G.

■ Puppy love gets a "gorgeous vintage Disney" spin in this "cute" canine romance awash in "lush animation" and lensed in "beautiful" CinemaScope; doggy devotees adore its fetching characters, "endearing story" and "great songs" ("highlighted by Peggy Lee's" sultry rendition of 'He's a Tramp'), though the most unforgettable moment has to be its "famous spaghetti kiss."

LADY EVE, THE ◑ 28 | 28 | 27 | 26

1941. Directed by Preston Sturges. With Barbara Stanwyck, Henry Fonda. 97 minutes. Not Rated.

■ "Steamy innuendo" and "wacky" "pratfalls" coexist in this "smart" "Preston Sturges romp" about a "scheming con artist" out to "snare an unsuspecting" "wealthy geek", aided by an "outstanding supporting cast" of "cardsharps"; a "sassy", "shameless" Stanwyck does "that sultry thing" so well that Fonda's "bumbling" "rube" "doesn't stand a chance" in this "slyly" "amusing" "screwball comedy" that many pronounce "perfect."

Lady from Shanghai, The ◑ 25 | 23 | 22 | 26

1948. Directed by Orson Welles. With Orson Welles, Rita Hayworth, Everett Sloane. 87 minutes. Not Rated.

◪ "Another Orson Welles achievement", this "bravura" "B movie" is "completely enjoyable" for many, thanks to some memorable "stand-out scenes": the "shootout in the hall of mirrors", "Rita Hayworth speaking Chinese"; still, skeptics shrug the plot is a "confusing mess" that "looks like it's been cut to death"; your call.

La Femme Nikita F 23 | 22 | 24 | 23

1991. Directed by Luc Besson. With Anne Parillaud, Jean-Hugues Anglade, Jeanne Moreau. 115 minutes. Rated R.

■ The "intelligent foreign film" gets a "violent jolt of adrenaline" in this "fast-paced" but "thought-provoking" "tough chick" flick about a punk junkie turned professional "assassin"; as the "kick-ass" lead, the "mesmerizing" Parillaud performs "spectacular stunts" that "hold your attention" so completely that it's more than "worth the effort to read the subtitles"; P.S. just forget about the "pathetic American remake."

Last Emperor, The ✉ 26 | 24 | 25 | 28

1987. Directed by Bernardo Bertolucci. With John Lone, Joan Chen, Peter O'Toole. 160 minutes. Rated PG-13.

■ "Truly an epic, and a darned good one" at that, this "sweeping", "large-scale" bio tells the story of China's "final monarch" from his ascent to the throne at age 3 through war, occupation and "revolutionary changes" in his kingdom; credit "lavish" sets, "spectacular scenery" and "outstanding" acting by Lone and O'Toole for its winning an impressive "nine Academy Awards"; N.B. the running time can vary, since several versions exist, but all are on the "long" side.

Last of the Mohicans, The 22 | 22 | 22 | 25

1992. Directed by Michael Mann. With Daniel Day-Lewis, Madeleine Stowe, Russell Means. 122 minutes. Rated R.

■ For a "realistic portrayal of the French and Indian War", this "historical adventure set in the battle-torn American colonies" doesn't stint on the "atrocities and barbarism", though they're tempered by "beautiful scenery" and an "incredible score"; "truly evil villains and larger-than-life heroes" make this "wonderful realization of James Fenimore Cooper's book" "top-notch filmmaking."

L.A. Story 20 | 20 | 20 | 19

1991. Directed by Mick Jackson. With Steve Martin, Victoria Tennant. 95 minutes. Rated PG-13.

■ "Every LA stereotype is played for laughs" in this "on-point" romantic comedy that's a "biting" if "loving put-down" of the "outrageous city" where people "really do drive down the road to get the mail"; Martin's "effortlessly" "intelligent" script throws "disarmingly wacky" curves – and foretells the Starbucks invasion with its priceless "half-caff-triple-shot-no-foam-cappuccino" scene.

Last Picture Show, The ◑Ⓘ 23 | 23 | 23 | 22

1971. Directed by Peter Bogdanovich. With Timothy Bottoms, Jeff Bridges, Cybill Shepherd, Ben Johnson. 118 minutes. Rated R.

■ This "gritty" "portrait of a small Texas town on the brink of extinction" is "stunningly realized" in Bogdanovich's "masterpiece" that captures the loss so well "you can practically hear the death rattle"; the "birthplace of many new stars", it features some mighty "raw performances" from its "marvelous ensemble", a "strong script" and ultra-"realistic production values"; in short, it's a "lovely" if "sad" tribute to "something intrinsically American."

LA STRADA ⊠◑🄵 27 | 28 | 26 | 25

1956. Directed by Federico Fellini. With Giulietta Masina, Anthony Quinn, Richard Basehart. 108 minutes. Not Rated.

■ Set in a "traveling circus", Fellini's "parable of goodness thwarted by cruelty" pairs a "strongman who's all muscle and no heart" with a "peasant girl who's nothing but heart"; the "waif-like" Masina is "luminous" opposite a "surprisingly good" Quinn, and combined with "beautiful imagery" and "sad" "music that will stay with you", it's plain to see why this "masterwork" won the very first Best Foreign Film Oscar.

Last Seduction, The Ⓘ∅ 22 | 24 | 22 | 20

1994. Directed by John Dahl. With Linda Fiorentino, Peter Berg, Bill Pullman. 110 minutes. Rated R.

■ "Fiorentino sizzles" as a "bad"-to-the-bone "femme fatale" in this "deliciously wicked" neo-noir crime thriller about a "very sexy" gal who rips off her husband and takes cover with a love-struck doofus; sure, it's "low budget" and there may be more than a few "holes in the plot", but "man, what a ride!"

Last Temptation of Christ, The 22 | 23 | 25 | 22

1988. Directed by Martin Scorsese. With Willem Dafoe, Harvey Keitel, Barbara Hershey. 164 minutes. Rated R.

◪ "Controversial" with a capital C, this "intriguing" drama "re-examines Christian faith" by portraying "one of the most humanizing perspectives on Jesus" ever filmed; of course, those who are "rigid on the Scriptures" consider it blasphemous (and it's still not available in certain video chains to this day), but believers say this "absorbing", "important" Scorsese drama must "be seen to be criticized."

Last Waltz, The 26 | - | 20 | 26

1978. Directed by Martin Scorsese. Documentary. With The Band. 117 minutes. Rated PG.

■ In the running for "best concert movie of all time", this renowned documentary "captures the end of a rock 'n' roll era" in its recording of The Band's last gasp, abetted by a musical "dream team" that includes, among others, Bob Dylan, Eric Clapton, Joni Mitchell, Muddy Waters, Ringo Starr and Van Morrison; a "classic" "high-water mark", it's "clearly a labor of love from Scorsese" that "shouldn't be this good, but it is."

Laura ◑∅ 27 | 25 | 27 | 26

1944. Directed by Otto Preminger. With Gene Tierney, Dana Andrews, Clifton Webb. 88 minutes. Not Rated.

■ A "suspenseful, elegant whodunit" "with a twist" – the "detective falls in love with the murder victim" – this "chic" take on film noir provides plenty of "romantic goose bumps" owing to the simmering "chemistry" between the "brooding" Andrews and "exquisite" Tierney; throw in some "haunting music" and a "nicely paced" if somewhat "silly plot", and the result is "Preminger's best flick."

Lavender Hill Mob, The ⊠◑∅ 25 | 26 | 23 | 22
1951. Directed by Charles Crichton. With Alec Guinness, Stanley Holloway. 78 minutes. Not Rated.
■ "Wittily whimsical", this British comic "gem" "helped introduce Alec Guinness" – an "actor's actor with the most expressive raised eyebrow in film" – to American audiences; the caper-gone-awry story involving a milquetoast bank clerk who dreams up the "perfect crime" is "delightfully funny" thanks to its "wonderful", Oscar-winning script.

LAWRENCE OF ARABIA ⊠ 29 | 28 | 27 | 29
1962. Directed by David Lean. With Peter O'Toole, Omar Sharif, Alec Guinness. 222 minutes. Rated PG.
■ The "biggest epic of them all", this bio of WWI British soldier T.E. Lawrence "sets the standard for large-scale" filmmaking with its "stunning" desert cinematography, "suspense by the duneful" and "stupendous cast", led by O'Toole in a "perfect" role; thanks to Lean's "painterly techniques", the "background is as consistently amazing as the foreground" in this "gold standard" of an Oscar magnet that "demands to be seen on the big screen."

League of Their Own, A 20 | 20 | 22 | 20
1992. Directed by Penny Marshall. With Geena Davis, Tom Hanks, Madonna, Lori Petty. 128 minutes. Rated PG.
■ "There's no crying in baseball", though this "nostalgic gem" about a WWII women's team has fans weeping with joy over its "groundbreaking" subject matter and "fantastic" ensemble cast ("even Madonna is good"); "bringing back the innocence" of simpler times, this "piece of history" might have a "sentimental epilogue", but the "brilliant Hanks" and its overall "feel-good" aura make it "highly rewatchable."

Leaving Las Vegas ⊠ 20 | 24 | 18 | 18
1995. Directed by Mike Figgis. With Nicolas Cage, Elisabeth Shue, Julian Sands. 111 minutes. Rated R.
◪ "Disturbing", "depressing" and "painful to watch", this "tragic love story" between a "suicidal alcoholic" and a "burned-out prostitute" is still "brilliant in all aspects", leaving viewers "emotionally drained"; while giddy fans agree the "damn good" Cage "deservedly won the Oscar" for his "best work thus far", soberer sorts bemoan this "feel-bad" flick as the "ultimate downer."

Legally Blonde 19 | 20 | 17 | 19
2001. Directed by Robert Luketic. With Reese Witherspoon, Luke Wilson. 96 minutes. Rated PG-13.
◪ The near-unanimous verdict on this "*Clueless*-goes-to-law-school" comedy: the "cute-as-a-button" Witherspoon is "irresistible" as a "Valley Girl" "bursting the stereotype" and proving that "anyone can achieve their dream"; though most jurors decree that "even an intellectual can like" this "pink puffball of a movie", the unconvinced harrumph "there ought to be a law" against such "derivative piffle."

Legend 18 | 15 | 18 | 22

1986. Directed by Ridley Scott. With Tom Cruise, Mia Sara, Tim Curry, David Bennent. 94 minutes. Rated PG.

◪ "Fantasy" fanatics adore this "mythical" tale of a quest to rescue an "innocent princess" and free the "last remaining unicorn" by a group of "bumbling elves" and a "forest boy" (Tom Cruise "before he became *the* Tom Cruise"); while it's "stylized" and "atmospheric" enough to be a "guilty pleasure" for some, the "dippy" dialogue makes it a "prize winner in the unintentional humor" department for others.

Legends of the Fall 20 | 21 | 20 | 23

1994. Directed by Edward Zwick. With Brad Pitt, Anthony Hopkins, Aidan Quinn, Julia Ormond. 133 minutes. Rated R.

■ This "sweeping epic" set in "untamed 19th-century America" chronicles "one family's struggle in times of political turmoil" and the "moving" story of a woman "tragically passed between three brothers"; sure, a few label it "pretentious" and "no threat to the best Westerns", but there are no complaints about the "fantastic scenery" (including a "gorgeous, captivating" Ormond) – and "nothing beats Pitt riding in on that horse!"

Lethal Weapon Ⓘ 21 | 19 | 20 | 21

1987. Directed by Richard Donner. With Mel Gibson, Danny Glover, Gary Busey. 112 minutes. Rated R.

■ "Top-notch" action peppered with "plenty of laughs" establishes this "classic buddy" flick as the "first and best of the franchise" (three sequels and counting); as "hard-bitten, job-weary" LA detectives, Gibson and Glover are "at the top of their form" with such "tremendous chemistry" that the picture became the "model for '80s cop movies", a "classic" of the genre.

Lifeboat ◑∅ 25 | 26 | 25 | 22

1944. Directed by Alfred Hitchcock. With Tallulah Bankhead, William Bendix, Walter Slezak. 96 minutes. Not Rated.

■ "Can a one-set movie hold your attention?": well, this "fascinating Hitchcock" war-era thriller does, providing "more drama per square inch", since the "entire picture takes place in a small lifeboat"; among the "bickering crew of castaways", Bankhead is "superb, dahling", but blink and you'll miss the director's "inspired" cameo appearance.

LIFE IS BEAUTIFUL ✉ F 27 | 27 | 27 | 25

1998. Directed by Roberto Benigni. With Roberto Benigni, Nicoletta Braschi. 118 minutes. Rated PG-13.

■ Simultaneously "heart-wrenching" and "uplifting", this "truly important" story about an Italian family's attempt to shelter their son from the Holocaust is a "bittersweet fable about the triumph of the human spirit"; the Oscar-winning Benigni provides an "emotional roller-coaster ride" with some "inspired comedic" touches, and though some "uncomfortable" viewers suggest a "trivialization" of a very serious subject, most agree "if you don't shed a tear, you're not human."

Life of Brian 23 | 21 | 23 | 20

1979. Directed by Terry Jones. With Monty Python. 94 minutes. Rated R.

■ "Profane, sacrilegious and really funny", this "hysterical" "cult classic" about a Holy Land sad sack mistaken for the Messiah is "as bitingly original a spoof as has ever been made" and "probably one of God's favorites"; only "Monty Python at their finest" could "get away with" the final scene that "sends you off singing 'Always Look on the Bright Side of Life.'"

Like Water for Chocolate F 25 | 24 | 25 | 25

1993. Directed by Alfonso Arau. With Lumi Cavazos, Marco Leonardi. 123 minutes. Rated R.

■ "Ahh, food and sex" make a "lip-smacking" combination in this "mouthwatering" Mexican "foodie classic" that serves up an "eccentric" love story that's "as pleasing to the eye as it is to the palate"; "deliciously" "true to the novel", it offers "magical realism at its best" and, "like a warm dessert", leaves one feeling so "content and hopeful" that many show up for "another helping"; P.S. "don't let the subtitles scare you off."

Lilies of the Field ✉◑ 25 | 26 | 24 | 23

1963. Directed by Ralph Nelson. With Sidney Poitier, Lilia Skala, Stanley Adams. 94 minutes. Not Rated.

■ With his "flawless" performance in this "quiet, simple" tale about a handyman who helps refugee nuns build a chapel, Poitier became the first African-American to win a lead-role Oscar and also helped "open up racial dialogue" in the Civil Rights era; the film's many admirers hail a "sweet story" told with "heart and charm" that delivers a "lesson in dignity and trust" – "raise the roof and your voice in song."

LION IN WINTER, THE ✉ 28 | 29 | 27 | 26

1968. Directed by Anthony Harvey. With Peter O'Toole, Katharine Hepburn. 134 minutes. Rated PG.

■ Hepburn and O'Toole give "performances so brilliant your eyes will hurt" as "two titans battling each other and history" in this "intelligent, delicious" drama that reigns as "one of the best historical films ever made"; indeed, this "masterful" look at Henry II and Eleanor of Aquitaine (the original "dysfunctional royal family") is so "superb" that it earned Kate her third Oscar, as well as statuettes for its "sparkling" screenplay and score.

Lion King, The ∅ 25 | – | 25 | 27

1994. Directed by Roger Allers, Rob Minkoff. Animated. 89 minutes. Rated G.

■ *Hakuna Matata!*: this "crowning achievement" garners roars of approval as one of "Disney's best" thanks to its "breakthrough animation techniques", "toe-tapping" music and "exceptional voice characterizations by Matthew Broderick and Jeremy Irons"; though this "heartwarming" tale about an exiled lion cub (sort of the "same story as *Bambi*") is "touching" and often "comedic", the film has some bona fide "scary moments" and "may be too intense" for smaller fry.

Little Big Man ∅ 24 | 25 | 24 | 23

1970. Directed by Arthur Penn. With Dustin Hoffman, Faye Dunaway, Chief Dan George. 147 minutes. Rated PG.

■ A "rousing" Wild West "saga", this "memorable" "period piece" concerns a "Forrest Gump–like" character with a knack for popping up at "famous historical moments"; plaudits go to its "engrossing blend of humor and drama" and "great" performances by George and Hoffman ("truly the man of 1,000 faces") – indeed, it's "one of the best looks at Native Americans" in moviedom.

Little Mermaid, The 24 | – | 23 | 25

1989. Directed by Ron Clements, John Musker. Animated. 82 minutes. Rated G.

■ This "first of the great second wave of Disney classics" manages to "hold its own against *Cinderella* and *Snow White*", what with its delightful cartoon "critters", "witty dialogue" and "upbeat", Oscar-winning music that "made animation sing again"; sure, feminists discern a "sexist message" ("why does the woman have to change for the man?"), but in the end "how could you not love this adorable redheaded mermaid?"

Little Shop of Horrors 19 | 19 | 20 | 21

1986. Directed by Frank Oz. With Rick Moranis, Ellen Greene, Steve Martin. 94 minutes. Rated PG-13.

◪ If "campy" "sci-fi musicals" ring your bell, this "twisted" tale about a boy, a girl and a "smart-ass, man-eating plant" "ranks right up there with *The Rocky Horror Picture Show* as a cult classic"; credit the "great cast" and "humorously dark score" for the ensuing "goofy fun"; most "priceless" moment: Martin's "sadistic dentist" treating "masochist patient" Bill Murray.

Little Women 21 | 23 | 24 | 21

1994. Directed by Gillian Armstrong. With Winona Ryder, Susan Sarandon. 115 minutes. Rated PG.

◪ Surveyors are split on this "feminist" adaptation of Louisa May Alcott's classic novel about a Civil War–era family: partisans of George Cukor's 1933 version dismiss this remake as "unnecessary", harrumphing that "Ryder can't compare to Katharine Hepburn", yet others swear it's "worth watching for Sarandon's" performance alone; there's no debate, however, that its "great message" – about a "family loving each other no matter what" – is "very well done."

Live and Let Die 19 | 17 | 20 | 21

1973. Directed by Guy Hamilton. With Roger Moore, Jane Seymour, Yaphet Kotto. 119 minutes. Rated PG.

◪ Expect "beautiful women, fast cars", "snakes, voodoo and Yaphet Kotto" in this "exotic" James Bond caper set in the Caribbean and the "sultry South"; "nonstop" action sequences ("particularly the bayou boat chase"), "humor that's shaken (not stirred)" and Moore's "first and best" 007 impersonation make it worth watching – even if Sean Connery loyalists label it the "beginning of the decline."

Local Hero 26 | 24 | 26 | 23

1983. Directed by Bill Forsyth. With Burt Lancaster, Peter Riegert, Peter Capaldi. 111 minutes. Rated PG.

■ "The little people triumph over the money people" in this "understated but brilliant" comedy contrasting the differences between a "quaint Scottish town" and the "corporate world"; its "engaging characters", "quirky" storyline and Mark Knopfler's "great soundtrack" make for such "bighearted", "whimsical" fun that many argue it "deserves a larger following."

Lock, Stock and Two Smoking Barrels 23 | 22 | 25 | 23

1998. Directed by Guy Ritchie. With Jason Flemyng, Dexter Fletcher, Nick Moran. 105 minutes. Rated R.

■ "First-time director" Ritchie does a "brilliant job co-opting every gangster flick cliché" in this "violent but riveting" thriller that's a "Cockney" take on "*Pulp Fiction*"; agreed, it's "hard to understand the accents", but the "acting, setting and soundtrack are dead-on" and "super plot surprises" abound; all in all, this "fun romp with guns" is "lean", mean and "wonderfully produced."

Lolita ◑ 24 | 24 | 24 | 23

1962. Directed by Stanley Kubrick. With James Mason, Sue Lyon, Shelley Winters, Peter Sellers. 152 minutes. Not Rated.

■ Though this "fine adaptation of the Nabokov classic" might be somewhat "sanitized" ("it was made in 1962, after all"), it's still "slyly dirty" enough for its very adult subject, a middle-aged man's obsession with a barely teenaged girl; though ageists argue Lyon is "too old" for the title role, there still are plenty of "choice moments" supplied by Winters, who "gives the performance of her life", and an "extremely funny" Sellers.

Lone Star 25 | 25 | 25 | 22

1996. Directed by John Sayles. With Kris Kristofferson, Matthew McConaughey. 135 minutes. Rated R.

■ Director Sayles' "overlooked masterpiece" is a "flawless murder mystery that digs deep into the American psyche" and "takes a hard look at race relations"; following the discovery of a buried skeleton in a small Texas town, the plot goes through "more twists and turns than the Rio Grande" but still "works on multiple levels" as it "seamlessly interweaves multiple characters" – and that "ending will make your jaw drop."

Longest Day, The ◑ 24 | 20 | 25 | 26

1962. Directed by Ken Annakin, Andrew Marton et al. With John Wayne, Rod Steiger. 180 minutes. Rated G.

■ As far as "war-as-spectacle" epics go, this "sweeping" chronicle of the Normandy invasion sets the "standard by which all others are measured"; D-day devotees dig the "superb dedication to detail" and "all-star cast" that "really gets into their characters" thanks to a script that intelligently "includes the point of view of everyone involved"; still, foes snipe "too many cameos" turn it into a "cattle call."

Looking for Mr. Goodbar ∅ 18 | 21 | 19 | 18

1977. Directed by Richard Brooks. With Diane Keaton, Tuesday Weld, Richard Gere. 135 minutes. Rated R.

■ Powered by Keaton's "brilliant" turn as a "sexually repressed" teacher by day who "trolls the bars by night", this "sobering tale of '70s promiscuity" is a "dark" "primer for single women" that "sends chills down your spine" – with a "gruesome ending" delivered "like a sledgehammer upside the head"; P.S. yes, that's Richard Gere ("before he became a big star") as a "charming but unstable rascal."

LORD OF THE RINGS: THE FELLOWSHIP OF THE RING, THE ⓫ 27 | 25 | 27 | 29

2001. Directed by Peter Jackson. With Elijah Wood, Ian McKellen, Viggo Mortensen. 178 minutes. Rated PG-13.

■ This "enthralling", "true-to-the-book" retelling of Tolkein's classic epic "transcends the genre" and "sets the benchmark for fantasy films to come" with its "lovingly crafted" visualization of Middle Earth; despite a somewhat "slow beginning", "three hours of brilliant bliss" ensue that are "exhilaratingly" perfect, "right down to the hairy Hobbit feet"; indeed, the main downside is "waiting for the future episodes to be released."

Lost Horizon ◑ 25 | 24 | 26 | 22

1937. Directed by Frank Capra. With Ronald Colman, Jane Wyatt, Margo, Sam Jaffe. 138 minutes. Not Rated.

■ A "nostalgic reminder of Hollywood's Golden Age", this "moving" adaptation of James Hilton's best-seller still "casts a spell" thanks to an "irresistible" conceit, the utopia known as "Shangri-la"; sure, this "fairy tale" of a picture may seem rather "quaint" and "dated" now, but Colman's performance is "as contemporary as if it were made today."

Lost in America 20 | 20 | 21 | 17

1985. Directed by Albert Brooks. With Albert Brooks, Julie Hagerty, Garry Marshall. 91 minutes. Rated R.

■ Brooks' "seriously underrated" satire about a yuppie couple who chuck it all and hit the road is dryly "hilarious" filmmaking boasting what may be the "funniest first 45 minutes in movie history"; though a few lost souls protest the "premise doesn't quite get there", the majority reports the "situations, characters and jokes are all in sync."

Love Bug, The ⓘ 18 | 15 | 16 | 17

1969. Directed by Robert Stevenson. With Dean Jones, Michele Lee, Buddy Hackett. 107 minutes. Rated G.

■ "They don't get much sillier" than this "imaginative", "live-action" "Disney oldie" about Herbie, a "sweet" talking VW bug that supplies boomers with plenty of "fond memories"; it still "stands the test of time" well enough for it to be a perennial "rainy-afternoon" rental.

Love Is a Many-Splendored Thing 22 | 23 | 22 | 21

1955. Directed by Henry King. With Jennifer Jones, William Holden. 102 minutes. Not Rated.

■ "What drama! what heartbreak!" sigh admirers of this "classic" romantic "tearjerker", an "ahead-of-its-time" tale about an affair between a "liberated" Eurasian woman and a conflicted American war correspondent; ok, it's a tad "soppy" and "Jones isn't believable as a Eurasian", but the "breathtaking" Hong Kong scenery and "memorable", Oscar-winning theme song "make the whole thing worth it."

Love Story 19 | 18 | 20 | 18

1970. Directed by Arthur Hiller. With Ali MacGraw, Ryan O'Neal, Ray Milland. 99 minutes. Rated PG.

◪ "Get out the Kleenex" – this "three-hanky chick flick" about a "rich boy, a poor girl" and an incurable disease is applauded for its "adorable" leads, the "cute" O'Neal and "divine" MacGraw; critics of this "shameless" "schmaltz"-fest sneer that "love means having to say you're sorry every five minutes", but even they admit "30 years of soggy-eyed females can't be wrong."

M ◑ 🅵 26 | 26 | 26 | 23

1931. Directed by Fritz Lang. With Peter Lorre, Ellen Widmann, Gustaf Gründgens. 99 minutes. Not Rated.

■ Still "frightening seven decades later", this crime thriller from "brilliant" director Lang features Lorre as a "nervous, sweaty little child killer" in a "riveting" performance that evokes "horror and pity at the same time"; set in "'30s Berlin" "plunging headlong into fascism", it's known for its "expressionistic" camerawork and montage sequences that "set the benchmark for film editing"; N.B. this "masterwork" works best "in German with subtitles."

Mad Max ⓘ 20 | 17 | 19 | 19

1980. Directed by George Miller. With Mel Gibson, Joanne Samuel, Hugh Keays-Byme. 93 minutes. Rated R.

■ "Raw" and thrillingly "underproduced", this "seminal" tale of "post-apocalyptic", "Darwinian" "doom" is one of the "all-time great low-budget fantasies", done with "conviction and style"; it pits a "fabulous Mel in tight black leather" against some "truly bad bad guys" and is so "ultimately effective" that it spawned two sequels (though connoisseurs claim the first is "the best").

Madness of King George, The 22 | 26 | 23 | 24

1994. Directed by Nicholas Hytner. With Nigel Hawthorne, Helen Mirren, Ian Holm. 107 minutes. Rated PG-13.

■ "Insightful", "worthwhile" bio of the "mad, irascible" British monarch who, among other things, lost the American colonies; though "history buffs" declare the "accuracy is debatable", there's no debate about Hawthorne's "superb" performance (that "almost makes George III sympathetic"), nor that it's "visually stunning", with an Art Direction Oscar as proof.

Magnificent Seven, The Ⓘ 26 | 22 | 25 | 23

1960. Directed by John Sturges. With Yul Brynner, Steve McQueen, Eli Wallach. 128 minutes. Not Rated.

■ "Gunfighter cool" is alive and well in this "magnificent remake" of *The Seven Samurai* that "stands on its own" despite being "translated into a Western" and cast with "big stars of the '60s"; those who "never tire of watching it" "enjoy the adventure", "love the score" and attempt to "memorize the dialogue" that's become "fodder for countless movie trivia questions."

Magnolia 20 | 23 | 18 | 21

1999. Directed by Paul Thomas Anderson. With Tom Cruise, Julianne Moore, Philip Seymour Hoffman, Jason Robards Jr., John C. Reilly. 188 minutes. Rated R.

◪ "Love-it-or-hate-it" filmmaking from auteur Anderson that's either a "compelling" study of "unforgettable", "intersecting lives" in the San Fernando Valley or a "never-ending" "letdown" about a "bunch of dysfunctional people"; still, the direction is "energetic" and "Cruise actually acts", though some ask "what's up with the frogs?"

Malcolm X 23 | 26 | 23 | 23

1992. Directed by Spike Lee. With Denzel Washington, Angela Bassett, Al Freeman Jr. 194 minutes. Rated PG-13.

■ In this "galvanizing", "probing" bio, the "transformation" of Malcolm X from "young hustler" to "outspoken" "Civil Rights leader" is portrayed by an "emotional" Washington in such a "bravura", "sympathetic" way that many say he was "robbed of an Oscar"; still, this "profound" (if "slightly sanitized") film is a "time capsule of black American style" that resolutely "captivates and educates."

MALTESE FALCON, THE ◑ 28 | 27 | 27 | 25

1941. Directed by John Huston. With Humphrey Bogart, Mary Astor, Peter Lorre. 101 minutes. Not Rated.

■ The "stuff movies should be made of", this "vintage noir" "gem" boasts an "unforgettable Bogie" as the "hard-boiled detective" Sam Spade, plus a "blue-ribbon" supporting cast of "creeps and crooks", all searching for a mysterious "rara avis"; although its "taut script" that "runs like a Swiss watch" and "keeps you guessing to the end" is "often imitated", this "perfect rendering" of Dashiell Hammett's novel has been "never duplicated."

Man and a Woman, A ✉ Ⓘ F ∅ 24 | 24 | 24 | 24

1966. Directed by Claude Lelouch. With Anouk Aimée, Jean-Louis Trintignant. 102 minutes. Not Rated.

■ For "romance par excellence", this "touching", "very French" '60s "classic" is served with "panache" and is "still worth seeing" today – indeed, the "music alone can make you fall in love"; detailing an affair between a widow and widower, it stars a "beautiful Aimée" opposite "Trintignant at his best"; "see it with someone special" and you may produce your own little sequel.

MANCHURIAN CANDIDATE, THE ◑ 27 | 26 | 28 | 25

1962. Directed by John Frankenheimer. With Frank Sinatra, Laurence Harvey, Angela Lansbury. 126 minutes. Rated PG-13.

■ As "perfectly paranoid" "Cold War" filmmaking, this "provocative" "conspiracy thriller" about Korean War–era "brainwashing" still packs a "wallop" due to a "twist"-laden scenario culminating in a "take-your-breath-away" ending; Sinatra and Harvey are "electrifying", but the real revelation is Lansbury as a "diabolically evil", solitaire-playing mommy.

MAN FOR ALL SEASONS, A ✉ 28 | 28 | 27 | 27

1966. Directed by Fred Zinnemann. With Paul Scofield, Wendy Hiller, Robert Shaw. 120 minutes. Rated G.

■ "Intelligent" and "riveting in a quiet way", this "literate" historical drama about the "conflict between conscience and convenience" between Henry VIII and Sir Thomas More garnered six Oscars, including Best Actor for the "magnificent Scofield"; a "rare film about integrity", "loyalty and betrayal", it serves as a "reminder of the days when the movies enlightened."

Manhattan ◑ 26 | 24 | 23 | 24

1979. Directed by Woody Allen. With Woody Allen, Diane Keaton, Michael Murphy. 96 minutes. Rated R.

■ "Even NYers get all mushy" about this "love letter to the Big Apple" filmed in "fantastic black and white" and set to a thrilling "Gershwin soundtrack"; a romance laced with "angst", it appeals to those who like their "philosophy mixed with a little comedy" and is "more fully realized than *Annie Hall*"; in a nutshell, "it can be fun to be depressive."

Man Who Fell to Earth, The 18 | 18 | 20 | 17

1976. Directed by Nicolas Roeg. With David Bowie, Rip Torn, Candy Clark. 140 minutes. Rated R.

◪ Followers of this "way-ahead-of-its-time" sci-fi fantasy about an extraterrestrial "searching for water" to save his planet say it's "still relevant", citing its "inventive" storyline and "perfect casting" ("Bowie has no trouble playing a trippy alien"); however, some dismiss it as an "incoherent", "unwatchable mess" that's too "creepy and weird."

Man Who Knew Too Much, The 24 | 24 | 25 | 24

1956. Directed by Alfred Hitchcock. With James Stewart, Doris Day, Brenda de Banzie. 120 minutes. Rated PG.

■ A "Hitchcock remake of an earlier Hitchcock" thriller, this "more commercial" version plays up the "amazing ordinariness" of its "everyman" stars as they seek their kidnapped son; for most, it's "very exciting" – especially the "unbearably suspenseful" "scene in Royal Albert Hall" – though a few "could do without" Day's "cornball" rendition of 'Que Sera, Sera' (which still snagged a Best Song Oscar).

Man Who Shot Liberty Valance, The ◑ 25 | 24 | 25 | 23

1962. Directed by John Ford. With John Wayne, James Stewart, Vera Miles. 123 minutes. Not Rated.

■ The formidable Ford's "darkest Western" is illuminated by a "star-studded" cast featuring "all-time bad guy" Lee Marvin in his "finest performance", with "dynamic" backup from Wayne and Stewart; though a bit "claustrophobic" (it was filmed "mostly on soundstages"), this is still "mythic" moviemaking that "works like a huge, sprawling novel"; biggest surprise: "Wayne loses the girl."

Man Who Wasn't There, The ◑ 21 | 25 | 19 | 25

2001. Directed by Joel Coen. With Billy Bob Thornton, Frances McDormand, James Gandolfini. 116 minutes. Rated R.

■ This "quirky, haunting" take on film noir ("as only the Coen brothers can recreate it") charts the last days of a "hapless" small-town barber whose "decline is a metaphor for modern alienation"; the "stylistically incredible" cinematography is "so colorful you forget it's filmed in black and white", while Thornton's titular turn nearly "out-Bogarts Bogart."

Man Who Would Be King, The 25 | 26 | 26 | 25

1975. Directed by John Huston. With Sean Connery, Michael Caine, Christopher Plummer. 129 minutes. Rated PG.

■ Based on Kipling's "epic of friendship and heroism", this "classic adaptation" is a "ripsnorting", "good-time adventure" chronicling the perils of a pair of "opportunistic" "British rogues" on a "grand lark" in 19th-century "colonial India"; the combination of "sweeping vistas", "incandescent chemistry" between Connery and Caine and a "haunting ending" make for a "buddy flick that rises above the genre."

Man with the Golden Gun, The 18 | 17 | 17 | 20

1974. Directed by Guy Hamilton. With Roger Moore, Christopher Lee, Britt Ekland. 125 minutes. Rated PG.

◪ "Moore almost redeems himself" in his second stab at 007 ("much better than his debut"), though Lee steals the show as a "droll" assassin boasting "three nipples" as well as a golden gun; still, despite the sizzle supplied by Ekland and some "great Asian scenery", foes dismiss it as a "disjointed, inferior" misfire in the Bond canon.

Marathon Man 24 | 27 | 24 | 22

1976. Directed by John Schlesinger. With Dustin Hoffman, Laurence Olivier, Roy Scheider. 125 minutes. Rated R.

■ "Just when you thought it was safe to go back to the dentist" comes this "nasty" little thriller about a "totally mad", "tooth-drilling" "Nazi on the loose" hell-bent on retrieving ill-gotten loot; the "huffing, puffing" Hoffman is "superlative" as a man "drawn into something way beyond his control", while set pieces like the "whining drill" scene and the "diamond-swallowing" finale raise enough "goose bumps" to make most "swear off checkups for life."

Mark of Zorro, The ◑ 22 | 19 | 22 | 19

1940. Directed by Rouben Mamoulian. With Tyrone Power, Linda Darnell, Basil Rathbone. 94 minutes. Not Rated.

■ This "rousing adventure" tale of "double identity and romance" has "hardly dated" thanks to the "dashing", buckle-swashing Power's "sexy" "sword-fighting"; "lady-in-distress" Darnell is "unbelievably lovely", "fop" Rathbone "as dastardly as ever" and a "marvelous" Alfred Newman score provides the cinematic coup de grace.

Marty ✉◑ 25 | 27 | 24 | 21

1955. Directed by Delbert Mann. With Ernest Borgnine, Betsy Blair, Esther Minciotti. 91 minutes. Not Rated.

■ Ok, the story of a "sloppy butcher" who finds love with a "mousy clerk" might "never play", but this "poignant" Paddy Chayefsky drama proved naysayers wrong, garnering four Oscars (including Best Actor for Borgnine, who's "perfect" as an ordinary Brooklynite); shot in moody black and white, its "realistic style" "never gets old" – so long as you're prepared for a feeling of "hopelessness" throughout.

Mary Poppins ✉ 27 | 24 | 25 | 27

1964. Directed by Robert Stevenson. With Julie Andrews, Dick Van Dyke, David Tomlinson. 140 minutes. Rated G.

■ Blend a "perky" Andrews (as a "decidedly odd" nanny boasting "magical powers") with a "cheeky" Van Dyke, "fantastic animation" and "catchy tunes", add a "spoonful of sugar" and the result is a "super-duper" Disney "treat"; a "technical marvel of its time", this "jolly" production "makes you feel good at any age" and serves as a dandy "introduction to musicals for kids."

MASH ✉ 26 | 25 | 26 | 24

1970. Directed by Robert Altman. With Donald Sutherland, Elliott Gould, Sally Kellerman. 116 minutes. Rated PG.

■ "War is hell (and funny)" in this "groundbreaking" "black" satire about a dysfunctional Korean War medical unit that still "holds up" as "one of the smartest comedies ever written" – "once you get past all the blood", that is; maybe the "last third" goes "downhill" during the "lame" football game, but there's no doubt this is "Altman's breakthrough."

Mask 21 | 24 | 23 | 19

1985. Directed by Peter Bogdanovich. With Cher, Sam Elliott, Eric Stoltz. 120 minutes. Rated PG-13.

■ Proof that "Cher can act", this "touching" "tearjerker" showcases the diva in "top form" as a single biker mom "in a tough situation with a challenged child" who's horribly disfigured; as the "grotesque" teen who just "wants to be treated normally", an "amazing" Stoltz radiates enough "inner beauty" to remind the rest of us "how lucky we are."

Mask of Zorro, The 18 | 17 | 18 | 21

1998. Directed by Martin Campbell. With Antonio Banderas, Catherine Zeta-Jones. 136 minutes. Rated PG-13.

◪ This "big-budget" "spin on the Zorro legend" provokes dueling opinions: zealots dig its "old-school movie style" ("great swordfights", "breathtaking" production values) and ask "is there a better-looking cast ever assembled?" – especially the "hot", "show-stealing" Zeta-Jones; but critics parry it's "lightweight" "fluff" that might work well with "popcorn" but "doesn't hold a candle to the 1940 version."

Matrix, The 25 | 19 | 25 | 28

1999. Directed by Andy Wachowski, Larry Wachowski. With Keanu Reeves, Laurence Fishburne, Carrie-Anne Moss. 136 minutes. Rated R.

■ "Move over, *Star Wars*"; not even Reeves' "leaden", "dime-store-Indian" acting can sink this "mind-bending, reality-rocking" "new modern myth" of a movie that "raised the bar on special effects" and "revolutionized hand-to-hand combat in filmmaking"; even if its "intricate" plot (something about a computer hacker turned "humanity's last hope") verges on "incoherence", this "sci-fi shoot-'em-up for people with brains" just "gets better every time you see it."

Maverick 18 | 20 | 17 | 19

1994. Directed by Richard Donner. With Mel Gibson, Jodie Foster, James Garner. 127 minutes. Rated PG.

◪ As TV shows morphed into movies go, this "laid-back piece of Western fluff" based on ABC's '50s series "works well" by loading the deck with "escapism", "modern twists" and Gibson as a "tall, dark stranger" who might be "having more fun than the audience"; but it's the "effortless style" of Garner (the original Maverick) that wins big.

McCabe & Mrs. Miller 23 | 23 | 23 | 24

1971. Directed by Robert Altman. With Warren Beatty, Julie Christie, Shelley Duvall. 120 minutes. Rated R.

■ Decidedly "not for conventional Western" fans, this "brilliantly directed", "postmodern deconstruction" of the genre "eliminates the clichés" and "faithfully recreates" "what the West was really like": namely, "harsh, cruel and lacking true heroes"; despite one major drawback – "you can't understand what anyone is saying" – it's more than evident that Beatty and Christie are "achingly, tragically, impossibly in love."

Meatballs Ⓘ 18 | 15 | 17 | 14

1979. Directed by Ivan Reitman. With Bill Murray, Harvey Atkin, Kate Lynch. 99 minutes. Rated PG.

◪ A pre-"*Caddyshack*" Murray plays a wisecracking "summer camp counselor everyone would love to have" in this "underrated", lowbrow "comedy staple", later "ruined" by three sequels; sure, it might be a "little dated" and "poor production quality" detracts, but overall it conveys the "experience every camper hopes for."

Mediterraneo ✉ F ∅ 21 | 21 | 20 | 23

1991. Directed by Gabriele Salvatores. With Diego Abatantuono, Claudio Bigagli. 96 minutes. Rated R.

◪ Sure, this "sweet" comedy about a group of WWII Italian soldiers "stranded" on a Greek isle is a "trifle", but the "beautiful cinematography" and "sweep-you-away" soundtrack nicely complement its assortment of "cute characters"; some report the story "drags in some parts" (resulting in "awkward" scenes), but it offers enough "great escapism" to make for a primo "date flick."

Meet Me in St. Louis ∅ 26 | 24 | 23 | 26

1944. Directed by Vincente Minnelli. With Judy Garland, Margaret O'Brien, Mary Astor. 113 minutes. Not Rated.

■ Clang, clang, clang, here comes Garland "at her radiant finest" as a girl who "adores the boy next door" in this musical "treasure" about a "delightfully offbeat" "turn-of-the-century" American family; fans laud its "sumptuous" Technicolor production and "unforgettable" tunes, while brainiacs hint it's "darker and deeper than its rep suggests."

Meet the Parents 19 | 21 | 19 | 19

2000. Directed by Jay Roach. With Robert De Niro, Ben Stiller, Blythe Danner. 108 minutes. Rated PG-13.

◪ "Every guy's worst nightmare" about being introduced to his "prospective in-laws" comes true in this very "watchable" comedy that succeeds mainly because of the "brilliant pairing of Stiller and De Niro"; though the unamused frown it "relies too much on slapstick" and repeats the "same joke for two hours straight", most say it "pinpoints" an "all-too-real" situation.

Memento 26 | 25 | 27 | 25

2000. Directed by Christopher Nolan. With Guy Pearce, Carrie-Anne Moss. 113 minutes. Rated R.

■ "Bring your brain to the theater, you'll need it" for this "exquisitely existential" "mind-bender" about a man who loses his "short-term memory" following his wife's murder; it "turns traditional narrative on its head" by telling the story "in reverse" – so it may "require several viewings to get it all straight"; though there's applause for the "stunning" Pearce, befuddled folks "still trying to figure it out" wail it's too "gnisufnoc."

Men in Black Ⓘ 21 | 20 | 21 | 24

1997. Directed by Barry Sonnenfeld. With Tommy Lee Jones, Will Smith. 98 minutes. Rated PG-13.

◪ "Wisecracking" Smith and "deadpan" Jones show "great chemistry" as they battle "slime, aliens and explosions" in this "action-packed" sci-fi "blockbuster" that's "delicious fun"; a "kids' movie for adults", it's a "hugely enjoyable" "spoof" that some find "silly" and may be a "little gross."

METROPOLIS ◑ 27 | 22 | 24 | 28

1927. Directed by Fritz Lang. With Alfred Abel, Gustav Froelich, Brigitte Helm. 153 minutes. Not Rated.

■ A "visionary" film of "magnitude, imagination and depth", this "chilling" "sci-fi social commentary" about "oppression and uprising" set in a "futuristic city" "still retains its visual impact" seven decades later; indeed, Lang's "man-vs.-machine" story (embodied by a "fetishized woman robot") remains "revolutionary in every sense of the word" – this is a "movie everybody should watch at least once."

Midnight Cowboy ✉ 26 | 28 | 24 | 24

1969. Directed by John Schlesinger. With Dustin Hoffman, Jon Voight, Sylvia Miles. 113 minutes. Rated R.

■ "Still as gritty as ever", this "unvarnished look at NYC street life" is a "touching" if "depressing" depiction of a pair of "down-and-out" losers "spiraling downward" that turns the "buddy-flick concept" on its ear; the first "X-rated" film to take Best Picture honors (and since re-rated), it continues to wow with "inner beauty", "haunting music" and "brilliant" turns from Hoffman and Voight – and that "ending on the bus is unforgettable."

Midnight Express ✉ 24 | 24 | 25 | 22

1978. Directed by Alan Parker. With Brad Davis, Randy Quaid, John Hurt. 120 minutes. Rated R.

■ This "frighteningly realistic" drama about a not-so-innocent American abroad imprisoned for smuggling hash "should be required viewing for teens and travelers", even though this "eye-opener" might "induce nightmares for years to come"; it probably "did more to stop kids from doing drugs" than all of "Nancy Reagan's" efforts combined.

Mighty Aphrodite 18 | 21 | 18 | 18

1995. Directed by Woody Allen. With Woody Allen, Mira Sorvino, Michael Rapaport. 98 minutes. Rated R.

■ Maybe "not as deep or incisive" as Allen's "best", this "minor Woody" work still exudes plenty of "inventive" "charm" in its story of a sportswriter seeking the biological mother of his adopted child; throw in an "inspired Greek chorus" providing commentary and Sorvino's Oscar-winning turn as a "ditzy hooker", and the result is "painless fun."

Mildred Pierce ⊠◑∅ 26 | 25 | 25 | 24

1945. Directed by Michael Curtiz. With Joan Crawford, Jack Carson, Ann Blyth. 111 minutes. Not Rated.

■ Oscar-winner Crawford is in "full weeper bloom" (with "shoulder pads for days" and "star lighting to make sure you get the point") in this noir "sudser" based on the James M. Cain novel about a "mother who sacrifices everything for her daughter"; "camp" followers crack up over Eve Arden's "witty repartee" (which "would put any drag queen to shame") and "rent it as a double feature with *Mommie Dearest* for full impact."

Miller's Crossing ∅ 22 | 23 | 22 | 22

1990. Directed by Joel Coen. With Gabriel Byrne, Albert Finney, Marcia Gay Harden. 115 minutes. Rated R.

■ "Don't give the high hat" to this "subtle", "criminally underrated" early Coen brothers "gem" about a gangland war between Irish and Italian mobsters that proves "betrayal can come back to haunt you"; devotees declare it "deserves to be up there with *Goodfellas*", given the worthiness of the "broody" Byrne, "knockout Finney" and "deliciously tangled" plot "larded with obscure underworld slang."

Miracle on 34th Street ⊠◑ 25 | 23 | 26 | 23

1947. Directed by George Seaton. With Maureen O'Hara, Natalie Wood, Edmund Gwenn. 96 minutes. Not Rated.

■ It "can't be Christmas" without a screening of this "schmaltzy", "charming fantasy" that embodies a "child's belief in Santa Claus" so well that it's become an enduring "seasonal favorite" for "every generation"; true believers say the Oscar-winning screenplay is the key behind this "perfect" "holiday classic" that puts the remakes to shame.

Miracle Worker, The ⊠◑ 25 | 28 | 24 | 22

1962. Directed by Arthur Penn. With Anne Bancroft, Patty Duke, Victor Jory, Inga Swenson. 106 minutes. Not Rated.

■ "Beautifully transferred from stage to screen" by director Penn, this "moving" account of deaf-and-blind Helen Keller and her teacher Annie Sullivan garnered Oscars for both leads (who reprised their Broadway roles); while Duke is undeniably "superb", it's Bancroft who "dominates" this "fiercely acted", "exceptional" film; most memorable moment: at the water pump.

Misery ⊠ 21 | 24 | 23 | 19

1990. Directed by Rob Reiner. With James Caan, Kathy Bates, Richard Farnsworth. 107 minutes. Rated R.

■ This "freaky" yarn about an injured writer "rescued" from a snowstorm by a "seriously deranged" fan is a "hobbling", "cracking-with-tension" experience that really "packs a wallop"; Oscar-winner Bates is "mesmerizing" as the "obsessed", "sledgehammer-swinging" captor opposite Caan's "excellent" hostage, though diehards say the real credit goes to Reiner's "great hand when it comes to directing Stephen King stories."

Mission, The 24 | 24 | 22 | 25

1986. Directed by Roland Joffé. With Robert De Niro, Jeremy Irons, Liam Neeson. 126 minutes. Rated PG.

◪ "Beautifully shot", Oscar-winning cinematography nearly steals the show in this "intriguing drama" about an 18th-century struggle between missionaries and mercenaries over the riches of South America; even though evangelist Irons and reformed slave trader De Niro turn out their usual "amazing" work, unfazed foes claim that Ennio Morricone's "soundtrack is far better" than the picture itself.

Mississippi Burning 23 | 24 | 23 | 22

1988. Directed by Alan Parker. With Gene Hackman, Willem Dafoe, Frances McDormand. 128 minutes. Rated R.

◪ A "story that needed to be told", this "powerful" depiction of '60s "racial unrest" focuses on an "intense" Hackman's investigation of the murder of three "civil rights" workers; yet despite an "all-too-real glimpse of life in the Deep South", critics say it overemphasizes "white hate" to the point that there are few "speaking parts for black actors."

Mister Roberts ⓫ 27 | 27 | 24 | 23

1955. Directed by John Ford, Mervyn LeRoy. With Henry Fonda, James Cagney, Jack Lemmon. 123 minutes. Not Rated.

■ A Broadway hit transposed to the big screen, this "heartfelt" story about the misadventures of a WWII supply ship crew delivers "wonderful acting all around", from the "unforgettable" Cagney to the "perfect" Fonda and "no-slouch" Lemmon; a "great wartime comedy with a serious side", it leaves even tough guys with a "lump in their throat."

MODERN TIMES ◑ 28 | 26 | 26 | 25

1936. Directed by Charles Chaplin. With Charles Chaplin, Paulette Goddard. 87 minutes. Not Rated.

■ "Timelessly funny and resonant", this "man-vs.-machine" story runs on a "blend of slapstick and pathos" guaranteed to make you "smile . . . though your heart is breaking"; there's "little dialogue" (save for Chaplin's "singing waiter" "gibberish number"), but his "heartwarming" performance and sharp "swipes at the age of technology" transcend words; in short, this one's a "must-see in *these* times."

Monsters, Inc. 26 | – | 25 | 28

2001. Directed by Peter Docter, David Silverman, Lee Unkrich. Animated. 92 minutes. Rated G.

■ "Pixar does it again" with this "innovative" "animation gem" that "shows kids that the monsters in their closets are really harmless"; this time around, the "*Toy Story*" tech team alloy an "original" plot, "amazing attention to detail" and "ugly" but "cute" characters to create an "endearing" entertainment that works "for adults" too; P.S. the "blow-you-away" "flying door" sequence has got "theme-park ride" written all over it.

Monty Python & the Holy Grail 26 | 22 | 23 | 21

1975. Directed by Terry Gilliam, Terry Jones. With Monty Python. 91 minutes. Rated PG.

■ By dint of "sheer tasteless genius", this "absurdly wacky" "burlesque of the King Arthur legend" turns "historic reverence" on its ear and rules among "true" Pythonettes as the "movie of a thousand quotes" ("bring out your dead!"); granted, it may be comprised of a series of "strung-together skits" involving "killer bunnies" and "knights who say 'ni'", but the array of "knee-slapping" characters provides enough "lunacy to last the ages."

Moonstruck ✉ 24 | 25 | 24 | 22

1987. Directed by Norman Jewison. With Cher, Nicolas Cage, Olympia Dukakis. 102 minutes. Rated PG.

■ Both "Italians and wanna-be Italians" fall for this "totally charming" "romp" that shows how "love can be found in the least likely places" – even Brooklyn; a "phenomenal" Cher and Cage (making *amore* at such "full throttle" that the "heat between them could peel wallpaper") combine with a "dead-on", "star-studded" ensemble to keep this "romance classic" shining bright; fave scene: the "snap-out-of-it" slap.

Moulin Rouge ∅ 21 | 22 | 20 | 26

1952. Directed by John Huston. With José Ferrer, Zsa Zsa Gabor, Colette Marchand. 119 minutes. Not Rated.

■ "Drenched in color and the excitement of belle époque Paris", this "original" look at the tortured life of artist Toulouse-Lautrec is the "lush" product of an era when "movies were movies"; Ferrer's "completely entertaining" performance as the "completely odd" painter is the glue here, even if his gloomy portrayal might be at odds with the "eye-candy" production values.

Moulin Rouge! 23 | 23 | 20 | 27

2001. Directed by Baz Luhrmann. With Nicole Kidman, Ewan McGregor. 127 minutes. Rated PG-13.

◪ This "dizzying, decadent" "fever dream of a musical" set in "bohemian Paris" earned a clutch of Oscar nominations and may have "single-handedly revived and recreated the genre" for the "new millennium"; the ever-"ravishing" Kidman "sheds her icy image" in a "kaleidoscopic" turn as a notorious "shady lady" smitten by a "naive poet", and it turns out "McGregor can sing", but naysayers call it a "confusing", "overedited" "mishmash" that's "all glitter, no substance."

Mouse That Roared, The Ⓘ∅ 23 | 23 | 24 | 19

1959. Directed by Jack Arnold. With Peter Sellers, Jean Seberg, David Kossoff. 83 minutes. Not Rated.

■ "British humor has never been better" than in this "priceless" Cold War–era import about a tiny, impoverished nation that declares war on America, planning to lose in exchange for foreign aid; an "ingenious" satire that "pokes lots of holes" in a lot of targets, it's well "worth seeing" for "Sellers' expert multiple performances alone."

Mr. Blandings Builds His Dream House ◑∅ 23 | 24 | 23 | 21

1948. Directed by H.C. Potter. With Cary Grant, Myrna Loy, Melvyn Douglas. 94 minutes. Not Rated.

■ "If you're thinking of building or remodeling your home", "there's no funnier movie" than this "timeless" "cautionary tale" that proves the "perils haven't changed" "in the last 50 years"; "fixer-uppers" "laugh along" with this amusing view of the "suburban dream gone askew", most notably "Myrna's painting-the-living-room" sequence.

Mr. Holland's Opus 21 | 22 | 21 | 19

1995. Directed by Stephen Herek. With Richard Dreyfuss, Glenne Headly. 143 minutes. Rated PG.

■ "Sweet, funny and insightful", this "uplifting" opus chronicles the career of an "originally reluctant" high-school music teacher "who makes a difference in the lives of his students" while "struggling to come to terms with his deaf son"; though the hard-hearted fuss it's too "saccharine" and "preachy", most swear this "inspirational" story is worth seeing for Dreyfuss' "superb" performance alone.

Mr. Mom 18 | 18 | 20 | 17

1983. Directed by Stan Dragoti. With Michael Keaton, Teri Garr, Martin Mull. 91 minutes. Rated PG.

■ Mom and pop "switch roles" in this "fish-out-of-water" comedy detailing the misadventures of a "stay-at-home dad" reduced to "ironing grilled-cheese sandwiches" and "playing poker" with housewives for "shopping coupons"; but even though Keaton is a "likable" enough "slob" in the title role, rewinders report this "guilty pleasure" "doesn't hold up" to repeated viewings.

Mrs. Brown 22 | 28 | 23 | 23

1997. Directed by John Madden. With Judi Dench, Billy Connolly, Geoffrey Palmer. 103 minutes. Rated PG.

■ "Not widely seen", this "intelligent" drama detailing the platonic relationship between Queen Victoria and her groomsman shows that "even the most hardened heart can be changed by love"; naturally, many say that the "amazing" "Dench is *the* reason to see it", given her "poignant" take on the monarch "as a woman", though the "intriguing" plot and "subtle" work from Connolly are equally "wonderful."

Mrs. Doubtfire 20 | 23 | 20 | 20

1993. Directed by Chris Columbus. With Robin Williams, Sally Field, Pierce Brosnan. 125 minutes. Rated PG-13.

◪ This "laugh-out-loud" story of a man attempting to "win back his ex and kids" by impersonating a "nanny" manages to be "over-the-top", "subversive" and "endearing" all at once; sure, doubters snipe the "far-fetched" screenplay "can't decide if it's a farce" "or a tearjerker", but it's agreed that "riot" Williams is "at his manic best" when in "drag."

Mr. Smith Goes to Washington ✉◑ 26 | 27 | 25 | 22

1939. Directed by Frank Capra. With James Stewart, Jean Arthur, Claude Rains. 125 minutes. Not Rated.

■ "As American as two slices of apple pie", Frank Capra's "rousing" "political fairy tale" about "one man's belief in goodness" and his eventual "triumph" "appeals to the idealist in each of us"; "corny", perhaps, but "you can't help but be moved" by Stewart waging the "filibuster to beat all filibusters" – and proving "you *can* beat City Hall."

Mulan 23 | – | 23 | 24

1998. Directed by Tony Bancroft, Barry Cook. Animated. 88 minutes. Rated G.

■ An "underrated" rarity, this "gorgeously realized" animated "Chinese folk tale" features a Disney heroine "who can carry a movie on her own"; its mix of "family honor" and "women power" make it "good for a girl's self-esteem", while "just the right balance of seriousness and humor" "delivers its message without preaching."

Mulholland Dr. 20 | 22 | 19 | 22

2001. Directed by David Lynch. With Naomi Watts, Laura Harring, Justin Theroux. 145 minutes. Rated R.

◪ "Another confusing but consuming Lynch production", this "intriguing", "utterly disquieting" "portrait of Hollywood losers" "requires contemplation" since it's "hard to follow"; sure, fans say its "smoldering" leads are so "beautiful" that their presence alone makes the film "visually worth it", but cynics feel "totally ripped off" by this "weird" "nonsense."

Mummy, The Ⓘ 19 | 16 | 18 | 24

1999. Directed by Stephen Sommers. With Brendan Fraser, Rachel Weisz. 124 minutes. Rated PG-13.

◪ Archeologists ravage Egyptian tombs to disastrous results in this "cornball" "modern B movie" featuring "fancy CGI effects" and a plot that lurches between "scary and funny"; but foes who dis its "ridiculous" premise suggest you "rent the original – *Raiders of the Lost Ark.*"

Muppet Movie, The Ⓘ 24 | 23 | 23 | 25

1979. Directed by James Frawley. With Charles Durning, Austin Pendleton. 97 minutes. Rated G.

■ "You're never too old" to enjoy this "goofy" but "utterly delightful" romp that might unleash your "inner kid" thanks to some "wonderful puppetry" abetted by an array of star-studded cameos from everyone from Milton Berle to Steve Martin; fans say it's the "best" of the Muppet oeuvre, crediting the "genius" of "national treasure" Jim Henson for the "successful transition" of *Sesame Street*'s denizens to the big screen.

Murder by Death 21 | 21 | 22 | 19

1976. Directed by Robert Moore. With Peter Falk, Peter Sellers, Maggie Smith. 94 minutes. Rated PG.

◪ A "kooky lampoon that hits the spot", this Neil Simon–penned whodunit "spoof" places a "diverse" group of private eyes in a castle where murder ensues; given the efforts of a Charlie Chan–esque Sellers and a Bogart-channeling Falk, this "madcap" exercise is a "must-see satire for mystery lovers", even if some gumshoes turn up evidence of too many "good actors playing useless parts."

Murder on the Orient Express ∅ 23 | 23 | 26 | 24

1974. Directed by Sidney Lumet. With Albert Finney, Lauren Bacall, Ingrid Bergman. 128 minutes. Rated PG.

■ "Agatha Christie has never been done better" than in this "fascinatingly complex, lushly produced" Hercule Poirot mystery set onboard the Orient Express; boasting a "crisply directed" "all-star" ensemble cast that "looks like they're having the time of their lives", this "luxuriously funny" "perfect thriller" certainly "won't bore you" – and "you'll never guess whodunit."

Music Man, The 25 | 24 | 25 | 26

1962. Directed by Morton DaCosta. With Robert Preston, Shirley Jones, Buddy Hackett. 151 minutes. Rated G.

■ Making an "exquisite, seamless transition from Broadway to screen", this slice of "pure Americana" about a "traveling con man" let loose in River City, Iowa, hits "classic" notes with its "catchy" Meredith Willson score; thanks to a "tour-de-force" turn by a "mesmerizing" Preston, this "family treat" "never grows old."

Mutiny on the Bounty ✉◑∅ 25 | 25 | 25 | 23

1935. Directed by Frank Lloyd. With Charles Laughton, Clark Gable, Franchot Tone. 132 minutes. Not Rated.

■ Despite being "a bit creaky" after all these years, this original version of a legendary clash of egos on the high seas remains "the one and only" simply because "you don't get acting like this anymore": Laughton is "grand" as "definitive villain" Captain Bligh, and "Gable is, well, Gable" as Mr. Christian, his second-in-command.

Mutiny on the Bounty ∅ 22 | 24 | 24 | 22

1962. Directed by Lewis Milestone. With Marlon Brando, Trevor Howard, Richard Harris. 178 minutes. Not Rated.

■ Ultra-"fabulous scenery" that will surely make you "want to move to Tahiti" and a "cast of thousands" collide in this "big-budget" MGM remake about an uprising at sea; Brando turns in "one of his most controversial roles" as a "foppish" Fletcher Christian, even if foes harrumph "I'll take Gable."

My Best Friend's Wedding 19 | 19 | 19 | 19

1997. Directed by P.J. Hogan. With Julia Roberts, Dermot Mulroney, Rupert Everett. 105 minutes. Rated PG-13.

◪ Ok, there's "no thinking required" in this "enjoyable if predictable" "chick flick" about a single gal bent on preventing her best male friend from "getting hitched"; while a "surprisingly funny Roberts" and "yummy Everett" "chew up the scenery" entertainingly, those through with love find this "anti-romance" "contrived" and "obvious" – except for the winning "'Say a Little Prayer'" sing-along.

My Bodyguard 18 | 18 | 19 | 16

1980. Directed by Tony Bill. With Chris Makepeace, Adam Baldwin, Matt Dillon. 96 minutes. Rated PG.

■ The "ultimate teenage revenge fantasy", this "feel-good" flick about a "underdog" high-schooler who hires a tough classmate to protect him from a bully "rings true" with "anyone who was ever picked on"; sure, there's a "silly, irrelevant" subplot about "eccentric grown-ups", but overall this "endearing" "coming-of-age saga" is "well done."

My Cousin Vinny 22 | 24 | 21 | 19

1992. Directed by Jonathan Lynn. With Joe Pesci, Ralph Macchio, Marisa Tomei. 120 minutes. Rated R.

■ "Fuhgeddaboudit": this "laugh-out-loud", "quotable" "courtroom classic" about a novice "Noo Yawk lawyer" representing his cousin in an Alabama murder trial is a "cleverly written" comic look at "Southern justice"; a "perfect" Pesci "carries the show", amply assisted by Tomei, who earned a "well-deserved Oscar" just by "making a Brooklyn accent the sexiest sound around"; P.S. it works best with "ordered-in pizza."

My Dinner with André 21 | 21 | 18 | 19

1981. Directed by Louis Malle. With Wallace Shawn, Andre Gregory. 110 minutes. Not Rated.

■ Who'd have thought a movie that "consists entirely of a dinner conversation" between two acquaintances could keep you entertained for two hours?; yet with talk "spanning every philosophical topic" that "captures the magic in the ordinary", Shawn and Gregory do just that; "remarkable for how little it works with", this "simple, unpretentious" art-house hit is "oddly fascinating" to those who wish their own dining companions "could be as interesting."

MY FAIR LADY ⊠ 27 | 27 | 27 | 27

1964. Directed by George Cukor. With Audrey Hepburn, Rex Harrison, Stanley Holloway. 170 minutes. Rated G.

■ "Hollywood couldn't have done a better job" than this "grand, classy" version of Broadway's Lerner and Loewe musical "based on *Pygmalion*"; a "breathtaking" (but "dubbed") Hepburn is "incomparable" as the Cockney "guttersnipe turned into a lady", while Oscar-winner Harrison "at his tweedy best" plays her "superior yet vulnerable" teacher; "infectious" tunes and costumes that "leave you weak-kneed" ("those hats!") make this "luscious production" all the more "loverly."

My Favorite Year 22 | 25 | 22 | 20

1982. Directed by Richard Benjamin. With Peter O'Toole, Mark Linn-Baker. 92 minutes. Rated PG.

■ This "winning comedy" about the "early days of TV" involves a boozy matinee idol's appearance on a program that's a "great riff on the old Sid Caesar show"; although "O'Toole playing a drunk might not be a stretch", he "nails every nuance", turning this "affectionate" "period piece" into "one of the funniest movies no one has ever seen."

My Girl Ⓘ 20 | 18 | 19 | 18

1991. Directed by Howard Zieff. With Dan Aykroyd, Jamie Lee Curtis, Anna Chlumsky. 102 minutes. Rated PG.

■ Get out your handkerchiefs: this "make-you-cry" dramedy pulls out all the stops in its depiction of a motherless girl dealing with emotional awakening (and her father's new girlfriend); Chlumsky's "sweet", "heart-wrenching" turn nails the "innocence and complexity of childhood" so well that many would like to "have her as a daughter."

My Left Foot ✉ 25 | 28 | 25 | 23

1989. Directed by Jim Sheridan. With Daniel Day-Lewis, Brenda Fricker, Hugh O'Conor. 98 minutes. Rated R.

■ It "could have been sappy and overly sentimental", but this "stereotype-smashing" true account of an Irish man born with cerebral palsy is "handled with unvarnished dignity" thanks to the Oscar-winning Day-Lewis, who "maintains the contorted body and emotional scars" of his condition so adeptly that "you forget you're watching an actor"; "very moving", this film's a "beacon of light for all."

My Life As a Dog F 25 | 24 | 25 | 22

1987. Directed by Lasse Hallström. With Anton Glanzelius, Melinda Kinnaman. 101 minutes. Rated PG-13.

■ "For once, an adult really gets into a child's head" in this "enchanting" Swedish "coming-of-age" drama that devotees deem director "Hallström's best"; the "puckish" lead is both "complex" and "cute", his fellow villagers "wacky" and the story "heart-tugging" without a "single false note" – no wonder many say it's "goose bump–worthy."

My Man Godfrey ◑ 25 | 25 | 23 | 21

1936. Directed by Gregory La Cava. With William Powell, Carole Lombard, Eugene Pallette. 94 minutes. Not Rated.

■ As an "unconventional love-struck heiress", Lombard displays "impeccable timing" opposite the "masterful"

Powell as the "hobo hired to be the family butler" in this "ultimate screwball comedy", the standard by which "all others are measured"; of course, the "fast-paced", fast-talking "plot is absurd" (that's "precisely the point"), but the "charming" principals "make it look convincing."

My Own Private Idaho ∅ 19 | 21 | 19 | 19

1991. Directed by Gus Van Sant. With River Phoenix, Keanu Reeves, William Richert. 102 minutes. Rated R.

◪ "Beautiful boys" work the streets of Portland in this "original modern romance" about a "narcoleptic" "hustler" (Phoenix, in a "heartbreaking" turn) who falls for a "man he can never have"; once the plot drifts off into a "pretentious" takeoff of "*Henry IV*", some say it becomes "overreaching" and downright "depressing", though overall there are "enough good moments to make it worthwhile."

Naked Gun, The Ⓘ 20 | 17 | 17 | 18

1988. Directed by David Zucker. With Leslie Nielsen, Priscilla Presley. 85 minutes. Rated PG-13.

◪ This "laugh-a-minute" "cop spoof" from the minds behind *Airplane!* stars a "deadpan" Nielsen, who "raises the bar for satirical comedy" with his "terrific" performance; sure, the "brilliantly dumb characters" and "loopy overlapping dialogue" are equally "riotous", but ultimately "you have to be a guy to enjoy this much stupidity"; P.S. some find it "discomfortingly amusing" when O.J. Simpson appears.

Nashville 23 | 23 | 22 | 24

1975. Directed by Robert Altman. With Ronee Blakley, Keith Carradine, Lily Tomlin. 159 minutes. Rated R.

■ It's the "wonderful ensemble" cast that makes this comic "portrait of '70s America" played out over a "few Nashville days and nights" "richer and funnier with every viewing"; though some find it "frustrating" ("too many people talking at once"), "black humor" fans dub it "Altman's best", with enough "interesting characters" and "smart observations" to make it the "country cousin of *Gosford Park*."

National Lampoon's Vacation Ⓘ 22 | 17 | 20 | 17

1983. Directed by Harold Ramis. With Chevy Chase, Beverly D'Angelo, Randy Quaid. 98 minutes. Rated R.

■ "Bad taste has never been funnier" than in this "vacation-from-hell" comedy recounting a "dysfunctional family's" cross-country "road trip"; as the beleaguered dad, Chase is at the "pinnacle of his career", though many say he's upstaged by those all-too-fleeting glimpses of the white-"hot" "Christie Brinkley in a red sports car."

National Velvet Ⓘ 24 | 24 | 24 | 22

1945. Directed by Clarence Brown. With Elizabeth Taylor, Mickey Rooney, Anne Revere. 123 minutes. Rated G.

■ The movie equivalent of "comfort food", this "classic" "coming-of-age story" about a "girl and her horse" stars a "dazzlingly young Taylor" and a "scene-stealing" Rooney in a "feel-good" parable of "surmounting obstacles to make dreams come true"; maybe it's "corny", but any young lady "who ever dreamed of having a pony" can't help but "gush" over that climatic steeplechase race.

Natural, The 23 | 21 | 23 | 22

1984. Directed by Barry Levinson. With Robert Redford, Robert Duvall, Glenn Close. 134 minutes. Rated PG.

■ "Every Little Leaguer's favorite flick", this mix of "magic" and "major league baseball" stars a "rugged Redford" as a "middle-aged rookie" who hits a "chill"-inducing "home run into the lights"; though some sigh it's too "sentimental", fans cheer this "solid" "period drama" (that's all the more "awe-inspiring" thanks to Randy Newman's "unforgettable score").

Network ✉ 24 | 25 | 24 | 22

1976. Directed by Sidney Lumet. With Faye Dunaway, William Holden, Peter Finch, Beatrice Straight. 120 minutes. Rated R.

■ Even 25 years later, newscaster Howard Beale's "fateful cry, 'I'm mad as hell, and I'm not going to take it anymore'" is still "relevant" to proponents of this "prophetic" dramedy about television's "battle between news and entertainment"; "expertly written" by Paddy Chayefsky and "brilliantly acted" by Finch, Dunaway and Straight (who all won Oscars), this "biting" dark comedy has surveyors citing "*Jerry Springer*" and sighing "it's all true now."

Never on Sunday ◑∅ 24 | 26 | 23 | 21

1960. Directed by Jules Dassin. With Melina Mercouri, Jules Dassin. 91 minutes. Not Rated.

■ A "sensuous" Mercouri became an international star after illuminating the screen in this "delightful" drama about a "earthy" Greek prostitute and an uptight American (played by director Dassin) who tries to pull a Pygmalion on her; though once "shocking" and now "delightfully dated", every-nighters could "watch it anytime – even on a Sunday."

Never Say Never Again 18 | 20 | 17 | 19

1983. Directed by Irvin Kershner. With Sean Connery, Klaus Maria Brandauer, Barbara Carrera. 134 minutes. Rated PG.

◪ Live-and-let-diehards declare it's "fun to see Connery reprise the role that made him famous (and rich)" in this "rehash of *Thunderball*" featuring an "older" though "still studly" 007 who's "stunningly" teamed with Carrera; but nonfans say this "disappointing" picture "shouldn't be considered a Bond film", since it lacks the "appropriate music" and panache of producer Albert Broccoli.

Night at the Opera, A ◑ 26 | 25 | 22 | 22

1935. Directed by Sam Wood. With the Marx Brothers, Kitty Carlisle, Margaret Dumont. 96 minutes. Not Rated.

■ "Inspired insanity" meets "Marxist lunacy" in this "nutty" comedy (the "origin of the term 'laugh riot'") from the brothers Marx, wherein Groucho persuades a social-climbing Dumont to invest in an opera production; fans fast-forward through the "saccharine musical moments" in favor of the "verbal dazzle" of the "contract routine", the "baseball-in-the-orchestra-pit" bit and, of course, that "not-to-be-believed stateroom scene."

Nightmare Before Christmas, The 24 | – | 22 | 28

1993. Directed by Henry Selick. Animated. 76 minutes. Rated PG.

◪ The "perfect antidote to the holidays" may well be this "magical", "macabre" "masterpiece" of stop-motion animation that epitomizes the "bizarre genius" of producer Tim Burton; with a "cool storyline" – Halloween meets Christmas – "interesting characters" and "Danny Elfman's great score", it's a "must-see for kids of all ages" (though some of the "dark" moments may "disturb" the littlest ones).

Nightmare on Elm Street, A Ⓘ 19 | 14 | 19 | 18

1984. Directed by Wes Craven. With John Saxon, Ronee Blakley, Johnny Depp. 91 minutes. Rated R.

■ Built around the "concept that your nightmares are real", this "original, intelligent splatter" flick "did for sleeping what *Jaws* did for swimming" thanks to Freddy Krueger, its "pizza-faced" villain who sports "knives for fingers"; the "first of the series" from director Craven, this "darn scary" picture is now recognized as a "modern horror classic."

NIGHT OF THE HUNTER, THE ◑ 27 | 28 | 25 | 26

1955. Directed by Charles Laughton. With Robert Mitchum, Shelley Winters, Lillian Gish. 93 minutes. Not Rated.

■ Playing a "semi-psychotic preacher" "personifying pure evil", the "mesmerizing" Mitchum "terrorizes a bunch of kids" (and "invents tattooed knuckles") in this "strange – and strangely affecting" – film noir frightfest; it's a "pity this was Laughton's only directorial" effort, given the "exquisite cinematography" and "unforgettable" performances that add up to "stunningly innovative cinema."

Night of the Living Dead ◑Ⓘ 22 | 13 | 19 | 16

1968. Directed by George A. Romero. With Duane Jones, Judith O'Dea, Russ Streiner. 96 minutes. Not Rated.

■ Director Romero "does zombies right" in this "zero-budget" indie "landmark" that proves that even "schlocky" special effects, a "shabby story line" and "bad acting" can produce what living dead–heads call the "scariest movie ever made"; the "grainy black-and-white film used adds to the creepy aura", right down to the "freak-you-out", "pj-wetting" finale.

NIGHTS OF CABIRIA ✉◑🄵 27 | 28 | 25 | 24

1957. Directed by Federico Fellini. With Giulietta Masina, François Périer. 117 minutes. Not Rated.

■ "Post-WWII Italy" as viewed "through the eyes of a streetwalker" is the premise of this "simple, heartfelt" drama that's one of Fellini's "most moving" (and least "bizarre") films; as the "lovable girl of the streets", the "radiant" Masina is nothing less than a "female Charlie Chaplin", rendering an "amazing" performance that "ranges from tragedy to transcendence to flat-out comedy."

9 to 5 18 | 18 | 19 | 17

1980. Directed by Colin Higgins. With Jane Fonda, Lily Tomlin, Dolly Parton. 110 minutes. Rated PG.

◪ "Every secretary's dream" of "getting even with the boss" comes true in this "silly, laugh-aloud comedy", a "feminist classic" with a "message relevant to its time" (though chauvinists snicker it's "proof that women's lib can be sexist too"); nevertheless, its "strong", "sassy" protagonists exhibit "amazing chemistry and are a joy to watch", and Parton's theme song sure is "catchy."

Norma Rae ✉ 24 | 27 | 24 | 21

1979. Directed by Martin Ritt. With Sally Field, Beau Bridges, Ron Leibman. 110 minutes. Rated PG.

■ A "stirring tale about the courage of ordinary people", this "uplifting" drama "based on a true story" is a "painfully accurate look" at a "courageous" mill worker's "fight for justice" when caught between "unions and management"; in the title role, the "superb" Field really "earned her Oscar", and the "image of her holding up that sign" has become iconically "indelible."

NORTH BY NORTHWEST 28 | 26 | 27 | 27

1959. Directed by Alfred Hitchcock. With Cary Grant, Eva Marie Saint, James Mason. 136 minutes. Not Rated.

■ "James Bond, eat your heart out" – "no one is cooler than Cary Grant" in this "incredibly stylish" Hitchcock thriller, a "twisting story of mistaken identity" set "all over the country" involving a "cool blonde", a "smooth villain" and a "malevolent crop duster"; despite some "holes in the script", there's ample distraction via that "exhilarating" climb down Mount Rushmore and the "double entendre" scenario (e.g. the shot of the "train entering a tunnel" at the climax).

No Time for Sergeants ◑∅ 23 | 22 | 22 | 19

1958. Directed by Mervyn LeRoy. With Andy Griffith, Myron McCornick, Nick Adams. 119 minutes. Not Rated.

■ Managing to be "endearing without being annoying", Griffith "delivers the goods" in this "hilarious" comedy about a "dim hayseed who nearly destroys the U.S. Air Force", abetted by "perfect foil" Don Knotts; the infamous "toilet-seat scene" is a "display of American ingenuity" at its finest.

NOTORIOUS ◑ 27 | 27 | 26 | 26

1946. Directed by Alfred Hitchcock. With Cary Grant, Ingrid Bergman, Claude Rains. 101 minutes. Not Rated.

■ "Fetching" "Ingrid Bergman goes under the sheets for her country and gets Cary Grant as a reward" in this "brilliantly subversive" Hitchcock spy thriller featuring "suspense", "suspicion", "hurt pride" and "Nazis too"; best remembered for the leads' "lingering, smoldering love scene", it also boasts "top-notch" supporting work from Rains, who has the best line: "mother, I'm married to an American agent."

Notting Hill 19 | 19 | 18 | 19

1999. Directed by Roger Michell. With Julia Roberts, Hugh Grant, Rhys Ifans. 124 minutes. Rated PG-13.

◪ "Straight-up chick flick" about a "hair-flicking" "movie star" who finds love with an "endearing" bookseller; though rotters relate it's "lame" and "formulaic" (with "Roberts playing herself" and Grant in his "typical" "stammering ingénue" mode), at least the supporting cast is "brilliantly funny", while the London scenery provides the "charm."

No Way Out 20 | 19 | 23 | 19

1987. Directed by Roger Donaldson. With Kevin Costner, Gene Hackman, Sean Young. 114 minutes. Rated R.

■ Perhaps "Costner's finest hour", this "entirely enjoyable military thriller" offers "wonderful intrigue" in its way-out plot, something to do with the KGB, the Pentagon, the backseat of a limousine and a classy call girl (the "very hot" Young); while coolly "tense" throughout, the "unexpected", "twisty" ending is a "shocker no matter how many times you see it."

Now, Voyager ◑ 27 | 28 | 26 | 25

1942. Directed by Irving Rapper. With Bette Davis, Paul Henreid, Claude Rains. 117 minutes. Not Rated.

■ "Break out the hankies" – this "chick flick extraordinaire" features "the moon, the stars and Bette Davis", who effects an "appealing" "transformation" as an "old maid" defecting from a "demanding mother" to find kismet with a "perfect" Henreid; though the "two-cigarette scene" is decidedly un-PC today, it's become a "sacred" (and paradoxically "life-affirming") moment in this "classy" "mature love story."

Nutty Professor, The 21 | 19 | 18 | 18

1963. Directed by Jerry Lewis. With Jerry Lewis, Stella Stevens, Del Moore. 107 minutes. Not Rated.

◪ Jerry's "finest hour", this "can't-be-improved-upon" "wacky" comedy concerns a nerdy college prof who is transformed from Dr. Jerk-yll into Mr. Hyde after guzzling an exotic tonic; fans find it "sweet", foes shrug "typical Lewis shtick" and deep thinkers deem it a "metaphor for the monsters inside the greatest comedians"; your call.

O Brother, Where Art Thou? 22 | 23 | 22 | 24

2000. Directed by Joel Coen. With George Clooney, John Turturro, John Goodman. 106 minutes. Rated PG-13.

■ "Who else but the Coen brothers could combine Greek mythology, bluegrass and George Clooney?" ask fans of this picaresque, "perversely funny" satire "based on Homer's

Odyssey" that details the adventures of three Depression-era "hayseeds" who bust out of prison; though a bit too "highbrow" for some, the "beautiful period detail" and "best roots music soundtrack ever" keep this "sweet" if "strange" genre-bender accessible.

Ocean's Eleven 19 | 19 | 19 | 22

2001. Directed by Steven Soderbergh. With George Clooney, Brad Pitt, Andy Garcia. 116 minutes. Rated PG-13.

◪ "Fluffy fun" that "goes down smooth like a good martini", this "breezy" "caper" flick is "more stylish than the original" version with its "great shots of Vegas", "never-a-dull-moment" plot and "lots of eye candy for the ladies"; ok, it might be "really silly" (verging on "vapid"), but the "slick", "all-star cast" and "genius director du jour Soderbergh" serve up something "wonderfully entertaining."

Odd Couple, The Ⓘ 25 | 27 | 25 | 21

1968. Directed by Gene Saks. With Jack Lemmon, Walter Matthau, John Fiedler. 105 minutes. Rated G.

■ Lemon and Matthau are "brilliant" in this "timeless" Neil Simon "classic" (which spawned both a sequel and a TV series) that poses the question 'can two divorced men share an apartment without driving each other crazy?'; the ensuing dilemma makes for "unbeatable" comedy that'll make your "sides hurt from nonstop laughter."

Officer and a Gentleman, An 22 | 21 | 21 | 20

1982. Directed by Taylor Hackford. With Richard Gere, Debra Winger, Louis Gossett Jr. 122 minutes. Rated R.

◪ "What gal doesn't dream" of Richard Gere "sweeping" her into his arms and lifting her up where she belongs?; this "quintessential" '80s "date movie" provides plenty of fodder for "guilty-pleasure" fantasizing with its oh-"so-romantic" love story between a "young enlisted man" and a "poor" working girl, even if pacifists pan it as "a bit lame" and advise "fast-forward to the last scene – it actually makes the rest worthwhile."

Oklahoma! 24 | 22 | 23 | 25

1955. Directed by Fred Zinnemann. With Gordon MacRae, Shirley Jones, Gloria Grahame. 145 minutes. Rated G.

◪ "Every single song" in this "sprawling" Rodgers and Hammerstein musical/Western "makes you want to sing along" with the "lovely" voices of Jones and MacRae, plus there are "rousing dance numbers"; though modernists malign it as a "little dated", for most it's a whole lot "more than O-K", it's a pure "C-L-A-S-S-I-C."

Old Yeller Ⓘ 24 | 20 | 24 | 20

1957. Directed by Robert Stevenson. With Dorothy McGuire, Fess Parker, Tommy Kirk. 83 minutes. Rated G.

◪ "You can't help but cry your eyes out" after watching this "outstanding" Disney "tearjerker" about a "boy and his big yellow dog"; if a few find the acting "formulaic" and the plot "sappy", most agree it's an "all-time" children's "standard" that even adults "never tire of watching" – despite that gosh-darned "sad ending."

Oliver! ✉ 24 | 23 | 24 | 26

1968. Directed by Carol Reed. With Mark Lester, Ron Moody, Shani Wallis, Oliver Reed. 153 minutes. Rated G.

■ Dickens' "bleak yet hopeful" novel is "lovingly brought to the screen" in this Oscar-winning adaptation of the stage "classic" musical; it's such a "plucky" "film for all ages" with "incredible" production numbers, a "wonderful" score and a "just-about-perfect" cast that "English orphan" wanna-bes beg 'please, sir can we watch it again?'

Omen, The Ⓘ 21 | 21 | 22 | 20

1976. Directed by Richard Donner. With Gregory Peck, Lee Remick, David Warner. 111 minutes. Rated R.

■ This "genuinely spooky" thriller has a "brilliant premise" – a couple unwittingly adopts the devil's child – and features an appropriately "satanic" storyline, "eerie" music and a "scrumptiously frightening" turn by the "scariest kid ever to be in a horror movie" (Harvey Stephens); thrill-seekers also quiver in delight at its "terrifying" special effects that make the "unbelievable believable."

Once Upon a Time in America ∅ 24 | 26 | 24 | 24

1984. Directed by Sergio Leone. With Robert De Niro, James Woods, Elizabeth McGovern. 227 minutes. Rated R.

◪ Some of De Niro's "most subtle and effective" acting is on display in this "unfairly neglected" crime epic spanning four decades, which hard-core cineasts hail as "truly remarkable" when "seen in the long [227-minute] director's cut"; but despite a "top-drawer cast" and "magnificent" direction by Leone, others are less enthused about the "flawed" end result that's awash in "too much blood."

ONE FLEW OVER THE CUCKOO'S NEST ✉ 27 | 29 | 27 | 25

1975. Directed by Milos Forman. With Jack Nicholson, Louise Fletcher, Will Sampson. 133 minutes. Rated R.

■ "Life in a mental ward" gets the "stand-up-for-your-rights" treatment in this "absorbing, disturbing" and "influential" drama starring "national treasure" Nicholson at his "ornery best", backed up by an "amazing" ensemble cast; no surprise, it took five major Oscars, made Nurse Ratched a household name and is "hard to top" – folks are just plain "nuts about it."

101 Dalmatians 24 | – | 22 | 24

1961. Directed by Wolfgang Reitherman, Clyde Geronimi, Hamilton Luske. Animated. 79 minutes. Rated G.

■ Puppy proponents put their paws together for Pongo, Perdita and their prolific progeny when watching this "fast, funny" piece of Disney animation that proves "cartoon dogs can have emotional depth"; its "hugely entertaining" tale of a klatch of "cute" canines outrunning über-villainess Cruella De Vil appeals to the "little kid in everyone" and makes this one an "enduring" "winner."

101 Dalmatians Ⓘ 18 | 19 | 19 | 22

1996. Directed by Stephen Herek. With Glenn Close, Jeff Daniels, Joely Richardson. 103 minutes. Rated G.

◪ "*The* reason" to see Disney's "cute" live-action "update" of their earlier animated feature is the "over-the-top" Close as the "truly wicked" Cruella De Vil (though there's also "dry humor" courtesy of the largely British supporting cast); still, cynics nix this "wholly unnecessary remake" as "not nearly as good as the original."

On Golden Pond ✉ 24 | 27 | 23 | 23

1981. Directed by Mark Rydell. With Katharine Hepburn, Henry Fonda, Jane Fonda. 109 minutes. Rated PG.

■ A "beautiful tale of growing old and looking back on life", this "brilliant" drama features the "stunning", Oscar-winning Hank and Kate "pulling out all the stops" as an elderly couple coming to terms with their child and each other over one golden summer; the "real-life tension" between the real-life father-and-daughter Fondas supplies some "electric" moments, while its timeless theme about the "strength of the human spirit" "will appeal to all."

On Her Majesty's Secret Service 19 | 15 | 21 | 20

1969. Directed by Peter R. Hunt. With George Lazenby, Diana Rigg, Telly Savalas. 140 minutes. Rated PG.

◪ "James Bond gets married" in this "respectable" flick featuring "astonishing ski chases", "spectacular views of the Swiss Alps" and a "believable love story" for a change; still, opinion splits on Lazenby's one-time-only impersonation of 007 ("wooden" vs. "formidable"), and as for the end result, it's either "highly underrated" or "the worst" in the series.

On the Town 23 | 23 | 21 | 25

1949. Directed by Stanley Donen, Gene Kelly. With Gene Kelly, Frank Sinatra, Jules Munshin. 98 minutes. Not Rated.

■ Despite "wonderful dancing by Kelly" and some "funny" bits from the ensemble cast, "NYC is the real star" of this "exuberant" musical "celebrating the American spirit in the '40s"; "filmed partially on location" and juiced up by a "great Leonard Bernstein score", it follows three sailors at liberty on the town, and although rather "silly", it effortlessly radiates the "pure joy" of simpler times.

ON THE WATERFRONT ✉◑ 28 | 29 | 26 | 26

1954. Directed by Elia Kazan. With Marlon Brando, Karl Malden, Eva Marie Saint. 108 minutes. Not Rated.

■ Most decidedly a "contender for all-time greatest" film, this "gritty tale of corruption on the docks of NJ" is a "movie to turn you onto movies", with Oscar-winning turns by the "phenomenal Brando" (as a "washed-up", "Palookaville"-bound boxer) and a "knockout" Saint (in her screen debut); indeed, this "gutsy", "brutal masterwork" "rings so true" and is so "emotionally satisfying" that it's "nothing less than brilliant"; best line: "I coulda been a contender."

Operation Petticoat 19 | 19 | 18 | 19

1959. Directed by Blake Edwards. With Cary Grant, Tony Curtis. 124 minutes. Not Rated.

◪ "Feel-good" WWII comedy having to do with a Navy captain's "emergency" efforts to keep a gaggle of army nurses and a "pink submarine" afloat; despite smooth "chemistry" between Grant and Curtis resulting in some pretty "funny" situations (i.e. lots of tight-quarters gags), the unamused torpedo it as "ancient and contrived."

Ordinary People ✉ 25 | 27 | 25 | 23

1980. Directed by Robert Redford. With Donald Sutherland, Mary Tyler Moore, Timothy Hutton. 124 minutes. Rated R.

■ "Every parent's nightmare" – the death of a child – is dissected in this "disturbingly" "devastating" drama that goes below the "veneer of an upper middle-class family" to plumb the "dysfunction" below; Redford's "deserving" directorial debut copped a Best Picture Oscar, but it's Moore's "playing-against-type" role as a "classy" but "coldhearted" mom that "steals the movie."

Others, The 23 | 25 | 23 | 24

2001. Directed by Alejandro Amenábar. With Nicole Kidman, Fionnula Flanagan. 101 minutes. Rated PG-13.

■ A "dynamic" Kidman delivers an "old-school movie star turn" in this "grand, gothic ghost story" about a "mother protecting" her children who suffer from a rare "photosensitive" condition (an "excellent excuse to keep the house dark and murky"); "wonderfully atmospheric" and "deliciously scary", it's a "highbrow horror" show with a "jeepers-creepers" "surprise ending" that's a "real shocker."

Outlaw Josey Wales, The 25 | 23 | 24 | 23

1976. Directed by Clint Eastwood. With Clint Eastwood, Sondra Locke, Chief Dan George. 135 minutes. Rated PG.

■ Playing a renegade Confederate soldier seeking revenge after his wife and children are murdered, Eastwood is his "usual unreadable self" (though you "feel for his plight") in this "quirky" Western that's ultimately a "rural version of *Death Wish*"; fans rate it "better-than-usual Clint", given its "classic lines" and "profound issues."

Out of Africa ✉ 25 | 25 | 24 | 27

1985. Directed by Sydney Pollack. With Meryl Streep, Robert Redford, Klaus Maria Brandauer. 150 minutes. Rated PG.

■ Supporters are "spellbound" by this "splendiferous" "love story played out against the mysterious continent" starring a "radiant" Streep as Danish writer Karen Blixen (aka Isak Dinesen) and a "great-looking" Redford as her paramour; the "beauty" of Africa and "soaring score" "amplify the emotion", and even though it's a "real tearjerker", armchair amorists eat up this "treat" "again and again."

Out of Sight 21 | 21 | 21 | 22

1998. Directed by Steven Soderbergh. With George Clooney, Jennifer Lopez, Ving Rhames. 123 minutes. Rated R.

■ "Clooney and Lopez generate electricity aplenty" in this "smart caper" flick that "oozes cool" in its depiction of a "cocksure" "con artist", his "eye-candy" "police pursuer" and "one of the sexiest love scenes" ever; a "crackling" story (via Elmore Leonard's novel) and "brilliant" direction from Soderbergh make this one an "overlooked gem."

Out-of-Towners, The ∅ 20 | 22 | 22 | 18

1970. Directed by Arthur Hiller. With Jack Lemmon, Sandy Dennis, Sandy Baron. 98 minutes. Rated G.

■ "They don't make comedies" like this Neil Simon–scripted "classic" anymore, the saga of an Ohio couple visiting "Fun City" only to discover that it's their "worst nightmare" as they endure one "hilariously miserable" mishap after another; "Lemmon and Dennis are perfection as the tortured" tourists, leading many to wonder "why they remade this movie" at all.

Outsiders, The 22 | 21 | 22 | 19

1983. Directed by Francis Ford Coppola. With C. Thomas Howell, Matt Dillon, Ralph Macchio. 91 minutes. Rated PG.

■ Coppola "paints a great picture" of "teen angst" in this "coming-of-age story" that limns the "problems" between adolescent gangs in a '50s Oklahoma hamlet; what seems like the "entire brat pack" delivers such "outstanding" work (with an especially "excellent" turn from a "young Dillon") that the end result is "almost as good" as S.E. Hinton's enduring novel.

Paper Moon ◑∅ 22 | 23 | 21 | 22

1973. Directed by Peter Bogdanovich. With Ryan O'Neal, Tatum O'Neal, Madeline Kahn. 102 minutes. Rated PG.

■ Have "fun watching Ryan and Tatum acting together" in this "absolutely delightful" "father/daughter bonding flick", the "charming" story of a Depression-era con man and his equally manipulative offspring who "drift" through the Midwest in glorious black and white; though some say this "sweet little comedy" was "stolen by Madeline Kahn", it was the younger O'Neal who copped the Oscar.

Papillon 26 | 27 | 26 | 24

1973. Directed by Franklin J. Schaffner. With Steve McQueen, Dustin Hoffman. 150 minutes. Rated R.

■ It's hard to escape from this "powerful" tale of prisoners scheming to break out of "Devil's Island", the "French

Guiana penal colony" that makes "HBO's *Oz* look like Club Med"; a "consistently cool McQueen" and "heavyweight Hoffman" play "mistreated-but-not-defeated" inmates "determined to be free" in this "tight", taut drama that's all the more "scary" because it's "based on a true story."

Parenthood 22 | 22 | 22 | 20

1989. Directed by Ron Howard. With Steve Martin, Mary Steenburgen, Dianne Wiest. 124 minutes. Rated PG-13.
■ "Modern family life" gets "compelling" treatment in this "affectionate if harrowing look at being a parent", a "feel-good" dramedy that confirms "you need a sense of humor" when you have kids; "smart, insightful" and briskly paced thanks to "multiple plotlines", it features "one of Martin's better performances" and "sweet" direction from Howard.

Parent Trap, The 23 | 21 | 23 | 21

1961. Directed by David Swift. With Hayley Mills, Maureen O'Hara, Brian Keith. 129 minutes. Rated G.
■ "Hayley Mills and Hayley Mills" star as "twins separated at birth plotting to bring their estranged parents together" in this "Disney non-animated classic", an "entertaining romp" that serves up plenty of "warmhearted family fare" "for any age"; one of the "most remembered" movies in boomerdom, it boasts such a "timeless story" that most "stick to the original", having "no need for the remake."

PATHS OF GLORY ◑ 28 | 27 | 28 | 26

1957. Directed by Stanley Kubrick. With Kirk Douglas, Ralph Meeker, George Macready. 86 minutes. Not Rated.
■ "All the hopelessness", "folly" and "stupidity" of WWI is "dramatically" depicted in Kubrick's "devastating" "anti-war" picture that "ruthlessly" depicts "corrupt" officers deploying "scapegoated enlisted men" as "cannon fodder"; even though this "grim" yet "moving" film is "in black and white", the "story is full color", and it "really makes its point" and "stands the test of time."

Patriot, The 21 | 21 | 21 | 23

2000. Directed by Roland Emmerich. With Mel Gibson, Heath Ledger, Joely Richardson. 164 minutes. Rated R.
◪ Present-day patriots salute this "epic in the Gibson tradition" as an "inspiring portrait" of a reluctant American "hero" enmeshed in "gruesome Revolutionary War battles"; though turncoats dismiss it as typical "Hollywood good guy/bad guy nonsense" ("Lethal Musket"), they're outvoted by partisans who "feel liberated" by this "heartfelt" history jazzed up with some "entertainment value."

Patriot Games 21 | 21 | 22 | 21

1992. Directed by Phillip Noyce. With Harrison Ford, Anne Archer, Patrick Bergin. 117 minutes. Rated R.
◪ "Harrison gets cool again" as a "humble hero whose life is turned upside down by a crazed IRA terrorist" in this

"slick" action-adventurer known for its "mind-spinning chase across oceans and freeways"; though it's as "thrilling on the screen as on the written page", traitors contend it's "cookie-cutter espionage" and say that Alec Baldwin is the "more believable Jack Ryan."

PATTON ✉ 27 | 28 | 26 | 27

1970. Directed by Franklin J. Schaffner. With George C. Scott, Karl Malden. 170 minutes. Rated PG.

■ Legions salute "one of the best biopics ever made", this "hauntingly mounted character study" of fabled WWII General Patton, who's "superbly fleshed out" as both "monstrous and human"; though there's "lots of drama" throughout, it "doesn't get much better than that opening speech" by "Old Blood and Guts", probably the most "memorable" scene in the picture; P.S. the "convincing" portrayal won Scott an Oscar, which he famously rejected.

Pawnbroker, The ◑∅ 26 | 28 | 24 | 22

1965. Directed by Sidney Lumet. With Rod Steiger, Geraldine Fitzgerald. 116 minutes. Not Rated.

■ This "disturbing", "depressing message" picture, expertly rendered in "chilling black and white", shows the "horrors of the Holocaust" by focusing on one survivor, the owner of a Harlem pawnshop; in "one of the all-time great screen performances", Steiger is nothing short of "mesmerizing" in the title role – too bad it's been so "sadly neglected" over the years.

Pee-wee's Big Adventure Ⓘ 19 | 17 | 17 | 20

1985. Directed by Tim Burton. With Paul Reubens, Elizabeth Daily, Diane Salinger. 90 minutes. Rated PG.

■ "Wacky", "campy", maybe even "inspired", this comic "cult classic" is a "work of the sublime from the ridiculous" team of "twisted" director Burton and "genius" performer Reubens; though ostensibly aimed at small fry, "adults love it" too, yet the pleasure is bittersweet for those who "miss Pee-wee" and "wish for another" installment; P.S. "Large Marge is worth the price of admission."

Peggy Sue Got Married 19 | 20 | 21 | 18

1986. Directed by Francis Ford Coppola. With Kathleen Turner, Nicolas Cage. 104 minutes. Rated PG-13.

◪ Unhappily married Peggy Sue "magically enters her teenage self's world" in this "timeless" "back-in-time" comedy "with a heart and a brain"; though ageists say Turner is "too old" for the role, the "original premise" and overall "nostalgic" mood provide ample distraction.

People vs. Larry Flynt, The 18 | 21 | 18 | 18

1996. Directed by Milos Forman. With Woody Harrelson, Courtney Love, Edward Norton. 129 minutes. Rated R.

■ Forman's "daring movie" creates an unlikely "hero" out of a "less than excellent subject", "pornographer" Larry Flynt, whose "rags-to-riches-to-ruin story" is rendered in such "heartbreaking" but "inspiring" terms that you wind up "loving the bad guy"; Harrelson is "first-rate" in the title role, Love "really can act" and you might just come away with a "whole new outlook" on smut.

Peter Pan ⓫ 25 | – | 25 | 25

1953. Directed by Clyde Geronimi, Wilfred Jackson, Hamilton Luske. Animated. 76 minutes. Rated G.

■ Lost boys and girls who "never want to grow up" fly to this "simple", pixie dust–peppered tale concerning the eternally youthful Peter's adventures in "Neverland"; a "true classic" of Disney animation from the days when "Walt was running the show", it remains enough of an "important childhood film" for latter-day critics to ask "why did they bother with a remake?"

Pete's Dragon 20 | 17 | 20 | 21

1977. Directed by Don Chaffey. With Helen Reddy, Jim Dale, Mickey Rooney. 128 minutes. Rated G.

◪ Surveyors slayed by this "Disney classic" combining both animation and live action cheer its "heartwarming" story of a runaway orphan and his sometimes-invisible dragon companion; though fire-breathers blast it as "overlong" and "unmemorable", most agree the "kids will dig it", which is all that matters.

Philadelphia ✉ 24 | 27 | 25 | 23

1993. Directed by Jonathan Demme. With Tom Hanks, Denzel Washington. 125 minutes. Rated PG-13.

■ "Hollywood takes on AIDS" in this "extraordinarily powerful and poignant" drama that "puts a human face" on a "depressing" subject via Hanks' "brave", Oscar-winning portrayal of a gay lawyer battling the "double-edged sword of discrimination and physical deterioration"; the final result "resonates" with "thought-provoking" issues, but "bring the tissues – it's painful to watch."

PHILADELPHIA STORY, THE ✉◑ 27 | 28 | 26 | 25

1940. Directed by George Cukor. With Cary Grant, Katharine Hepburn, James Stewart. 112 minutes. Not Rated.

■ For the "sheer joy" of "listening to fast, furious dialogue" that "doesn't insult your intelligence", this "laugh-out-loud" "screwball" "comedy of manners" provides a "wild ride"; "you'll need a scorecard to keep up" with the "banter and spark" between the "classy" Kate, "acerbic" Grant and "underplaying" Stewart, uttered in settings so "perfectly frothy" that many wish that "life was really like that."

Piano, The ✉ 21 | 24 | 19 | 22

1993. Directed by Jane Campion. With Holly Hunter, Harvey Keitel, Sam Neill. 121 minutes. Rated R.

◪ "Each frame could be a painting" in this "exquisitely shot" drama set in 19th-century New Zealand concerning a "mute woman" and her "search for fulfillment"; though Hunter delivers an "expressive", Oscar-winning performance (despite very "limited dialogue") opposite Keitel at his "sensual", "full-frontal" best, critics contend the "contrived" plot strikes flat notes.

Picnic 24 | 24 | 24 | 24

1955. Directed by Joshua Logan. With William Holden, Kim Novak, Rosalind Russell. 115 minutes. Not Rated.

■ Darn "sexy for its time", this "star-crossed", "moonglow"-drenched romance relates the havoc that a "handsome drifter" wreaks upon a group of "small-town" gals; fans say it "retains its charm", since it "epitomizes the lush storytelling of the '50s", but admit it may be a "little too theatrical to appeal to today's audiences"; hottest scene, no contest: Novak and Holden's "sizzling dance on the bridge."

Pillow Talk ✉ 20 | 20 | 17 | 19

1959. Directed by Michael Gordon. With Doris Day, Rock Hudson, Tony Randall. 103 minutes. Not Rated.

◪ The "first – and best – of the Rock-Doris bedroom farces", this "gloriously goofy" romantic comedy about an "unlikely" pair who share a telephone party line is "good clean fun" with "no laugh track needed"; alright, the "setup is a bit dated" (verging on "insipid"), but more than a few fess up it's a "true guilty pleasure" that they "never tire of watching."

Pink Panther, The Ⓘ 24 | 24 | 21 | 21

1964. Directed by Blake Edwards. With Peter Sellers, David Niven, Robert Wagner. 113 minutes. Not Rated.

■ "Hilarity abounds" – "starting with the opening credits" – in this "outlandish" caper flick, the first production by the "comedy dream team" of director Edwards and actor Sellers (in his "brilliant" debut as "bumbling Inspector Jacques Clouseau"); "funny to this day", it marked the start of a "sequel brigade" that marched along for years afterward.

Pinocchio 26 | – | 26 | 26

1940. Directed by Hamilton Luske, Ben Sharpsteen. Animated. 88 minutes. Rated G.

■ "Forget the wooden kid with the schnoz" (who's a bit "dull" anyway) – this "wonderful" animated fantasy is more memorable for its introduction of the "classic" character of Jiminy Cricket and its Oscar-winning song, 'When You Wish Upon a Star'; otherwise, this story of a puppet transformed into a boy still "combines some of the sweetest and scariest scenes" in all of Disneydom.

Place in the Sun, A ✉◑ 27 | 27 | 27 | 24

1951. Directed by George Stevens. With Montgomery Clift, Elizabeth Taylor, Shelley Winters. 122 minutes. Not Rated.

■ This "classic American" love triangle from Oscar-winning director Stevens might be a "glamorized version of the Dreiser novel" but was still rather daring for its time given the unwed-mother subplot; while it's hard to miss the "radiant Clift and Taylor" (thanks to some swoonworthy giant close-ups), "poor Shelley Winters'" role as the third wheel may well be the best performance; most famous line: Liz's smoldering "'tell mama all.'"

Places in the Heart ⊠ 20 | 22 | 20 | 18

1984. Directed by Robert Benton. With Sally Field, Lindsay Crouse, Ed Harris, Danny Glover. 112 minutes. Rated PG.

◪ Softhearted souls really, really like this "moving Depression-era tale" of a Texas "woman alone with kids, a farm, a mortgage" and, thankfully, plenty of "courage"; though both Field and screenwriter Benton snagged Oscars for this "heartwarming" study of "struggle, conquest and forgiveness", the hard-hearted nix it as too "depressing."

Planet of the Apes Ⓘ 23 | 20 | 25 | 23

1968. Directed by Franklin J. Schaffner. With Charlton Heston, Roddy McDowall, Kim Hunter. 112 minutes. Rated G.

■ "Darwin would have loved" this "thought-provoking" stew of "science fiction and pop culture" about an American astronaut who crashes on a simian-ruled planet; Heston's "brawny", "over-the-top" performance brings equal parts "paranoid power" and "Republican campiness" to the leading role, while that "wallop" of an ending remains one of the "most talked-about ever."

Platoon ⊠ 25 | 25 | 24 | 26

1986. Directed by Oliver Stone. With Tom Berenger, Willem Dafoe, Charlie Sheen. 120 minutes. Rated R.

■ "Disturbing" yet "unforgettable", this "almost-too-real" war picture offers a "raw" view of the Vietnam conflict as seen "through the eyes of a recruit just arrived in the jungle"; granted, it "fails to offer the slightest glimmer of hope", but it "captures the desperation" of battle "better than any other movie", with a clutch of Oscars (including Best Picture and Best Director) to prove it.

Player, The 23 | 23 | 23 | 22

1992. Directed by Robert Altman. With Tim Robbins, Greta Scacchi, Fred Ward. 124 minutes. Rated R.

■ "People who love movies about movies" love this ultra-"scathing" "satire" of "cutthroat" Hollywood, "perfectly directed" by "genius" Altman; cineasts cite the "excellent opening shot" (eight minutes "without a cut") and the "wonderful" all-star "cameo" appearances peppered throughout, but zero in on Robbins' "marvelous" portrayal of a "ne'er-do-well producer" as the real standout.

Play It Again, Sam 22 | 21 | 23 | 20

1972. Directed by Herbert Ross. With Woody Allen, Diane Keaton, Tony Roberts. 85 minutes. Rated PG.

◪ Woody's "wonderful" in this "fine early comedy" adapted from his Broadway hit about a "lovable", lovelorn film critic so enamored with *Casablanca* that he conjures up an imaginary Bogey for advice; though this "funny" "spoof" "works on every level" for "hard-core" Allenites, purists protest it "suffers because he didn't direct it."

Play Misty for Me 22 | 20 | 23 | 19

1971. Directed by Clint Eastwood. With Clint Eastwood, Jessica Walter, Donna Mills. 102 minutes. Rated R.

■ The "original – and much creepier" – version of "*Fatal Attraction*", this "scary", "suspenseful" erotic thriller concerns a 'Misty'-spinning DJ "stalked by a deranged radio listener" (who supplies the "jump-out-at-you" moments); fans "get a thrill" out of Eastwood playing the "hunted instead of the hunter" for a change and dub his directorial debut "must-see" material.

Pleasantville 20 | 21 | 22 | 23

1998. Directed by Gary Ross. With Tobey Maguire, Jeff Daniels, Joan Allen, Reese Witherspoon. 124 minutes. Rated PG-13.

◪ "Two modern teens" are magically transported into the "world of a '50s sitcom" in this "totally disarming" parable about "American family" life that's enlivened by some high-"tech tricks" (notably the "imaginative" use of "color vs. black and white"); though a bit "heavy-handed" for some, its "clever premise" and "memorable Randy Newman score" make for "unique" moviemaking.

Pollock 22 | 26 | 21 | 22

2000. Directed by Ed Harris. With Ed Harris, Marcia Gay Harden, Amy Madigan. 122 minutes. Rated R.

■ "Harris is uncanny" capturing the "essence of dark genius" Jackson Pollock, the "misunderstood" "20th-century artist"/"self-destructive" individual who's the subject of this "unflashy" biopic; as his mate and fellow painter, "Harden matches him every step of the way" in a "deservedly Oscar-winning" performance that further transforms this "amazing life" story into a "real work of art."

Poltergeist Ⓘ 22 | 20 | 23 | 24

1982. Directed by Tobe Hooper. With JoBeth Williams, Craig T. Nelson, Beatrice Straight. 114 minutes. Rated PG.

■ "Half social satire, half haunted-house tale", this "vivid" "roller-coaster ride" of a horror flick has a "pure Spielberg" premise: "affluent parents and cute children" living in a home "built over a graveyard" chock-full of "pesky ghosts"; the "strong story", "ahead-of-its-time special effects" and that "little voice" squeaking "they're he-ere" still startle boo-mers "20 years later."

Poseidon Adventure, The Ⓘ 19 | 18 | 20 | 22

1972. Directed by Ronald Neame. With Gene Hackman, Ernest Borgnine, Red Buttons. 117 minutes. Rated PG.

◪ A "boat flips over" and the "actors flip out" in this "topsy-turvy" "granddaddy" of "Hollywood all-star disaster flicks" that's "more fun in a campy way than you'd expect"; sure, the "phenomenal underwater footage" and "unforgettable (if not completely subtle) performances" are "entertaining" enough, but foes sneer this "kitschy" "sinking ship" defines the "true meaning of 'all wet.'"

Postcards from the Edge 18 | 23 | 19 | 18

1990. Directed by Mike Nichols. With Meryl Streep, Shirley MacLaine, Dennis Quaid. 101 minutes. Rated R.

■ Edgy types tout this "Hollywood insider story" as a "terrifically funny" look at the relationship between a "recovering-druggie" movie star and her scenery-chewing movie-star mom; though both the "biting" MacLaine and "brilliant" Streep "shine", fans single out scenarist Carrie Fisher, whose "sharp", vaguely "autobiographical" script is as acidly "amusing" as they come.

Postman Always Rings Twice, The ◑∅ 25 | 25 | 25 | 24

1946. Directed by Tay Garnett. With John Garfield, Lana Turner, Cecil Kellaway. 113 minutes. Not Rated.

■ "Garfield and Turner set off the smoke alarms" in this "steamy" slice of film noir, a "deliciously sinful" saga about a "hot" "married femme fatale", a "sexy" "streetwise vagabond" and their simmering affair that "boils over into murderous passion"; though this "twisting" tale of "love, betrayal" and "homicide" is pretty "wonderful", one burning question remains: "didn't people know about divorce in those days?"

Postman Always Rings Twice, The 20 | 23 | 22 | 19

1981. Directed by Bob Rafelson. With Jack Nicholson, Jessica Lange, John Colicos. 122 minutes. Rated R.

◩ Maybe it's "not as good as the original", but this "decent" enough remake of the film noir classic features "real sex" scenes instead of "implied" ones, most notably that display of "countertop love" that inspired many to install "butcher blocks in their kitchens"; "Jack is as creepy as ever" and Jessica's "good" as well, though purists pout "there's too much emphasis on sex at the expense of characterization" here.

POTEMKIN ◑ 27 | 22 | 25 | 27

1925. Directed by Sergei Eisenstein. With Aleksandr Antonov, Vladimir Barsky. 75 minutes. Not Rated.

■ More than 75 years later, cineasts are still electrified by director Eisenstein's "influential" "triumph" that "put 'montage' into the filmmaking lexicon" and "forever set the standards for camerawork"; recounting the failed 1905 uprising against the Czar, it's best known for its "often copied" "baby-carriage-on-the-Odessa-steps sequence" that "paved the way for edit-happy MTV directors"; indeed, it's so "viscerally exciting" that many insist it "should be mandatory moviegoing."

Presumed Innocent 20 | 21 | 22 | 18

1990. Directed by Alan J. Pakula. With Harrison Ford, Brian Dennehy, Raul Julia. 127 minutes. Rated R.

■ Based on Scott Turow's best-seller, this "darkly powerful courtroom thriller" features an "excellent" Ford as a Philadelphia prosecutor whose life takes a "roller-coaster" turn after he's accused of murder; jurists say its "cliff-hanger" storyline boasts a "perfect surprise ending" that "keeps you guessing up till the last frame."

Pretty in Pink 19 | 18 | 19 | 18

1986. Directed by Howard Deutch. With Molly Ringwald, Harry Dean Stanton, Jon Cryer. 96 minutes. Rated PG-13.

◪ For an "entertaining" "glimpse into the horrors of teenage dating", try this "brat pack" comedy "classic" starring Ringwald ("at her poutiest") as an "angst"-ridden gal from the "wrong side of the tracks" who falls for a "rich preppie"; ok, it's "sappy" and "not too original", but given all the "cute touches" and that "killer soundtrack", many call it a "guilty pleasure to the nth degree."

Pretty Woman 23 | 22 | 22 | 22

1990. Directed by Garry Marshall. With Richard Gere, Julia Roberts, Jason Alexander. 119 minutes. Rated R.

■ Despite a hoary premise that lies somewhere between "Cinderella" and "Eliza Doolittle", this story of a "hooker with a heart of gold" who bags "Prince Charming" is a "dreamy", "happily-ever-after" romance that "put Julia (and her smile) on the map and the rest of us on Rodeo Drive"; credit the "dizzying charisma" and "palpable" "chemistry between its stars" for its "believability", and though the "glamorization-of-prostitution" angle turns off bluenoses, "hopeless romantics" insist it will "steal your heart."

Pride of the Yankees, The ◑ 22 | 22 | 23 | 20

1942. Directed by Sam Wood. With Gary Cooper, Teresa Wright, Walter Brennan. 127 minutes. Not Rated.

■ A "must" for both "baseball and Yankee fans", this "best sports" biopic virtually guarantees a "lump in the throat" as it delineates the life story of the "great Lou Gehrig" and his courage in the face of death; in the title role, Cooper is so effectively "self-effacing" that repeat viewers "cry every time" they hear his "farewell speech."

Primal Fear 22 | 25 | 23 | 21

1996. Directed by Gregory Hoblit. With Richard Gere, Laura Linney, Edward Norton. 129 minutes. Rated R.

■ The verdict's in: an "amazing" Norton "hits a home run" in his "stunning debut" as a "timid, stuttering" altar boy accused of killing an archbishop in this "unsettling" murder mystery/courtroom drama; otherwise, the "acting is on-point all around" (even "Gere is less dull than usual"), though the performances are nearly "blown away" by that "shocking", "knock-you-for-a-loop" "surprise ending."

Prince of Egypt, The 19 | – | 19 | 23

1998. Directed by Simon Wells, Brenda Chapman, Steve Hickner. Animated. 99 minutes. Rated PG.

◪ Respondents part like the Red Sea over this "history/cartoon combo" from the "then-fledgling Dreamworks": yeasayers insist it's a "fascinating" "modern Bible retelling" of the story of Moses' exodus with the Jews from Egypt, with "terrific animation" and "beautiful songs", but apostates opine it's an "overwrought" derivation of the "Disney formula" that "lacks" in all areas "except special effects."

Prince of Tides, The 19 | 21 | 21 | 20

1991. Directed by Barbra Streisand. With Barbra Streisand, Nick Nolte, Blythe Danner. 132 minutes. Rated R.

◪ In this "interesting story" about a "Southern football coach, his dysfunctional family" and the "NYC psychiatrist who sorts it all out", the "convincing" "Nolte really gives his all"; however, despite the drama's "lyricism" and "stunning scenery", some say the "self-important" Babs "never should have directed herself" in this "vanity" production.

PRINCESS BRIDE, THE 27 | 23 | 27 | 24

1987. Directed by Rob Reiner. With Cary Elwes, Mandy Patinkin, Robin Wright. 98 minutes. Rated PG.

■ Despite the "chick-flick title", this "lighthearted" but "fractured fairy tale" defies "categorization" and is admired by "even the most macho" guys for its "swordfights" and "verbal jousting"; thanks to an "intelligent" William Goldman script, "masterful" direction by Reiner and an "incredibly talented" cast, "finding a better movie is inconceivable" – "plus, it's got André the Giant."

Princess Diaries, The 18 | 19 | 17 | 18

2001. Directed by Garry Marshall. With Julie Andrews, Anne Hathaway, Hector Elizondo. 114 minutes. Rated G.

◪ It's "every girl's dream" – to discover she's "actually a princess" (albeit of "some little country you've never heard of") – and this "wholesome" "mom-and-daughter" comedy follows newcomer Hathaway's transformation from "high-school dork" to crowned head amusingly enough; but even though this "feel-good" flick appeals to the "teenager inside us all", critics complain it's a "little flat for older audiences."

Prizzi's Honor 21 | 24 | 21 | 19

1985. Directed by John Huston. With Jack Nicholson, Kathleen Turner, Anjelica Huston. 130 minutes. Rated R.

■ This "terrific black comedy about a dysfunctional mob family" anticipates *The Sopranos* with "cynical", "give-and-take" dialogue delivered by the "perfect cast" (a "bright" Jack, a "perfect" Kathleen and a "stellar", Oscar-copping Anjelica); one of director Huston's "last masterpieces", this "whacked-out" "gangster farce" wrings laughs via a "play-it-straight" script peppered with "in-jokes"; best line: "let's do it right here on the oriental – with all the lights on."

Producers, The ✉ 26 | 26 | 26 | 23

1968. Directed by Mel Brooks. With Zero Mostel, Gene Wilder, Kenneth Mars. 88 minutes. Rated PG.

■ Flaunting "silly and shocking" "originality" "long before" the "Broadway hoopla", this "anarchic", "appallingly funny" comedy boasts Mostel and Wilder "at their best" as perps of a "Ponzi scheme" to produce an "unbelievably over-the-top" musical winningly titled *Springtime for Hitler* and cash in on its failure; it earns a standing ovation as "unrelenting" "inspired lunacy" from Brooks' "warped mind" that "holds up" as a manic "masterpiece."

PSYCHO ◑ⓘ 28 | 26 | 27 | 27

1960. Directed by Alfred Hitchcock. With Anthony Perkins, Vera Miles, John Gavin, Janet Leigh. 109 minutes. Rated R.

■ "Generations of moviegoers started double-locking their bathroom doors" after one look at the "famous shower scene" in this "classic Hitchcock" "psycho-logical thriller" that was "quite a shocker in its day" and "still packs a wallop" – "without the gross violence of modern flicks"; standouts include Bernard Herrmann's "scariest film score ever" and Perkins' "twitchy", "tour-de-force" performance as the ultimate "mama's boy."

Pulp Fiction ✉ 26 | 26 | 25 | 25

1994. Directed by Quentin Tarantino. With John Travolta, Samuel L. Jackson, Uma Thurman, Bruce Willis, Amanda Plummer, Tim Roth, Ving Rhames. 154 minutes. Rated R.

■ A "pioneer of plot shuffling" and "twisty chronology", this "propulsive", "in-your-face" thriller is a "true original" with an "unpredictable storyline" and "dialogue that's like a punch in the face"; recounting the affairs of some "charming hit men", it stars a "rogue's gallery of actors" in memorable bits ("Travolta's dancing", Uma's overdose, Plummer's "psychotic rant") played out with "dark humor", "intense violence" and "foul language"; not only did it "put the brilliant Tarantino on the map", it's in a "genre all by itself."

Purple Rose of Cairo, The 21 | 21 | 24 | 21

1985. Directed by Woody Allen. With Mia Farrow, Jeff Daniels, Danny Aiello. 84 minutes. Rated PG.

■ The Woodman rises to the occasion with this "clever", "not-self-absorbed" comedy, a "bittersweet tale" featuring some of "Farrow's best" work as an escapist Depression-era moviegoer whose "fantasy world" merges with "real life" when an RKO star walks off the screen into her life; the "imaginative" plot takes an "inside-out" look at "love of the movies", with a last reel calculated to "break your heart."

QUIET MAN, THE ✉ 27 | 25 | 25 | 27

1952. Directed by John Ford. With John Wayne, Maureen O'Hara, Barry Fitzgerald. 129 minutes. Not Rated.

■ Begosh, "every Irish" cliché is "alive and well" in this "romanticized" drama, starring the Duke as an American boxer who hangs up his gloves and settles in his Hibernian "ancestral home" only to be a-smitten by the "beautiful", "feisty O'Hara"; presenting a "postcard" Ireland populated by "enchanting townspeople", it's "witty" and – despite a wee bit o' "blarney" – judged "worthy of a yearly viewing."

Quiz Show 21 | 23 | 21 | 20

1994. Directed by Robert Redford. With Ralph Fiennes, John Turturro, Rob Morrow. 133 minutes. Rated PG-13.

■ "Say it isn't so", Bob: "America's loss of innocence" is the subtext for this "intelligent", "underappreciated" drama chronicling the '50s TV quiz-show scandals, an "engaging" but "blistering" commentary on the "mania for celebrity and money"; Turturro is the cast's "bright spot" as a bought-off contestant in a rigged highbrow showdown, and nostalgists prize the "vivid picture of the era", long before *Millionaire* – the "kicker is it really happened."

Radio Days 23 | 23 | 23 | 23

1987. Directed by Woody Allen. With Mia Farrow, Julie Kavner, Dianne Wiest. 85 minutes. Rated PG.

■ Tune in for "fond memories" to this "charming" "family comedy", a "low-key", "affectionate period piece" set in "late-'30s" Rockaway Beach, where "childhood innocence, neurotic relatives" and golden-age radio fill the airwaves in a series of "warm vignettes"; touted for "top-to-bottom acting excellence", it's a "funny", "free-form" sampler of "Allen at his sunniest" and "most enjoyable."

Raging Bull ⊠◑ 26 | 28 | 24 | 26

1980. Directed by Martin Scorsese. With Robert De Niro, Cathy Moriarty, Joe Pesci. 129 minutes. Rated R.

■ Perhaps the "best boxing movie of all time", this "brutal" but "riveting" biopic "charts the rise and fall" of former middleweight champion Jake LaMotta, whose toughest opponents were his own "self-destructive tendencies"; shot in "beautiful black and white", it features a "primo De Niro" (who won the Oscar), ably directed by the "incredible Scorsese"; sure, it can be "as painful as an open wound" to watch, but most judges agree this is "knockout" filmmaking.

RAIDERS OF THE LOST ARK ⓫∅ 28 | 24 | 27 | 28

1981. Directed by Steven Spielberg. With Harrison Ford, Karen Allen, Paul Freeman. 115 minutes. Rated PG.

■ It doesn't get "more exciting" than this "benchmark" of "nonstop" "pulp-fiction action", Spielberg's "roller-coaster" "homage" to "Saturday matinee" serials that introduces the "rakish" Indiana Jones, a tweedy archaeologist with a "strapping-hero" alter ego who scraps with the Nazis over an "all-powerful artifact"; chock-full of "retro" delights like "tongue-in-cheek" humor, "improbable" "cliff-hanger" "escapes" and a "love interest" amid the "snakes, whips and guns", it's a "rousing" "blockbuster" that proves the "'80s weren't all bad."

Rain Man ✉ 25 | 27 | 24 | 23

1988. Directed by Barry Levinson. With Dustin Hoffman, Tom Cruise, Valeria Golino. 133 minutes. Rated R.

■ This Best Picture winner is an unconventional "brothers bonding" drama driven by a Oscar-winning performance from Hoffman, who's "nothing short of incredible" as a full-grown "autistic savant" blessed with an endless supply of "quirky mannerisms" and "memorable lines"; Cruise shows off his own "acting chops" as the "scheming" sibling angling for half his inheritance, bringing on showers of "insight" that clear up to let a "feel-good" resolution shine through.

Raising Arizona 23 | 23 | 23 | 21

1987. Directed by Joel Coen. With Nicolas Cage, Holly Hunter, John Goodman. 94 minutes. Rated PG-13.

■ For a "completely original" and truly "bizarre" screwball comedy, check out this "hilarious white-trash" "cult classic" about a "childless", "criminal-class" couple (a policewoman married to a "failed convenience-store thief") that kidnaps a kid; Cage and Hunter are drolly "deadpan" delivering "dialogue that can't be beat", while the plot is typical Coen brothers: "goofy", "quirky" and gosh "darn funny."

RAN F 27 | 25 | 27 | 29

1985. Directed by Akira Kurosawa. With Tatsuya Nakadai, Mieko Harada, Daisuke Ryu. 160 minutes. Rated R.

■ "Big, bold and beautiful", Kurosawa's "swan song" shows his "deft touch" intact in this "expansive retelling of *King Lear*" transformed into a "riveting" samurai "epic" involving a "Shogun" warlord whose decision to sheath his sword for good leads to intra-clan "betrayals and eventual downfall"; suitably "Shakespearean" in its "grand scale", with "visually stunning" depictions of "feudal society" and "incredible" "battle scenes", it's "slow"-running but hailed as "brilliant almost beyond belief."

RASHOMON ✉ ◐ F 29 | 27 | 29 | 25

1951. Directed by Akira Kurosawa. With Toshiro Mifune, Machiko Kyo, Masayuki Mori. 88 minutes. Not Rated.

■ Surely "truth is in the eye of the beholder", but most agree that Kurosawa's "superb" "head-twister" of a Japanese drama should be "required viewing"; aided by "exquisite" camerawork and "fine medieval embellishments", it's a "simple story" about an ambush in the forest told from "four different" points of view, proving that "self-interest" amounts to "nine-tenths of everything"; in sum, this "seminal" tale of "fallibility" has been tirelessly "copied but never equaled."

Reality Bites 19 | 18 | 18 | 17

1994. Directed by Ben Stiller. With Winona Ryder, Ethan Hawke, Janeane Garofalo. 99 minutes. Rated PG-13.

■ "Escape with the losers" in this romantic comedy of "post-college" Gen-X existence as Winona and company find themselves "going nowhere" but obliged to deal when faced with "job woes", tainted love and "utter annoyance with life"; vets of the day say as a "portrayal of MTV and other pop-culture" touchstones (from couture to tunes to "attitude"), "nothing represents the '90s more accurately."

REAR WINDOW 28 | 27 | 28 | 27

1954. Directed by Alfred Hitchcock. With James Stewart, Grace Kelly, Thelma Ritter. 112 minutes. Rated PG.

■ "Voyeurism" meets "suspense" in this "snooper's dream" about a "wheelchair-bound" photographer "spying on his neighbors" and trying to "trap a killer" while fending off his girlfriend, who's tempting him into "another trap – marriage"; while the "crisp script" and "great NY" set draw huzzahs, fans tout its "perfectly cast" leads, the "solid" Stewart and "deeelicious" Kelly; so many find it "unsurpassed" that it was voted the top Hitchcock flick in this *Survey.*

Rebecca ✉◑ 27 | 27 | 27 | 25

1940. Directed by Alfred Hitchcock. With Laurence Olivier, Joan Fontaine, Judith Anderson. 130 minutes. Not Rated.

■ Based on Daphne du Maurier's "ultimate romance novel", "Hitchcock's first American film" is a "dark, moody" tale of a woman living in the shadow of her new husband's old wife; "haunting" and "eerily captivating", it showcases an "excellent" Olivier and a "gorgeous" Fontaine, but it's the "over-the-top" Anderson who's the real "hoot" here.

Rebel Without a Cause 24 | 24 | 21 | 22

1955. Directed by Nicholas Ray. With James Dean, Natalie Wood, Sal Mineo. 111 minutes. Not Rated.

■ A "lost generation lives on" in this "terse drama" of "disaffected youth" and "family conflict", which elevated Dean to "icon" status as a "rebellious" juvenile delinquent who leads a "great cast" as they cope with "hope, fear and love" in the "inchoate LA" of the '50s; if all that acting out is a bit "dated", most maintain it "lives up to its rep" as the "ultimate" ode to "teen alienation."

Red River ◑ 26 | 25 | 25 | 27

1948. Directed by Howard Hawks. With John Wayne, Montgomery Clift, Joanne Dru. 133 minutes. Not Rated.

■ "Perhaps the grandest" Western of all, this cowpuncher "classic" breaks into a gallop when "lots of hunky men" saddle up for a dangerous cattle drive along the Chisholm Trail; Wayne "excels in an unsympathetic role" as a "stolid" rancher who turns against Monty, who "holds his own" as a buckaroo of "brooding sensitivity"; the result is a horn-lock that fans brand a grade-A prime "rewatcher."

Reds ✉∅ 21 | 21 | 20 | 22

1981. Directed by Warren Beatty. With Warren Beatty, Diane Keaton, Jack Nicholson. 194 minutes. Rated PG.

◪ Agitprop meets "epic romance" in this "impressive" bio of writers John Reed and Louise Bryant that chronicles their courtship and activities as bolshie sympathizers during the Russian Revolution; "Beatty's labor of love" "celebrating American radicalism", it's an "excellent recreation" of the time, framed by "remembrances" of "largely forgotten men and women", but "major themes" or no, critics call it a "big production" that's "too long to keep you interested."

Red Shoes, The 26 | 24 | 24 | 26

1948. Directed by Michael Powell, Emeric Pressburger. With Anton Walbrook, Moira Shearer. 133 minutes. Not Rated.

■ With a tip of the slipper to Hans Christian Andersen, this "ageless" drama of "romance and ballet" "takes a fairy tale and creates magic" around the story of a young dancer who joins a celebrated troupe only to enter into a pas de deux with a composer; "sumptuous" staging and "dreamy choreography" make it a terpsichorean "benchmark", and dance-lesson vets "love every bit of it."

Red Violin, The F 24 | 23 | 24 | 24

1999. Directed by François Girard. With Samuel L. Jackson, Greta Scacchi. 131 minutes. Rated R.

■ A "symphony" recounting the "many tales of a violin's life", this "smart", "intricate" drama uses an "international cast" to "follow the path" of a "fabulous instrument" from its creation in Renaissance Italy though various owners, countries and epochs, up to Jackson's encounter as a present-day appraiser; in spite of "art-house" airs, boosters bow to a "twisting" story that "keeps you guessing" – backed by a "stunning" soundtrack featuring "real music by a real composer."

Remains of the Day, The 24 | 27 | 23 | 25

1993. Directed by James Ivory. With Anthony Hopkins, Emma Thompson, Christopher Reeve. 138 minutes. Rated PG.

■ "If you loved *Howards End*", you'll dig this "complex and entertaining" drama of "two fragile souls" on a British estate in the late '30s; "repressed" head butler Hopkins "puts duty above all else", even his yen for housekeeper Thompson, and both give "precise, controlled performances" filled with "gripping silences" to suit its "nuanced" story of "unfulfilled love", "class-system" bias and the "obtuseness of the upper crust" – just "don't expect action."

Remember the Titans 20 | 21 | 21 | 19

2000. Directed by Boaz Yakin. With Denzel Washington, Will Patton, Wood Harris. 113 minutes. Rated PG.

◪ "Denzel is the man" to knock a ball team into shape while tackling "racial fault lines" in this "inspirational" family drama about a black high-school coach taking over a newly integrated football squad; if the "feel-good" theme of "tolerance and social understanding" on and off the field plays out as "hokey" and "about as deep as astroturf", fans "cheer anyway" for a "sleeper" that never fumbles its underlying "hope."

Requiem for a Dream 25 | 27 | 24 | 25

2000. Directed by Darren Aronofsky. With Ellen Burstyn, Jared Leto, Jennifer Connelly. 102 minutes. Not Rated.

■ "Heavy" and "altogether devastating", this "bleak" "druggy" drama "spirals into the depths of hell" on the back of some "scary", strung-out imagery and Burstyn's "amazing" turn as a magenta-maned diet-pill popper with a none-too-swift junkie son; a "stomach-churning" depiction of "major drug use" that pushes Aronofsky to the "cutting edge" of "directing talents", it's "not subtle" but lingers like a "brilliant", "unnerving" "nightmare" – "be prepared" for some "grueling" going.

Reservoir Dogs 24 | 25 | 24 | 22

1992. Directed by Quentin Tarantino. With Harvey Keitel, Tim Roth, Michael Madsen. 99 minutes. Rated R.

◪ The Tarantino "template" for a "new" style of crime thriller splices "hip, sharp" dialogue with "hard-core violence" as a "dream cast" sporting two-tone threads turns a jewel heist into a "riveting" "bloody spectacle"; the "clever" script relies on diced chronology, "sly riffs" on pop culture and "psychological twists" to lend heart to the "vicious" gang, though many howl the "nasty" bits ("ear removal", anyone?) are still "painful to watch."

Return of the Jedi ∅ 24 | 20 | 23 | 28

1983. Directed by Richard Marquand. With Mark Hamill, Harrison Ford, Carrie Fisher, Billy Dee Williams. 134 minutes. Rated PG.

◪ Either a "worthy sequel" or "leftovers", this "wrap-up" episode of the *Star Wars* original trilogy finds the now-classic cast "comfortable in their roles", mugging their way through a "patented good-wins-over-evil storyline" with ample space for "cool special effects" and an "amazing" "final battle"; loyalists say the force is with it, but skeptics see a "weak entry" overrun with "cute, furry Ewoks", foreshadowing "toy tie-ins" and the "beginnings of Jar Jar."

Right Stuff, The 26 | 24 | 26 | 26

1983. Directed by Philip Kaufman. With Sam Shepard, Scott Glenn, Ed Harris. 193 minutes. Rated PG.

■ "Exuberant", "involving" and "proud to be American", this "triumphant" drama "never flags" in launching Tom Wolfe's "snarky yet sincere" "epic of the space age" onto the big screen; a "retelling of true events" surrounding the evolution of test pilots into astronauts in the Mercury program, it takes "historical" stuff and pushes the envelope with "adventure, humor" and an "ensemble cast" that's "A-ok in every way."

Risky Business 20 | 18 | 19 | 18

1983. Directed by Paul Brickman. With Tom Cruise, Rebecca De Mornay. 98 minutes. Rated R.

■ "Every boy's dream" comes true in this "smart, sexy" "coming-of-age" comedy, with Cruise as the high-schooler who turns chez suburbia into party central when the 'rents leave town – only to fall into "the arms of a beautiful hooker" and venture into the brothel biz; it's a "funny" jibe at "upper-middle-class teen life" and "raging hormones", with a celebrated scene of "Tom dancing in his Jockeys" that's nothing short of "starmaking."

River Runs Through It, A 22 | 23 | 21 | 25

1992. Directed by Robert Redford. With Brad Pitt, Craig Sheffer, Tom Skerritt. 123 minutes. Rated PG.

■ Sounding "deep" waters with a "pastoral" tale of "life as we no longer know it", Redford's "elegiac" drama of "family bonds" takes a "moving", "candid" look at the sibling rivalry between two small-town minister's sons; the "smooth" pace is set by the stars' "subtle emotion" and "striking" cinematography that captures the "Montana wilderness" in full "majesty", though some clock-watchers find the running "too slow."

Road Warrior, The Ⓘ 22 | 18 | 21 | 20

(aka Mad Max 2)

1982. Directed by George Miller. With Mel Gibson, Bruce Spence, Mike Preston. 94 minutes. Rated R.

■ "Road rage" kicks into overdrive in this "raw" "Aussie action flick", with "lean, mean", "leather"-wrapped Gibson "at his baddest" as Mad Max, a "lone, reluctant cowboy" cruising a "post-apocalyptic" wasteland and upholding his "own brand of justice"; set in a "harsh", "nihilistic" near-future when barbaric gangs comb the desert pestering decent folk for petrol, its combo of an "intriguing" setup and "incredible car stunts" makes it a "visceral" "cult favorite"; gas up.

Rock, The 20 | 21 | 20 | 22

1996. Directed by Michael Bay. With Sean Connery, Nicolas Cage, Ed Harris. 136 minutes. Rated R.

■ Find out who's got the biggest "fireballs" in this "noisy" "juggernaut" of a "testosterone fix", bringing "slick", "edge-of-your-seat action" to Alcatraz as "crusty" ex-spy Connery and "bumbling" weapons expert Cage penetrate the prison walls to stop a mad general from blitzing the Bay Area with nerve gas; followers find the pair "amazing together", and despite the highly "not-likely" scenario, the "awesome locale" and "great FX" ensure a "kick-ass" "couch night."

Rocky ✉ Ⓘ 25 | 20 | 25 | 21

1976. Directed by John G. Avildsen. With Sylvester Stallone, Talia Shire, Burt Young. 119 minutes. Rated PG.

■ This "red-blooded" ring drama (and Oscar champ) "goes the distance" with an "underdog-makes-good" theme as "two-bit" boxer Sly "wins over everyone's heart" when he "gets his shot" at the title, works up "lots of sweat" and "finds true love" along the way; though part "hokey" "Hollywood" "fantasy", it's also a "stirring" "confidence-booster" that packs an everlasting "wallop" (and stands as the "only really good Stallone" pic).

Rocky Horror Picture Show, The 21 | 18 | 19 | 22

1975. Directed by Jim Sharman. With Tim Curry, Susan Sarandon, Barry Bostwick. 100 minutes. Rated R.

■ "Beyond weird" to the uninitiated, this "camp classic" "rock 'n' roll musical" is famed for the "floor show" put on at "midnight screenings" by costumed carousers who pronounce it the "best trash ever"; a "pure B-movie" spoof involving a pair of innocents who stumble into the lair of a "sweet transvestite", it's "silly" but "entertaining on its own bizarre level", so "get out your toast, rice and lighter" and "sing along" with this "legendary mess."

Roger & Me ∅ 24 | – | 24 | 20

1989. Directed by Michael Moore. Documentary. 91 minutes. Rated R.

■ "Laugh and cringe" at this salvo of "guerrilla filmmaking", an "eye-opening" documentary chronicling both the "disintegration" of a Michigan town after its GM plant pulls up stakes and "squeaky wheel" Moore's "quest to confront" the corporation's CEO; the "too-real" footage is "drop-dead funny" yet "sobering" ("rabbit lovers beware"), and if a few find the "irreverent" tone "annoying", "progressives everywhere" hail it as a "vital" "exposé" of the "new global economy" and a "stirring" fanfare for the "common man."

Romancing the Stone Ⓘ 20 | 19 | 21 | 20

1984. Directed by Robert Zemeckis. With Michael Douglas, Kathleen Turner, Danny DeVito. 105 minutes. Rated PG-13.

◪ This "poor man's *Raiders of the Lost Ark*" turns a "lighthearted" adventure into a "fast-paced, colorful crowd-pleaser", with Turner cast as a "nerdy" romance novelist who "makes good" when she hooks up with "tongue-in-cheek hero" Douglas down South America way; the two are "quite the duo", and some "humorous action sequences" with archrival DeVito "trying to keep up" make for "durable" "escapism" with the occasional "deft touch."

Roman Holiday ✉◑∅ 27 | 26 | 25 | 25

1953. Directed by William Wyler. With Gregory Peck, Audrey Hepburn. 118 minutes. Not Rated.

■ A "date movie without equal", this "frothy", "witty romance" presents a "radiant" Hepburn as the "rebellious" "gamine princess" with a "pixie cut" who "plays hooky" in the Eternal City, escorted by "charming", "not-so-hardboiled reporter" Peck; helped along by "wondrous" "Roman scenery", their "coy" exchanges lead things on their natural "exhilarating" course, making for a "captivating" "fantasy" that draws to a "bittersweet", "refreshingly realistic" ending ("awww!").

Romeo and Juliet 26 | 24 | 27 | 26

1968. Directed by Franco Zeffirelli. With Olivia Hussey, Leonard Whiting. 138 minutes. Rated PG.

■ "Achingly beautiful" and played with "youthful vigor", this "faithful Zeffirelli" reading renders the "grand" romance of star-crossed love so "accessible" that "even boys cry" during the tragic last act; the "classic" production stays "true to the Bard" with "so-cute" "teenage actors" and "gorgeous" sets, pleasing "purists" as the "definitive film version" and surviving as the odds-on favorite to be the Shakespeare everyone's "made to watch in school."

Romeo + Juliet 19 | 17 | 22 | 23

1996. Directed by Baz Luhrmann. With Leonardo DiCaprio, Claire Danes, John Leguizamo. 120 minutes. Rated PG-13.

◪ Flash master Luhrmann presents the ageless romance "in a different light" in this "daring" "updating", a "kinetic" "visual feast" that aims to please the "MTV generation" with "pop music" and "creative" "modern-day" staging; Leo and Claire lend the lovers "teen-idol" allure, and if some sniff at "style over substance" and say the "acting seriously lacks", those who are "ok with extravagance" find it "effective" and "really cool."

Room with a View, A ✉ 26 | 26 | 24 | 27

1986. Directed by James Ivory. With Maggie Smith, Helena Bonham Carter, Denholm Elliott. 117 minutes. Not Rated.

■ "Florence looks like heaven" in this "crisp" "costume drama" about a "proper Victorian girl's" sightseeing tour that's considerably perked up by "friendships that form in a pensione", leading to her "romantic" "awakening"; the "brilliant acting" brings "wit and energy" to a "sunny" "study of class and character" that finds all kinds of room for "superb" "fin de siècle" touches and "seductive" shots of the "Italian landscape" – "most enchanting" sigh the Merchant Ivory minions.

Rope 22 | 21 | 23 | 22

1948. Directed by Alfred Hitchcock. With Farley Granger, James Stewart, John Dall. 80 minutes. Rated PG.

◪ "One word – Hitchcock" – draws film buffs to this "chilling" reworking of the "Leopold and Loeb murder case" that's told with a "compelling" "gimmick": it was "shot entirely on one set" and "runs in real time" (without any visible cuts); though a few snore "slow and stagy", at least the master's "eye to detail" and "dark humor" make it an "interesting curiosity."

Rose, The ∅ 19 | 23 | 18 | 18

1979. Directed by Mark Rydell. With Bette Midler, Alan Bates, Frederic Forrest. 125 minutes. Rated R.

■ The "mesmerizing" Miss M makes the "most stunning movie debut since Streisand" in this rock-chanteuse drama, a "homage" to the wild-at-heart chronicling the life and times of a "self-destructive Janis Joplin type" as she barrels down the road to ruin; groupies who insist Midler's "strong performance" should have "won the Oscar" can always find consolation in that "great title song."

Rosemary's Baby Ⓘ 24 | 25 | 25 | 22

1968. Directed by Roman Polanski. With Mia Farrow, John Cassavetes, Ruth Gordon. 136 minutes. Rated R.

■ A "glamorous horror" flick about a "naive" housewife "duped" into bearing "Satan's child", this "gut-wrenching classic" still "scares the hell out" of nearly everybody; "pro-choice" types tout Farrow's "amazing" turn (and "faaabulous haircut") as well as Polanski's "very faithful adaptation" of Ira Levin's novel, but everyone says that the "devilishly good", Oscar-winning Gordon "steals the show."

Roxanne 21 | 21 | 21 | 19

1987. Directed by Fred Schepisi. With Steve Martin, Daryl Hannah, Rick Rossovich. 107 minutes. Rated PG.

■ Schnoz aficionados consider this "amusing" romance the "quintessential Martin vehicle": a "modernization" of *Cyrano de Bergerac* concerning a fire chief cursed with a prodigious proboscis but blessed with a "grab bag of comic devices" with which he helps a surrogate court the highly "watchable" Hannah; though some find it too "cute", "God nose" it's a "good-natured" yarn with a "ton of heart."

Royal Tenenbaums, The 20 | 24 | 18 | 21

2001. Directed by Wes Anderson. With Gene Hackman, Anjelica Huston, Ben Stiller, Gwyneth Paltrow. 109 minutes. Rated R.

◪ This "very black" yet colorful "character-driven" comedy delineates the "humorous side of dysfunctionality" within a "wacky" "family of overachievers"; while the "Oscar-worthy" script and "stellar ensemble cast" draw applause, some shrug it's a "movie about nothing" that's "too clever" and "cynical" – the "reviewers liked it more than I did."

Runaway Train 21 | 22 | 20 | 21

1985. Directed by Andrei Konchalovsky. With Jon Voight, Eric Roberts, Rebecca de Mornay. 111 minutes. Rated R.

■ "Surprisingly" stimulating despite "cheapish production values", this "stark", "existential actioner" keeps onlookers "enthralled" with a "twist on the prison-break" scenario as a freight train carrying a pair of fugitive cons careens through the Alaskan wild ("bring a parka") while the law looks on; though "over the top" enough to nearly hop the rails, it offers "powerful" performances and "dark" themes engineered into what backers call a "bleak" "masterwork."

Run Lola Run F 23 | 21 | 24 | 24

1999. Directed by Tom Tykwer. With Franka Potente, Moritz Bleibtreu, Herbert Knaup. 81 minutes. Rated R.

■ There's "never a dull moment" in this "amped-up" German import involving the "sweat-dripping" effort of a fleet-footed fräulein to hustle a big pile of cash to save her boyfriend from a nasty mobster; "strongly driven" by an "adrenaline"-pumping "techno soundtrack" and "video-game" vibe, the "breathless" "nonlinear" narrative forges "different perspectives" and "time repeats" into a "pulse-pounding" "original" that's as "ultra-watchable" as it is "quirky."

Rush Hour Ⓘ 19 | 17 | 16 | 20

1998. Directed by Brett Ratner. With Jackie Chan, Chris Tucker, Tom Wilkinson. 97 minutes. Rated PG-13.

◪ Formula "fluff" with "all the right moves", this actioner finds time for "comic relief" as a crime-fighting pair of "exact opposites" teams up to rescue a kidnapped kid; "high-kicking" Chan breaks out with some "inventive chop-socky sequences" and "exhilarating" stunts while playing it straight alongside outspoken "wild man" Tucker, so even if the "plot's not much", the "buddy pairing" offers enough crowd-pleasing "chemistry" to translate into "loads of fun."

Rushmore 23 | 25 | 22 | 22

1998. Directed by Wes Anderson. With Jason Schwartzman, Olivia Williams, Bill Murray. 93 minutes. Rated R.

■ A monument of "quality quirkiness", this "unabashedly" "unusual" comedy stars Schwartzman as an "arrogant and clever" but "dysfunctional" scholarship student at an elite prep school whose "coming of age" takes many a "droll" twist when he befriends a rich alumnus and falls for a teacher; the "smart", "character-driven" script is "expertly acted", leading to high marks for a "winning" "gem" with "real heart" "beneath the smarminess" – and how about that "killer soundtrack"?

Russians Are Coming, The Russians Are Coming, The ∅ 21 | 21 | 22 | 20

1966. Directed by Norman Jewison. With Alan Arkin, John Phillip Law, Jonathan Winters. 120 minutes. Not Rated.

■ Da, comrades, this "classic '60s comedy" is a "Cold War satire" that offers a "sweet take" on a paranoid period as a Red Navy sub goes aground off the Massachusetts coast and Soviet swabbie Arkin is sent into a Nantucket-like island community for a rescue boat, setting off rumors of an invasion; *Strangelove* it ain't, but the "very funny" situations are still "worth the time."

Ruthless People 20 | 19 | 19 | 17

1986. Directed by David Zucker, Jerry Zucker, Jim Abrahams. With Danny DeVito, Bette Midler. 93 minutes. Rated R.

■ *Echt* '80s in its send-up of "pure greed", this "crass" but "sidesplitting" "black comedy" gets going when a couple of "inept kidnappers" snatch Midler (carrying on at "her bitchy best") and demand ransom from DeVito, a "standout" as the "crude", double-dealing "spandex king" husband scheming to rid himself of a despised spouse; "lots of plot twists" ensue in a "silly", "hilarious" caper that anyone with a cynical side shouldn't "overlook."

Sabrina ◑ 25 | 25 | 25 | 23

1954. Directed by Billy Wilder. With Humphrey Bogart, Audrey Hepburn, William Holden. 113 minutes. Not Rated.

■ Like an order of "first-class everything", this "delicious" "rags-to-riches" romance "sparkles" with "wit and couture" as an "ethereal" Hepburn plays a "beguiling", love-struck "chauffeur's daughter" in a "little black dress"; the "modern Cinderella" scenario finds Bogie in a "comedic role" as an all-business heir determined to beat out his "younger playboy brother" for Audrey's affections; as for the 1995 remake, loyalists "consider it blasphemy."

Same Time, Next Year ∅ 22 | 24 | 25 | 21

1978. Directed by Robert Mulligan. With Ellen Burstyn, Alan Alda, Ivan Bonar. 119 minutes. Rated PG.

■ Expect to go from "laughter to tears and back again" in this "decade-spanning romance", featuring "convincing" turns from Alda and Burstyn as a couple of "married lovers who meet once a year"; adapted from the stage, the "annual adultery" device tracks the two as they "change with the times", making for "sweet", "warm" entertainment – even if it does "promote affairs."

Sand Pebbles, The 24 | 26 | 25 | 24

1966. Directed by Robert Wise. With Steve McQueen, Richard Crenna. 179 minutes. Rated PG-13.

■ An "epic of China" told from the point of view of Yank sailors knee-deep in the revolutionary turmoil of 1926, this "powerful, pertinent" war drama features "authentic hero" McQueen "smoldering in top form" as a "tough-guy" Navy mechanic "with a heart of gold", manning an American patrol boat; if the tale "meanders" "like the Yellow River", it's still a "must-see" for History Channel addicts.

Santa Clause, The ⓫ 19 | 17 | 19 | 19

1994. Directed by John Pasquin. With Tim Allen, Judge Reinhold, Wendy Crewson. 97 minutes. Rated PG.

◪ "Corny in a good way", this "enjoyable" holiday comedy packages the "fantastic" with the "real world" when exec Allen takes over the reins from an abruptly retired Kris Kringle, mysteriously begins "fattening" and meets with complications in the custody of his young son; though it sleds along on a "sappy story", consensus calls it rather "original" as far as Yuletide yarns go.

Saturday Night Fever ⓫ 22 | 19 | 20 | 22

1977. Directed by John Badham. With John Travolta, Karen Lynn Gorney. 118 minutes. Rated R.

■ A paean to the "polyester era" set to a "spectacular" beat, this romance "defines" the "days of disco" with an "electric" Travolta as the blow-dried mook who lives to "look good" and "shake his groove thing" but has to boogie to "improve his life" when love comes to town; iconic "dance scenes" accentuate an "affecting" story with "dark" undercurrents that "perfectly evokes" "real life in Brooklyn" circa '77, even if some survivors of those "cheesy times" "feel embarrassed" about it now.

Saving Private Ryan ✉ 26 | 26 | 24 | 28

1998. Directed by Steven Spielberg. With Tom Hanks, Tom Sizemore, Edward Burns. 170 minutes. Rated R.

■ "As intense as it gets", Spielberg's "stark" "celluloid monument" to WWII evokes the "fear and brotherhood" of war with "blazing", "in-your-face" footage like the "devastating" opening, a "masterful" montage of "graphic" death and mayhem on a D-day beachhead; thereafter Hanks leads a "superbly" cast unit through no-man's-land on a "compelling" quest for a missing grunt, and despite sniping that "the story bogs down", it's a "wrenching" oh-"so-real" reminder that "war is hell."

Scarface 22 | 23 | 22 | 22

1983. Directed by Brian De Palma. With Al Pacino, Steven Bauer, Michelle Pfeiffer. 170 minutes. Rated R.

◪ "Raw and fun all at once", this "benchmark" crime thriller about a Miami-based "Latin drug ring" is ultra-"intense" and "extravagantly bloody" ("close your eyes when they bring out that chainsaw!"); addicts attest that it's worth seeing for Pacino's "over-the-top" turn as the "kind of bad guy you could really like", but the unmoved sneer it's "ultimately unredeeming" – and too "profane" to boot ("how many times can you say the F-word?").

Scent of a Woman ✉ 21 | 25 | 21 | 21

1992. Directed by Martin Brest. With Al Pacino, Chris O'Donnell, Philip Seymour Hoffman. 157 minutes. Rated R.

◪ Pacino's "bravura" Best Actor bit has him cast as a retired military man "to be reckoned with", compensating for his visual impairment with an "abrasive personality" and "foghorn" pipes as he drags his "meek" preppy "babysitter" along for a wild weekend in the Naked City; where cynics see "hokum" that "tends to drag", fans of the "too-fabulous" Al find it worthwhile "for the tango scene" alone.

SCHINDLER'S LIST ✉◑∅ 29 | 29 | 28 | 29

1993. Directed by Steven Spielberg. With Liam Neeson, Ben Kingsley, Ralph Fiennes. 197 minutes. Rated R.

■ Embarking on a "tour-de-force" "journey through a dark period", Spielberg's "direct", "painful" wartime drama "crystallizes" the "real-life horror" of the Holocaust in "stunning" "quasi-documentary" black-and-white, with Neeson as the man of "moral conscience" dealing with the Nazis in "shattering" circumstances; "beyond moving" and "tough to watch" in spite of its "understatement" and "touches of grace", it's a top Oscar honoree that's all-but-unanimously cited as "unforgettable" "required viewing."

Scream Ⓘ 20 | 16 | 21 | 19

1996. Directed by Wes Craven. With David Arquette, Neve Campbell, Courteney Cox. 111 minutes. Rated R.

◪ In an "aptly titled" entry, *Nightmare on Elm Street*'s Craven "revives" the horror genre by aiming "clever" "potshots" at a host of hackneyed "slasher-film" clichés, lending a "humorously self-aware" "twist" to a "fast-paced" story of a "slice-and-dice" psycho at large among suburban teens; sure, the picture "makes fun of itself", but it's still "scary stuff" that sets a suitably "bloody and gross" "precedent" for a "slew of imitators."

SEARCHERS, THE 27 | 25 | 27 | 27

1956. Directed by John Ford. With John Wayne, Jeffrey Hunter, Vera Miles. 120 minutes. Not Rated.

■ "Not just a shoot-'em-up", this "thinking person's" Western features "peak" work from Wayne, who delivers a "gripping" portrayal of a "brooding" Civil War vet obsessed with tracking down his niece, abducted in a Comanche raid; with its "spectacular" backdrops and "controversial" handling of "kinship and racism", it's much mentioned as "Ford's masterpiece", "perhaps the finest in the genre."

Secret of NIMH, The Ⓘ 24 | – | 25 | 24

1982. Directed by Don Bluth. Animated. 82 minutes. Rated G.

■ From the all-pro pens of "former Disney artists" comes this "freaky", oft-"forgotten" "alternative to sugar-coated" animation, a "beautifully drawn" "gem" of a barnyard yarn about a mama mouse desperately seeking a new nest for her brood; the "captivating" depiction of farm life comes with "character development" and an "interesting" story designed to appeal to the "adult" in everyone.

Secrets and Lies 24 | 27 | 24 | 22

1996. Directed by Mike Leigh. With Brenda Blethyn, Marianne Jean-Baptiste. 136 minutes. Rated R.

■ Bad boy Leigh turns "accessible" in this "smart", "solid British drama" of "long-lost" family ties concerning a young black Londoner who "searches out her biological mother" only to find out that mum may be a working-class white woman; led by Blethyn's "pure, honest performance", the principals do a "terrific job" of making this "surprisingly" tip-top tale "involving" and "heartbreaking."

Sense and Sensibility ✉ 26 | 27 | 26 | 26

1995. Directed by Ang Lee. With Emma Thompson, Alan Rickman, Kate Winslet. 136 minutes. Rated PG.

■ "Jane Austen would have liked" this "bittersweet" story of two husband-hunting sisters that "captures the true flavor" of her novel "with wit and honesty" largely due to a "strong", Oscar-winning script from the "so-fine" Emma

Thompson; sensitive types tout the "beautiful" scenery, director Lee's "brilliant" job and an ensemble cast that "rises to the occasion" – "this is what moviemaking should be."

Serpico ∅ 23 | 26 | 24 | 21

1973. Directed by Sidney Lumet. With Al Pacino, John Randolph, Tony Roberts. 129 minutes. Rated R.

◪ Honesty "doesn't pay" in this "gritty" "true story" starring a "superb" Pacino as a whistle-blowing NYPD do-gooder who becomes a "man alone" when his exposure of "cop corruption" threatens to "bring down" the whole city; if all the "raw" "emotion" can grow "frustrating" and the milieu seems "a bit dated", it remains arresting as a "compelling" "commentary on the times."

Seven 23 | 23 | 24 | 23

1995. Directed by David Fincher. With Brad Pitt, Morgan Freeman, Kevin Spacey. 123 minutes. Rated R.

■ All the "elegant nastiness" of a "guided tour through hell" surfaces in this "macabre" "psychological thriller" about two big-city detectives on the trail of an "ingenious" serial killer who dreams up "genuinely disturbing" torments "based on the seven deadly sins"; an "unrelenting" dose of "creepy" "modern noir" at its "darkest", it's wickedly "riveting" and "impressive" but "hard-to-take" and "gruesome" – with "no happy ending."

Seven Brides for Seven Brothers 24 | 20 | 21 | 25

1954. Directed by Stanley Donen. With Howard Keel, Jane Powell, Russ Tamblyn. 103 minutes. Rated G.

■ Ok, it's "low on feasibility", but this "down-home" musical of "seven eligible backwoodsmen looking for love" with a septet of hillbilly "Sabine women" strikes "pure gold" with its "great Johnny Mercer" tunes and "extraordinary" choreography; fans dig its "exuberant","CinemaScope"-enhanced production numbers so "athletic" they "make dance macho", particularly that "barn-raising scene."

Seven Days in May ◑ 26 | 24 | 28 | 22

1964. Directed by John Frankenheimer. With Burt Lancaster, Kirk Douglas, Fredric March. 118 minutes. Not Rated.

■ "It could happen here", or so says this "riveting 'what-if' drama", a "scary" "Cold War story" about disgruntled Pentagon brass who lay plans for a "military takeover"; soldiering along with "well-plotted" plausibility and "Douglas and Lancaster turning up the star heat", it's a "powerful" "nail-biter" that "political junkies" consider – gulp – "as timely today as ever."

SEVEN SAMURAI, THE ◑ F 29 | 27 | 28 | 27

1956. Directed by Akira Kurosawa. With Toshiro Mifune, Takashi Shimura. 203 minutes. Not Rated.

■ Credited with "defining" its "own genre", Kurosawa's "awesome", "pivotal" Japanese adventure introduces the "original magnificent seven" as old-time samurai "warrior-heroes" who rise to the defense of a village menaced by a "vicious band of marauders"; the "epic" "running time melts away" before the "exciting" display of "honor", "courage" and "classic swordplay", and though there are "countless" reworkings, connoisseurs claim this "way-cool" "prototype" is "far superior."

1776 22 | 22 | 24 | 23

1972. Directed by Peter H. Hunt. With William Daniels, Howard da Silva, Blythe Danner. 142 minutes. Rated G.

■ Put away the books and take an "entertaining" "shortcut" to U.S. history via this "faithful" rendering of the Broadway musical, a "patriotic" "pageant" wherein periwigged radicals assemble in Philly and wrangle over the Declaration of Independence, backed up by "wonderful music and lyrics"; it's a "smart", "informative" way to "put a face" on "those lovable founding fathers", and they turn out to be "such great singers" – "who knew?"

SEVENTH SEAL, THE ◑ F 27 | 27 | 26 | 26

1957. Directed by Ingmar Bergman. With Max von Sydow, Gunnar Björnstrand, Nils Poppe. 96 minutes. Not Rated.

■ An utterly foreign flick and staple of "college days", Bergman's "challenging" drama is a "dark" "allegory" with von Sydow as a "knight returning from the Crusades to plague-swept Europe" only to hunker down for a high-stakes "chess game with Death"; as a "cerebral" meditation on the "meaning of existence", it seals the deal with "some of the greatest visuals ever" and a "symbolic story" that "makes everything else look like a game of checkers."

7th Voyage of Sinbad, The 20 | 12 | 20 | 22

1958. Directed by Nathan Juran. With Kerwin Mathews, Kathryn Grant, Torin Thatcher. 88 minutes. Rated G.

◪ "Amazing for its time", this "delightful" adventure "throwback" "makes myth real without computers" using '50s-era FX to summon up a host of "lovingly created monsters" for the "hammy" hero to hack away at; ok, the "Saturday-matinee" storyline is "standard" "cheese", but it's a "fondly remembered" "fantasy" for longstanding fans who happily "take it for what it is."

Seven Year Itch, The 23 | 23 | 20 | 20

1955. Directed by Billy Wilder. With Marilyn Monroe, Tom Ewell, Evelyn Keyes. 105 minutes. Not Rated.

■ Marilyn's billowing-dress "subway-grate scene" is the iconic moment in this "enjoyable" comedy, which finds "ordinary guy" Ewell "on his own" when the wife and kiddies split for summer vacation simultaneous with the arrival of his new neighbor, a most "memorable" Monroe in full "innocent"-"sexpot" mode, who brings on a major "midlife crisis"; sure, the repartee seems "dated and stagy", but it can still tickle the "funny" bone.

Sex, Lies and Videotape 19 | 20 | 20 | 18

1989. Directed by Steven Soderbergh. With James Spader, Andie MacDowell, Peter Gallagher, Laura San Giacomo. 98 minutes. Rated R.

◪ Wounded libidos fight the "battles of the sexes" in this "fresh take" on the "deterioration of relationships", a "simple", "well-crafted" drama about a college chum visiting an unhappily married couple and getting some spicy tell-all on tape; it's an "intelligent" look at the "permissive age" heated up by erotic "suspense" more than "actual" on-screen whoopee, though those who spurn "loser" characters find it "hard to care about."

Shadow of the Vampire 20 | 25 | 20 | 23

2000. Directed by E. Elias Merhige. With John Malkovich, Willem Dafoe, Cary Elwes. 92 minutes. Rated R.

◪ Maybe it's "not scary", but this "unusual", "behind-the-scenes" drama does apply a few shadowy "touches of horror" as it chronicles the "legendary production" of the fiendish '20s masterwork *Nosferatu*; Dafoe does a "great job" vamping as an undead actor with an "evil" hankering for hemoglobin, but foes call it a "disappointing" "art-house" "mess" that's "not sharp" enough to draw blood.

Shakespeare in Love ✉ 24 | 25 | 24 | 26

1998. Directed by John Madden. With Gwyneth Paltrow, Geoffrey Rush, Joseph Fiennes, Judi Dench. 122 minutes. Rated R.

■ "Whether it be true or not", this "lush, literate" romance is a "good-humored" "confection" that "lights up the screen" with "adorable" performances from Fiennes (an "ink-stained" Elizabethan scribe) whose "writer's block" is cleared by the "exquisitely attired" Paltrow (his not-so-secret admirer); a "rich" depiction of the age "laced with dialogue" from the plays, it's a "captivating", "rip-roaring" ride that's "accessible" at "any level."

Shane 26 | 25 | 25 | 25

1953. Directed by George Stevens. With Alan Ladd, Jean Arthur, Van Heflin. 118 minutes. Not Rated.

■ There's "always a nuance to savor" in this "towering", "classic" Western, telling the "mythical American" tale of a "world-weary gunslinger forced out of retirement" when he sides with a "homesteader" family menaced by "ruthless cattle ranchers"; the "poignant" setup pays off with a "great finale" as Ladd walks tall in a showdown with "no-good" varmint Jack Palance, leading many oater voters to name it "best" in the West.

SHAWSHANK REDEMPTION, THE 28 | 28 | 28 | 27

1994. Directed by Frank Darabont. With Tim Robbins, Morgan Freeman, Bob Gunton. 142 minutes. Rated R.

■ Finding the "stirring" in the stir and big hearts in the big house, this "first-rate" "gripper" of a "prison drama" goes behind the walls of a "dismal" state pen to follow "fellow lifers" Robbins and Freeman on a "long, dark journey" that pits "friendship", "ingenuity and inner strength" against a "brutal", "corrupt system"; besides the "marvelous acting", there's a last-reel "surprise" to add a "feel-good factor" and even some "hope."

She Wore a Yellow Ribbon 24 | 22 | 23 | 25

1949. Directed by John Ford. With John Wayne, Joanne Dru, John Agar, Ben Johnson. 103 minutes. Not Rated.

■ Ford's second bugle blast in his "cavalry trilogy" finds the director "at his best" in a tribute to the "honor and tradition" of horse soldiers posted to the ever-fleeting frontier; the Duke is typically "bigger than life" as a stiff-brimmed but sympathetic "old man" about to hang up his hat after a career in Injun territory, all portrayed against boundlessly "beautiful" big-sky scenery – "what else does a Western need?"

Shine ✉ 22 | 25 | 21 | 21

1996. Directed by Scott Hicks. With Geoffrey Rush, Armin Mueller-Stahl, Lynn Redgrave. 105 minutes. Rated PG-13.

◪ "Mad musician makes good" in this "enlightening", "uplifting true story" about a gifted Australian pianist who succeeds in the shadow of an inflexible father but succumbs to a "harrowing" bout with schizophrenia – only to return to the bench for a midlife comeback; Rush's "compelling" turn keeps things uptempo, and if some dub it an "overrated" "curiosity", more offer bravos for a portrait that "shines" from first movement to last.

Shining, The 25 | 26 | 25 | 25

1980. Directed by Stanley Kubrick. With Jack Nicholson, Shelley Duvall, Scatman Crothers. 146 minutes. Rated R.

■ The "supernatural and the psychotic" collide in this "revolutionary horror film", a "downright scary" story from the Stephen King novel about a "snowbound caretaker of an old hotel" running amok; though voters agree that the "elevator scene", "Diane Arbus twin girls" and "gloriously unhinged Nicholson" all shine, Duvall gets mixed marks: "intensely annoying" vs. "profoundly brilliant"; best line, no contest: "heeere's Johnny!"

Shipping News, The 18 | 21 | 17 | 21

2001. Directed by Lasse Hallström. With Kevin Spacey, Julianne Moore, Judi Dench. 111 minutes. Rated R.

◪ Based on the "best-selling book", this drama tells the "strange story" of a "hopeless mope" doing drudge work at a small-town gazette who gets a "second chance" when his wife dies and he ships out to the Newfoundland coast; though it reels in praise as an "ultimately optimistic" "gem", foes torpedo the "overblown", "contrived" production as a "lackluster" Miramax bid for the Oscar race.

Shirley Valentine ∅ 24 | 24 | 23 | 20

1989. Directed by Lewis Gilbert. With Pauline Collins, Tom Conti, Alison Steadman. 108 minutes. Rated R.

■ A real "charmer" with a "Liverpudlian accent", this "spirited" comedy sends a "terrific message" with its "sweet" "midlife" "fantasy" of a "bored English housewife" who flees to the Aegean "looking for love and adventure" and nets "Greek sailor" Conti; adapted from the "superb" stage show, it "loses nothing in the translation" as a "wise" celebration of "independence and self-respect."

SHOAH F ∅ 28 | – | 28 | 26

1985. Directed by Claude Lanzmann. Documentary. 563 minutes. Not Rated.

■ "Not a film to watch casually", this "groundbreaking documentary" addresses the "horror of the Holocaust" through "first-hand accounts" as a "necessary antidote" to "one of the worst episodes in human history"; Lanzmann uses witnesses from both sides of the "barbed-wire fence" to record their "intense", "shattering" memories of an entire society's "complicity", and "emotions pour out" over "eight hours of painful viewing" that are "impossibly sad and difficult" – but "worth all of it."

Shot in the Dark, A II 23 | 22 | 20 | 20

1964. Directed by Blake Edwards. With Peter Sellers, Elke Sommer, George Sanders. 102 minutes. Rated PG.

■ Sort of a cub *Pink Panther,* this "laugh-aloud funny" comedy features a "brilliant" Sellers in an early foray as the catastrophically clueless Inspector Clouseau, bumbling his way through a "delicious red-herring salad" of a plot that finds him assigned to solve a murder pinned on a Parisian chambermaid; if the "charmingly quirky" setup has its "slow" moments, the "master" makes it watchable "for his accent alone."

Show Boat 23 | 20 | 24 | 25

1951. Directed by George Sidney. With Kathryn Grayson, Ava Gardner, Howard Keel. 107 minutes. Not Rated.

◪ The "schmaltzy" but "fabulous" hit from the Broadway boards gets the "brightest Technicolor" treatment in this "sterling" "MGM musical" about a showgirl's "sentimental" entanglement with a riverboat gambler; the big wheel paddles along to "unforgettable" songs, "solid production numbers" and hoofers who "dance up a storm", and if purists prefer 1936's "glory-days" version, most can't help lovin' dat "beautiful, melodic" spectacle.

Shrek 26 | – | 25 | 28

2001. Directed by Andrew Adamson, Vicky Jenson. Animated. 90 minutes. Rated PG.

■ They "added a category" on Oscar night to honor this "playfully creative" "original" that uses "exceptional" CGI animation and "great voicing" to rework a "hoary storyline" about an ogre saving a princess into "highly entertaining" fare; it "challenges" the "Disney fairy-tale formula" with adult-level "parody" and "inside jokes" underscored with a "positive message" for all.

Sid & Nancy 18 | 20 | 18 | 16

1986. Directed by Alex Cox. With Gary Oldman, Chloe Webb, David Hayman. 112 minutes. Rated R.

■ An "absolutely demented but totally compelling love story", this "gripping" slice of "rock history" details the rise and fall of the "Sex Pistols' wildest member", featuring a "convincing Oldman" as Sid Vicious and the "scarily real" Webb as his "crazy girlfriend"; though the story of their downward, drug-laden spiral is not for the faint-hearted, groupies dig it 'cause it's "dark, ugly and vibrant all at once."

SILENCE OF THE LAMBS, THE ✉ Ⓘ 27 | 28 | 27 | 26

1991. Directed by Jonathan Demme. With Jodie Foster, Anthony Hopkins, Scott Glenn. 118 minutes. Rated R.

■ Every subsequent "psych-profiling" flick owes something to this "masterful", "profoundly creepy" thriller that combines "heart-thumping suspense" with "premier" performances as Foster, an FBI greenhorn on a "serial-killer hunt", is drawn into "intense mind games" with the "soft-spoken" madman Hopkins; its "well-deserved Oscars" speak for its "twisted", "truly terrifying" achievement, though some say it "gives fava beans a bad name."

Silkwood 22 | 26 | 25 | 21

1983. Directed by Mike Nichols. With Meryl Streep, Kurt Russell, Cher, Craig T. Nelson. 131 minutes. Rated R.

■ This "somewhat forgotten" drama generates a "great deal of tension" telling the fact-based story of a whistle-blowing nuclear plant worker who comes to a "mysterious end" when she tries to go public with hazardous goings-on at the facility; lit up by "terrific acting" from "marvelous" Meryl and "eye-opener" Cher, it's a "moving" depiction of blue-collar good guys vs. white-collar baddies.

Silverado 24 | 24 | 23 | 24

1985. Directed by Lawrence Kasdan. With Kevin Kline, Scott Glenn, Kevin Costner. 127 minutes. Rated PG-13.

■ Boys, the "fun Western" rides again in this "well-made" "modern horse opera", a "true homage" that "throws in all the clichés" and delivers some "slick sequences" and "great one-liners" of its own; a "tremendous" cast "manages to upstage the glorious scenery", though it's best appreciated on the "biggest screen you can find."

Silver Streak ∅ 19 | 19 | 18 | 19

1976. Directed by Arthur Hiller. With Gene Wilder, Richard Pryor, Jill Clayburgh. 114 minutes. Rated PG.

■ "One of the best comedy teams on film" gets its "first pairing" in this "slick" "takeoff" on Hitchcock-style "train capers", featuring a "restrained" Wilder in the "amusing" role of an innocent railroaded in an art-world murder only to find himself on the run along with the "beyond-funny" Pryor; aficionados call it "enjoyable" and "underappreciated."

Simple Plan, A 19 | 22 | 22 | 19

1998. Directed by Sam Raimi. With Bill Paxton, Bridget Fonda, Billy Bob Thornton. 121 minutes. Rated R.

■ B-movie maestro Raimi's "entry into respectable filmdom" is a "well-paced thriller" with a "entirely convincing" scenario about a rustic threesome in the frozen backwoods who stumble upon a wrecked plane and a big bag of cash; "plot-twisting" and "suspense" ensue as lives "unravel" in a "tragic" parable of the "evils of ill-gotten gain" that makes it the "*Treasure of the Sierra Madre*" for the "*Fargo*" crowd.

SINGIN' IN THE RAIN 28 | 26 | 25 | 28

1952. Directed by Stanley Donen, Gene Kelly. With Gene Kelly, Donald O'Connor, Debbie Reynolds. 103 minutes. Rated G.

■ "Giddy", "wet and wonderful", this "timeless" musical brightens the "worst day" with an "exuberant" "something-for-everyone" blend of "quintessential" "song and dance", "satire" and a "sappy, funny love story"; the "flawless" Kelly plays a silent movie star in a "sweet" "send-up" of Hollywood's early talkie days and effortlessly executes the puddle-hopping "title number", leaving admirers "awed."

Sister Act ⓫ 18 | 18 | 17 | 17

1992. Directed by Emile Ardolino. With Whoopi Goldberg, Maggie Smith, Kathy Najimy. 100 minutes. Rated PG.

■ Whoopi gets a witness protection program in this "engaging" "fish-out-of-water comedy" about a lounge diva who sings for the cops after her bad-boy beau commits homicide, only to find herself stashed in "nun other than" a convent; the verdict: a "guilty pleasure" that rises above the "run of the mill" with "really cool" musical interludes.

Six Degrees of Separation 21 | 24 | 23 | 20

1993. Directed by Fred Schepisi. With Will Smith, Stockard Channing, Donald Sutherland. 112 minutes. Rated R.

■ "Great performances" ensure this "intriguing" "stage-to-screen" drama "adjusts quite nicely" to celluloid as a "sublime" Channing offers an encore of her theatrical role opposite a "young" Smith in the "challenging" part of a "charming hustler" posing as Sidney Poitier's son; it draws applause as a "clever" critique of "moneyed values" that's "surprisingly strong."

Sixteen Candles 22 | 18 | 21 | 19

1984. Directed by John Hughes. With Molly Ringwald, Justin Henry, Anthony Michael Hall. 93 minutes. Rated PG.

■ "Ringwald will steal your heart" in this "sweet" "coming-of-age classic", a "day-in-the-life" comedy that conveys the "teen angst" of high school, "first love and puberty" as seen through the eyes of a 16-year-old "birthday girl whom everyone forgot"; though its "damn funny" "brat pack" cast "characterizes the '80s to a tee", modernists who "love" this "brilliant" send-up "can still relate to it."

Sixth Sense, The 26 | 25 | 27 | 25

1999. Directed by M. Night Shyamalan. With Bruce Willis, Haley Joel Osment, Toni Collette. 107 minutes. Rated PG-13.

■ A "tricky" one, this mega-hit thriller "surprises even the most astute" with its "perfectly crafted story" of a troubled boy with an "unwelcome gift" who finds a friend in Willis, leading to "really spooky" plot developments; it's hailed as an "unpredictable" sensation that "rewards" with "white-knuckle" "jolts" and a "stunning" "O. Henry"–esque ending that's among the "best-kept secrets ever."

Slap Shot Ⓘ 22 | 18 | 19 | 17

1977. Directed by George Roy Hill. With Paul Newman, Michael Ontkean, Strother Martin. 122 minutes. Rated R.

■ Right up there with the "funniest sports flicks", this puckish comedy finds "Newman on skates" as the "foul-mouthed coach" of a "dark horse" minor-league hockey team with a "strange way" of turning every face-off into a riot on ice; it "epitomizes the goonery" of the high-sticking "'70s", resulting in "crazy", "profane" and "fairly violent" fare that hard-core fans "cannot live without."

Sleeper 23 | 19 | 23 | 20

1973. Directed by Woody Allen. With Woody Allen, Diane Keaton, John Beck. 89 minutes. Rated PG.

■ Orwell's wake-up call has nothing on this "inspired" "sci-fi spoof", a "hilarious" comedy of a nebbishy NYer who's cryogenically preserved then "defrosted in the future"; "laced with fast-paced verbal" cracks, it's "vintage" Allen at his "goofiest" and "most slapsticky" in a romp that generates "nonstop laughs" – the "orgasmatron alone is worth the price of admission."

Sleeping Beauty 25 | – | 23 | 25

1959. Directed by Clyde Geronimi. Animated. 75 minutes. Rated G.

■ No snooze among the "old Disney greats", this "lushly animated" "princess movie" has a trio of good fairies protecting the titular knockout from an evil spell by zapping her into a sound nap, interrupted only after her true love battles it out with filmdom's most fearsome dragon lady; the very wicked witch may be "too scary for the little ones", but most say this "classic" only "gets better with age."

Sleepless in Seattle 21 | 22 | 22 | 21

1993. Directed by Nora Ephron. With Tom Hanks, Meg Ryan, Rosie O'Donnell. 105 minutes. Rated PG.

◪ Although pretty "predictable", this Ephron romance "works", renewing faith in the "soul-mate concept" as the "perfectly cast", "totally lovable" Hanks and Ryan make "a great match" in the story of a woman who pursues a lonely-hearts stranger cross country; sure, this "toothache"-"sweet" "trifle" is "a bit far-fetched" ("at least Harry *met* Sally"), but it's also a "funny", "male-tolerable" "chick flick" that's likely to spring eternal for "hopeless romantics."

Sleuth 25 | 28 | 26 | 23

1972. Directed by Joseph L. Mankiewicz. With Laurence Olivier, Michael Caine. 138 minutes. Rated PG.

■ It's no mystery why this stage-sired "suspense thriller" adapts "wonderfully to film": "masters-at-work" Olivier and Caine offer "witty", "subtle" work as a cuckolded writer and his rival engaged in a calculated confrontation in an English country manor; the "creative" story builds "numerous" "plot twists" that cross and double-cross, and "two of the greatest" muster up some of the liveliest back-and-forth "volleys" ever seen "outside of Wimbledon."

Sling Blade ✉ 25 | 27 | 25 | 22

1996. Directed by Billy Bob Thornton. With Billy Bob Thornton, Dwight Yoakam, J.T. Walsh. 135 minutes. Rated R.

■ "Too convincing" in the role that lands him "on the map", "creepy Billy Bob" is "brilliantly" "believable" in this "tragedy from the real world" playing a slow-witted country boy who's sprung from the state booby hatch and taken in by a single mom; a "unique, touching" drama of man trouble, it "earns every accolade" with "excellent acting" and an "unforgettable" "punch" at the climax.

Snatch 21 | 23 | 22 | 22

2000. Directed by Guy Ritchie. With Benicio Del Toro, Dennis Farina, Brad Pitt. 104 minutes. Rated R.

■ Fittingly "splashy" fare from Mr. Madonna, director Ritchie's "sophomore effort" is a "relentless crime comedy" with a substantial cast of "wild" London gangsters who follow "interacting storylines" in a "quick-witted" "mix-'em-up heist" caper centered around a stolen diamond; the results are "bloody" "hilarious", and though you might need "subtitles" to decipher Pitt's "crazy-man accent", at least it's "never boring."

SNOW WHITE & THE SEVEN DWARFS 27 | – | 26 | 27

1937. Directed by David Hand. Animated. 83 minutes. Rated G.

■ The "one that started it all", this "true classic" is the "*Citizen Kane* of animation", the "first full-length" feature from the Disney drawing boards and "still the finest" of them all; this tale of a fair maiden hiding in the forest with a band of "cute" "little guys" to escape a "terrifying" "wicked queen" is a "masterpiece" of "charm, simplicity and beauty" that continues to "entertain generations" and leave 'em humming "hi ho, hi ho!"

SOME LIKE IT HOT ◑ 28 | 27 | 26 | 26

1959. Directed by Billy Wilder. With Marilyn Monroe, Tony Curtis, Jack Lemmon. 120 minutes. Rated PG.

■ "Cross-dressing was never so hilarious" as in this "legendary" "laff riot" about "two patsies on the run from the mob" who don dresses and join an all-girl band as part of their escape plan; thanks to Wilder's "sure touch" and the "sidesplitting" script's "countless priceless scenes" ("Lemmon with the maracas", "Curtis' riff on Cary Grant", Monroe "running wild"), this is one hot contender for the "greatest comedy ever made" – with the "best closing line" in moviedom: "nobody's perfect."

Song of the South ∅ 23 | 21 | 22 | 26

1946. Directed by Wilfred Jackson, Harve Foster. With Ruth Warrick, James Baskett. 94 minutes. Rated G.

■ Yup, it's "corny and dated", but "Disney's version of the Uncle Remus stories" is also "one of the earliest" to offer an "animation–live action mix" as a young boy encounters Brers Rabbit, Fox and Bear, plus some "singing crows on telephone wires"; its "controversial" stereotyping of plantation life means it's currently "missing in action" at your video store, but music lovers say it will always be "tough to top 'Zip-A-Dee-Doo-Dah.'"

Sophie's Choice ✉ 26 | 28 | 26 | 24

1982. Directed by Alan J. Pakula. With Meryl Streep, Kevin Kline, Peter MacNicol. 150 minutes. Rated R.

■ A "luminous" Streep with a "faint Polish accent" "shows her stuff" in this "haunting", highly "emotional" drama, which draws its "powerful storyline" from William Styron's novel about an Auschwitz survivor; though "wrenching" at points and "difficult to watch", it's a "compelling" "tour de force" that many see as Oscar-winner Meryl's "finest" hour.

SOUND OF MUSIC, THE ✉ 28 | 25 | 27 | 28

1965. Directed by Robert Wise. With Julie Andrews, Christopher Plummer, Eleanor Parker. 174 minutes. Rated G.

■ "Admit it", everyone has an Alp-size "soft spot" for this "schmaltzy" Rodgers and Hammerstein musical, a "feel-good" smash wherein a "charming" governess marries into a "do-re-mi" singing family and "stands on principle" after the Huns invade; the only Best Picture winner to feature "nuns, Nazis" and "kids in lederhosen", it's also "shamelessly" "saccharine" but "beloved" for its "uplifting" story, "fantastic" songs and "lush" landscapes.

South Pacific 24 | 22 | 24 | 25

1958. Directed by Joshua Logan. With Mitzi Gaynor, Rossano Brazzi, John Kerr. 151 minutes. Not Rated.

◪ "Incomparable music" washes up in a "tropical paradise" in this Rodgers and Hammerstein songfest, which finds American sea dogs and dames living and loving and singing along to "beautiful orchestrations" on a WWII Pacific atoll;

though a huge hit in its day owing to those "eternal" tunes, some say it "doesn't hold up" anymore, pointing to the "filtered camera gels" that drown meaningful moments in "gaudy Technicolor" tints.

South Park 20 | – | 19 | 16

1999. Directed by Trey Parker. Animated. 81 minutes. Rated R.

◪ Don't "blame Canada" for the "tasteless glory" of this "obnoxious", full-length treatment of the "rude, crude" animated TV series, a "very un-PC" "equal-opportunity offender" offering a "raunchy" mix of "blush-worthy" "low-brow" laffs and "disturbing" but "catchy" musical interludes; "rated R for a reason", this "spoof" is "unbelievably funny" but "not for the kiddies" or "faint-of-heart" adults.

Spaceballs 18 | 15 | 17 | 17

1987. Directed by Mel Brooks. With Mel Brooks, John Candy, Rick Moranis. 96 minutes. Rated PG.

◪ "Brooks strikes again" in this "goofy" "takeoff on *Star Wars*" that skewers sci-fi as a couple of space cowboys rocket to the rescue of a princess when her planet is menaced, setting up "cornball" gags and "quick one-liners" that are the "hysterical" stuff of Mel's genre parodies; though hard-core fans find it "gets funnier every time", those unamused by the "tired", "obvious" humor contend it's "hard to believe" this is the work of a "genius."

Spartacus 26 | 24 | 25 | 26

1960. Directed by Stanley Kubrick. With Kirk Douglas, Laurence Olivier, Jean Simmons. 184 minutes. Rated PG-13.

■ "Elevated" by its "sweeping vision" and "superb" "all-star cast", Kubrick's "impressive" epic headlines Douglas as the "virile" leader of a "slave revolt against Rome"; matching a "psychologically complex" story with plenty of "gory but good" action, it's an "exciting" box-office big-timer that's "matched by few" in the "classic" spectacle sweeps.

Speed Ⓘ 18 | 14 | 19 | 20

1994. Directed by Jan de Bont. With Keanu Reeves, Dennis Hopper, Sandra Bullock. 116 minutes. Rated R.

◪ "*Die Hard* on a bus" is the "inanely simple" premise behind this "fast-moving" "high-concept actioner", with "sweetheart" Bullock and "studly SWAT boy" Reeves making a "cute and feisty" twosome as they find themselves "trapped" on a "tense", "nonstop" "thrill ride" aboard a "runaway bus" wired to "go boom"; though it's dismissed as "lightweight" "bubblegum" with "wooden" line readings from "Mr. Whoa", at least there's "no letup."

Spellbound ◑ 24 | 25 | 23 | 24

1945. Directed by Alfred Hitchcock. With Gregory Peck, Ingrid Bergman. 111 minutes. Not Rated.

◪ One of the first mainstream movies to tackle the theme of psychiatry, this "outstanding" Hitchcock thriller deals with unlocking a "repressed memory", and the "perfect Bergman" and "gorgeous Peck" are a "good match" as doctor and patient; but despite touches like the "ahead-of-its-time dream sequences" designed by Salvador Dali, some analysts dismiss it as "dated" "Freudian nonsense."

Splash Ⓘ 19 | 18 | 19 | 20

1984. Directed by Ron Howard. With Tom Hanks, Daryl Hannah, John Candy. 111 minutes. Rated PG.

■ More "sweet" than salty yet "not too mushy", this "fish-out-of-water love story" is an "engaging" comedy shored up by Hannah's "yummy", starmaking splash as a "sexy mermaid" whom Hanks courts and transports to NYC; the fantasy is buoyed by a cast of "charming" characters "you can't help but like", including some "sterling support" from a "scene-stealing" Candy – so dive in and "enjoy."

Splendor in the Grass ✉ 25 | 25 | 24 | 22

1961. Directed by Elia Kazan. With Natalie Wood, Warren Beatty, Zohra Lampert. 124 minutes. Not Rated.

■ There's "heartbreak" in the heartland as "yearning" breeds "teen angst" in this "bittersweet" romance set in "pre-Depression" Kansas; the very "young" and very "gorgeous" Wood and Beatty supply some "real acting" as a "modern Romeo and Juliet" driven to "wrenching" extremes in this drama of "stolen dreams" and "lost love" that makes some sob sisters "cry just thinking about it."

Spy Kids Ⓘ 19 | 17 | 19 | 21

2001. Directed by Robert Rodriguez. With Antonio Banderas, Carla Gugino. 88 minutes. Rated PG.

■ Look for "good clean spy fun" in this "appealing" family adventure that's "empowering for kids" in its story of a parental pair of agents "called back into duty" only to bungle the assignment, leaving it up to their "cute" tykes to "save the world"; there are plenty of "cool gadgets", so grown-ups might not want to "check their brain" after all.

Spy Who Loved Me, The 21 | 17 | 20 | 22

1977. Directed by Lewis Gilbert. With Roger Moore, Barbara Bach, Richard Kiel. 125 minutes. Rated PG.

■ When it comes to "popcorn" action fare, "nobody does it better" than Mr. Bond, and this is "one of Moore's better outings" as 007 pursues a nuclear blackmailer and fights off the "awesome", metal-mouthed nemesis Jaws; if by now the scripts are "superfluous", it's still the leading franchise for "fast cars, fast women" in "clingy clothes" ("oh, James!") and "lots of things that blow up."

Stagecoach ◑ 27 | 24 | 26 | 25

1939. Directed by John Ford. With John Wayne, Claire Trevor, John Carradine. 96 minutes. Not Rated.

■ "Wayne's grand entrance" alone immortalizes this "archetypal" Ford Western about a group of stock frontier types "traversing hostile Indian territory" by rickety stage; featuring the young Duke in his "breakthrough role" as a fugitive convict, it rolls along on "great dialogue" and "well-acted" ensemble work interrupted by "viscerally exciting" action scenes, making it the "classic" "source" of countless tumbleweed "clichés."

STALAG 17 ✉◑ 27 | 26 | 27 | 24

1953. Directed by Billy Wilder. With William Holden, Don Taylor, Otto Preminger. 120 minutes. Not Rated.

■ Wilder's "wonderful" adaptation of the stage drama supplies the "intrigue" of a "psychological thriller" with some comic relief in this story starring the "properly Oscarized" Holden as a "cynical prisoner" in a WWII POW camp who's "suspected of being a German spy"; thanks to "tremendous acting" and "tense" plotting that "keeps you guessing until the end", this study of military "camaraderie" and "mob judgment" is "not to be missed."

Stand and Deliver 20 | 22 | 22 | 17

1988. Directed by Ramon Menendez. With Edward James Olmos, Lou Diamond Phillips. 102 minutes. Rated PG.

■ Giving credit to the "common man", this "inspirational" drama presents Olmos as the real-life Jaime Escalante, a "math teacher who makes a difference" in a tough East LA school by engaging a class of bad-attitude kids and tutoring them to success; tough graders say this "good fun flick" also scores as an "underrated" self-esteem booster.

Stand by Me 24 | 23 | 25 | 23

1986. Directed by Rob Reiner. With Wil Wheaton, River Phoenix, Corey Feldman. 89 minutes. Rated R.

■ "Aren't those kids great?"; this "wholesome" "coming-of-age" drama focuses on four preadolescent "best buddies" in '50s Oregon who set out "in search of a missing boy", bonding in the face of various perils and learning about the "real stuff" along the way; a platform for "young talent", it carries a "strong message" about the "struggle to grow up."

Stargate 18 | 17 | 20 | 22

1994. Directed by Roland Emmerich. With Kurt Russell, James Spader, Jaye Davidson. 121 minutes. Rated PG-13.

◪ "Egypt" meets "outer space" in this "interesting" sci-fi flicker about a "portal" discovered in the desert that's an intergalactic wormhole to a "distant world" enslaved by the "sexy, powerful" Egyptian god Ra; the ensuing "face-off" is long on "thoughtless action" and "terrific" pyrotechnics but "never delivers" on the "great premise."

Star Is Born, A 25 | 26 | 26 | 26

1954. Directed by George Cukor. With Judy Garland, James Mason, Jack Carson. 181 minutes. Rated PG.

■ "Forget the other versions": this "heartbreaking" musical drama revisits the Tinseltown parable of fickle celebrity fortunes with the "best Judy ever", showcasing her "true range" as the nobody whose rise to fame is paralleled by her big-name hubby's descent; whether laughing, singing or "turning on the waterworks", the "mesmerizing" Garland gives the "performance of her life", leaving loyalists to lament the Oscar "that got away."

Starman 19 | 20 | 21 | 17

1984. Directed by John Carpenter. With Jeff Bridges, Karen Allen, Richard Jaeckel. 115 minutes. Rated PG-13.

■ A spacecraft falls to Earth and an "alien and earthling fall for each other" in this "overlooked" "date movie"; a "first-rate" Bridges plays an "E.T. in human form" who inhabits the bod of Allen's recently deceased husband, leading to "sentimental" getting-to-know-you sessions and a "romantic" road trip that draws to a "sweet" if "predictable" conclusion – "who says there aren't any sci-fi chick flicks?"

Star Trek II: The Wrath of Khan Ⓘ 23 | 19 | 24 | 24

1982. Directed by Nicholas Meyer. With William Shatner, Leonard Nimoy, DeForest Kelley. 113 minutes. Rated PG.

■ "Best villain + best story" = "best *Trek*": so say supporters of this "ripping" sci-fi sequel that hits warp speed when "scenery-chewing" outer-space outlaw Khan hijacks a starship and goes gunning for Admiral Kirk, back for yet one more mission with his familiar Starfleet crew; it offers all the "overblown acting" and "heart of the original", and the windup with Spock on the spot has enough "emotional punch" to "make a Trekkie out of anyone."

Star Trek IV: The Voyage Home Ⓘ 21 | 17 | 21 | 23

1986. Directed by Leonard Nimoy. With William Shatner, Leonard Nimoy, DeForest Kelley. 119 minutes. Rated PG.

◪ The final frontiersmen send us a "message from the future" in this "easygoing", "most accessible" of the sci-fi spin-offs, with Kirk and company "letting their hair down" to indulge in "tongue-in-cheek" interplay as they travel backward through the centuries to join a modern-day "scientific babe" in a mission to "save the whales"; it's a little "lightweight" despite the "timely ecological" theme, but as with the other "even-numbered" entries in the series, the voyaging is "not at all bad."

STAR WARS Ⓘ ∅ 28 | 22 | 28 | 29

1977. Directed by George Lucas. With Mark Hamill, Harrison Ford, Carrie Fisher. 121 minutes. Rated PG.

■ Lucas' "Force is strong" in this "visionary" blockbuster, the "quantum leap" that "redefined sci-fi" and established a "dynasty" by locating the "universal" in a "galaxy far, far away", where "original" "critters" and "futuristic samurais" side with a put-upon princess against a evil Empire; building to a boffo "black hats/white hats" showdown, it's a "vastly entertaining" mix of "modern myth" and "thrill-and-a-half" FX; subsequent space operas "can't touch" it.

Star Wars Episode 1: The Phantom Menace Ⓘ 18 | 16 | 18 | 26

1999. Directed by George Lucas. With Liam Neeson, Ewan McGregor, Natalie Portman. 133 minutes. Rated PG.

◪ "After all the hype", here's the "good-looking" sci-fi prequel, which finds an earlier Jedi generation aiding a "planet under blockade" while setting some backstory straight as Obi-Wan and Skywalker *père* are groomed for knighthood; though denounced as a "giant misstep" that makes do with "so-so" storytelling while "pandering" to the "kiddies" with CGI "overkill" and "irritating" cast members ("why Jar Jar?"), "it's still *Star Wars*", and many "escapists" welcome it as a "worthy addition."

Steel Magnolias 24 | 25 | 24 | 23

1989. Directed by Herbert Ross. With Sally Field, Dolly Parton, Shirley MacLaine. 117 minutes. Rated PG.

■ Break out the "Kleenex" for this "estrogen"-soaked drama, a "major tearjerker" smothered in "Southern-fried" "flavor", dashed with "laughs" and "memorable one-liners" and played "to the hilt and then some" by a "talented" bunch of "adorable" all-star "belles"; the story of "best girlfriends" in a Looziana beauty parlor bonding through "thick and thin", it's "captivating", "well-made" and "weepy" enough to qualify as the "ultimate chick flick."

STING, THE ✉Ⓘ 27 | 26 | 27 | 26

1973. Directed by George Roy Hill. With Paul Newman, Robert Redford, Robert Shaw. 129 minutes. Rated PG.

■ "Deftly" charming its way to Best Picture honors, this "classy" comedy "caper" "succeeds in spades" as a "likable", "fast-paced" "vehicle" for Newman and Redford, radiating "great rapport" as a pair of "grifters" playing a gangster for a sucker in "Depression-era Chicago"; a "funny, intriguing" "period piece" set to "elegant" "Joplin rags", it raises the "suspense" stakes with "masterful" plotting and a final "zinger" that saves the sharpest sting for last.

Stop Making Sense 25 | – | 14 | 24

1984. Directed by Jonathan Demme. Documentary. With the Talking Heads. 88 minutes. Not Rated.

■ "Turn up the sound", because Demme's "joyful" "alterna-rockumentary" presents a "superior" show from new wave faves the Talking Heads in their "heyday", burning down the house with some mighty "energetic music"; the flick proves the "exception to the rule that concerts don't translate" to the big screen and finds bandleader "David Byrne in top form", "swaying" in his trademark "enormous suit."

Straight Story, The 24 | 27 | 22 | 21

1999. Directed by David Lynch. With Richard Farnsworth, Sissy Spacek, Jane Galloway. 111 minutes. Rated G.

■ The "only G-rated" effort from malaise-meister Lynch goes straight for the "heart" in this "odd" but "compelling" drama of a septuagenarian "who rides his John Deere" power mower cross-country to mend fences with his infirm brother; this "interesting" "character study" is polished into an "absolute gem" by "brilliant performances" and a "lovely" meditation on the "ending of the life cycle", but be warned that "travel by tractor" can be a "slow" ride.

Strangers on a Train ◑ 26 | 24 | 27 | 24

1951. Directed by Alfred Hitchcock. With Farley Granger, Robert Walker, Ruth Roman. 101 minutes. Rated PG.

■ Be careful "what you wish for" is the underlying theme of this "fascinating", "forward-thinking" Hitchcock thriller wherein a flippant "promise to exchange murders" spirals out of control into a "dark tale of unwanted bedfellows"; "spine-tingler" aficionados single out Walker's "chilling" turn as a "wacko" mama's boy, and among the many "tense moments", the "carousel finale still amazes."

STREETCAR NAMED DESIRE, A ✉◑ 27 | 28 | 26 | 25

1951. Directed by Elia Kazan. With Vivien Leigh, Marlon Brando, Kim Hunter, Karl Malden. 125 minutes. Rated PG.

■ A drama destined to "hold great forever", this "brilliant interpretation" of Tennessee Williams' "overwrought classic" showcases the "amazing" Brando "exploding onto the scene" ("hey, *Stella!*") in the "legendary" role of a "rugged" slob who engages in "shattering" "psychological warfare" with his delicate sister-in-law (the "wonderful", "so-sad" Leigh); fans say it's worth watching if only for a look at the "virile" Marlon when he was "still acting."

Strictly Ballroom 23 | 21 | 23 | 22

1992. Directed by Baz Luhrmann. With Paul Mercurio, Tara Morice, Bill Hunter. 94 minutes. Rated PG.

■ This "quirky", on-the-ball dose of "flash and flamenco" is a surprise charmer of a romantic comedy pairing a "hot" Aussie hoofer with an "ugly duckling", who proceed to shake up a dance championship with the question "to tango or not to tango?"; a "delightful" "send-up" of the "viciousness of the competitive ballroom circuit", it amuses with "well-executed" moves, even if onlookers "kinda know" how the strictly by-the-numbers story will turn out.

Stripes 21 | 18 | 18 | 18

1981. Directed by Ivan Reitman. With Bill Murray, Harold Ramis, Warren Oates. 101 minutes. Rated R.

◪ "Red-blooded guys" are quick to salute this "service comedy" starring "cynical" Murray as a goldbricking civilian who joins the Army and endures basic training with the idea that it's "all about laughs"; with a "strong comic cast" and gags ranging from the truly "hilarious" to the sublimely "ridiculous", it ranks as "one of the funniest" in its class, though deserters say it "bogs down" midway and caution it's "no *Caddyshack*" – and "that's a fact, Jack."

Stuart Little Ⓘ 19 | 18 | 19 | 21

1999. Directed by Rob Minkoff. With Geena Davis, Hugh Laurie, Jonathan Lipnicki. 84 minutes. Rated PG.

◪ Adapted from E.B. White's "sweet" children's classic, this "cute production" craftily combines "amazing animation" and live action to tell the tale of an "adorable" "talking mouse" who's adopted by humans only to be claimed by a couple of rodents posing as his "birth parents"; most can't help "lovin'" its "warm" "poignancy", though a few whiskers twitch at the "piffle"-ridden plot that "mangles the original" into a flick "only a little kid could like."

Summer of '42 21 | 19 | 23 | 19

1971. Directed by Robert Mulligan. With Jennifer O'Neill, Gary Grimes, Jerry Houser. 103 minutes. Rated R.

■ Sentimental yearning and raging hormones drive this "coming-of-age" romance, which finds a trio of "pubescent boys" spending the first summer after Pearl Harbor goofing off until one of them hooks up with a young soldier's widow, who's "grasping at life"; the combination of "humor" and "heartbreak" is also a "moving" remembrance of a "time of war", while the Oscar-winning score alone is "worth the price of admission."

SUNSET BOULEVARD ⊠◑∅ 28 | 28 | 27 | 27

1950. Directed by Billy Wilder. With William Holden, Gloria Swanson, Erich Von Stroheim. 110 minutes. Not Rated.

■ "Some of the greatest dialogue ever" (most famously, "I'm ready for my close-up, Mr. DeMille") graces this hybrid of "gothic" and "film noir", a "scabrous take on Hollywood" from the standpoint of a "struggling screenwriter" trying to "resurrect the career of a silent movie star" who's "not exactly in touch with reality"; given Wilder's "acerbic" direction, an "'in'-joke"–laced script and "pitch-perfect" performances from a "larger-than-life Swanson" and "hunky Holden", "who needs a musical version?"

Sunshine Boys, The ∅ 21 | 23 | 19 | 18

1975. Directed by Herbert Ross. With Walter Matthau, George Burns, Richard Benjamin. 111 minutes. Rated PG.

◪ The radiant screen rendition of Neil Simon's Broadway comedy presents Matthau and Burns (who reappears after decades offscreen and snags an Oscar) as a couple of crusty "vaudeville greats who must work together" on a TV reunion show, even though they're given to much bickering; ok, the "funny story" makes for surefire yuks, but razzers report the act as a whole is "not so bright."

Superman Ⓘ 22 | 19 | 22 | 23

1978. Directed by Richard Donner. With Christopher Reeve, Margot Kidder, Gene Hackman. 143 minutes. Rated PG.

■ "You'll really believe a man can fly" after a look at this "ahead-of-its-time" superhero fantasy, the "delightful", "campy" saga of a survivor from a doomed planet who grows up to be a "man of steel"; even if the "comic-book sensibility" is "a little silly" and the line readings "stiff", a super "heart shines through" as Reeve turns in the "definitive", "true-blue portrayal" of "all things good" – when he's not "sizing up telephone booths", that is.

Sweet Charity ∅ 20 | 21 | 19 | 23

1969. Directed by Bob Fosse. With Shirley MacLaine, John McMartin, Chita Rivera. 149 minutes. Rated G.

◪ "Fosse's directorial debut" adapts a boffo Broadway show into an "exciting" musical featuring "MacLaine at her best" as a honey of a dance-hall damsel; look for "over-the-top" "production numbers" (especially Chita's raucous 'Big Spender') with "memorable staging" and "great tunes", and if the "quirky" story "drifts" when the music stops, charitable types cheer the players for "trying with all their might."

Sweet Hereafter, The 24 | 25 | 23 | 23

1997. Directed by Atom Egoyan. With Ian Holm, Sarah Polley, Bruce Greenwood. 112 minutes. Rated R.

■ "Haunting" in a "somber" way, this adaptation of Russell Banks' novel is a "beautifully shot", "terribly moving" drama about the "aftermath of a small-town tragedy" and the "dysfunction" it lays bare; the "terrific cast" sees the burg's "delicate balance" upset when a group of children die in a "bus crash", and the camera lends a "hypnotic" feel to material that's "smart" but "shrouded in sadness."

SWEET SMELL OF SUCCESS, THE ◑ 27 | 28 | 26 | 26

1957. Directed by Alexander Mackendrick. With Burt Lancaster, Tony Curtis. 96 minutes. Not Rated.

■ A "cookie full of arsenic" soaked in "hydrochloric acid", this extra-"tasty" morsel of "moody noir" unearths the "seamy side" of showbiz with its "cynical" "character study" of the "slimy" sorts working the "publicity end": a "superb" Lancaster as a "brutal", Winchell-esque columnist and the "unctuous Curtis" as his publicist toady; brace yourself for "crackling dialogue" and some "beyond beautiful" NYC "nighttime shots" in this "timeless" but never "more timely" picture.

Swept Away F 24 | 24 | 24 | 24

1975. Directed by Lina Wertmüller. With Mariangela Melato, Giancarlo Giannini. 116 minutes. Rated R.

■ Stranding strangers on a "sunbaked islet" long "before *Survivor*", Wertmüller's "unforgettable" Italian comedy "steams up the screen" as a snobbish socialite and a coarsely "expressive" boatman develop a "passionate" "love/hate relationship" alone on a Mediterranean cay; the "satire" "speaks volumes" as a "comment on class" and the "battle of the sexes", though there's a strong undercurrent of "violence" running beneath the beautiful "scenery"; P.S. look for Madonna in the remake playing opposite Giannini's son Adriano.

Swingers 23 | 22 | 23 | 20

1996. Directed by Doug Liman. With Jon Favreau, Vince Vaughn, Heather Graham. 96 minutes. Rated R.

■ "Hooking up in the '90s" gets a "hilarious" but "realistic" spin in this "hip, kinetic" buddy comedy–cum–"cultural phenomenon" about two single guys "finding their mojo" on the "LA dating scene"; it's "immensely funny", universally "accurate" in "defining a generation" and "'so money' that it spawned its own vernacular."

Take the Money and Run 21 | 18 | 21 | 17

1969. Directed by Woody Allen. With Woody Allen, Janet Margolin, Marcel Hillaire. 85 minutes. Rated R.

■ Woody's "first full-fledged feature" wings it with "pure slapstick" and "typical" self-deprecating "shtick" in its "rawest form", stringing together the escapades of a "hopeless nerd bank robber" into a phony documentary that's "basically a series of blackouts and sketches"; though a bit "threadbare" in between the "patches of brilliance", it packs in enough "anarchy and whimsy" to foretell things to come.

Talented Mr. Ripley, The 18 | 21 | 19 | 21

1999. Directed by Anthony Minghella. With Matt Damon, Jude Law, Gwyneth Paltrow. 139 minutes. Rated R.

◪ A "lush thriller of mistaken identity" set in "'50s Europe", this "unsettling", "underrated" study of a murderous "schmuck-turned-socialite" stars Damon as the "slippery" title character (in a performance that's either "unnervingly good" or totally "botched"); while the "disturbing storyline" played out against "spectacular scenery" enthralls many, critics see little talent in its "lack of warmth" and way-"too-long" running time.

Tarzan 22 | – | 21 | 24

1999. Directed by Chris Buck, Kevin Lima. Animated. 88 minutes. Rated G.

■ Some of "Disney's best work" "recreates the magic" of a "classic" in this jungly tale of man and monkey swinging through life via "phenomenally" "innovative" animation; a "fast-paced, thrilling adventure" that takes time out for "character" but "keeps things relatively lighthearted", it adds some "thoughtful" "modern" angles and a "great score", including an Oscar-winning song from Phil Collins.

Tarzan the Ape Man ◑Ⅱ∅ 21 | 16 | 21 | 18

1932. Directed by W.S. Van Dyke. With Johnny Weissmuller, Maureen O'Sullivan. 99 minutes. Not Rated.

■ An "old-fashioned" fave among the "first real adventure films", this "memorable" intersection of Hollywood and vine finds a Brit lady Jane abducted by the ape-bred hero only to civilize him (and catch a bit of jungle fever herself); Olympic swimmer Weissmuller brings "definitive" bravura to the title character, and thus this "campy" but "trendsetting original" "holds up better" than all the sequels you can shake a banana at.

TAXI DRIVER 27 | 29 | 25 | 25

1976. Directed by Martin Scorsese. With Robert De Niro, Jodie Foster, Harvey Keitel, Cybill Shepherd. 113 minutes. Rated R.

■ Confirming "non-NYers' greatest fears" about the "brutal" "underbelly" of "modern urban life", Scorsese's vividly "cerebral" thriller rolls through "sleazy" streets and "neon" nights charged by De Niro's "monumental performance" as a "creepy", insomniac hack – "you talking to me?" – whose live-wire issues build to "harrowing" magnum force in the "steam-filled" city; overall, its depiction of "urban decay, rage and alienation" is "top-class" but "lurid" and very "intense."

Ten Commandments, The 24 | 21 | 25 | 27

1956. Directed by Cecil B. DeMille. With Charlton Heston, Yul Brynner, Anne Baxter. 220 minutes. Rated G.

◪ "Let it be written" that DeMille's "over-the-top" biblical blockbuster is the "epic of all epics", a "Cliffs Notes" account of Exodus built on "Heston's finest" role as the "one and only Moses", performer of "monumental" miracles on land and Red Sea; though "fantastic sets" and Brynner's "badass" Egyptian king distract from the "kitschy" script and "overblown" production, it's "entertaining" enough to keep a "cast of thousands" in "constant circulation."

Terminator, The Ⓘ 24 | 18 | 24 | 24

1984. Directed by James Cameron. With Arnold Schwarzenegger, Michael Biehn, Linda Hamilton. 108 minutes. Rated R.

■ Buckle up for Cameron's "unstoppable" "breakthrough", this "sci-fi/action" "genre-maker" about an "evil cyborg sent from the future" to wreak havoc on the past via "Ah-nuld's" laconic, "seriously scary" "presence" alone; it "doesn't disappoint" in dispensing "awesome" "violent" mayhem all over '80s LA, and its most famous line – "I'll be back" – was a harbinger of the sequels to come.

Terms of Endearment ✉Ⓘ 25 | 26 | 24 | 22

1983. Directed by James L. Brooks. With Shirley MacLaine, Debra Winger, Jack Nicholson. 132 minutes. Rated PG.

■ A "four-hanky tearjerker" "worth its weight in Kleenex", this "engrossing" "weepie with a spine" starts off comically enough depicting a "tangled mother-daughter relationship" but takes a "serious" turn in the second act when "life-and-death" issues arise; quite the Oscar magnet, it took home Best Picture honors as well as statuettes for the "amazing" MacLaine and an "outstanding" Nicholson, who's a "hoot" as the "drunken" former astronaut who lives next door.

That's Entertainment! Ⓘ 25 | – | – | 25

1974. Directed by Jack Haley Jr. Documentary. With Gene Kelly, Fred Astaire. 127 minutes. Rated G.

■ This "remarkable" "survey of MGM musicals" lays out a "delicious", "crème-de-la-crème" "buffet" of glorious "old clips" set up with "narration by some mighty big stars"; showcasing the likes of Kelly and Astaire at their "thrilling" peak, this compilation is "desert-island" viewing for old-timers and a peerlessly "entertaining" "introduction" for "young folks" to the bygone days of "real talent."

Thelma & Louise ✉ 23 | 25 | 23 | 21

1991. Directed by Ridley Scott. With Susan Sarandon, Geena Davis, Brad Pitt, Harvey Keitel. 129 minutes. Rated R.

■ A "high-powered" "girl-power" flick focusing on a "feminist crime spree", this "groundbreaking" display of "female macho" "rocks" as two everyday gals "finally get back" at the men who've wronged them by becoming "devil-may-care" "outlaws" "on the lam"; the "superb storyline" and "stellar performances" keep things "involving" right up to the "heartbreaking", "*Butch Cassidy*"–esque "bad ending"; P.S. look for Pitt's "starmaking" breakout as the "sexy hitchhiker."

There's Something About Mary 21 | 19 | 20 | 19

1998. Directed by Bobby Farrelly, Peter Farrelly. With Cameron Diaz, Matt Dillon, Ben Stiller. 119 minutes. Rated R.

◪ Proceed "at your own risk" as the "ultra-crude" Farrelly brothers "push the limits" of "gross-out comedy" in this "tacky laugh riot" about a "loser with a heart of gold" and the "good-sport" girl he loves that's an "oh-my-gosh" compendium of "high-school humor" and "vulgar" "sight gags" (the "dog", the "zipper", the "hair gel"); foes moan this movie "made by morons for morons" is "even dumber than *Dumb and Dumber*"; your call.

They Shoot Horses, Don't They? 21 | 24 | 22 | 21

1969. Directed by Sydney Pollack. With Jane Fonda, Michael Sarrazin, Susannah York. 120 minutes. Rated PG.

■ "Jane Fonda at her world-weariest" provides the glue in this "classic" Depression drama about "desperate" marathon dancers frantically trying to make a buck; though the story's "small" and the sentiments grim, its ensemble cast is "unforgettable" – particularly the "superlative" Gig Young, who copped an Oscar for the role of the slimy emcee.

Thing, The ◑∅ 23 | 19 | 25 | 19

1951. Directed by Christian Nyby. With Kenneth Tobey, Margaret Sheridan. 87 minutes. Not Rated.

■ This "serious '50s sci-fi" suspenser "still holds up" as a "smart" "flying-saucer" shocker about a group of scientists driven to "creepy" extremes in a "claustrophobic, paranoid" encounter with a murderous alien found frozen in the Arctic ice; despite "skimpy" special effects, the "tight script" builds enough "tension" to frighten the "daylights" out of fans, who spurn the "gory remake" – there's nothing like "the real *Thing*."

Thing, The 23 | 19 | 23 | 23

1982. Directed by John Carpenter. With Kurt Russell, Wilford Brimley, David Clennon. 109 minutes. Rated R.

■ "Chills" abound in Carpenter's "excellent remake of the '51 classic", wherein the Antarctic's most "frigid science outpost" is beset by a "horrible alien" capable of "disguising itself" in human form; an "imaginative" contribution to the "sci-fi/horror pantheon", it supplies enough "true suspense" to keep the audience "guessing" as the "paranoia" mounts.

Thin Man, The ◑⓫∅ 26 | 25 | 23 | 23

1934. Directed by W.S. Van Dyke. With William Powell, Myrna Loy, Maureen O'Sullivan. 93 minutes. Not Rated.

■ "Break out the martini glasses": "mystery meets screwball" comedy in this "snazzy" flicker featuring "cool detective" Nick Charles and his "classy wife" Nora "drinking like fish" and "fluidly" spouting "snappy dialogue" ("double entendre, anyone?") as they investigate a murder; the "suave, sexy fun" is so "cosmopolitan" and "wonderfully evocative of the '30s" that it seems unsporting to point out that the "whodunit" plot is a bit thin.

Thin Red Line, The 19 | 21 | 17 | 22

1998. Directed by Terrence Malick. With Sean Penn, George Clooney, John Cusack. 170 minutes. Rated R.

◪ Malick's "experimental war epic" is made for those who "enjoy thinking" about "big questions", with Penn exuding "gravity" as a sarge facing the front lines at Guadalcanal with a "star-studded" company of "common soldiers"; "lavish", "stunning visuals" "attempt to poeticize" the "horror and beauty" of battle and warfare's "emotional effects", though detractors grunt it's "incoherent."

THIRD MAN, THE ◑ 28 | 28 | 27 | 28

1949. Directed by Carol Reed. With Joseph Cotten, Alida Valli, Orson Welles, Trevor Howard. 104 minutes. Not Rated.

■ "Oh, that zither!"; this "masterful" piece of "postwar" noir simmers with shadowy "intrigue" as an "alienated" Cotten encounters "romance" and "betrayal" while searching "bombed-out" Vienna for a "mysterious" black marketeer (played by Welles, who makes the most of a "small" role with an "arresting" entrance); graced with "expressionist" lensing, Graham Greene's "clever, dark script" and a "memorable" final fade, it's hailed as "all-around perfect."

39 Steps, The ◑ 27 | 25 | 27 | 24

1935. Directed by Alfred Hitchcock. With Robert Donat, Madeleine Carroll. 86 minutes. Not Rated.

■ "You can't go wrong" with this "classic" "British period" Hitchcock nail-biter, a "virtuoso" "thriller diller" wherein an "innocent man wrongly accused" of murder tries to clear his name amid "chase scenes, foreign spy intrigue and romance" (with a woman he winds up "handcuffed" to); sure, the "dated" special effects are on the low-tech side, but this "tense mystery" delivers enough suspense to "keep you on the edge of your seat."

This Is Spinal Tap 26 | 24 | 25 | 22

1984. Directed by Rob Reiner. With Christopher Guest, Michael McKean, Rob Reiner. 82 minutes. Rated R.

■ "VH1's *Behind the Music*" pales before this "hysterical" "rock mockumentary", an "unbelievably authentic-feeling" "send-up" of the music industry and superstar "pretensions" that follows an "aging heavy-metal band" taking its act "on the road"; the "stellar cast" plays an "unforgettable" group of clueless musicians, simulating a "sidesplitting insider's view" that's alarmingly "like the real thing" – except "every single second is funny."

Thomas Crown Affair, The 23 | 23 | 24 | 22

1968. Directed by Norman Jewison. With Steve McQueen, Faye Dunaway, Paul Burke. 102 minutes. Rated R.

■ This "slick", "grown-up romance" offers a "cat-and-mouse" plot as millionaire McQueen engineers a bank heist for kicks until he encounters Dunaway, a "knockout" insurance sleuth in mad pursuit; their "smoldering", "high-tension" affair is a "stylish" standoff down to the final "checkmate" in that famed chess match, and as for the recent remake, "do not accept imitations."

Thoroughly Modern Millie ∅ 18 | 19 | 16 | 21

1967. Directed by George Roy Hill. With Julie Andrews, Mary Tyler Moore, Carol Channing. 138 minutes. Rated G.

◪ "Roaring '20s" razzle-dazzle makes this musical comedy an "absolute hoot", with "Andrews at her peak" as a big-city rookie trying to land a man while coming to the rescue of her abducted chum Moore; it's played as a "slapstick farce set to song and dance" that alternates new tunes with "flapper-era" standards, and if it's a thoroughly unmodern "silly bit of fluff", all that "jazzy fun" is "entertaining nonetheless."

Three Faces of Eve, The ✉◑∅ 24 | 27 | 24 | 20

1957. Directed by Nunnally Johnson. With Joanne Woodward, David Wayne, Lee J. Cobb. 91 minutes. Not Rated.

■ "Incredible" Oscar-winner Woodward delivers a "tour-de-force" turn in this "breakthrough" "multiple-personality genre film", an "interesting drama" about a "woman tormented" by triple identities that she can't control; switching from subdued homemaker to brazen party girl in the bat of an eyelash, a "strong" Woodward does a "stellar" job of "bringing all three characters to life" in all their "schizoid" perplexity.

Three Kings 20 | 21 | 21 | 22

1999. Directed by David O. Russell. With George Clooney, Mark Wahlberg, Ice Cube. 114 minutes. Rated R.

◪ Opening at the close of Desert Storm, this "bold and different" war flick offers a combo of "crackerjack action" and "surprisingly good" acting as "irreverent army guy" Clooney assembles a team to take off across the dunes in a "chase for stolen Kuwaiti gold" that morphs into a "morality tale" midway through; the "exciting, insightful" scenario and "creative" visuals make it royally "enjoyable on many levels", though a few are "not impressed" by the "chaotic storyline" and "preachy dialogue."

Three Musketeers, The Ⓘ 22 | 22 | 22 | 23

1974. Directed by Richard Lester. With Oliver Reed, Raquel Welch, Richard Chamberlain, Michael York. 105 minutes. Rated PG.

■ A "rollicking rendition" of the "Dumas classic", this "rousing" "old-fashioned" adventure "stays faithful" to the original tale but spices up the swordplay with "slapstick" and "bawdy" humor as a brave band of swashbucklers defends the queen's honor against that crooked cardinal; the "lavish" 17th-century sets and all-for-one "charm" of the "great cast" ensure its place as the "quintessential" version by which all others "shall be judged."

Thunderball 22 | 21 | 21 | 23

1965. Directed by Terence Young. With Sean Connery, Claudine Auger, Adolfo Celi. 130 minutes. Rated PG.

■ Bringing the "basic Bond formula" to the Bahamas, this swimming entry in the superspy series has Connery breaking out his arsenal of "gadgets" and dry wisecracks against the "very real threat" of stolen nukes held for ransom; the "nonstop action" and "incredible underwater fight sequences" made it a thunderous success in its day, and if now "underappreciated", connoisseurs nevertheless rank it "near the top" of the 007 oeuvre.

Tie Me Up! Tie Me Down! F 20 | 21 | 20 | 20

1990. Directed by Pedro Almodóvar. With Victoria Abril, Antonio Banderas, Loles Leon. 111 minutes. Rated NC-17.

■ "Madcap" director Almodóvar strikes again in this naughty knotty comedy about a kidnapped, trussed-up B-movie star that's a cross between "*The Collector*" and a soft-core bondage flick; its "sexy", "vivid characters" and "nice" Ennio Morricone soundtrack further spice up a storyline that's already "hysterically funny – even if you don't speak Spanish."

Time After Time 23 | 23 | 25 | 21

1979. Directed by Nicholas Meyer. With Malcolm McDowell, Mary Steenburgen, David Warner. 112 minutes. Rated PG.

■ A "clever" bit of "brainy entertainment", this "charming" sci-fi thriller recounts "H.G. Wells chasing Jack the Ripper to modern-day San Francisco" via a "functioning time machine"; a "witty" romp expertly blending "romantic" interludes between McDowell and Steenburgen with "suspenseful" sequencing, it's "well worth seeing" for Warner's "helluva performance" alone.

Time Bandits 21 | 19 | 23 | 22

1981. Directed by Terry Gilliam. With John Cleese, Sean Connery, Shelley Duvall. 116 minutes. Rated PG.

■ Terry Gilliam's "warped-mind" "genius" shines in this "bittersweet" time-travel "fantasy" about the "classic struggle between good and evil", with a sprawling cast that includes a "band of midgets", a "fantastic villain" and the director's trademark parade of "delightful" cameos (i.e. the "standout" Connery and "funny-as-anything" Cleese); though the visual effects may be showing their age, there are enough "juicy moments" to justify its "cult-classic" status.

Time Machine, The 22 | 17 | 26 | 23

1960. Directed by George Pal. With Rod Taylor, Alan Young, Yvette Mimieux. 103 minutes. Rated G.

■ "Faithful to both the letter and spirit of H.G. Wells' novel", this "granddaddy of time-travel movies" concerning a 19th-century scientist flabbergasted by the future is "nicely paced" and "fondly remembered" for its "thought-provoking storyline" and "good special effects for the era" (which won an Oscar); though the "remake isn't bad", the "much-better" original is prized as a real "gem."

Time to Kill, A 18 | 18 | 22 | 19

1996. Directed by Joel Schumacher. With Matthew McConaughey, Sandra Bullock, Samuel L. Jackson. 149 minutes. Rated R.

■ "Very adult" and "suspenseful to the end", this "hard-hitting" "Mississippi courtroom drama" about racist violence and retribution is a "solid adaptation of the John Grisham novel"; despite the very "Hollywood ending", it's ever "captivating" thanks to "intelligent" turns from Bullock and McConaughey ("his best role").

Titanic ✉ 19 | 16 | 18 | 26

1997. Directed by James Cameron. With Leonardo DiCaprio, Kate Winslet, Billy Zane. 194 minutes. Rated PG-13.

◪ Ok, it's "not highbrow stuff", but this "over-the-top" "spectacular" detailing a "doomed love story" aboard a "doomed ocean liner" thrills with "dazzling" special effects, including a "fantastic" "re-creation of the original ship" and icebergs so real "you can almost touch" them; some torpedo the "shallow" "cardboard characters", "soap opera"–esque script and "weak acting" as "all wet", and whether it's "deserving of its Oscars" – all 11 of them – is still hotly debated.

To Catch a Thief ∅ 25 | 25 | 24 | 25

1955. Directed by Alfred Hitchcock. With Grace Kelly, Cary Grant, Jesse Royce Landis. 106 minutes. Not Rated.

■ "Slick, sophisticated and oh-so-cool", this "stylish" romantic thriller may be "Hitchcock lite", but Grant and Kelly provide plenty of "dazzle" in an amusing trifle about a cat burglar prowling the "south of France"; maybe the "plot is secondary" to the "enjoyable scenery" and "fab clothes", but there's snappy patter aplenty, notably Grace's classic picnic query "would you prefer a leg or a breast?"

To Die For 18 | 21 | 19 | 18

1995. Directed by Gus Van Sant. With Nicole Kidman, Matt Dillon, Joaquin Phoenix. 106 minutes. Rated R.

■ A "true tabloid story" becomes "cuttingly observed satire" in this drama about "America's obsession with fame", a "wicked black comedy" due to "Buck Henry's brilliant script" and Van Sant's "incisive" direction; in her "most original role", Kidman "positively shines" as an "ambitious" TV weathergirl "trying to get ahead in her job and out of her marriage" – many say her performance alone is the "reason to see it."

To Have and Have Not ◑∅ 26 | 27 | 24 | 24

1944. Directed by Howard Hawks. With Humphrey Bogart, Lauren Bacall, Walter Brennan. 100 minutes. Not Rated.

■ Bacall (in her screen debut) teams with future real-life hubby Bogart to "define star chemistry" in this dramatization of the Hemingway novel about WWII resistance runners; Martinique supplies a sultry backdrop for the two stars to "smolder", especially when Lauren "steams up the screen" with her legendary question "you know how to whistle, don't you?"

TO KILL A MOCKINGBIRD ✉◑ 29 | 29 | 29 | 26

1962. Directed by Robert Mulligan. With Gregory Peck, Mary Badham, Robert Duvall. 129 minutes. Not Rated.

■ "After all these years", this Southern courtroom drama about racism and prejudice "told from the point of view of a young girl" "still packs the same emotional punch"; kudos go to Oscar-winning screenwriter Horton Foote, "for not having strayed" from Harper Lee's "original text", and to an "im-peck-able" Peck at his "peak" as the "father we all wish we had"; in short, "Hollywood got this one right."

Tombstone 21 | 22 | 21 | 21

1993. Directed by George P. Cosmatos. With Kurt Russell, Val Kilmer, Sam Elliott. 130 minutes. Rated R.

■ More than an ok rendition of the "O.K. Corral story", this "slick retelling" brings legends Wyatt Earp and Doc Holliday up to date with plenty of good old "modern-day violence"; starring a pistol-packing Russell and "fun-to-watch" Kilmer, it's a "worthy" enough stab at pure "entertainment" – "even if you don't like Westerns."

Tom Jones ✉ 25 | 24 | 24 | 25

1963. Directed by Tony Richardson. With Albert Finney, Susannah York, Hugh Griffith. 121 minutes. Not Rated.

■ "Richly crafted and craftily acted" – with four Oscars to prove it – this hilariously "bawdy" "period piece par excellence" might be set in 18th-century England but moodwise is more like a "snapshot of the Swinging Sixties"; devotees are ever smitten with its "clever script", "lively direction" and Finney's "lusty" title turn, while gourmands eat up that "sexy" "food-seduction scene."

Tomorrow Never Dies 20 | 20 | 17 | 21

1997. Directed by Roger Spottiswoode. With Pierce Brosnan, Jonathan Pryce, Michelle Yeoh. 119 minutes. Rated PG-13.

◪ ". . . and neither does James" joke 007 junkies of the juggernaut's 18th entry, wherein "Brosnan fills Connery's" custom-made shoes and "brings back" the secret agent's "cruel streak"; the "thoughtful plot" (something about a mad "media magnate" bent on starting WWIII) is buoyed by "high-tech special effects", though Bond-girl watchers say the picture belongs to the "fabulous" Yeoh.

Tootsie 25 | 27 | 24 | 23

1982. Directed by Sydney Pollack. With Dustin Hoffman, Jessica Lange, Bill Murray. 119 minutes. Rated PG.

■ "Cross-dressing doesn't get much better" than this "brilliantly funny" comedy about a long-"struggling actor" who finally achieves success – "as an actress"; though Hoffman might be "one ugly" broad, his "sublime", "think-out-of-the-box" performance mixing "humor with humanity" is beautiful, while a "slick" but "unpredictable script" and an "outstanding" supporting cast make this one a "keeper, not a renter."

Top Gun 22 | 18 | 20 | 24

1986. Directed by Tony Scott. With Tom Cruise, Kelly McGillis, Val Kilmer. 110 minutes. Rated PG.

◪ "Sexy fighter pilots" populate this "absolutely irresistible" "'80s action" "icon", a roiling mix of "testosterone", "noise", "romance" and "aerial maneuvers"; the "cocky" Cruise "looks great in uniform" and that "volleyball scene" sure is "hot", but foes dis the "hokey" plot and "intermittent acting" and can't fathom why it's so "inexplicably popular."

TOP HAT ◑ 27 | 23 | 21 | 26

1935. Directed by Mark Sandrich. With Fred Astaire, Ginger Rogers. 101 minutes. Not Rated.

■ "Heaven, I'm in heaven" sigh fans of this "classic" "'30s musical" spotlighting the charms of a "debonair Astaire" opposite a "feather"-gowned Rogers; sure, there's an "all-hit Irving Berlin score", "amazing production numbers" and a "witty French farce of a script" rife with "mistaken-identity" gags, but in the end, it's "Fred and Ginger dancing cheek-to-cheek" that catapults it to "sublime" status.

Topkapi 24 | 22 | 25 | 21

1964. Directed by Jules Dassin. With Melina Mercouri, Peter Ustinov. 119 minutes. Not Rated.

■ Director "Dassin's '60s caper holds up well", managing to "avoid clichés the same way" its jewel-thief cast "avoid traps" as they engineer a heist in Istanbul; owing to a "clever script" and some "beautifully drawn characters" (like the "sophisticated" Mercouri and "priceless", "Oscar-winning" Ustinov), this "taut" but "fun" thriller/comedy is reminiscent of an erstwhile "*Mission: Impossible.*"

Topper ◑ⓘ∅ 20 | 21 | 21 | 19

1937. Directed by Norman Z. McLeod. With Roland Young, Constance Bennett, Cary Grant. 97 minutes. Not Rated.

■ Grant and Bennett "never miss a beat" in this "smart" romantic comedy about a pair of martini-swilling, madcap ghosts who must do a good deed to go to heaven; expect lots of laughs when the "delightful" phantoms select uptight banker Cosmo Topper as the beneficiary of their largesse in this "lighthearted" bit of "whimsy."

Topsy-Turvy 23 | 25 | 23 | 26

1999. Directed by Mike Leigh. With Jim Broadbent, Allan Corduner, Timothy Spall. 160 minutes. Rated R.

◪ This "finely observed backstage story about the stormy partnership of Gilbert and Sullivan" provides a "window into the Victorian age" as well as a "fascinating" glimpse into the "creative process" via a subplot about the first staging of *The Mikado*; "superb" acting (with an especially "grand Broadbent") and a "gorgeous production" make it a "joy to watch" for most, though a few yawn "boring."

Tora! Tora! Tora! 23 | 19 | 25 | 24

1970. Directed by Richard Fleischer, Kinji Fukasaku, Toshio Masuda. With Martin Balsam, Jason Robards, Joseph Cotten. 144 minutes. Rated G.

◪ Surveyors split on this "intricate" war chronicle of the "Japanese attack on Pearl Harbor": defenders say this "ultimate docudrama" is "well done historically", citing its "bilingual plotlines" and over-the-top "stunning" special effects, but curmudgeons counter it's a "comic-book" look at the tragedy (although "light years ahead" of the 2001 version); your call.

To Sir, With Love ⓘ 22 | 23 | 24 | 20

1967. Directed by James Clavell. With Sidney Poitier, Judy Geeson, Christian Roberts. 105 minutes. Not Rated.

■ The "always-excellent" Poitier stars in this "nice little piece of '60s" nostalgia as a "London high school teacher" passing on life lessons to "inner-city punks"; "sweet" and "timeless", it deals with "still-relevant" issues – "race, family conflicts, respect for authority" – in a "genuinely moving" fashion, and Lulu's smashing rendition of the title song "makes the movie."

Total Recall 18 | 14 | 21 | 22

1990. Directed by Paul Verhoeven. With Arnold Schwarzenegger, Rachel Ticotin, Sharon Stone. 113 minutes. Rated R.

◪ "One of Ah-nuld's better" efforts may be this "exciting sci-fi adventure" flick, one of those "is-it-all-a-dream" stories about a secret agent implanted with someone else's memory chip; filmed "just before the age of digital effects" dawned, this "visual tour de force" inspires diverse reactions – "original" vs. "mediocre" – though pacifists are peeved by all that "gratuitous violence."

Touch of Evil ◑ 26 | 24 | 25 | 26

1958. Directed by Orson Welles. With Charlton Heston, Janet Leigh, Orson Welles. 95 minutes. Rated PG-13.

■ "Proof that Welles was more than a one-hit wonder", this "rococo" "pinnacle of film noir" stars the director as a "bloated" "Texas border town" cop feuding with his south-of-the-border counterpart (Heston in "Mexican blackface"); among its many memorable touches are the "sweeping" "opening sequence" and the "effortless scene-stealing" by Marlene Dietrich, who has the picture's best line: "lay off the candy bars"; P.S. the "restored version" is "much better" than the original release.

Towering Inferno, The 18 | 17 | 18 | 22

1974. Directed by John Guillermin, Irwin Allen. With Steve McQueen, Paul Newman, William Holden. 165 minutes. Rated PG.

◪ "Make sure you know where all the exits are" before settling into this "big, bad '70s disaster" flick starring a skyscraper, a fire and a "rogue's gallery of great actors", led by a "kick-ass McQueen"; although the "passable" "special effects were top-drawer for its time", cynical sorts snort it's more of a "made-for-TV movie" by modern standards.

Toy Story (II) 27 | – | 25 | 28

1995. Directed by John Lasseter. Animated. 81 minutes. Rated G.

■ Ushering in a "new era of animation" with "breakthrough" computer-generated effects, this Pixar-produced "instant classic" is a bona fide "technical wonder"; its "humorous" storyline, "lovable characters" and the "great concept" of walking, talking toys add up to a picture that's not only "equally entertaining for adults and kids" but also "deserving of the franchise it started."

Trading Places ∅ 23 | 22 | 23 | 20

1983. Directed by John Landis. With Dan Aykroyd, Eddie Murphy, Jamie Lee Curtis. 118 minutes. Rated R.

■ This "hysterical" treatment of the "classic" "rags-to-riches" "switcheroo" has "pauper" Murphy turned into "prince" Aykroyd and vice-versa; "quickly paced and never boring", it's memorable for "early vintage" Eddie moments, some "funny" business from Dan and the spectacle of Jamie Lee's "exposed breasts."

Traffic ✉ 23 | 24 | 23 | 25

2000. Directed by Steven Soderbergh. With Michael Douglas, Benicio Del Toro, Catherine Zeta-Jones. 147 minutes. Rated R.

■ Maybe "more realistic than you want", this "eye-opening" "portrait of the drug wars" is simultaneously "poignant", "intelligent" and "troubling", using "multiple storylines" to create a "stunning" hybrid of "thriller" and "cautionary tale"; the "amazing use of color", "documentary-like" "handheld" camerawork and Del Toro's deft, Oscar-winning turn all get the green light, though the highest praise is reserved for its "absolutely brilliant" director.

Training Day ✉ 20 | 27 | 19 | 22

2001. Directed by Antoine Fuqua. With Denzel Washington, Ethan Hawke. 120 minutes. Rated R.

■ "Denzel shows his scary side" as a "profoundly bad" LA cop with enough "charisma to convince you that his skewed view of the world makes sense" in his Oscar-winning role as a detective who has "one day to teach the ropes" to a "rookie" (played by a "holding-his-own" Hawke); the "twisting" plot "grabs you from the very beginning" and takes you on one "wild ride."

Trainspotting 22 | 22 | 20 | 22

1996. Directed by Danny Boyle. With Ewan McGregor, Ewen Bremner, Robert Carlyle. 94 minutes. Rated R.

■ "Giddy and witty" but also "harrowing and intense", this "graphic" British drama depicting the "daily life of drug addicts" has a "kinetic" "rawness" about it that "gets right under your skin"; while "not for everyone", its "quirky" cinematography, "outstanding" score and "breakthrough" turn from McGregor make for "reality-check" viewing, but bring an "interpreter" – the "Scottish accents are thick."

TREASURE OF THE SIERRA MADRE, THE ✉◑∅ 27 | 27 | 26 | 24

1948. Directed by John Huston. With Humphrey Bogart, Walter Huston, Tim Holt. 126 minutes. Not Rated.

■ "Human nature" "poisoned by greed" is the theme of this "archetypal treasure hunt", a "wonderfully old-fashioned adventure" that won Oscars for the father-and-son Hustons; Bogart exudes "masculine energy" showing "what gold will do to a man" in an "unforgettably powerful" performance that devolves into "paranoia" – and as for the "stunning" photography, purists say "we don't need no stinkin' color."

TRIUMPH OF THE WILL ◑F 27 | – | 17 | 27

1935. Directed by Leni Riefenstahl. Documentary. 114 minutes. Not Rated.

■ "Perhaps the most powerful (and immoral) documentary" ever made, this "Leni Riefenstahl masterpiece" was commissioned to honor Germany's 1934 National Socialist Party Congress and the metaphorical "enthronement of Hitler"; the "superb" camerawork is "way ahead of its time", leading reluctant admirers to admit this "artful" propaganda piece is indeed a "triumph of filmmaking", if not subject matter.

Tron 18 | 14 | 18 | 22

1982. Directed by Steven Lisberger. With Jeff Bridges, Bruce Boxleitner, David Warner. 96 minutes. Rated PG.

■ Wired types tout this "underappreciated forerunner to today's special-effects" extravaganzas by dubbing it the "first real geek movie", owing to a storyline that posits what could happen "if you got sucked into your Nintendo"; ok, it could be a tad "dated" now, but it was the "coolest thing since sliced bread when it came out."

True Grit ✉ Ⓘ 22 | 23 | 21 | 22

1969. Directed by Henry Hathaway. With John Wayne, Glen Campbell, Kim Darby. 128 minutes. Rated G.

■ "Another Western for your library", this "classic" oater is made "especially for Wayne fans" because the Duke took home his first (and only) Oscar for his role as U.S. Marshall Rooster Cogburn; otherwise, it's standard stuff about a vengeful lawman, though early-in-their-career performances by Dennis Hopper and Robert Duvall keep things lively.

True Lies 19 | 16 | 20 | 22

1994. Directed by James Cameron. With Arnold Schwarzenegger, Jamie Lee Curtis. 144 minutes. Rated R.

■ "Arnold is Bond, James Bond" in this "tongue-in-cheek spy" flicker that's a "wonderful combo" of "comedy, action and intrigue"; as his "frumpy wife" turned "drop-dead gorgeous" siren, Jamie Lee is "smoking", while Tom Arnold's a "gas" as the "not-so-super secret-agent sidekick"; throw in "lots of explosions and weapons" and you've got a true "blockbuster" "blastfest."

Truman Show, The 21 | 22 | 23 | 22

1998. Directed by Peter Weir. With Jim Carrey, Laura Linney, Ed Harris. 103 minutes. Rated PG.

◪ This "original", "thought-provoking" fantasy/comedy offers a "departure" for Carrey, who's "unusually restrained" (i.e. "doesn't act like a moron") in the role of an unwitting star of a 24/7 reality TV show set in a "phony world"; though some lookers find "little content" among all the "hype", intellectuals enthuse that this "Big Brother"–ish "allegory" leaves you "questioning what reality is."

Tucker: The Man and His Dream 20 | 21 | 23 | 21

1988. Directed by Francis Ford Coppola. With Jeff Bridges, Joan Allen, Martin Landau. 110 minutes. Rated PG.

■ For a "revealing look beneath the hood of the American auto industry", this "colorful", "stylish" film features a "terrific" Bridges in the "true-ish story" of a "visionary '40s car maker and his sad defeat" at the hands of competitors and politicians; Coppola-ficionados are convinced this "underrated" film "deserves more notice."

12 ANGRY MEN ◑ 28 | 28 | 27 | 23

1957. Directed by Sidney Lumet. With Henry Fonda, Martin Balsam, Lee J. Cobb, E.G. Marshall. 96 minutes. Not Rated.

■ "Human nature at its best and worst" is on display in this "brilliant" "courtroom drama", wherein an "all-star cast" enact the "hidden agendas" and "biases" of jurors deciding the fate of a murder defendant; thanks to its "taut" script, an "appropriately claustrophobic" "one-room setting" and an "unforgettable Fonda", this "study of American democracy" is alternately "suspenseful" and "compelling."

Twelve Monkeys 22 | 23 | 24 | 23

1995. Directed by Terry Gilliam. With Bruce Willis, Madeleine Stowe, Brad Pitt. 129 minutes. Rated R.

■ Gilliam's "master-of-the-bizarre" status is reinforced by this "complex", "super-ingenious" "time-travel tale" about the "release of a deadly virus" followed by a "post-apocalyptic" attempt to "save the world"; the sets are "dazzling", Brad 'n' Bruce prove they can "actually act" and if the "*Terminator*-meets-*Brazil*" sci-fi storyline is "confusing", it's "wonderfully" so.

Twelve O'Clock High ◑ 26 | 25 | 26 | 23

1949. Directed by Henry King. With Gregory Peck, Hugh Marlowe, Dean Jagger. 132 minutes. Not Rated.

■ "Peck is marvelous" as a WWII Brigadier General "placing terrible pressure on young American pilots" in this "accurate" depiction of the "burdens of command" and the "human side of war"; a "perfect screenplay" "rooted in historical reality" "manipulates the tension" right up to the compelling climax.

20,000 Leagues Under the Sea 22 | 18 | 25 | 23

1954. Directed by Richard Fleischer. With Kirk Douglas, James Mason, Peter Lorre. 127 minutes. Rated G.

■ "Disney's live-action adaptation of the Jules Verne classic" is a "fabulous" "undersea adventure" starring a "singing", "tight shorts"–wearing Douglas as the heroic 19th-century seafarer who battles both Captain Nemo and a "scary" "giant squid" who "should have received an Oscar"; even though the special effects look "cheesy" today, overall it's a "real old-fashioned hoot."

Two for the Road ∅ 24 | 27 | 24 | 24

1967. Directed by Stanley Donen. With Albert Finney, Audrey Hepburn. 111 minutes. Not Rated.

■ "Love isn't always easy" in this "bittersweet travelogue of the ups and downs of a married couple" that "jumps back and forth in time" as they "find, lose and rekindle" their relationship; Audrey's at her "most charming", "hopelessly glamorous" best and "marvelous together" with Finney amid all that "unmatched European scenery"; meanwhile, the "mesmerizing, melodious" Mancini music "sustains the poignant mood."

2001: A Space Odyssey Ⓘ 26 | 19 | 24 | 27

1968. Directed by Stanley Kubrick. With Keir Dullea, Gary Lockwood, William Sylvester. 139 minutes. Rated G.

◪ The "*Citizen Kane* of science-fiction films", this "era-defining" Kubrick "interpretation of an Arthur C. Clarke" story "changed movies forever" with its "haunting view" of a future world of "machine domination"; sure, some modernists find it "slow" and "ponderous", but even those who have "no clue what it all means" say this "coldly magnificent" epic is "undeniably influential" – and add "you'll never hear Strauss' 'Blue Danube Waltz' the same way again"; P.S. "don't bother trying to figure out the ending."

Umbrellas of Cherbourg, The 🅵 24 | 22 | 21 | 26

1964. Directed by Jacques Demy. With Catherine Deneuve, Nino Castelnuovo. 87 minutes. Not Rated.

■ Ultra-"bright Technicolor" and "captivating" music from Michel Legrand provide the uplift in this "sad story" of love in vain, an idiosyncratic French bonbon that's "entirely sung" (a "risky" proposition that ultimately "works"); starring a "fetching" "young Deneuve", it has the "courage" to turn a potentially "cheesy" premise into "inspiring" filmmaking.

Unbearable Lightness of Being, The 21 | 24 | 21 | 21

1988. Directed by Philip Kaufman. With Daniel Day-Lewis, Juliette Binoche, Lena Olin. 171 minutes. Rated R.

◪ "Romance amid revolution" is the theme of this erudite picture about the "erotic" misadventures of a young Czech surgeon swept up in the '68 Russian invasion of Prague; while the light-headed like the "hottie" cast's "compelling" work, cynics sneer this "yawner" "leaves a lot to be desired" and suggest the title be cut to just plain "*Unbearable.*"

Unforgiven ✉ 26 | 26 | 24 | 25

1992. Directed by Clint Eastwood. With Clint Eastwood, Gene Hackman, Morgan Freeman. 131 minutes. Rated R.

■ "Clint directs, Clint scores, Clint wins" a Best Picture statuette with this "grim" "anti-Western" that manages to "revise every convention and cliché of the genre" with a "superb script" and cast of "unforgivable", "unforgettable" characters (especially the Oscar-winning Hackman); indeed, it's so "powerful" and "dark", you'll find "no white hats here."

Unmarried Woman, An ∅ 20 | 25 | 21 | 19

1978. Directed by Paul Mazursky. With Jill Clayburgh, Alan Bates, Michael Murphy. 130 minutes. Rated R.

■ This "very-much-of-its-time" portrait of a "New Yorkey" divorcée "in transition" offers a "thoughtful", "emotional" examination of a '70s "woman's lib"–style "romance"; the picture broke "new ground" when originally released, thanks to the "excellent" Clayburgh as the recently "single" gal, though postfeminists posit it may "seem dated now."

Unsinkable Molly Brown, The ∅ 21 | 20 | 20 | 21

1964. Directed by Charles Walters. With Debbie Reynolds, Harve Presnell, Ed Begley. 128 minutes. Not Rated.

■ "Think of it as the last big" MGM musical and "you'll be in for a good evening's entertainment" with this "rollicking" bio of a turn-of-the-century "bawdy broad who wants it all and gets it"; warblers "enjoy singing along" with all the "great numbers" and adore the "rip-roarin'" Reynolds in the title role, who drowns all doubts about how "she got the name 'unsinkable.'"

Untouchables, The 22 | 22 | 22 | 22

1987. Directed by Brian De Palma. With Kevin Costner, Sean Connery, Robert De Niro. 119 minutes. Rated R.

■ "Sassy" '30s crime drama recounting the epic "good-vs.-evil" struggle between Eliot Ness and Al Capone, as interpreted by Costner and De Niro (wearing "amazing Armani suits" that nearly upstage them); while this "period piece" has "exciting action" and "style to spare", the most "compelling" work comes from the Oscar-winning Connery as a streetwise copper.

Urban Cowboy 18 | 17 | 16 | 17

1980. Directed by James Bridges. With John Travolta, Debra Winger, Scott Glenn. 132 minutes. Rated PG.

■ Travolta "in tight jeans" plays opposite Winger at her most "adorable" in this "highly watchable" honky-tonk romance about "beer-swigging", "mechanical bull–riding" men and the women who love them; although Debra nearly "steals the show", she's bested by a Houston setting so appealing that it inspired a vogue for all things Texan at the time.

USUAL SUSPECTS, THE ✉ 27 | 28 | 28 | 25

1995. Directed by Bryan Singer. With Gabriel Byrne, Kevin Spacey, Benicio Del Toro. 106 minutes. Rated R.

■ "Don't blink" or you'll risk missing one of the many "imaginative" twists in this "tricky-as-hell" "instant classic" that may be one of the finest "whodunit" "thrill rides" "ever made"; hard-core types advise "watching it at least twice" to absorb the "brilliant" story, admire the "flawless" Spacey and figure out what the heck "Benicio's saying"; as for that "unpredictable finale", you'll "never see it coming."

Verdict, The 23 | 25 | 23 | 20

1982. Directed by Sidney Lumet. With Paul Newman, Charlotte Rampling, Jack Warden. 129 minutes. Rated R.

■ A "David-vs.-Goliath" legal struggle is the underpinning of this "underrated" courtroom drama about a "burned-out lawyer trying one last case to keep from going under"; Newman's "intense", "tour-de-force" turn is one of his "greatest" roles (leaving many "stunned" that the Oscar eluded him), while the "mesmerizing" Rampling "excels" as the love interest.

VERTIGO 27 | 26 | 27 | 26

1958. Directed by Alfred Hitchcock. With James Stewart, Kim Novak, Tom Helmore. 128 minutes. Rated PG.

■ "Don't look down": this "dizzyingly complex" thriller offers lots of "twists and turns" as it details the "haunting" tale of an "obsessive" man who "tries to mold a woman into a vision of his lost love"; many call it "Hitchcock's crowning achievement" thanks to a Bernard Herrmann score that's "like perfume" as well as "spellbinding" work from a "bewitching Novak" and "Stewart at his darkest"; as for that "fever dream" of a plot, "it's not supposed to make sense."

Victor/Victoria 23 | 24 | 23 | 23

1982. Directed by Blake Edwards. With Julie Andrews, James Garner, Robert Preston. 132 minutes. Rated PG.

■ "What a hoot!" holler fans who "never tire of watching" this "hilarious" musical "farce" about Parisian nightlife denizens in the '30s; "Andrews lights up the screen" as the titular double-crossed cross-dresser, while Leslie Ann Warren's fabulous floozie is deliciously "over-the-top"; in sum, this "fast-paced", "madcap" tale of "jazz-age gender bending" is "just plain fun."

WAGES OF FEAR ◑ F 27 | 26 | 27 | 24

1953. Directed by Henri-Georges Clouzot. With Yves Montand, Charles Vanel. 148 minutes. Not Rated.

■ "Fasten your seatbelts for a bumpy" ride via this "nerve-racking" "nail-biter" about "down-and-outers" racing a "nitroglycerine-loaded truck" across the mountains of South America; Clouzot's knack for "heart-stopping", "oh-my-God" suspense and "gripping" "social commentary" makes it one of the "best art-house" "action" flicks around.

Wag the Dog 19 | 22 | 22 | 19

1997. Directed by Barry Levinson. With Dustin Hoffman, Robert De Niro, Anne Heche. 97 minutes. Rated R.

■ Pundits praise this "biting" "black comedy" that "makes light (and dark) of media-oriented politics" via a "surreal" story about a "nonexistent war created by the government to divert attention" from a presidential scandal; though some wonder if it's a "documentary", others tout this "underrated" political satire for Hoffman and De Niro's "standout" turns.

Wait Until Dark ∅ 25 | 26 | 27 | 23

1967. Directed by Terence Young. With Audrey Hepburn, Alan Arkin, Richard Crenna. 107 minutes. Not Rated.

■ This "unforgettable" thriller posits a "simple, nerve-shattering premise": a "blind woman", all alone in her apartment, in a "game of cat-and-mouse" with a "brutal psychopath"; gird yourself for an "eerie Henry Mancini soundtrack" and a "twists-and-turns"–laden scenario with "one particularly electrifying moment" that's guaranteed to "have you out of your seat."

Wall Street ✉ 22 | 23 | 22 | 21

1987. Directed by Oliver Stone. With Michael Douglas, Charlie Sheen, Martin Sheen. 125 minutes. Rated R.

■ "Greed is good" in this "quintessential" "insider's view" of the "go-go '80s" as personified by "ruthless financier" Gordon Gecko, an "ever-so-cool" piece of "Wall Street slime", "brilliantly executed" by the Oscar-winning Douglas; the "world of high finance" in all its "moneymaking" excess is captured here "like in no other film."

War of the Worlds, The 23 | 16 | 24 | 23

1953. Directed by Byron Haskin. With Gene Barry, Ann Robinson, Les Tremayne. 85 minutes. Rated G.

◪ Although the "Orson Welles radio broadcast" is "more famous", this "faithful" filming of the H.G. Wells "sci-fi classic" still clearly telegraphs its "frightening premise" of Martians run amok on Planet Earth; ok, it may be a bit "overstated" and "unintentionally funny today", but boob-tubers tune in "every time it's on television."

Way We Were, The 24 | 25 | 25 | 23

1973. Directed by Sydney Pollack. With Barbra Streisand, Robert Redford, Bradford Dillman. 118 minutes. Rated PG.

■ "Still a tearjerker after all these years", this "improbable romance" pits a "brainy" "Jewish girl" opposite a "golden Wasp boy" and "tugs every heartstring available" in its "realistic" depiction of their "ill-fated" affair; Streisand and Redford "at their peak" are "beyond delicious" together, though the most indelible "memories" involve the "famous final scene" at the "Plaza Hotel" with that "sad", Oscar-winning song playing in the background.

Wedding Banquet, The F ∅ 22 | 21 | 25 | 21

1993. Directed by Ang Lee. With Winston Chao, May Chin, Mitchell Lichtenstein. 106 minutes. Rated R.

■ "Family dynamics" get a "touching" twist in this "gently told" Taiwanese tale about a "marriage of convenience" between a "gay man" hoping to make his "parents happy" and his green card–seeking bride; this "funny charade" comes to a climax at the titular feast, where "unconditional love" comes "out of the closet" in a "warmhearted" if "bittersweet finale."

Welcome to the Dollhouse 22 | 21 | 21 | 19

1995. Directed by Todd Solondz. With Heather Matarazzo, Matthew Faber, Eric Mabius. 88 minutes. Rated R.

■ A "dead-on look at the horrors" of junior high, this "scathing" study of a "dorky adolescent" "hits close to home" thanks to an "eerily real" performance by Matarazzo as the "picked-on" protagonist; both "cruelly funny" and "disturbingly accurate", it makes some oldsters "worry about young people today."

WEST SIDE STORY ✉ 27 | 24 | 27 | 27

1961. Directed by Jerome Robbins, Robert Wise. With Natalie Wood, Richard Beymer, Rita Moreno, George Chakiris. 151 minutes. Not Rated.

■ Starting with that "opening bird's-eye view of Manhattan", this "remarkable musical" that transposes "*Romeo and Juliet*" to "urban" turf is "sheer perfection" thanks to "fiery acting", Robbins' "superb" streetwise choreography and the "dynamic" Leonard Bernstein/Stephen Sondheim score; sure, Beymer might be "miscast" and it's "too bad they wouldn't let Natalie sing", but otherwise this Oscar magnet – 10 statuettes including Best Picture – is "forever fabulous."

Westworld Ⓘ 19 | 16 | 21 | 20

1973. Directed by Michael Crichton. With Yul Brynner, Richard Benjamin, James Brolin. 88 minutes. Rated PG.

◪ You can "see where *Jurassic Park* came from" in this sci-fi thriller whose "irresistible premise" involves a futuristic resort where vacationers live out their Wild West fantasies with robot stand-ins; though sharp-shooters say Brynner is "perfect" as an "android gunslinger" gone haywire, critics ponder the idea of a "wooden actor playing an automaton."

What About Bob? 18 | 19 | 18 | 17

1991. Directed by Frank Oz. With Bill Murray, Richard Dreyfuss, Julie Hagerty. 99 minutes. Rated PG.

◪ Proving that "life is indeed baby steps", this "dark" comedy about a "shrink driven nuts" by a "psycho patient" pairs the "screwball" Murray with the "hilarious" Dreyfuss; though the picture might be "as irritating as it is funny", your "sides will hurt" from laughter all the same.

Whatever Happened to Baby Jane? ◑ 22 | 25 | 23 | 21

1962. Directed by Robert Aldrich. With Bette Davis, Joan Crawford, Victor Buono. 134 minutes. Not Rated.

■ "Campy and creepy", this "classic" exercise in Grand Guignol is the last hurrah of Hollywood's "two queen bees" in a "frightening" story of the "hate-hate relationship" between a pair of movie-star sisters; expect an "audacious" Crawford facing off against an "over-the-top" Davis, whose "grotesque" appearance is "too scary to think about" for too long; most memorable scene: Joan's "rat à-la-carte" din-din.

What's Eating Gilbert Grape 22 | 25 | 22 | 21

1993. Directed by Lasse Hallström. With Johnny Depp, Juliette Lewis, Leonardo DiCaprio. 118 minutes. Rated PG-13.

■ An "original" study of an ultra-"dysfunctional" family, this "weirdly winning" dramedy features a "quietly intense"

Depp opposite a "brilliant" DiCaprio "before he became a celebrity teen idol"; its "loving look at two fringe groups – the obese and the mentally challenged" – turns this "quirky" "coming-of-age" tale into "surprisingly good" moviemaking.

What's Love Got to Do with It 22 | 26 | 22 | 21

1993. Directed by Brian Gibson. With Angela Bassett, Laurence Fishburne. 118 minutes. Rated R.

■ That Tina Turner "never did anything nice and easy" is plain to see in this "perfect" biopic depicting how a "gifted" gal from Nuttbush, Tennessee, "got the strength to move on" from an abusive marriage to super-duper stardom; in a picture that's "all about the acting", both Bassett and Fishburne are "outstanding", but be warned that it can be "painful to watch."

What's Up, Doc? ∅ 21 | 20 | 21 | 20

1972. Directed by Peter Bogdanovich. With Barbra Streisand, Ryan O'Neal, Madeline Kahn. 94 minutes. Rated G.

■ "Streisand's like butter" in this "zany" "modern screwball comedy" "reminiscent of *Bringing Up Baby*" wherein some "terrific Ryan-Babs chemistry" is brought to bear on a nutty storyline involving "igneous rocks", identical plaid suitcases and a "fantastic comic car chase through San Francisco"; P.S. "Kahn's a scream" in her film debut.

When Harry Met Sally . . . 26 | 25 | 25 | 24

1989. Directed by Rob Reiner. With Billy Crystal, Meg Ryan, Carrie Fisher, Bruno Kirby. 96 minutes. Rated R.

■ "Can a man and a woman be just friends?"; this romantic comedy – the "king of all date movies" – attempts to answer that question as it details a "terrific take on relationships" that "rings true for many"; written by Nora Ephron as an "ode to Manhattan", it stars an "adorable", "pre–pixie cut" Ryan opposite a "perfect" Crystal, both "forever remembered" for the "infamous orgasm scene" in Katz's Deli that inspired one of the best lines in moviedom: "I'll have what *she's* having."

While You Were Sleeping 18 | 19 | 20 | 18

1995. Directed by Jon Turteltaub. With Sandra Bullock, Bill Pullman, Peter Gallagher. 103 minutes. Rated PG.

◪ "Token-booth worker" Bullock "falls in love with two brothers" in this "tender" romantic comedy, an "engaging", "Cinderella"-like "fairy tale" trading on "mistaken identity"; sure, it's "feel-good fluff", but the "unique storyline", "sweet" performances and "great chemistry" between the principals add up to an "all-around cute movie."

White Christmas 25 | 21 | 22 | 24

1954. Directed by Michael Curtiz. With Bing Crosby, Danny Kaye, Rosemary Clooney. 120 minutes. Not Rated.

■ "It wouldn't be Christmas" without a peek at this "sentimental" favorite, a virtual holiday "requirement" with "all the trimmings": "wonderful dance numbers", "essential" Irving Berlin tunes and "Der Bingle" crooning "kringle jingles"; in short, this "classic" is so "charming", it's almost "un-American not to love it"; P.S. sticklers note that Bing originally "made the title song famous in *Holiday Inn*."

White Heat ◑ ∅ 25 | 28 | 24 | 23

1949. Directed by Raoul Walsh. With James Cagney, Virginia Mayo, Edmond O'Brien. 114 minutes. Not Rated.

■ One part "descent into madness", one part "valentine to mom", this schizophrenic, noirish thriller represents the "classic gangster film refined to the nth degree"; as a "homicidal nut job" "mama's boy", Cagney turns in one of his "greatest performances", though the flick's most remembered for the "best last line in movie history": 'made it, ma! top of the world!'

Who Framed Roger Rabbit 24 | 22 | 23 | 27

1988. Directed by Robert Zemeckis. With Bob Hoskins, Christopher Lloyd. 103 minutes. Rated PG.

■ This "one-of-a-kind" "treat" featuring a "glorious mix of live action and animation" boasts an all-star cartoon cast, with appearances by every 'toon from Mickey and Minnie to Bugs and Woody (though the "seductive" Jessica Rabbit runs away with the picture); set in the Hollywood of yore, the "classic" noir plot has Hoskins investigating a murder case, with "wonderfully entertaining" results.

Who's Afraid of Virginia Woolf? ✉ ◑ 25 | 27 | 25 | 23

1966. Directed by Mike Nichols. With Elizabeth Taylor, Richard Burton, George Segal, Sandy Dennis. 134 minutes. Not Rated.

■ Maybe "Liz made up to look frumpy is a laugh", but otherwise this "scalding adaptation" of Edward Albee's "masterpiece" about an "unraveling marriage" is pretty serious stuff, "brilliantly acted" and "brutally honest"; it's "funny and mean and sad" all at once – "never has a play been converted into a movie" with such "power."

WILD BUNCH, THE 27 | 26 | 25 | 27

1969. Directed by Sam Peckinpah. With William Holden, Ernest Borgnine, Robert Ryan. 134 minutes. Rated R.

■ Not for the faint of heart, this "blood-and-guts" Peckinpah "epic" is a "Western to end all Westerns" that "transcends the genre" with an "in-your-face style" that turns "violence into poetry"; starring Holden as the leader of a band of "honorable outlaws" on the run, it depicts a "changing world" at the "end of an era" in "unsentimental" terms and manages to be both "noble and perverse at the same time."

Wild Strawberries ◑ F 26 | 26 | 24 | 25

1959. Directed by Ingmar Bergman. With Victor Sjöström, Bibi Andersson, Ingrid Thulin. 91 minutes. Not Rated.

■ "Essential Bergman" that's not just for "art movie" mavens, this "elegiac" "road film about life, death and redemption" "continues to hold up well"; a "bittersweet" story of an "elderly doctor who learns how to love at the last minute of his life", it's ultimately "cathartic and hopeful", even if it occasionally displays the director's signature "depressive" streak.

Willow 20 | 18 | 20 | 22

1988. Directed by Ron Howard. With Val Kilmer, Joanne Whalley, Warwick Davis. 130 minutes. Rated PG.

◪ "If you like *Princess Bride*", you'll like this "intelligent", "wonderfully escapist" "fantasy" featuring "appealing" characters in a sword-and-sorcery story that "seems familiar" to those who dub it a "*Lord of the Rings*" clone; "Kilmer's gorgeous" and there's plenty of "excitement", but some weep that it's a "formulaic" "disappointment."

Willy Wonka and the Chocolate Factory 26 | 22 | 26 | 26

1971. Directed by Mel Stuart. With Gene Wilder, Jack Albertson, Peter Ostrum. 100 minutes. Rated G.

■ Chocoholics cheer this "delicious family classic" adeptly adapted from the "brilliant Roald Dahl book" about an "underdog" kid who gets a "once-in-a-lifetime" chance to tour a "curious candy factory"; it's such a "blast to watch" (thanks to "psychedelic" sets, "imaginative" vignettes and "great songs") that it's almost become a "rite of passage" for the stroller set.

Wind and the Lion, The ∅ 24 | 25 | 24 | 24

1975. Directed by John Milius. With Sean Connery, Candice Bergen, Brian Keith. 119 minutes. Rated PG.

■ This "old-fashioned, character-driven adventure" about an Arab chieftain's abduction of an American widow is loosely "based on a real incident during Teddy Roosevelt's presidency"; despite the "wonderful" "desert romance" that blooms between the "charismatic" Connery and "watchable" Bergen, there's "still enough action for the guys" in this "obscure history lesson."

Wings of Desire ◑ Ⅱ F ∅ 24 | 24 | 22 | 25

1988. Directed by Wim Wenders. With Bruno Ganz, Solveig Dommartin. 127 minutes. Rated PG-13.

■ A "charming meditation" about the "angels who watch over us", "longing to be human", this "haunting" German film "celebrates the human condition"; "sumptuous", "dreamy cinematography" and an "amazing" cast elevate it to "pure poetry" – but don't "judge it by its self-conscious remake", Hollywood's "unfortunate" *City of Angels.*

Witness ✉ 23 | 24 | 23 | 22

1985. Directed by Peter Weir. With Harrison Ford, Kelly McGillis, Lukas Haas. 112 minutes. Rated R.

■ "One of Weir's finest", this "quiet" film offers a "sensitive portrayal" of a "small Amish community" that "collides with the violent outside world" in the aftermath of a murder; the actors have "perfect pitch" (particularly the "workmanlike" Ford, who "sizzles" against the "luminous McGillis"), and even if the story's somewhat "improbable", its overall "excellence sneaks up on you."

WITNESS FOR THE PROSECUTION ◑ 27 | 28 | 28 | 25

1957. Directed by Billy Wilder. With Tyrone Power, Marlene Dietrich, Charles Laughton. 116 minutes. Not Rated.

■ Perhaps the "best murder mystery ever", this "superb Agatha Christie puzzler" is one of "Wilder's wiliest", featuring "two legends" – an "incredible" Laughton and an "outstanding" Dietrich – complemented by a courtroom-full of "compelling characterizations"; the dialogue "crackles" and the "plot twists and double twists" right up to the "still shocking ending."

WIZARD OF OZ, THE 28 | 26 | 28 | 29

1939. Directed by Victor Fleming. With Judy Garland, Ray Bolger, Jack Haley, Bert Lahr. 101 minutes. Rated G.

■ A "star is born" – the "iconic" "Judy, Judy, Judy" – in this "timeless", "transporting" musical about a Kansas girl "off to see the Wizard" that's been "adored for decades" thanks to its "tremendous" cast, "glorious", "rainbow"-hued score and "inspired" moments involving a pair of "ruby slippers", a pack of "scary" "flying monkeys" and that "magical", "hello-Technicolor" transition; in Toto, this "landmark in family entertainment" is the ultimate proof that "there's no place like home."

Wolf Man, The ◑Ⓘ 20 | 19 | 22 | 19

1941. Directed by George Waggner. With Lon Chaney Jr., Claude Rains, Ralph Bellamy. 70 minutes. Not Rated.

◪ This "classic" "Universal monster" flicker set the "standard for fright" in its day with a hair-raising mix of ominous gypsies, howling werewolves and foreboding full moons; a "superb" Chaney stars as the fuzzy-faced lead – "what a disguise!" – though a few howl about his "hammy" acting chops and "special effects that look damn silly" now.

WOMAN OF THE YEAR ✉◑ 27 | 28 | 26 | 26

1942. Directed by George Stevens. With Katharine Hepburn, Spencer Tracy. 114 minutes. Not Rated.

■ The "war between the sexes was never more fun" than in this first matchup of legendary duo Hepburn and Tracy in what some call the "best" of their eight films together; its Oscar-winning script pits the "right-on" Kate as a hard-driving, "ahead-of-her-time" foreign correspondent against Spence's laid-back sportswriter, but the hands-down winner in this battle of wills is clearly the audience; best moment: the "breakfast scene."

Women on the Verge of a Nervous Breakdown 🄵 24 | 24 | 23 | 22

1988. Directed by Pedro Almodóvar. With Carmen Maura, Antonio Banderas. 90 minutes. Rated R.

■ Forget the "depressing" title: this "campy", "door-slamming farce" "put director Almodóvar on the map" and is one of the "funniest foreign films" ever made; a "wacky" story of "neurotic characters with different agendas", it introduced "eye-candy" "Banderas to the Western world" and also offered "new ideas on how to make gazpacho."

Wonder Boys 21 | 24 | 21 | 20

2000. Directed by Curtis Hanson. With Michael Douglas, Tobey Maguire, Frances McDormand. 111 minutes. Rated R.

◪ Douglas shines in this "intelligent" if "overlooked" dramedy as a "humpy-shlumpy" college professor stultified by writer's block compounded by a "midlife crisis"; a "funny, smart and caring" piece of moviemaking, it supplies "many different interwoven storylines" – though calculators say its "parts prove greater than the sum of the whole."

Woodstock 24 | – | 21 | 23

1970. Directed by Michael Wadleigh. Documentary. With Jimi Hendrix, The Who. 184 minutes. Rated R.

◪ "Drop out, turn on and tune in" to this "seminal pop-culture event", a "groundbreaking" rockumentary about the fabled "peace-and-love" concert that's a "near-perfect snapshot" of the era, "minus the bad acid"; though ticked-off "tie-dyed" "flower children" sniff the "split-screen stuff gets old" and find "too much mud and not enough Hendrix", peaceniks maintain that this "marathon" movie provides "evidence that the summer of love was no pipe dream."

Working Girl 20 | 20 | 21 | 19

1988. Directed by Mike Nichols. With Harrison Ford, Sigourney Weaver, Melanie Griffith. 109 minutes. Rated R.

■ "Workplace revenge" was never funnier than in this "Cinderella-by-way-of-Wall-Street" "chick flick" that "empowers" "every woman who's had to put up with a difficult boss"; Griffith's at her "dumb girl/smart girl best", Weaver's "delightfully loathsome" and Ford's "adorable" "not playing an action hero for a change"; favorite line: "I've got a head for business and a bod for sin."

World According to Garp, The 21 | 23 | 22 | 19

1982. Directed by George Roy Hill. With Robin Williams, Mary Beth Hurt, Glenn Close. 131 minutes. Rated R.

■ An "unforgettable", "modern-day fairy tale" full of "bizarre characters", this adept adaptation of John Irving's best-seller relates the "weird life" of T.S. Garp, beginning with his conception "when his mother sleeps with a man on his death bed"; though "unusual" is putting it mildly, this "unforgettable" tale is ultimately "affecting" – and worth seeing for Close's (Oscar-nominated) screen debut alone.

World Is Not Enough, The 19 | 19 | 18 | 21

1999. Directed by Michael Apted. With Pierce Brosnan, Denise Richards. 128 minutes. Rated PG-13.

◪ Though admittedly "pure escapism", 007's 19th trip to the big screen divides voters: loyalists like its "never-a-dull-moment" pace and vow that Pierce is "as good as Sean", but foes growl that "gadgets have replaced characterization and plot" and snicker at the "ludicrous" Richards playing a "short-shorts–wearing nuclear physicist."

Wuthering Heights ◑ 27 | 27 | 27 | 24

1939. Directed by William Wyler. With Laurence Olivier, Merle Oberon, David Niven. 103 minutes. Not Rated.

■ This "dark", "despairing" "gothic romance" is a "charter" member of the "pantheon" of "silver screen" weepies and the "ultimate" adaptation of the Brontë tale; Olivier's "soulful brooding" as a spurned, lower-caste lover is so "brilliantly intense" that it's inspired generations of maidens to "waste away from heartbreak on the moors" ever after.

X-Men Ⓘ 19 | 18 | 18 | 23

2000. Directed by Bryan Singer. With Patrick Stewart, Hugh Jackman, Ian McKellen. 104 minutes. Rated PG-13.

■ Even those "who've never read the comic book" chime in with their "ringing endorsement" of this "true-to-the-source" adaptation of the "Marvel" sci-fi series; most memorable for Jackman's "starmaking turn", it's such an obvious "setup for a franchise" that many "popcorn" eaters are hungrily "awaiting the sequels."

Yankee Doodle Dandy ✉◑∅ 25 | 25 | 23 | 25

1942. Directed by Michael Curtiz. With James Cagney, Joan Leslie, Walter Huston. 126 minutes. Not Rated.

■ "Flag-waving", "red-white-and-blue" musical bio of the "all-American" "showman George M. Cohan", starring Cagney in full "hoofer" bloom; the story's "whitewashed", but after a few bars of its "patriotic tunes" you'll understand why the "4th of July wouldn't be the same without it."

Year of Living Dangerously, The 24 | 25 | 25 | 24

1983. Directed by Peter Weir. With Mel Gibson, Sigourney Weaver, Linda Hunt. 117 minutes. Rated PG.

■ An outbreak of "civil war" during the "Sukarno regime" in "'60s Indonesia comes alive" in this "captivating" "political" drama following a journalist who's covering the conflict; though the "compelling" Gibson and Weaver cast "steamy" "sparks", Hunt took home an Oscar for her "tour-de-force", "gender-bending role" in this "tense" thriller.

Yellow Submarine 22 | – | 18 | 23

1968. Directed by George Dunning. Animated. 90 minutes. Rated G.

■ "Contagiously fun", this "lighthearted" "hallucination" of a "cartoon" supplies "eye-popping" "psychedelic" imagery aplenty in recounting a story about the Fab Four's battle to save Pepperland from the Blue Meanies; though the "actual Beatles don't provide" the speaking parts, their performance on the "foot-tapping" soundtrack is "more than enough" – and the music "won't drive parents crazy."

Yentl ∅ 18 | 19 | 19 | 20

1983. Directed by Barbra Streisand. With Barbra Streisand, Mandy Patinkin, Amy Irving. 132 minutes. Rated PG.

◪ "La Streisand" does it all – "acts, sings and directs" – in this "underrated", "impeccably made" musical about a turn-of-the-century Jewish girl masquerading as a "boy in order to study the Talmud"; though foes call it Babs at her "self-indulgent, overproduced worst", fans counter her "incredible talent" and "amazing" "attention to detail" make this "emotionally stirring" picture "deserving of more credit."

You Can Count on Me 23 | 26 | 22 | 20

2000. Directed by Kenneth Lonergan. With Laura Linney, Mark Ruffalo, Matthew Broderick. 109 minutes. Rated R.

■ Freshman director Lonergan "doesn't take a false step" in this "compelling", "character-driven" "indie film" about the "family bonds" between a "messed-up brother and sister"; you can count on lots of "terrific acting" (with a "breakout performance from Linney") and a "lifelike lack of final resolution" that makes this a "sleeper with a heart."

YOUNG FRANKENSTEIN ◑ 27 | 26 | 25 | 25

1974. Directed by Mel Brooks. With Gene Wilder, Peter Boyle, Marty Feldman, Madeline Kahn. 108 minutes. Rated PG.

■ "Frankenstein Sr. would be proud" of this "insanely hysterical" "spoof of the Mary Shelley" horror classic that's Mel Brooks' "high-water mark" ("who else would have the monster" perform 'Puttin' on the Ritz?'); Wilder is "pure genius" in the title role backed up by an "endlessly amusing" cast spouting some of the "most quoted" dialogue in movie history; best line: a toss-up between "walk this way", "what big knockers" and "hump? what hump?"

You Only Live Twice 22 | 21 | 20 | 22

1967. Directed by Lewis Gilbert. With Sean Connery, Mie Hama, Donald Pleasence. 117 minutes. Rated PG.

◪ "Despite the absurdity of a six-foot-plus Scotsman as a spy in Japan", diehards declare this espionage flicker one of the "better Connery Bonds", given its amusing "'60s Tokyo" settings and that "great Nancy Sinatra" theme song; ok, it might be "cheesy" and "doesn't age well", but camp followers claim that's what makes it "all the more fun now."

Z ✉ F 26 | 25 | 26 | 24

1969. Directed by Costa-Gavras. With Yves Montand, Irene Papas, Jean-Louis Trintignant. 127 minutes. Rated PG.

■ Unfortunately "all too true", this fact-based story of the assassination of a left-leaning scientist in a right-wing country is a crackerjack "political thriller" that's "deeply affecting" and "not easy to watch"; Montand is "nothing less than superb" in the title role, while Costa-Gavras makes this "documentary-like" "exposé" of "corruption" "captivating from the first scene."

Zelig ◑ 20 | 20 | 21 | 21

1983. Directed by Woody Allen. With Woody Allen, Mia Farrow. 79 minutes. Rated PG.

◪ "Forrest Gump's ancestor" is the much "more charming (and neurotic) Zelig", a human chameleon who somehow plays a prominent role in 20th-century world events with "dryly comedic" results; it's a "technically complex" outing for Allen that "warps history" by "digitally" inserting our hero into vintage "newsreel footage"; cynics say this "curiosity piece" has only "one clever idea" and "should have been funnier."

Zorba the Greek ◑∅ 25 | 27 | 25 | 23

1964. Directed by Michael Cacoyannis. With Anthony Quinn, Alan Bates, Irene Papas, Lila Kedrova. 142 minutes. Not Rated.

■ There's ex-zorba-tant praise for this "still-fresh" drama about an Englishman visiting Crete on an existential quest, only to fall under the spell of a "person full of passion"; Quinn's "breakout" turn, plus some "memorable" "theme music" and "dancing", keep this "feel-good" "affirmation of life" so "exciting and entertaining" that repeaters "see it every year."

Zulu Ⓘ 24 | 24 | 25 | 24

1964. Directed by Cy Endfield. With Stanley Baker, Jack Hawkins, Michael Caine. 138 minutes. Not Rated.

■ The "true story of valor in the face of incredible odds", this "epic treatment of a 19th-century British military disaster" is played out against the "broad canvas of Africa" and features an "unknown Caine" in his "first big film"; "visually and viscerally stunning", it's "historically accurate without sacrificing dramatic appeal", and the "tension's unrelenting."

Indexes

GENRES
DECADES
SPECIAL FEATURES

Indexes list the best of many within each category.

GENRES

Action/Adventure

Abyss, The
Adventures of Robin Hood
Air Force One
Apocalypse Now
Around the World in 80 Days
Backdraft
Back to the Future
Batman
Beau Geste
Ben-Hur
Benji
Beverly Hills Cop
Black Stallion
Blade Runner
Braveheart
Bullitt
Butch Cassidy
Captain Blood
Captains Courageous
Cast Away
City Slickers
Clear and Present Danger
Close Encounters
Contact
Crimson Tide
Crouching Tiger
Dances with Wolves
Deliverance
Diamonds Are Forever
Die Hard
Dirty Dozen
Diva
Dr. No
Easy Rider
Empire Strikes Back
Enemy of the State
Enter the Dragon
Evil Dead
Face/Off
Fantastic Voyage
Fifth Element
First Blood: Rambo
Fistful of Dollars
Flight of the Phoenix
Fly Away Home
48 HRS.
For Whom the Bell Tolls
For Your Eyes Only
French Connection
From Russia With Love
Fugitive, The
Gladiator
Gods Must Be Crazy
GoldenEye
Goldfinger
Goonies
Great Escape
Great Race
Gunga Din
Guns of Navarone
Hatari!
Heat
Hunt for Red October
Independence Day
Indiana Jones/Last Crusade
Indiana Jones/Temple of Doom
In the Line of Fire
Journey to the Center
Jumanji
Jurassic Park
King Kong
King Solomon's Mines
Lawrence of Arabia
Legend
Lethal Weapon
Live and Let Die
Lord of the Rings/Fellowship
Mad Max
Magnificent Seven
Man Who Would Be King
Man with the Golden Gun
Mark of Zorro
Mask of Zorro
Matrix, The
Men in Black
Mission, The
Mummy, The
Mutiny on the Bounty (1935)
Mutiny on the Bounty (1962)
Never Say Never Again
O Brother, Where Art Thou?

Americana

Animated

Biography

Children/Family

Comedy

(See also Dramedy, p. 245, Screwball Comedy, p. 250)

No Time for Sergeants
Notting Hill
Nutty Professor
O Brother, Where Art Thou?
Odd Couple
101 Dalmatians (1961)
101 Dalmatians (1996)
Operation Petticoat
Out-of-Towners, The
Paper Moon
Parent Trap
Pee-wee's Big Adventure
Peggy Sue Got Married
Pillow Talk
Pink Panther
Play It Again, Sam
Postcards from the Edge
Pretty in Pink
Pretty Woman
Princess Bride
Princess Diaries
Producers, The
Purple Rose of Cairo
Radio Days
Risky Business
Rocky Horror Picture Show
Roger & Me
Roman Holiday
Roxanne
Rush Hour
Russians Are Coming . . .
Ruthless People
Santa Clause
Sevon Brides/Seven Brothers
Seven Year Itch
Shirley Valentine
Shot in the Dark
Silver Streak
Singin' in the Rain
Sister Act
Sixteen Candles
Slap Shot
Sleeper
Sleepless in Seattle
Some Like It Hot
South Park
Spaceballs
Splash
Stalag 17
Sting, The
Strictly Ballroom
Stripes
Sunshine Boys
Sweet Charity
Swept Away
Swingers
Take the Money and Run
There's Something About Mary
This is Spinal Tap
Thoroughly Modern Millie
Tie Me Up! Tie Me Down!
Time Bandits
Tom Jones
Tootsie
Topkapi
Topper
Trading Places
Two for the Road
Unmarried Woman
Victor/Victoria
Wedding Banquet
What About Bob?
When Harry Met Sally . . .
While You Were Sleeping
Woman of the Year
Working Girl
Young Frankenstein
Zelig

Crime

(See also Film Noir, p. 246)

Anatomy of a Murder
Angels with Dirty Faces
Badlands
Basic Instinct
Big Lebowski
Bonnie and Clyde
Boyz N the Hood
Bullitt
Casino
Clockwork Orange
Death on the Nile
Dirty Harry
Dog Day Afternoon
Donnie Brasco
Fargo
Fletch
48 HRS.

Documentary

Drama

(See also Crime, p. 241, Dramedy, p. 245, Film Noir, p. 246)

Lone Star
Looking for Mr. Goodbar
Love Is a Many Splendored
Love Story
Madness of King George
Magnolia
Malcolm X
Man for All Seasons
Marty
Mask
McCabe & Mrs. Miller
Midnight Cowboy
Miracle on 34th Street
Miracle Worker
Mission, The
Mississippi Burning
Moulin Rouge (1952)
Mr. Holland's Opus
Mrs. Brown
Mr. Smith Goes to Washington
Mulholland Dr.
Mutiny on the Bounty (1935)
Mutiny on the Bounty (1962)
My Bodyguard
My Dinner with André
My Left Foot
My Life As a Dog
My Own Private Idaho
National Velvet
Natural, The
Never on Sunday
Nights of Cabiria
Norma Rae
Now, Voyager
One Flew Over Cuckoo's Nest
On Golden Pond
On the Waterfront
Ordinary People
Out of Africa
Outsiders, The
Paths of Glory
Pawnbroker, The
Philadelphia
Piano, The
Place in the Sun
Places in the Heart
Pollock
Pride of the Yankees
Primal Fear
Prince of Tides
Quiet Man
Quiz Show
Raging Bull
Rain Man
Rashomon
Rebel Without a Cause
Red Shoes
Red Violin
Remains of the Day
Remember the Titans
Requiem for a Dream
Right Stuff
River Runs Through It
Rocky
Romeo and Juliet
Room with a View
Rose, The
Run Lola Run
Sand Pebbles
Schindler's List
Secrets and Lies
Seven Days in May
Seventh Seal
Sex, Lies and Videotape
Shadow of the Vampire
Shawshank Redemption
Shine
Shipping News
Silkwood
Six Degrees of Separation
Sling Blade
Sophie's Choice
Splendor in the Grass
Stand and Deliver
Stand by Me
Star Is Born
Straight Story
Streetcar Named Desire
Sweet Hereafter
Talented Mr. Ripley
Taxi Driver
Ten Commandments
Thelma & Louise
They Shoot Horses, Don't They?
Three Faces of Eve
Time to Kill
To Have and Have Not
To Kill a Mockingbird

Topsy-Turvy
Tora! Tora! Tora!
To Sir, With Love
12 Angry Men
Unbearable Lightness of Being
Urban Cowboy
Verdict, The
Wall Street
What's Love Got to Do with It
Who's Afraid of Virginia Woolf?
Wild Strawberries
Witness
Witness for the Prosecution
Wuthering Heights
Year of Living Dangerously
Yentl
You Can Count on Me
Zorba the Greek

Dramedy

(Part Comedy, part Drama)
After Hours
All About My Mother
Almost Famous
American Beauty
American Graffiti
Apartment, The
As Good As It Gets
Barton Fink
Being There
Big Chill
Big Night
Brazil
Broadcast News
Butch Cassidy
Charade
Cool Hand Luke
Crimes and Misdemeanors
Diner
Do the Right Thing
Erin Brockovich
Fargo
Fight Club
Fisher King
Five Easy Pieces
Forrest Gump
Fried Green Tomatoes
Ghost World
Good Morning, Vietnam
Good Will Hunting
Gosford Park
Guess Who's Coming to Dinner
Hannah and Her Sisters
Happiness
Harold and Maude
Heathers
Heaven Can Wait
Jerry Maguire
King of Comedy
League of Their Own
Life Is Beautiful
Lolita
Man Who Wasn't There
Moonstruck
Murder on the Orient Express
My Girl
Nashville
Network
Parenthood
People vs. Larry Flynt
Player, The
Pleasantville
Prizzi's Honor
Reality Bites
Royal Tenenbaums
Rushmore
Same Time, Next Year
Scent of a Woman
Sense and Sensibility
Shakespeare in Love
Snatch
Steel Magnolias
Terms of Endearment
Three Musketeers
To Die For
Trainspotting
Truman Show
Wag the Dog
Welcome to the Dollhouse
What's Eating Gilbert Grape
Wonder Boys
World According to Garp

Epic

Alexander Nevsky
Around the World in 80 Days
Ben-Hur
Birth of a Nation

Bridge on the River Kwai
Cleopatra
Dances with Wolves
Doctor Zhivago
El Cid
Empire of the Sun
Evita
Exodus
Gandhi
Giant
Gladiator
Gone with the Wind
It's a Mad Mad Mad World
Last Emperor
Lawrence of Arabia
Legends of the Fall
Longest Day
Lord of the Rings/Fellowship
Man Who Would Be King
Mutiny on the Bounty (1962)
Once Upon a Time in America
Patriot, The
Ran
Reds
Sand Pebbles
Seven Samurai
Spartacus
Ten Commandments
Titanic
Tora! Tora! Tora!
Zulu

Fantasy

Back to the Future
Batman
Beauty and the Beast
Beetlejuice
Being John Malkovich
Brazil
Christmas Carol
Cinderella
Contact
Crouching Tiger
Dark Crystal
Edward Scissorhands
Eraserhead
Fantastic Voyage
Field of Dreams
Fisher King
Ghost
Ghost and Mrs. Muir
Ghostbusters
Gremlins
Harry Potter/Sorcerer's Stone
Harvey
Heaven Can Wait
Heavenly Creatures
Heavy Metal
Hunger, The
Indiana Jones/Last Crusade
Indiana Jones/Temple of Doom
It's a Wonderful Life
James and the Giant Peach
Jumanji
King Kong
Legend
Lord of the Rings/Fellowship
Lost Horizon
Mad Max
Man Who Fell to Earth
Mary Poppins
Miracle on 34th Street
Nightmare Before Christmas
Nutty Professor
Peggy Sue Got Married
Pete's Dragon
Pleasantville
Princess Bride
Purple Rose of Cairo
Raiders of the Lost Ark
7th Voyage of Sinbad
Splash
Stuart Little
Superman
Time Bandits
Topper
Truman Show
Willow
Willy Wonka
Wings of Desire
Wizard of Oz

Film Noir

Asphalt Jungle
Big Sleep
Blade Runner
Blood Simple
Body Heat

Horror

James Bond

Musical

Romance

(See also Chick Flick, p. 266)

Sci-Fi

Screwball Comedy

Silent

Thriller

Vertigo
Wages of Fear
Wait Until Dark
Westworld
Whatever Happened to . . .
Z

War

Alamo, The
Alexander Nevsky
All Quiet on the Western Front
Apocalypse Now
Beau Geste
Born on the Fourth of July
Braveheart
Bridge on the River Kwai
Caine Mutiny
Casablanca
Coming Home
Das Boot
Deer Hunter
Diary of Anne Frank
Dirty Dozen
El Cid
Empire of the Sun
Exodus
For Whom the Bell Tolls
Full Metal Jacket
Gallipoli
Glory
Good Morning, Vietnam
Good, the Bad and the Ugly
Grand Illusion
Gunga Din
Guns of Navarone
Henry V
Killing Fields
Last of the Mohicans
Longest Day
MASH
Mister Roberts
Paths of Glory
Patriot, The
Patton
Platoon
Potemkin
Ran
Sand Pebbles
Saving Private Ryan
Schindler's List
Stalag 17
Thin Red Line
Three Kings
Tora! Tora! Tora!
Twelve O'Clock High
Year of Living Dangerously

Western

Alamo, The
Blazing Saddles
Butch Cassidy
Cat Ballou
City Slickers
Dances with Wolves
Fistful of Dollars
Fort Apache
Good, the Bad and the Ugly
Gunfight at the O.K. Corral
High Noon
High Plains Drifter
Jeremiah Johnson
Legends of the Fall
Little Big Man
Magnificent Seven
Man Who Shot Liberty Valance
Maverick
McCabe & Mrs. Miller
Oklahoma!
Outlaw Josey Wales
Red River
Searchers, The
Shane
She Wore a Yellow Ribbon
Silverado
Stagecoach
Tombstone
True Grit
Unforgiven
Wild Bunch

DECADES

1910s/1920s

Birth of a Nation
Cabinet of Dr. Caligari
Cocoanuts, The
General, The
Metropolis
Potemkin

1930s

Adventures of Robin Hood
Alexander Nevsky
All Quiet on the Western Front
Angels with Dirty Faces
Animal Crackers
Babes in Toyland
Blue Angel
Bride of Frankenstein
Bringing Up Baby
Captain Blood
Captains Courageous
City Lights
Dark Victory
Day at the Races
Dracula
Duck Soup
42nd Street
Frankenstein
Gone with the Wind
Gunga Din
Horse Feathers
Invisible Man
It Happened One Night
King Kong
Lost Horizon
M
Modern Times
Mr. Smith Goes to Washington
Mutiny on the Bounty
My Man Godfrey
Night at the Opera
Snow White
Stagecoach
Tarzan the Ape Man
Thin Man
39 Steps
Top Hat
Topper
Triumph of the Will
Wizard of Oz
Wuthering Heights

1940s

Adam's Rib
All the King's Men
Arsenic and Old Lace
Bambi
Beauty and the Beast
Best Years of Our Lives
Bicycle Thief
Big Sleep
Bishop's Wife
Brief Encounter
Buck Privates
Casablanca
Children of Paradise
Citizen Kane
Double Indemnity
Dumbo
Easter Parade
Fantasia
Fort Apache
For Whom the Bell Tolls
Gaslight
Ghost and Mrs. Muir
Gilda
Grand Illusion
Grapes of Wrath
Great Dictator
His Girl Friday
Holiday Inn
It's a Wonderful Life
Jane Eyre
Key Largo
Killers, The
Kind Hearts and Coronets
Lady Eve
Lady from Shanghai
Laura
Lifeboat
Maltese Falcon
Mark of Zorro
Meet Me in St. Louis
Mildred Pierce
Miracle on 34th Street

1950s

1960s

1970s

Slap Shot
Sleeper
Sleuth
Spy Who Loved Me
Star Wars
Sting, The
Summer of '42
Sunshine Boys
Superman
Swept Away
Taxi Driver
That's Entertainment!
Three Musketeers
Time After Time
Tora! Tora! Tora!
Towering Inferno
Unmarried Woman
Way We Were
Westworld
What's Up, Doc?
Willy Wonka
Wind and the Lion
Woodstock
Young Frankenstein

1980s

Absence of Malice
Abyss, The
Accidental Tourist
Accused, The
After Hours
Agnes of God
Airplane!
Akira
Aliens
Altered States
Amadeus
American Tail
American Werewolf in London
Annie
Arthur
Atlantic City
Au Revoir Les Enfants
Babette's Feast
Baby Boom
Back to the Future
Batman
Beetlejuice
Beverly Hills Cop
Big
Big Chill
Blade Runner
Blood Simple
Blues Brothers
Blue Velvet
Body Heat
Born on the Fourth of July
Brazil
Breaker Morant
Breakfast Club
Broadcast News
Broadway Danny Rose
Bull Durham
Caddyshack
Chariots of Fire
Children of a Lesser God
Christmas Story
Clear and Present Danger
Cocoon
Color Purple
Coming to America
Crimes and Misdemeanors
Dangerous Liaisons
Dark Crystal
Das Boot
Dead Poets Society
Dead Ringers
Die Hard
Diner
Dirty Dancing
Diva
Do the Right Thing
Dressed to Kill
Driving Miss Daisy
Drugstore Cowboy
Eating Raoul
Educating Rita
Elephant Man
Empire of the Sun
Empire Strikes Back
E.T. The Extra-Terrestrial
Evil Dead
Fabulous Baker Boys
Fame
Fanny and Alexander
Fast Times at Ridgemont High
Fatal Attraction
Ferris Bueller's Day Off

1990s

Dances with Wolves
Dave
Dead Again
Dead Man Walking
Donnie Brasco
Dracula
Eat Drink Man Woman
Edward Scissorhands
Ed Wood
Election
Elizabeth
Emma
Enchanted April
End of the Affair
Enemy of the State
English Patient
Evita
Face/Off
Fantasia 2000
Farewell My Concubine
Fargo
Father of the Bride
Few Good Men, A
Fifth Element
Fight Club
Fisher King
Fly Away Home
Forrest Gump
Four Weddings and a Funeral
Fried Green Tomatoes
Fugitive, The
Full Monty
Ghost
Girl, Interrupted
Glengarry Glen Ross
Gods and Monsters
GoldenEye
Goodfellas
Good Will Hunting
Grand Canyon
Green Mile
Grifters, The
Groundhog Day
Grumpy Old Men
Hamlet
Happiness
Heat
Heavenly Creatures
Hilary and Jackie
Home Alone
Hoop Dreams
Howards End
Hunchback of Notre Dame
Hunt for Red October
Hurricane, The
Il Postino
Independence Day
Indochine
Insider, The
Interview with the Vampire
In the Line of Fire
In the Name of the Father
Iron Giant
James and the Giant Peach
Jerry Maguire
JFK
Jumanji
Jurassic Park
L.A. Confidential
La Femme Nikita
Last of the Mohicans
L.A. Story
Last Seduction
League of Their Own
Leaving Las Vegas
Legends of the Fall
Life Is Beautiful
Like Water for Chocolate
Lion King
Little Women
Lock, Stock and Two...
Lone Star
Madness of King George
Magnolia
Malcolm X
Mark of Zorro
Matrix, The
Maverick
Mediterraneo
Men in Black
Mighty Aphrodite
Miller's Crossing
Misery
Mr. Holland's Opus
Mrs. Brown
Mrs. Doubtfire
Mulan
Mummy, The

2000s

SPECIAL FEATURES

Adults Only

American History X
Bad Seed
Basic Instinct
Belle de Jour
Blue Velvet
Body Heat
Boogie Nights
Carnal Knowledge
Dead Ringers
Eating Raoul
Fight Club
Grifters, The
Happiness
Hunger, The
Last Seduction
Last Temptation of Christ
Leaving Las Vegas
Lolita
Looking for Mr. Goodbar
Midnight Cowboy
Requiem for a Dream
Reservoir Dogs
Seven
Sid & Nancy
Taxi Driver
Tie Me Up! Tie Me Down!

Box Office Champ

(Among the Top 3 grossing movies in first year of release)

Aladdin
American Graffiti
Animal Crackers
Animal House
Around the World in 80 Days
Back to the Future
Batman
Beauty and the Beast (1991)
Ben-Hur
Best Years of Our Lives
Beverly Hills Cop
Birth of a Nation
Blazing Saddles
Bonnie and Clyde
Butch Cassidy
Cast Away
Cat on a Hot Tin Roof
Cheaper By the Dozen
Close Encounters
Coming to America
Dances with Wolves
Dirty Dozen
Dirty Harry
Doctor Zhivago
Easy Rider
El Cid
Empire Strikes Back
E.T. The Extra-Terrestrial
Exodus
Exorcist, The
Fatal Attraction
Fiddler on the Roof
Forrest Gump
For Whom the Bell Tolls
French Connection
From Here to Eternity
Fugitive, The
Funny Girl
Ghost
Ghostbusters
Giant
Godfather
Goldfinger
Gone with the Wind
Graduate, The
Grease
Great Dictator
Guess Who's Coming to Dinner
Guns of Navarone
Harry Potter/Sorcerer's Stone
Home Alone
Independence Day
Indiana Jones/Last Crusade
Indiana Jones/Temple of Doom
It Happened One Night
It's a Mad Mad Mad World
Jaws
Jerk, The
Jurassic Park
King Kong
King Solomon's Mines
Kramer vs. Kramer

Camp Classic

Caper

Topkapi
White Heat

Chick Flick

(See also Romance, p. 248)

Affair to Remember
Amélie
Baby Boom
Breakfast at Tiffany's
Bridges of Madison County
Bridget Jones's Diary
Clueless
Dirty Dancing
Enchanted April
English Patient
Father of the Bride (1991)
Four Weddings and a Funeral
Fried Green Tomatoes
Ghost
Legally Blonde
Little Women
Love Is a Many Splendored
Love Story
My Best Friend's Wedding
Notting Hill
Now, Voyager
Officer and a Gentleman
Out of Africa
Pretty Woman
Roman Holiday
Sense and Sensibility
Shakespeare in Love
Sleepless in Seattle
Splendor in the Grass
Steel Magnolias
Terms of Endearment
Thelma & Louise
Unmarried Woman
Way We Were
When Harry Met Sally . . .
Working Girl

City Setting

LA Stories

Barton Fink
Beverly Hills Cop
Big Sleep
Boogie Nights
Boyz N the Hood
Chinatown
Clueless
D.O.A.
Ed Wood
Gods and Monsters
Grand Canyon
L.A. Confidential
L.A. Story
Mulholland Dr.
Player, The
Postcards from the Edge
Pretty Woman
Princess Diaries
Reservoir Dogs
Singin' in the Rain
Sunset Boulevard
Swingers

London Stories

Alfie
American Werewolf in London
Austin Powers
Bedazzled
Blowup
Bridget Jones's Diary
Elephant Man
End of the Affair
Fish Called Wanda
Gaslight
Lock, Stock and Two...
Man Who Knew Too Much
Mary Poppins
My Fair Lady
Notting Hill
101 Dalmatians (1996)
Patriot Games
Secrets and Lies
Snatch

New York Stories

Affair to Remember
After Hours
Age of Innocence
All About Eve
All That Jazz
Angels with Dirty Faces
Annie Hall
Apartment, The
Arthur
Bells Are Ringing
Big
Breakfast at Tiffany's

Comic Book Adaptation

Cross-Dressing

Adventures of Priscilla
All About My Mother
Birdcage, The
Boys Don't Cry
Celluloid Closet
Crying Game
Ed Wood
Farewell My Concubine
Hairspray
Kind Hearts and Coronets
La Cage aux Folles
Life of Brian
Monty Python & the Holy Grail
Mouse that Roared
Mrs. Doubtfire
Psycho
Rocky Horror Picture Show
Some Like It Hot
Tootsie
Victor/Victoria
World According to Garp
Yentl

Cult Film

Adventures of Priscilla
After Hours
All About Eve
Being John Malkovich
Big Lebowski
Blade Runner
Blue Velvet
Brazil
Casablanca
Children of Paradise
Clerks
Clockwork Orange
Crying Game
Dr. Strangelove
Eating Raoul
8½
Enter the Dragon
Eraserhead
Evil Dead
Fantasia
Ferris Bueller's Day Off
Fight Club
Gods Must Be Crazy
Grease
Harold and Maude
Heavy Metal
It's a Wonderful Life
Life of Brian
Little Shop of Horrors
Mad Max
Manchurian Candidate
Monty Python & the Holy Grail
Mulholland Dr.
My Dinner with André
Night of the Living Dead
Pee-wee's Big Adventure
Princess Bride
Psycho
Raising Arizona
Red Shoes
Road Warrior
Rocky Horror Picture Show
Sound of Music
Star Wars
Time Bandits
Welcome to the Dollhouse
Wizard of Oz

Date Movie

Amélie
Annie Hall
Big Chill
Bull Durham
Casablanca
Chocolat
Dirty Dancing
Fabulous Baker Boys
Four Weddings and a Funeral
Ghost
Jerry Maguire
Love Story
Man and a Woman
Mediterraneo
Moonstruck
Notting Hill
Officer and a Gentleman
Pretty Woman
Prince of Tides
Romancing the Stone
Roman Holiday
Romeo and Juliet
Saturday Night Fever
Shakespeare in Love

Food-Themed

Foreign Film

Australian

British

Guy Movie

(See also Sports, p. 283, War, p. 252)

Independent Film

(Other than documentaries)

Literary Adaptation

Movies About Movies

Occupation

Education

Patton (1970)
Platoon (1986)
Rain Man (1988)
Rebecca (1940)
Rocky (1976)
Schindler's List (1993)
Shakespeare in Love (1998)
Silence of the Lambs (1991)
Sound of Music (1965)
Sting, The (1973)
Terms of Endearment (1983)
Titanic (1997)
Tom Jones (1963)
Unforgiven (1992)
West Side Story (1961)

Best Actor

African Queen
  Humphrey Bogart
All the King's Men
  Broderick Crawford
Amadeus
  F. Murray Abraham
American Beauty
  Kevin Spacey
As Good As It Gets
  Jack Nicholson
Ben-Hur
  Charlton Heston
Best Years of Our Lives
  Fredric March
Bridge on the River Kwai
  Alec Guinness
Captains Courageous
  Spencer Tracy
Cat Ballou
  Lee Marvin
Charly
  Cliff Robertson
Coming Home
  Jon Voight
Elmer Gantry
  Burt Lancaster
Forrest Gump
  Tom Hanks
French Connection
  Gene Hackman
Gandhi
  Ben Kingsley
Gladiator
  Russell Crowe
Godfather
  Marlon Brando
Goodbye Girl
  Richard Dreyfuss
High Noon
  Gary Cooper
In the Heat of the Night
  Rod Steiger
It Happened One Night
  Clark Gable
King and I
  Yul Brynner
Kiss of the Spider Woman
  William Hurt
Kramer vs. Kramer
  Dustin Hoffman
Leaving Las Vegas
  Nicolas Cage
Life Is Beautiful
  Roberto Benigni
Lilies of the Field
  Sidney Poitier
Man for All Seasons
  Paul Scofield
Marty
  Ernest Borgnine
My Fair Lady
  Rex Harrison
My Left Foot
  Daniel Day-Lewis
Network
  Peter Finch
One Flew Over Cuckoo's Nest
  Jack Nicholson
On Golden Pond
  Henry Fonda
On the Waterfront
  Marlon Brando
Patton
  George C. Scott
Philadelphia
  Tom Hanks
Philadelphia Story
  James Stewart
Raging Bull
  Robert De Niro

Rain Man
Dustin Hoffman
Scent of a Woman
Al Pacino
Shine
Geoffrey Rush
Silence of the Lambs
Anthony Hopkins
Stalag 17
William Holden
To Kill a Mockingbird
Gregory Peck
Training Day
Denzel Washington
True Grit
John Wayne
Wall Street
Michael Douglas
Yankee Doodle Dandy
James Cagney

Best Actress

Accused, The
Jodie Foster
Alice Doesn't Live Here
Ellen Burstyn
Anastasia
Ingrid Bergman
Annie Hall
Diane Keaton
As Good As It Gets
Helen Hunt
Born Yesterday
Judy Holliday
Boys Don't Cry
Hilary Swank
Cabaret
Liza Minnelli
Children of a Lesser God
Marlee Matlin
Coal Miner's Daughter
Sissy Spacek
Coming Home
Jane Fonda
Dead Man Walking
Susan Sarandon
Driving Miss Daisy
Jessica Tandy
Erin Brockovich
Julia Roberts
Fargo
Frances McDormand
Funny Girl
Barbra Streisand
Gaslight
Ingrid Bergman
Gone with the Wind
Vivien Leigh
Guess Who's Coming to Dinner
Katharine Hepburn
Howards End
Emma Thompson
It Happened One Night
Claudette Colbert
Klute
Jane Fonda
Lion in Winter
Katharine Hepburn
Mary Poppins
Julie Andrews
Mildred Pierce
Joan Crawford
Miracle Worker
Anne Bancroft
Misery
Kathy Bates
Moonstruck
Cher
Network
Faye Dunaway
Norma Rae
Sally Field
One Flew Over Cuckoo's Nest
Louise Fletcher
On Golden Pond
Katharine Hepburn
Piano, The
Holly Hunter
Places in the Heart
Sally Field
Roman Holiday
Audrey Hepburn
Shakespeare in Love
Gwyneth Paltrow
Silence of the Lambs
Jodie Foster
Sophie's Choice
Meryl Streep

Streetcar Named Desire
  Vivien Leigh
Terms of Endearment
  Shirley MacLaine
Three Faces of Eve
  Joanne Woodward
Who's Afraid of Virginia Woolf?
  Elizabeth Taylor

Best Director

All About Eve
All Quiet on the Western Front
Amadeus
American Beauty
Annie Hall
Apartment, The
Beautiful Mind
Ben-Hur
Best Years of Our Lives
Born on the Fourth of July
Braveheart
Bridge on the River Kwai
Cabaret
Casablanca
Dances with Wolves
Deer Hunter
English Patient
Forrest Gump
French Connection
From Here to Eternity
Gandhi
Giant
Gigi
Godfather Part II
Gone with the Wind
Graduate, The
Grapes of Wrath
It Happened One Night
Kramer vs. Kramer
Last Emperor
Lawrence of Arabia
Man for All Seasons
Marty
Midnight Cowboy
My Fair Lady
Oliver!
One Flew Over Cuckoo's Nest
On the Waterfront
Ordinary People
Out of Africa
Patton
Place in the Sun
Platoon
Quiet Man
Rain Man
Reds
Rocky
Saving Private Ryan
Schindler's List
Silence of the Lambs
Sound of Music
Sting, The
Terms of Endearment
Titanic
Tom Jones
Traffic
Treasure of the Sierra Madre
Unforgiven
West Side Story

Best Screenplay

All About Eve
Almost Famous
Amadeus
American Beauty
American in Paris
Annie Hall
Apartment, The
Around the World in 80 Days
Beautiful Mind
Becket
Best Years of Our Lives
Breaking Away
Bridge on the River Kwai
Butch Cassidy
Candidate, The
Casablanca
Chariots of Fire
Chinatown
Cider House Rules
Citizen Kane
Coming Home
Crying Game
Dances with Wolves
Dangerous Liaisons
Dead Poets Society
Doctor Zhivago
Dog Day Afternoon
Driving Miss Daisy
Elmer Gantry

Best Foreign Language Film

Other Great Films

(Films that just missed our cut-off; not reviewed in this book)

David Copperfield (1935)
Dinner at Eight (1933)
Front Page (1931)
Gentleman's Agreement (1947)
Gold Rush (1925)
Goodbye, Mr. Chips (1939)
Grand Hotel (1932)
Greed (1924)
Hamlet (1948)
Hunchback Notre Dame (1939)
Intolerance (1916)
Juliet of the Spirits (1965)
Lady Vanishes (1938)
Last Tango in Paris (1973)
L'Avventura (1960)
Letter, The (1940)
Little Foxes (1941)
Lost Weekend (1945)
Love in the Afternoon (1957)
Magnificent Ambersons (1942)
Man Who Came to Dinner (1942)
Mean Streets (1973)
Napoleon (1927)
Ninotchka (1939)
Nosferatu (1922)
Nothing Sacred (1937)
Open City (1945)
Persona (1966)
Public Enemy (1931)
Repulsion (1965)
Rules of the Game (1939)
Scenes from a Marriage (1973)
Sullivan's Travels (1942)
Thief of Bagdad (1924)
To Be or Not To Be (1942)
Two Women (1960)
Women, The (1939)

Religion

Agnes of God
Ben-Hur
Elmer Gantry
Exorcist, The
Jesus Christ Superstar
Last Temptation of Christ
Life of Brian
Prince of Egypt
Ten Commandments
Yentl

Remake

(Both versions reviewed herein)

Anastasia
Beauty and the Beast
Birdcage, The
Cape Fear
Dracula
Father of the Bride
Invasion/Body Snatchers
La Cage aux Folles
Moulin Rouge
Mutiny on the Bounty
101 Dalmatians
Postman Always Rings Twice
Romeo and Juliet
Tarzan
Thing, The

Rock 'n' Roll

Almost Famous
Blues Brothers
Bye Bye Birdie
Fame
Gimme Shelter
Grease
Hair
Hard Day's Night
Help!
Jesus Christ Superstar
Last Waltz
Rocky Horror Picture Show
Rose, The
Saturday Night Fever
Sid & Nancy
Stop Making Sense
This is Spinal Tap
What's Love Got to Do with It
Woodstock
Yellow Submarine

Soundtrack

(See also Musical, p. 247; *Best Score Oscar winner)

Adventures of Robin Hood*
Aladdin*
Alexander Nevsky
Alfie
All That Jazz*

Sports

Stage Adaptation